Blank Canvas
My So-Called Artist's Journey

4

STORY &
ART

**Akiko
Higashimura**

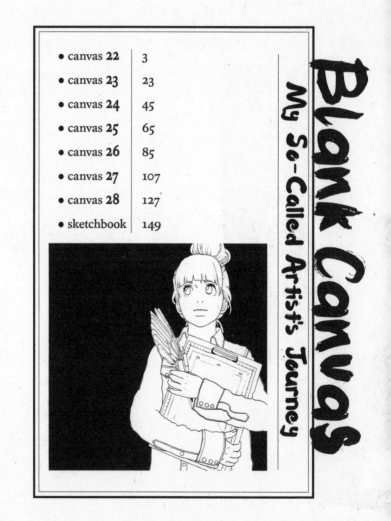

Blank Canvas

My So-Called Artist's Journey

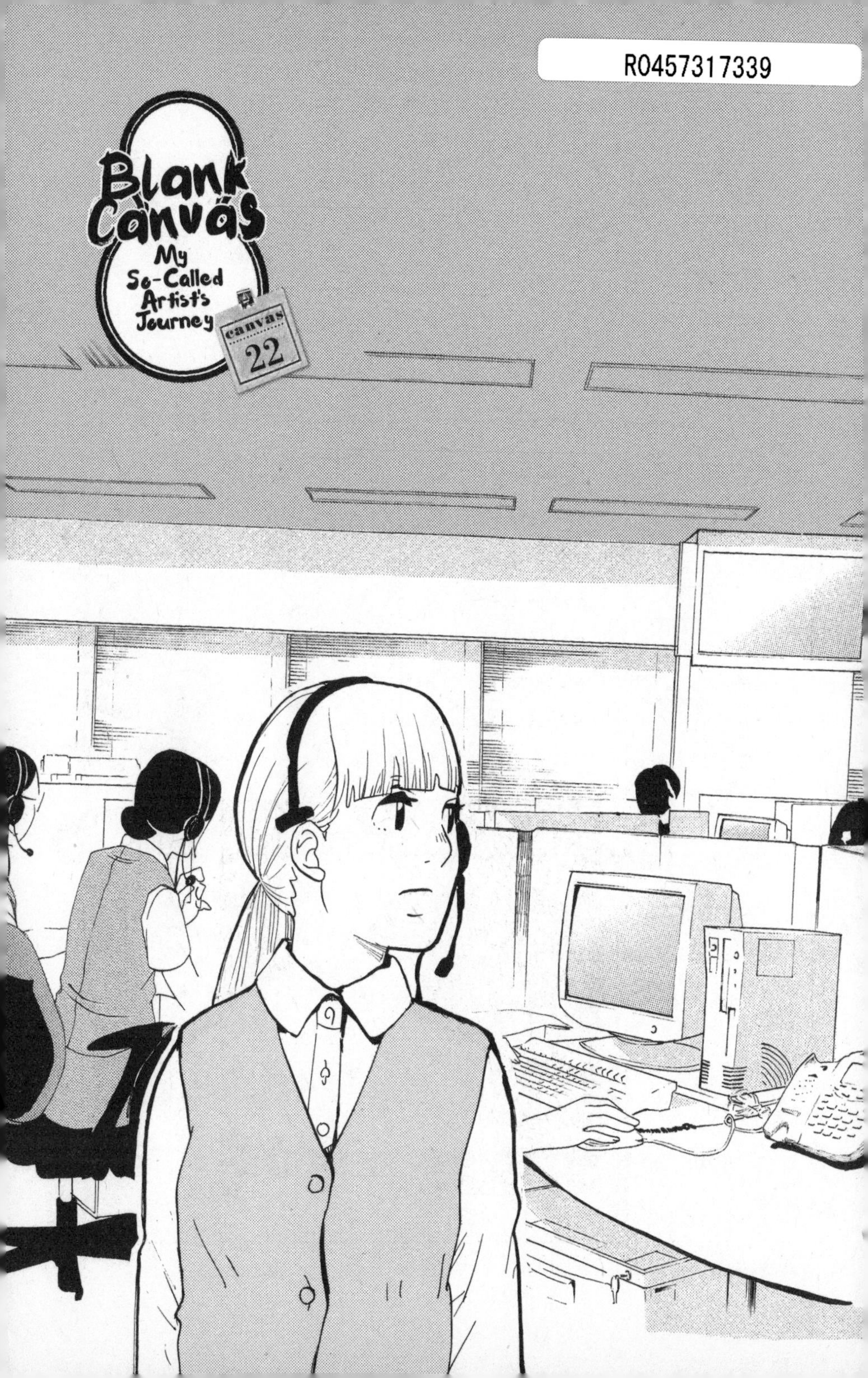
Blank Canvas
My So-Called Artist's Journey
canvas
22

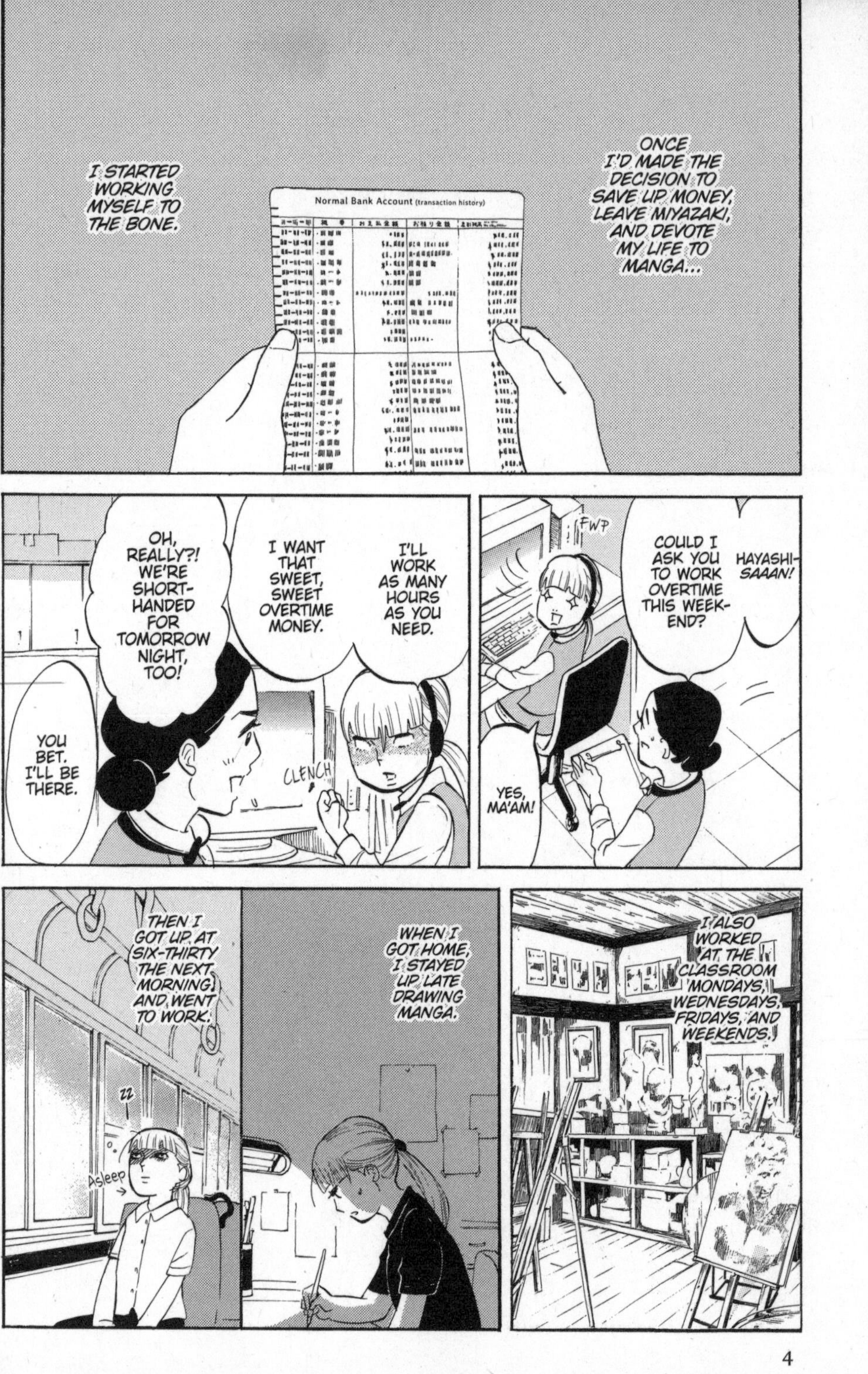
ONCE I'D MADE THE DECISION TO SAVE UP MONEY, LEAVE MIYAZAKI, AND DEVOTE MY LIFE TO MANGA...
Normal Bank Account (transaction history)
I STARTED WORKING MYSELF TO THE BONE.
HAYASHI-SAAAN!
COULD I ASK YOU TO WORK OVERTIME THIS WEEK-END?
FWP
YES, MA'AM!
I'LL WORK AS MANY HOURS AS YOU NEED.
I WANT THAT SWEET, SWEET OVERTIME MONEY.
OH, REALLY?! WE'RE SHORT-HANDED FOR TOMORROW NIGHT, TOO!
CLENCH
YOU BET. I'LL BE THERE.
I ALSO WORKED AT THE CLASSROOM MONDAYS, WEDNESDAYS, FRIDAYS, AND WEEKENDS.
WHEN I GOT HOME, I STAYED UP LATE DRAWING MANGA.
THEN I GOT UP AT SIX-THIRTY THE NEXT MORNING AND WENT TO WORK.
zz
Asleep →

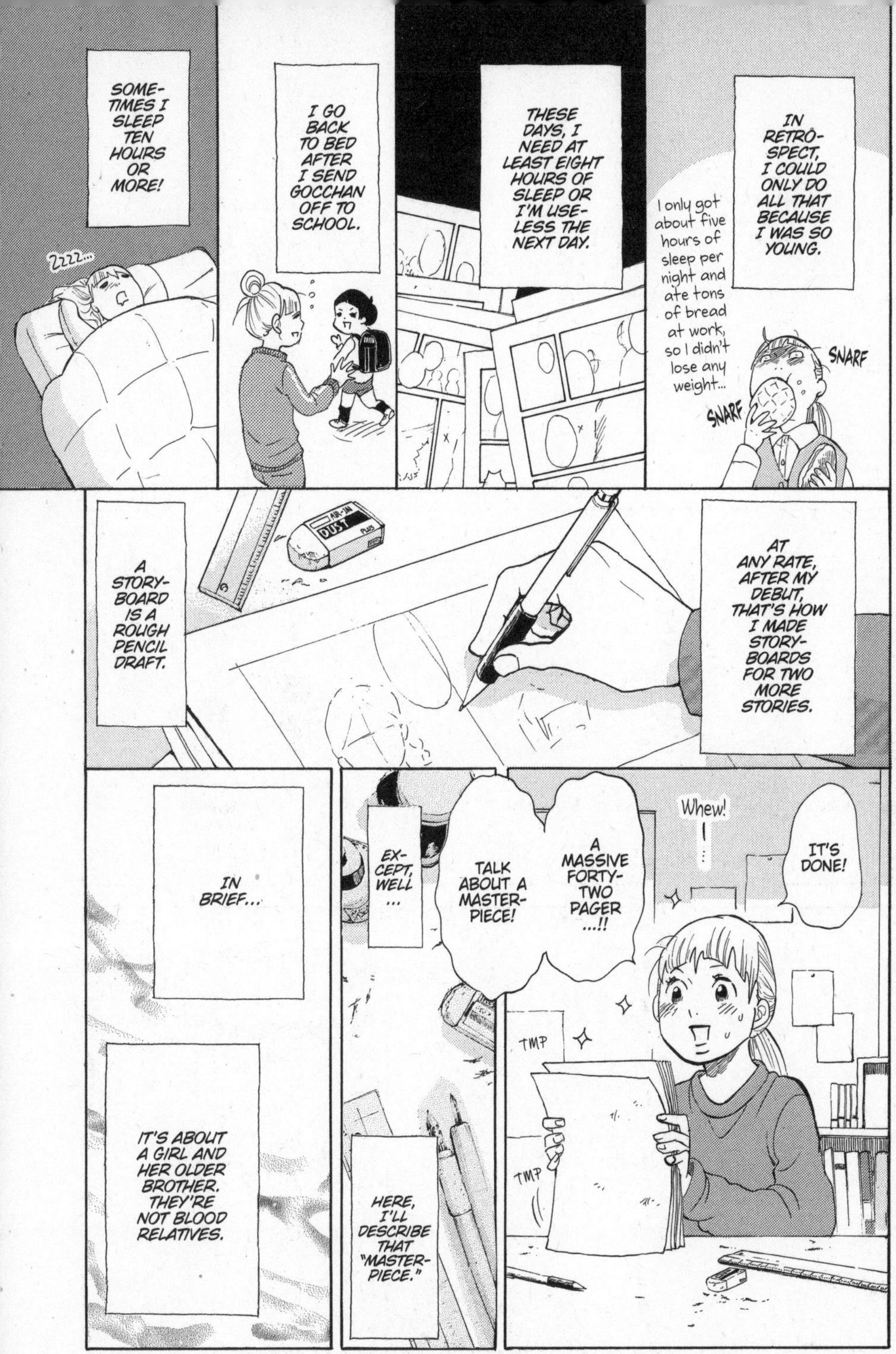

IN RETROSPECT, I COULD ONLY DO ALL THAT BECAUSE I WAS SO YOUNG.
I only got about five hours of sleep per night and ate tons of bread at work, so I didn't lose any weight...
SNARF
SNARF
THESE DAYS, I NEED AT LEAST EIGHT HOURS OF SLEEP OR I'M USELESS THE NEXT DAY.
I GO BACK TO BED AFTER I SEND GOCCHAN OFF TO SCHOOL.
SOMETIMES I SLEEP TEN HOURS OR MORE!
Zzzz...
AT ANY RATE, AFTER MY DEBUT, THAT'S HOW I MADE STORYBOARDS FOR TWO MORE STORIES.
A STORYBOARD IS A ROUGH PENCIL DRAFT.
IT'S DONE!
Whew! ...
A MASSIVE FORTY-TWO PAGER ...!!
TALK ABOUT A MASTERPIECE!
TMP
TMP
EXCEPT, WELL ...
HERE, I'LL DESCRIBE THAT "MASTERPIECE."
IN BRIEF...
IT'S ABOUT A GIRL AND HER OLDER BROTHER. THEY'RE NOT BLOOD RELATIVES.

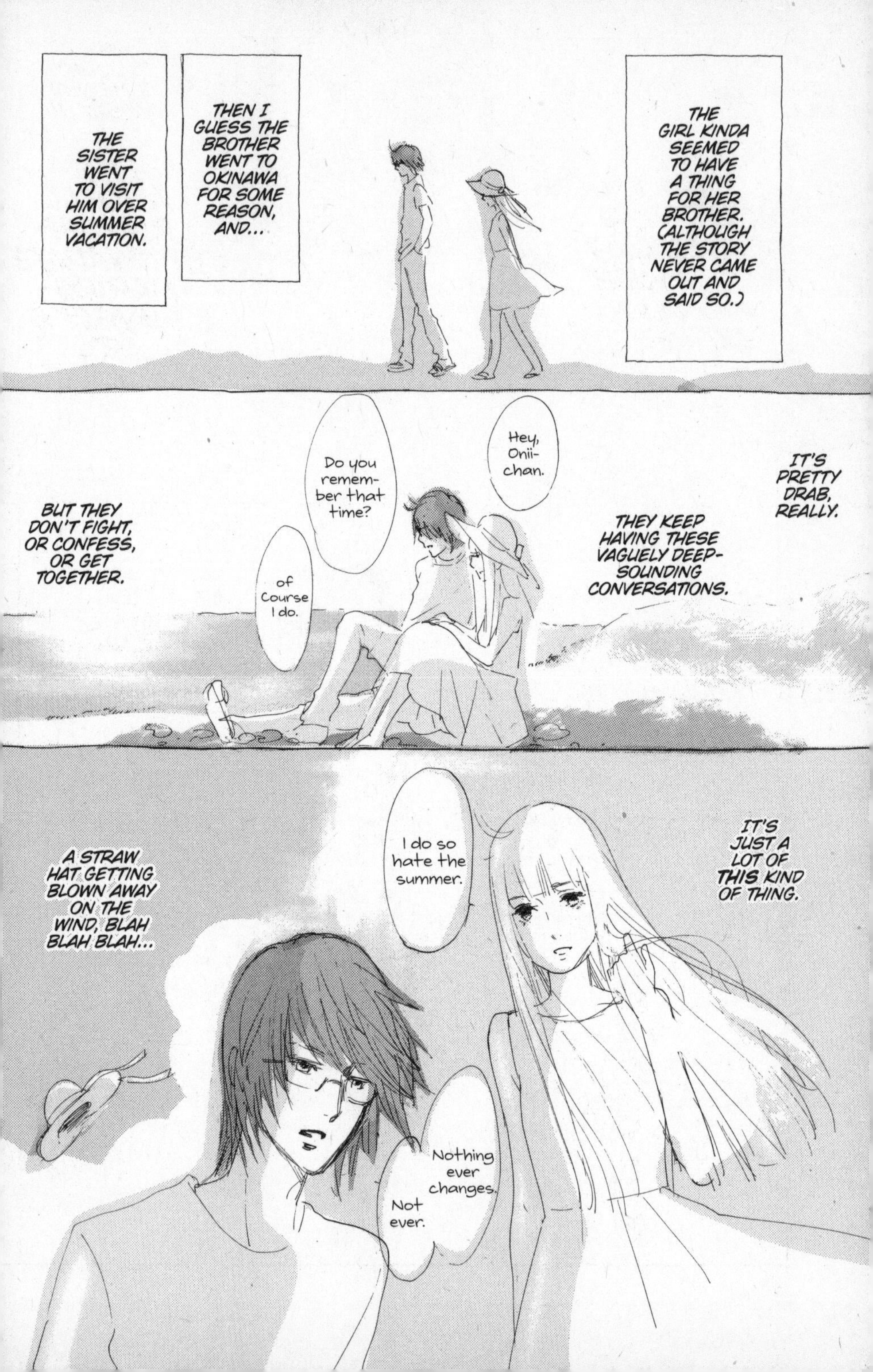
THE GIRL KINDA SEEMED TO HAVE A THING FOR HER BROTHER. (ALTHOUGH THE STORY NEVER CAME OUT AND SAID SO.)
THEN I GUESS THE BROTHER WENT TO OKINAWA FOR SOME REASON, AND...
THE SISTER WENT TO VISIT HIM OVER SUMMER VACATION.
IT'S PRETTY DRAB, REALLY.
Hey, Onii-chan.
THEY KEEP HAVING THESE VAGUELY DEEP-SOUNDING CONVERSATIONS.
Do you remem-ber that time?
of Course I do.
BUT THEY DON'T FIGHT, OR CONFESS, OR GET TOGETHER.
IT'S JUST A LOT OF THIS KIND OF THING.
I do so hate the summer.
A STRAW HAT GETTING BLOWN AWAY ON THE WIND, BLAH BLAH BLAH...
Nothing ever changes.
Not ever.

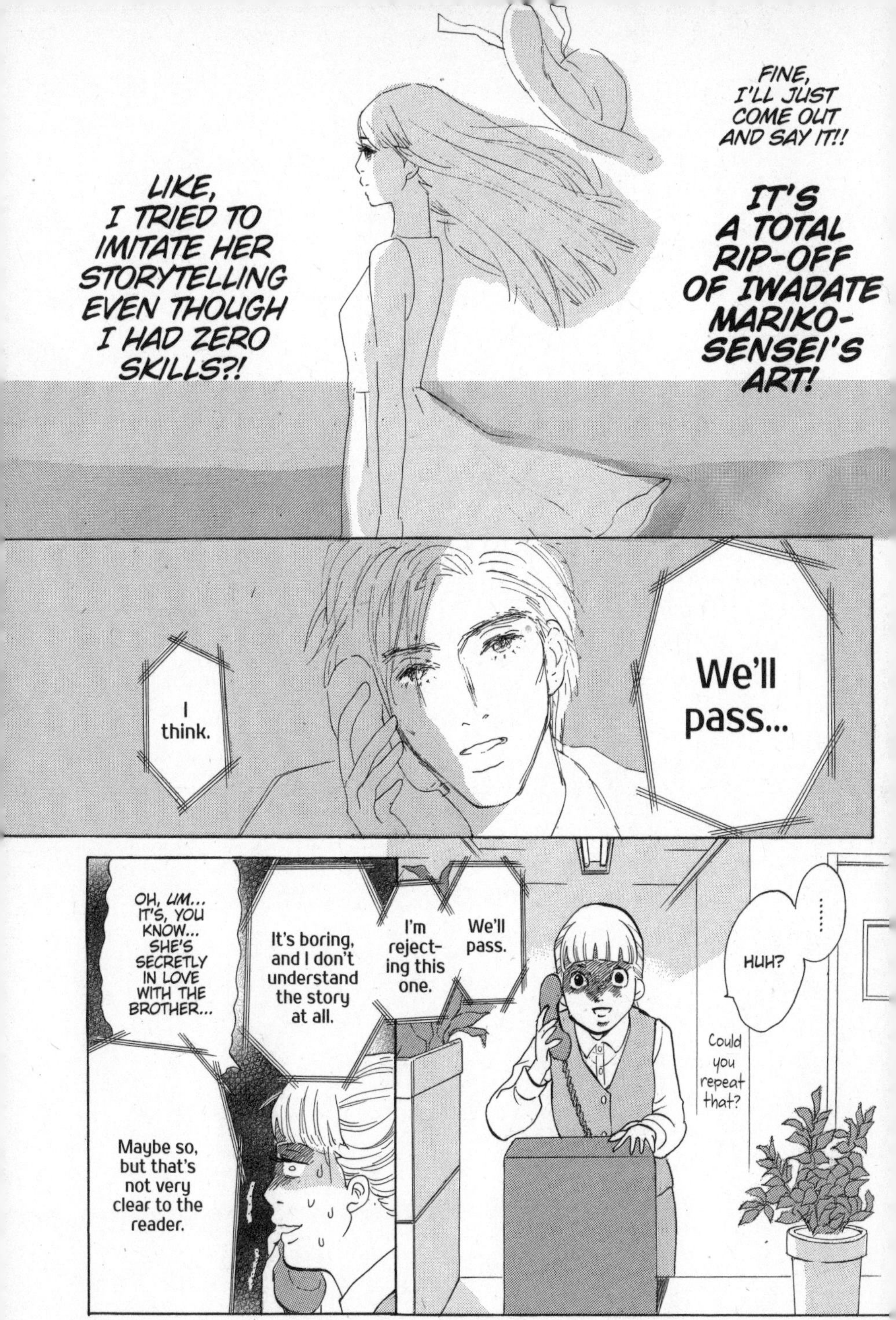
FINE, I'LL JUST COME OUT AND SAY IT!!
IT'S A TOTAL RIP-OFF OF IWADATE MARIKO-SENSEI'S ART!
LIKE, I TRIED TO IMITATE HER STORYTELLING EVEN THOUGH I HAD ZERO SKILLS?!
We'll pass...
I think.
......
HUH?
Could you repeat that?
We'll pass.
I'm rejecting this one.
It's boring, and I don't understand the story at all.
OH, UM... IT'S, YOU KNOW... SHE'S SECRETLY IN LOVE WITH THE BROTHER...
Maybe so, but that's not very clear to the reader.

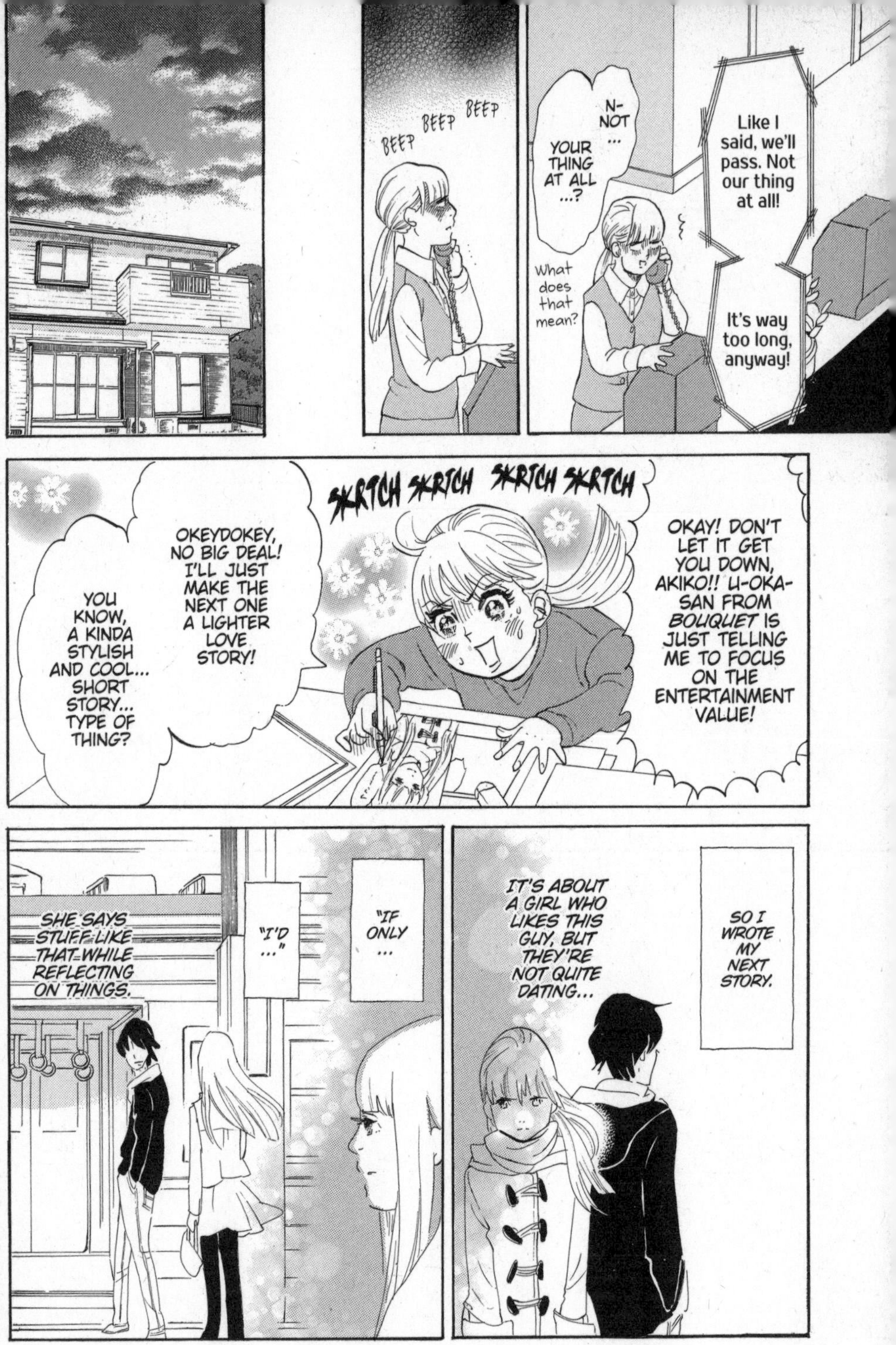
Like I said, we'll pass. Not our thing at all!
It's way too long, anyway!
N-NOT ...
YOUR THING AT ALL ...?
What does that mean?
BEEP BEEP BEEP
SKRTCH SKRTCH SKRTCH SKRTCH
OKAY! DON'T LET IT GET YOU DOWN, AKIKO!! U-OKA-SAN FROM *BOUQUET* IS JUST TELLING ME TO FOCUS ON THE ENTERTAINMENT VALUE!
OKEYDOKEY, NO BIG DEAL! I'LL JUST MAKE THE NEXT ONE A LIGHTER LOVE STORY!
YOU KNOW, A KINDA STYLISH AND COOL... SHORT STORY... TYPE OF THING?
SO I WROTE MY NEXT STORY.
IT'S ABOUT A GIRL WHO LIKES THIS GUY, BUT THEY'RE NOT QUITE DATING...
"IF ONLY ..."
"I'D ..."
SHE SAYS STUFF LIKE THAT WHILE REFLECTING ON THINGS.

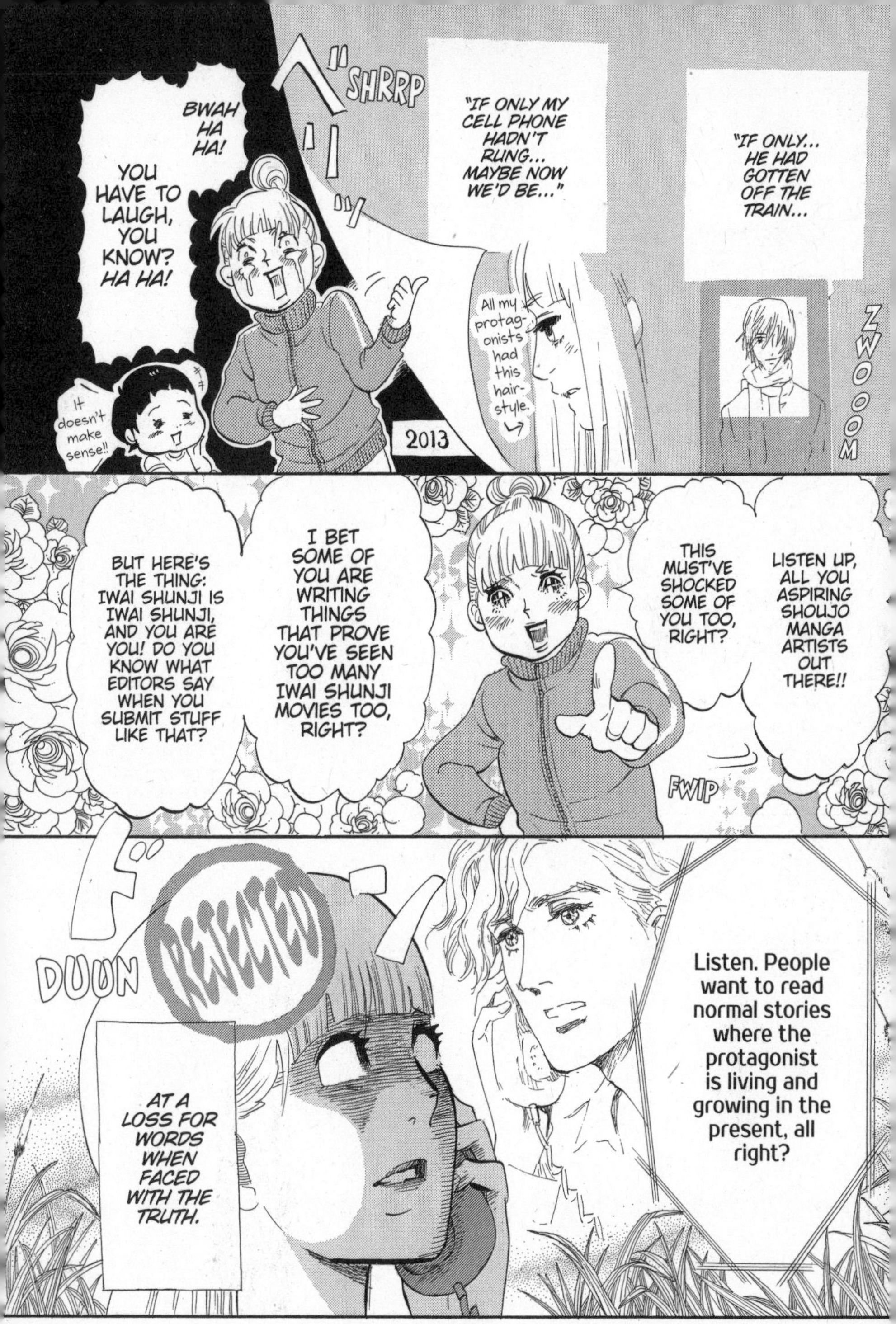

"IF ONLY... HE HAD GOTTEN OFF THE TRAIN..."
ZWOOOOM
"IF ONLY MY CELL PHONE HADN'T RUNG... MAYBE NOW WE'D BE..."
All my protagonists had this hairstyle.
SHRRP
BWAH HA HA!
YOU HAVE TO LAUGH, YOU KNOW? HA HA!
It doesn't make sense!!
2013
LISTEN UP, ALL YOU ASPIRING SHOUJO MANGA ARTISTS OUT THERE!!
THIS MUST'VE SHOCKED SOME OF YOU TOO, RIGHT?
FWIP
I BET SOME OF YOU ARE WRITING THINGS THAT PROVE YOU'VE SEEN TOO MANY IWAI SHUNJI MOVIES TOO, RIGHT?
BUT HERE'S THE THING: IWAI SHUNJI IS IWAI SHUNJI, AND YOU ARE YOU! DO YOU KNOW WHAT EDITORS SAY WHEN YOU SUBMIT STUFF LIKE THAT?
Listen. People want to read normal stories where the protagonist is living and growing in the present, all right?
REJECTED
DUUN
AT A LOSS FOR WORDS WHEN FACED WITH THE TRUTH.

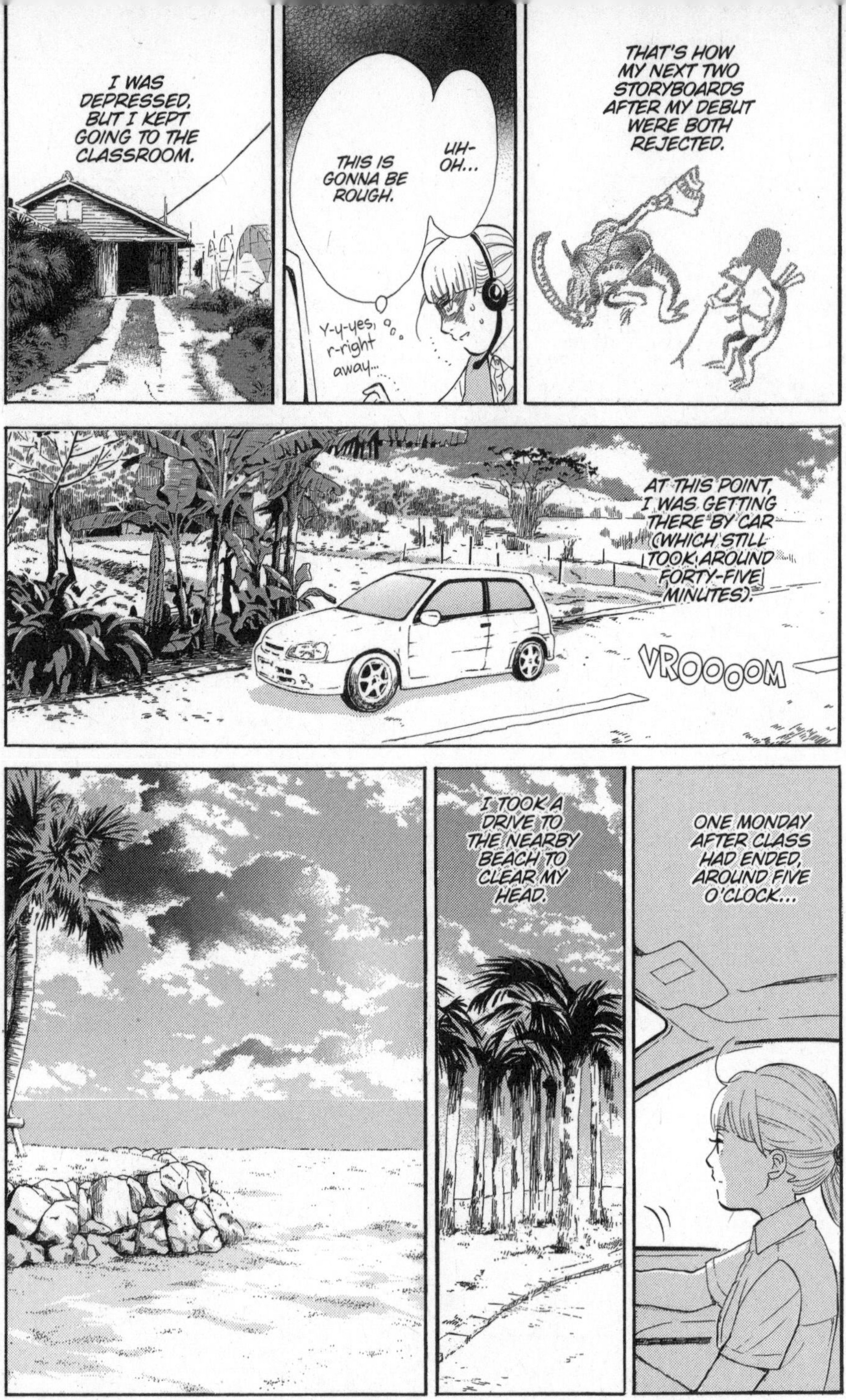
THAT'S HOW MY NEXT TWO STORYBOARDS AFTER MY DEBUT WERE BOTH REJECTED.
UH-OH...
THIS IS GONNA BE ROUGH.
Y-y-yes, r-right away...
I WAS DEPRESSED, BUT I KEPT GOING TO THE CLASSROOM.
AT THIS POINT, I WAS GETTING THERE BY CAR (WHICH STILL TOOK AROUND FORTY-FIVE MINUTES).
VROOOOM
ONE MONDAY AFTER CLASS HAD ENDED, AROUND FIVE O'CLOCK...
I TOOK A DRIVE TO THE NEARBY BEACH TO CLEAR MY HEAD.

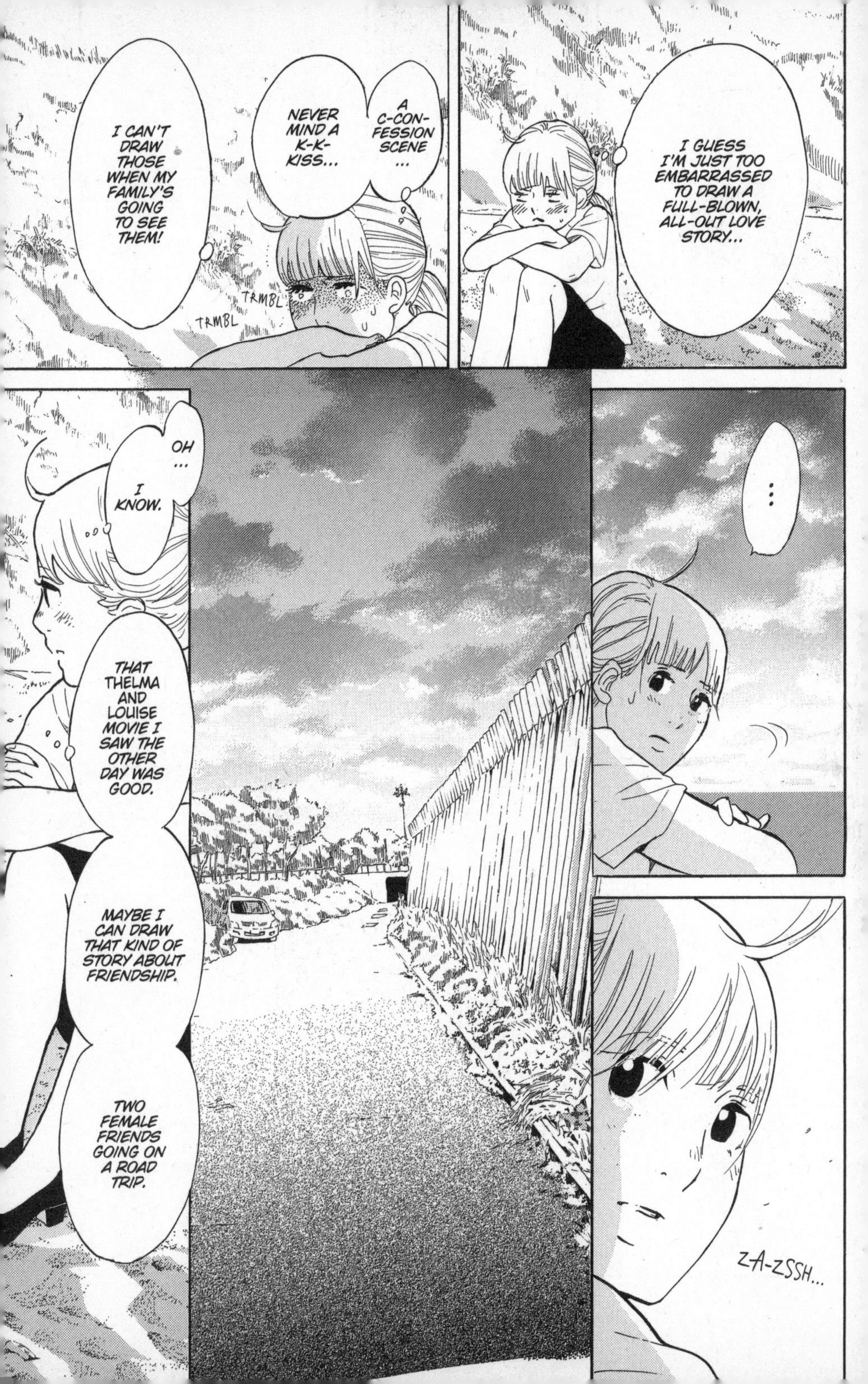
I GUESS I'M JUST TOO EMBARRASSED TO DRAW A FULL-BLOWN, ALL-OUT LOVE STORY...
A C-CON-FESSION SCENE ...
NEVER MIND A K-K-KISS...
I CAN'T DRAW THOSE WHEN MY FAMILY'S GOING TO SEE THEM!
TRMBL
TRMBL
...
Z-A-ZSSH...
OH ...
I KNOW.
THAT THELMA AND LOUISE MOVIE I SAW THE OTHER DAY WAS GOOD.
MAYBE I CAN DRAW THAT KIND OF STORY ABOUT FRIENDSHIP.
TWO FEMALE FRIENDS GOING ON A ROAD TRIP.

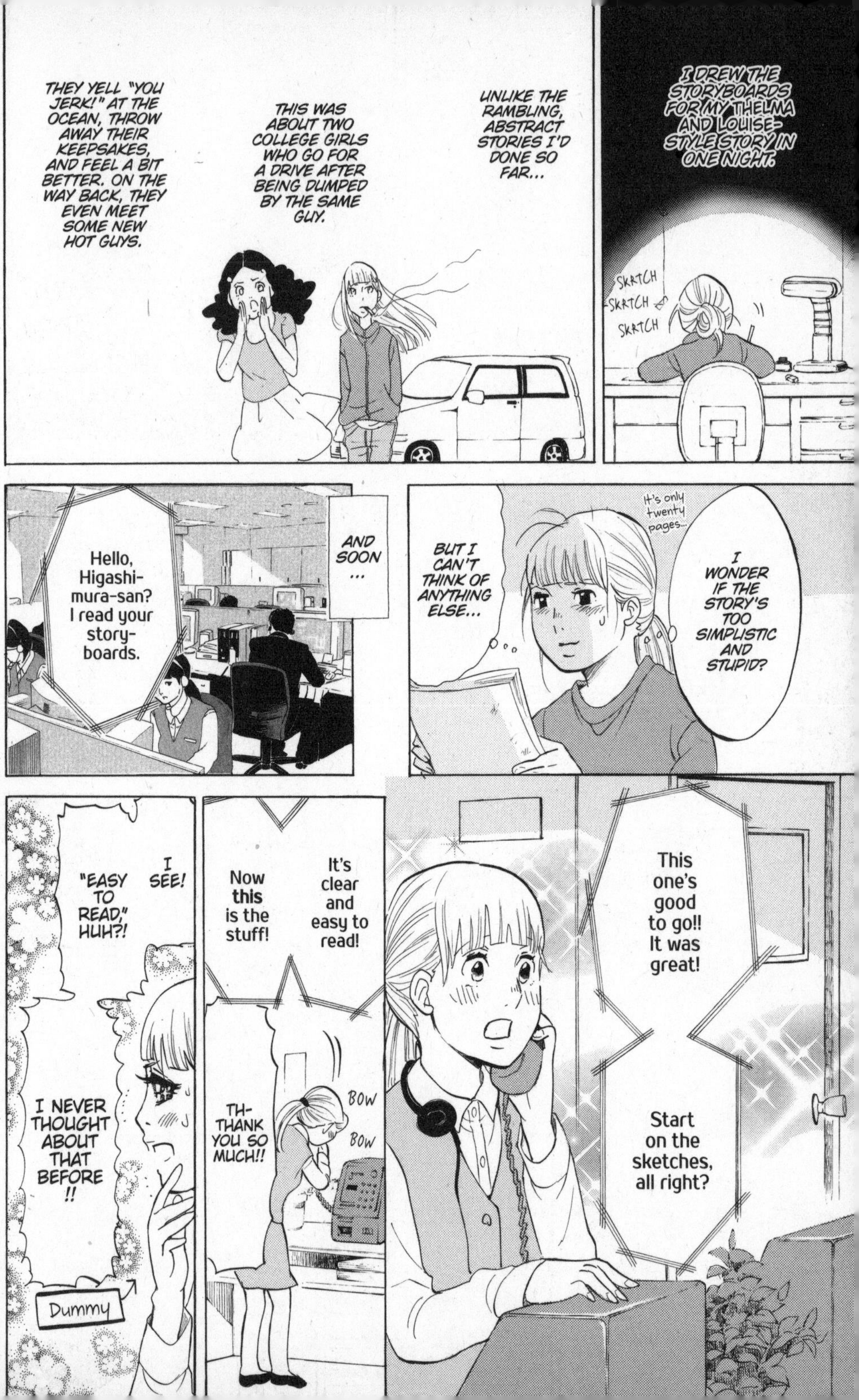
I DREW THE STORYBOARDS FOR MY THELMA AND LOUISE-STYLE STORY IN ONE NIGHT.
SKRTCH
SKRTCH
SKRTCH
UNLIKE THE RAMBLING, ABSTRACT STORIES I'D DONE SO FAR...
THIS WAS ABOUT TWO COLLEGE GIRLS WHO GO FOR A DRIVE AFTER BEING DUMPED BY THE SAME GUY.
THEY YELL "YOU JERK!" AT THE OCEAN, THROW AWAY THEIR KEEPSAKES, AND FEEL A BIT BETTER. ON THE WAY BACK, THEY EVEN MEET SOME NEW HOT GUYS.
It's only twenty pages...
I WONDER IF THE STORY'S TOO SIMPLISTIC AND STUPID?
BUT I CAN'T THINK OF ANYTHING ELSE...
AND SOON...
Hello, Higashimura-san? I read your storyboards.
This one's good to go!! It was great!
Start on the sketches, all right?
It's clear and easy to read!
Now **this** is the stuff!
TH- THANK YOU SO MUCH!!
BOW
BOW
I SEE!
"EASY TO READ," HUH?!
I NEVER THOUGHT ABOUT THAT BEFORE!!
Dummy

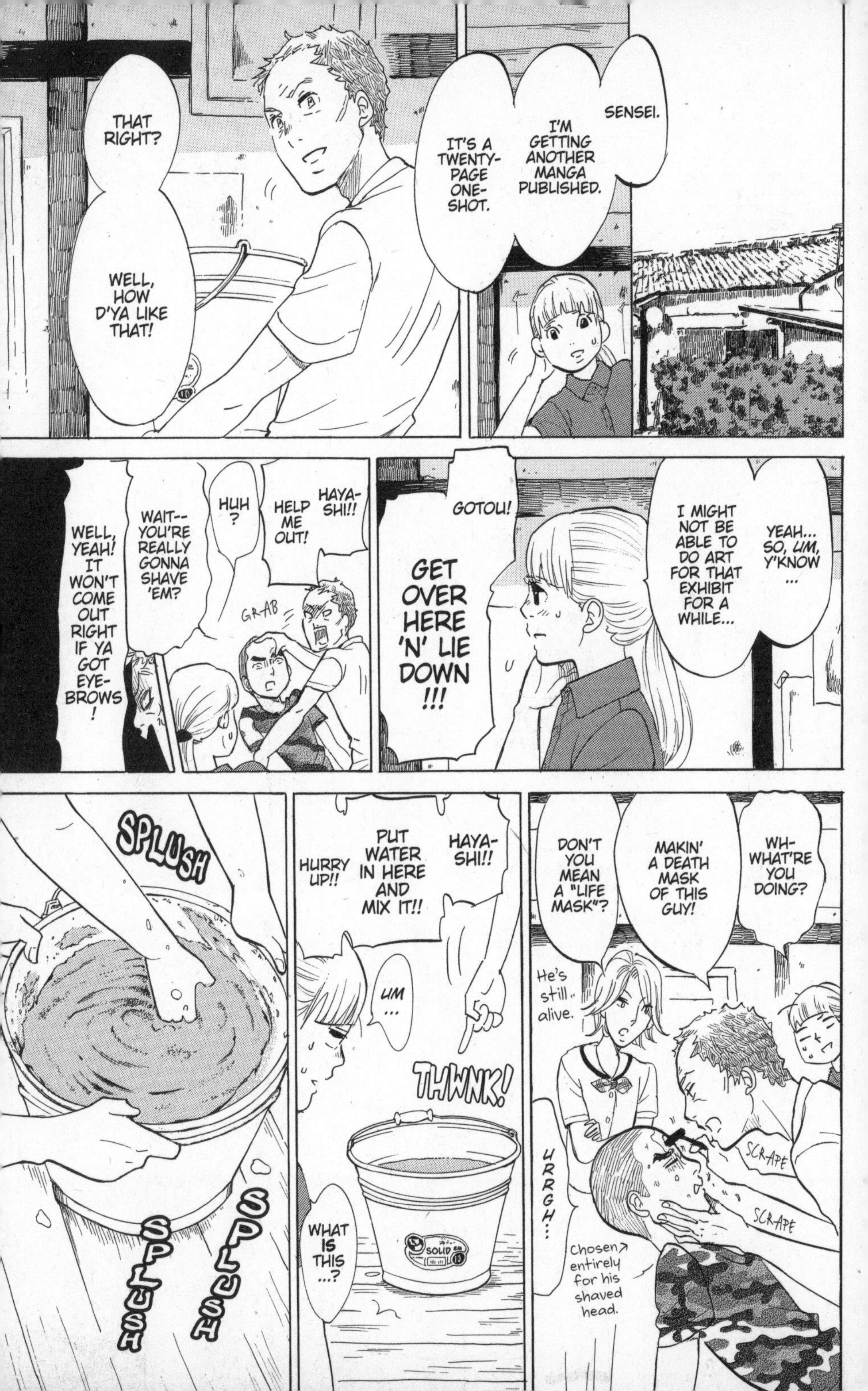
SENSEI.
I'M GETTING ANOTHER MANGA PUBLISHED.
IT'S A TWENTY-PAGE ONE-SHOT.
THAT RIGHT?
WELL, HOW D'YA LIKE THAT!
YEAH... SO, UM, Y'KNOW...
I MIGHT NOT BE ABLE TO DO ART FOR THAT EXHIBIT FOR A WHILE...
GOTOU!
GET OVER HERE 'N' LIE DOWN!!!
HAYA-SHI!!
HELP ME OUT!
HUH?
WAIT-- YOU'RE REALLY GONNA SHAVE 'EM?
WELL, YEAH! IT WON'T COME OUT RIGHT IF YA GOT EYE-BROWS!
GRAB
WH-WHAT'RE YOU DOING?
MAKIN' A DEATH MASK OF THIS GUY!
DON'T YOU MEAN A "LIFE MASK"?
He's still alive.
SCRAPE
SCRAPE
URRGH...
Chosen entirely for his shaved head.
HAYA-SHI!!
PUT WATER IN HERE AND MIX IT!!
HURRY UP!!
UM...
THWNK!
WHAT IS THIS...?
SPLUSH
SPLUSH
SPLUSH

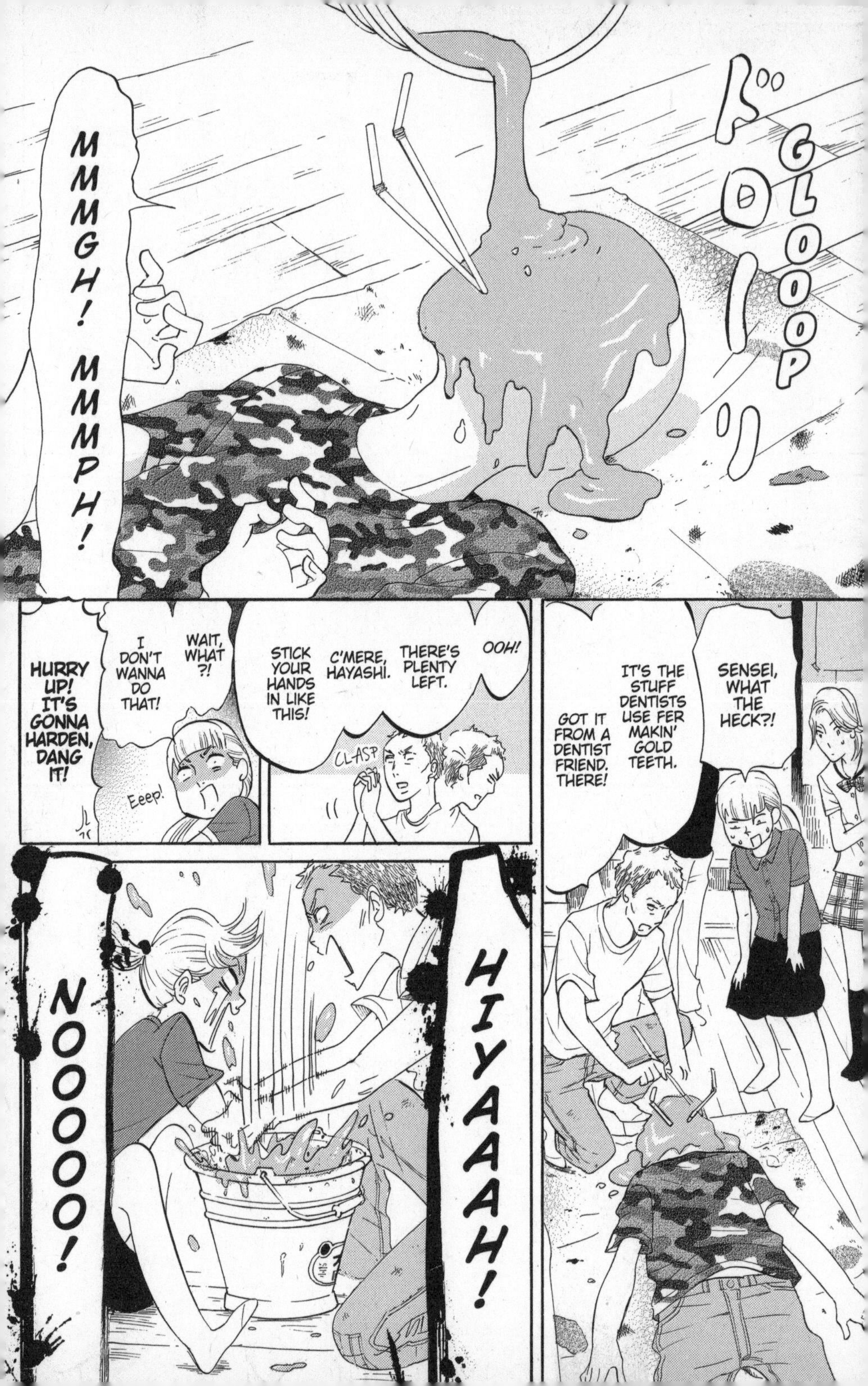
GLOOOP
ドローリ
MMMGH! MMMMPH!
SENSEI, WHAT THE HECK?!
IT'S THE STUFF DENTISTS USE FER MAKIN' GOLD TEETH.
GOT IT FROM A DENTIST FRIEND. THERE!
OOH!
THERE'S PLENTY LEFT.
C'MERE, HAYASHI.
STICK YOUR HANDS IN LIKE THIS!
CL-ASP
WAIT, WHAT?!
I DON'T WANNA DO THAT!
HURRY UP! IT'S GONNA HARDEN, DANG IT!
Eeep!
HIYAAAH!
NOOOOOO!

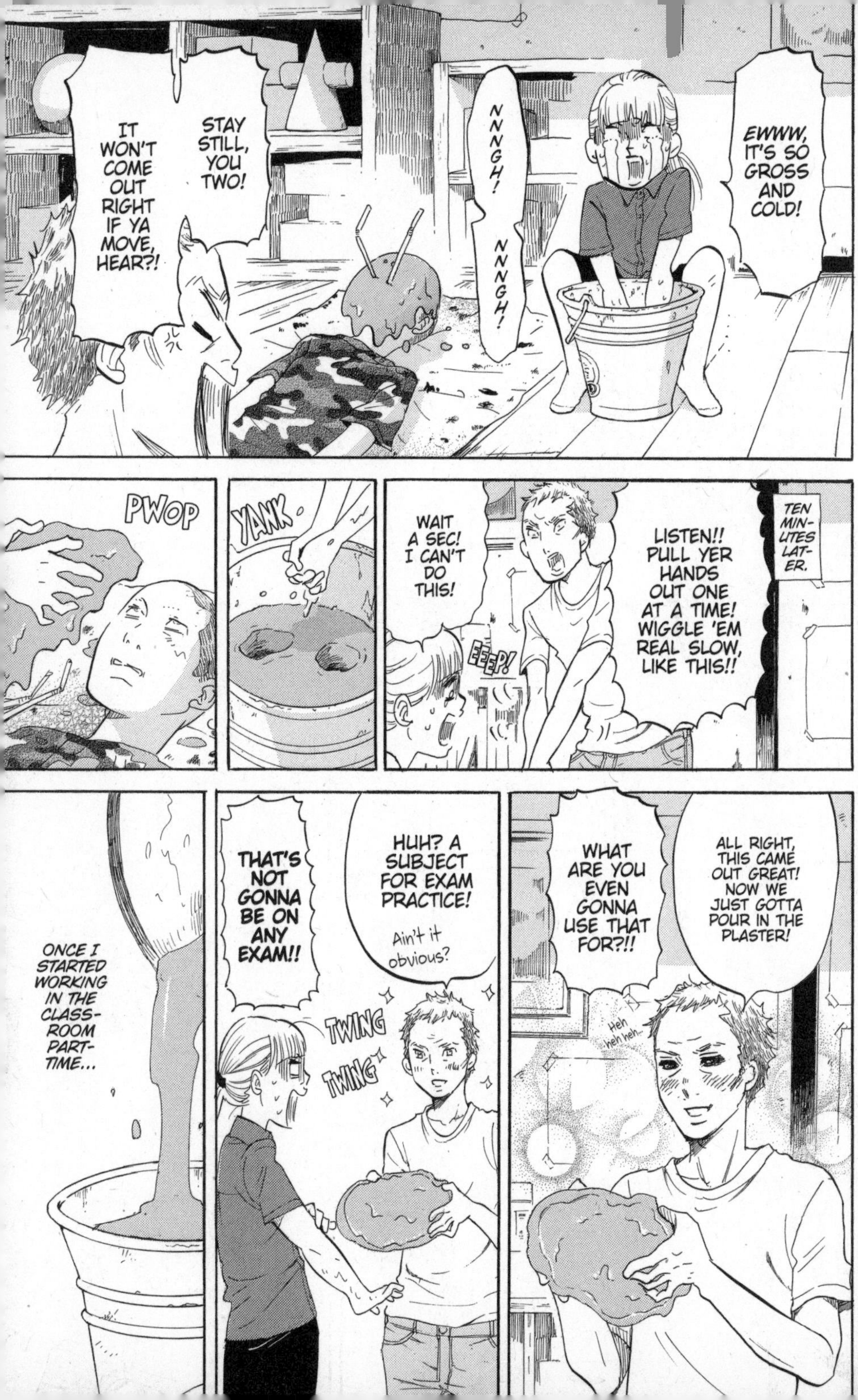
EWWW, IT'S SO GROSS AND COLD!
NNNGH! NNNGH!
STAY STILL, YOU TWO!
IT WON'T COME OUT RIGHT IF YA MOVE, HEAR?!
TEN MIN-UTES LAT-ER.
LISTEN!! PULL YER HANDS OUT ONE AT A TIME! WIGGLE 'EM REAL SLOW, LIKE THIS!!
WAIT A SEC! I CAN'T DO THIS!
EEEP!
YANK
PWOP
ALL RIGHT, THIS CAME OUT GREAT! NOW WE JUST GOTTA POUR IN THE PLASTER!
WHAT ARE YOU EVEN GONNA USE THAT FOR?!!
Heh heh heh...
HUH? A SUBJECT FOR EXAM PRACTICE!
Ain't it obvious?
THAT'S NOT GONNA BE ON ANY EXAM!!
TWING
TWING
ONCE I STARTED WORKING IN THE CLASS-ROOM PART-TIME...

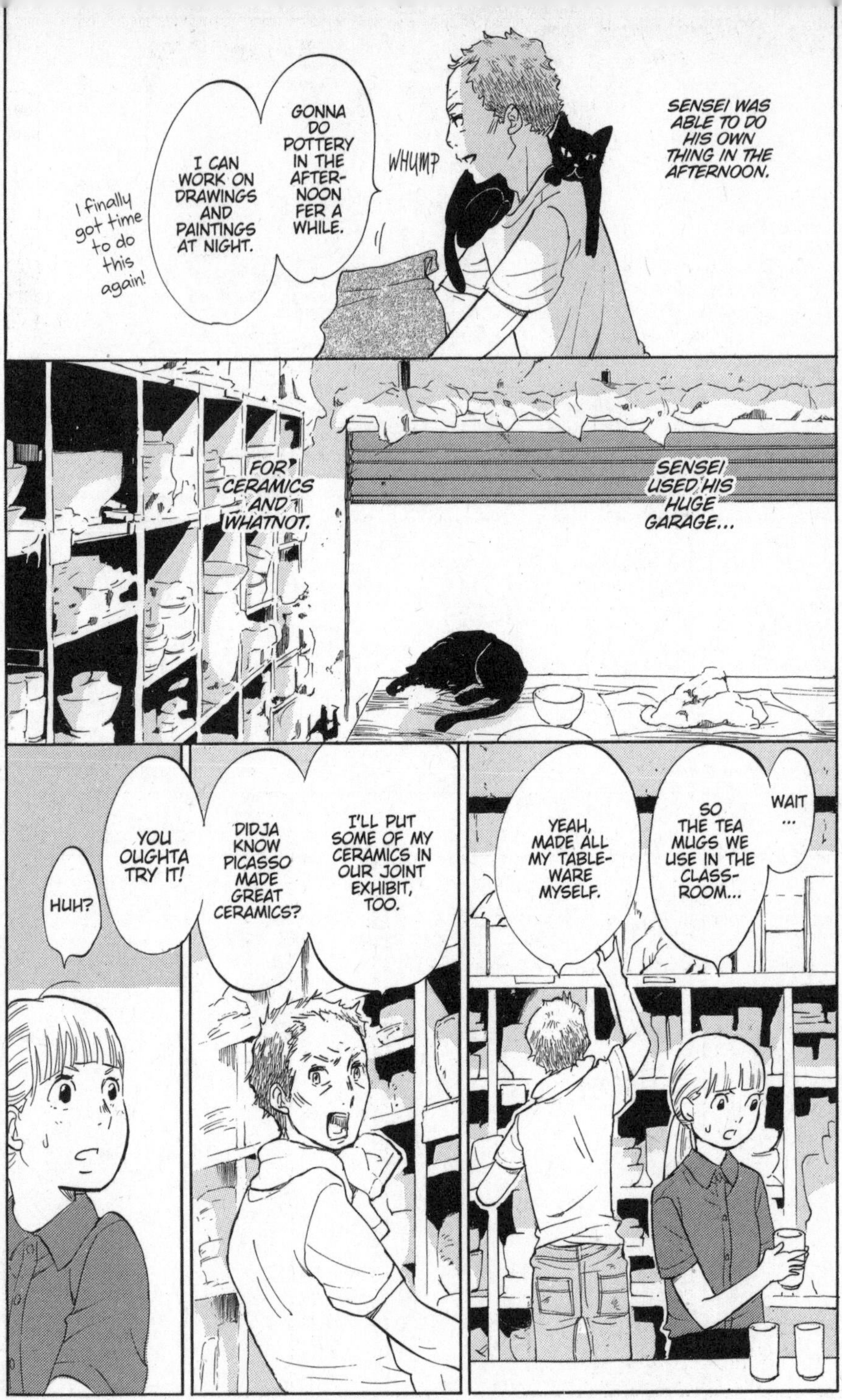
SENSEI WAS ABLE TO DO HIS OWN THING IN THE AFTERNOON.
WHUMP
GONNA DO POTTERY IN THE AFTERNOON FER A WHILE.
I CAN WORK ON DRAWINGS AND PAINTINGS AT NIGHT.
I finally got time to do this again!
SENSEI USED HIS HUGE GARAGE...
FOR CERAMICS AND WHATNOT.
WAIT ...
SO THE TEA MUGS WE USE IN THE CLASSROOM...
YEAH, MADE ALL MY TABLEWARE MYSELF.
I'LL PUT SOME OF MY CERAMICS IN OUR JOINT EXHIBIT, TOO.
DIDJA KNOW PICASSO MADE GREAT CERAMICS?
YOU OUGHTA TRY IT!
HUH?

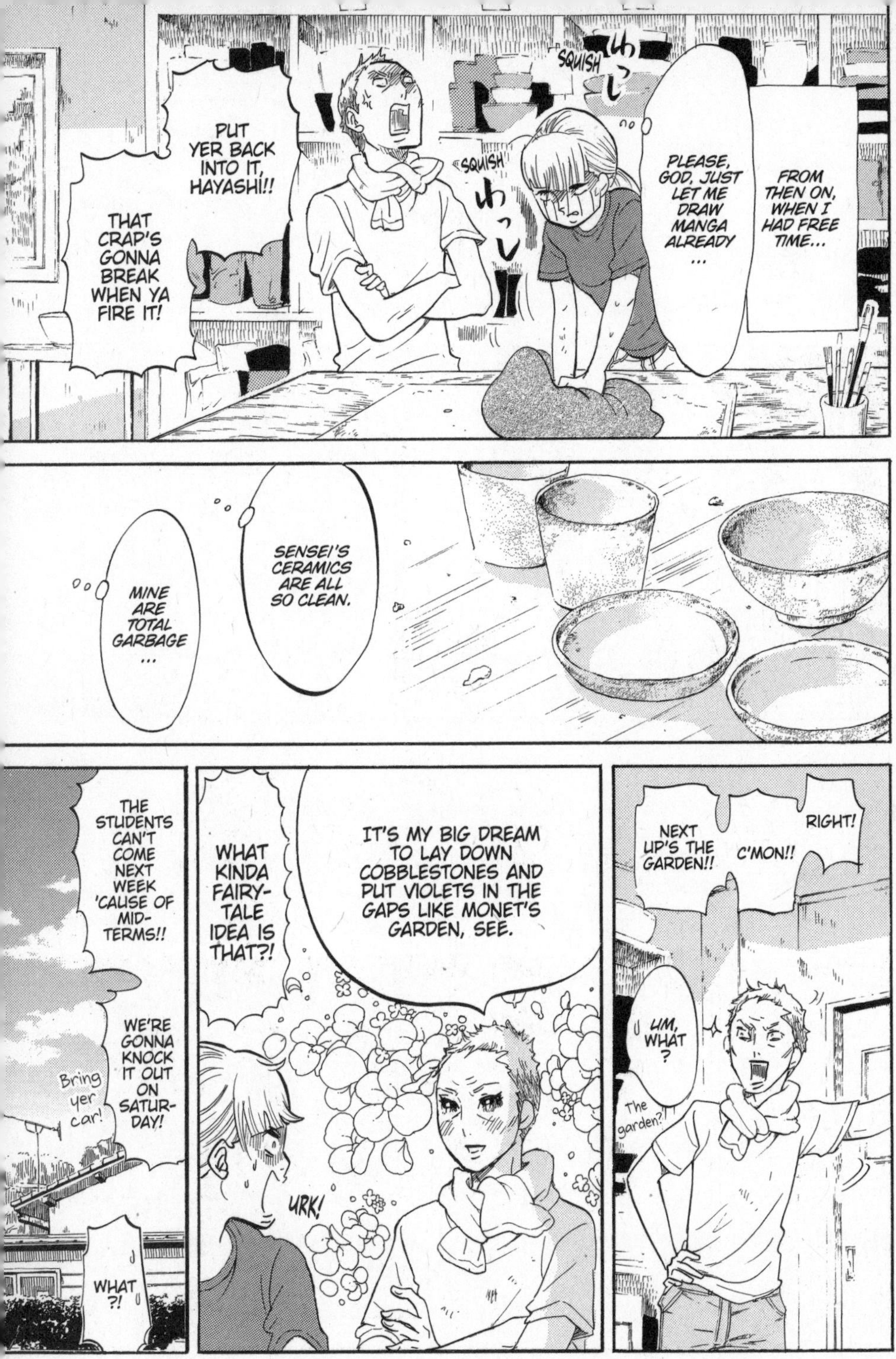
FROM THEN ON, WHEN I HAD FREE TIME...
PLEASE, GOD, JUST LET ME DRAW MANGA ALREADY...
SQUISH
SQUISH
PUT YER BACK INTO IT, HAYASHI!!
THAT CRAP'S GONNA BREAK WHEN YA FIRE IT!
SENSEI'S CERAMICS ARE ALL SO CLEAN.
MINE ARE TOTAL GARBAGE...
RIGHT!
NEXT UP'S THE GARDEN!!
C'MON!!
UM, WHAT?
The garden?
IT'S MY BIG DREAM TO LAY DOWN COBBLESTONES AND PUT VIOLETS IN THE GAPS LIKE MONET'S GARDEN, SEE.
WHAT KINDA FAIRY-TALE IDEA IS THAT?!
URK!
THE STUDENTS CAN'T COME NEXT WEEK 'CAUSE OF MID-TERMS!!
WE'RE GONNA KNOCK IT OUT ON SATUR-DAY!
Bring yer car!
WHAT?!

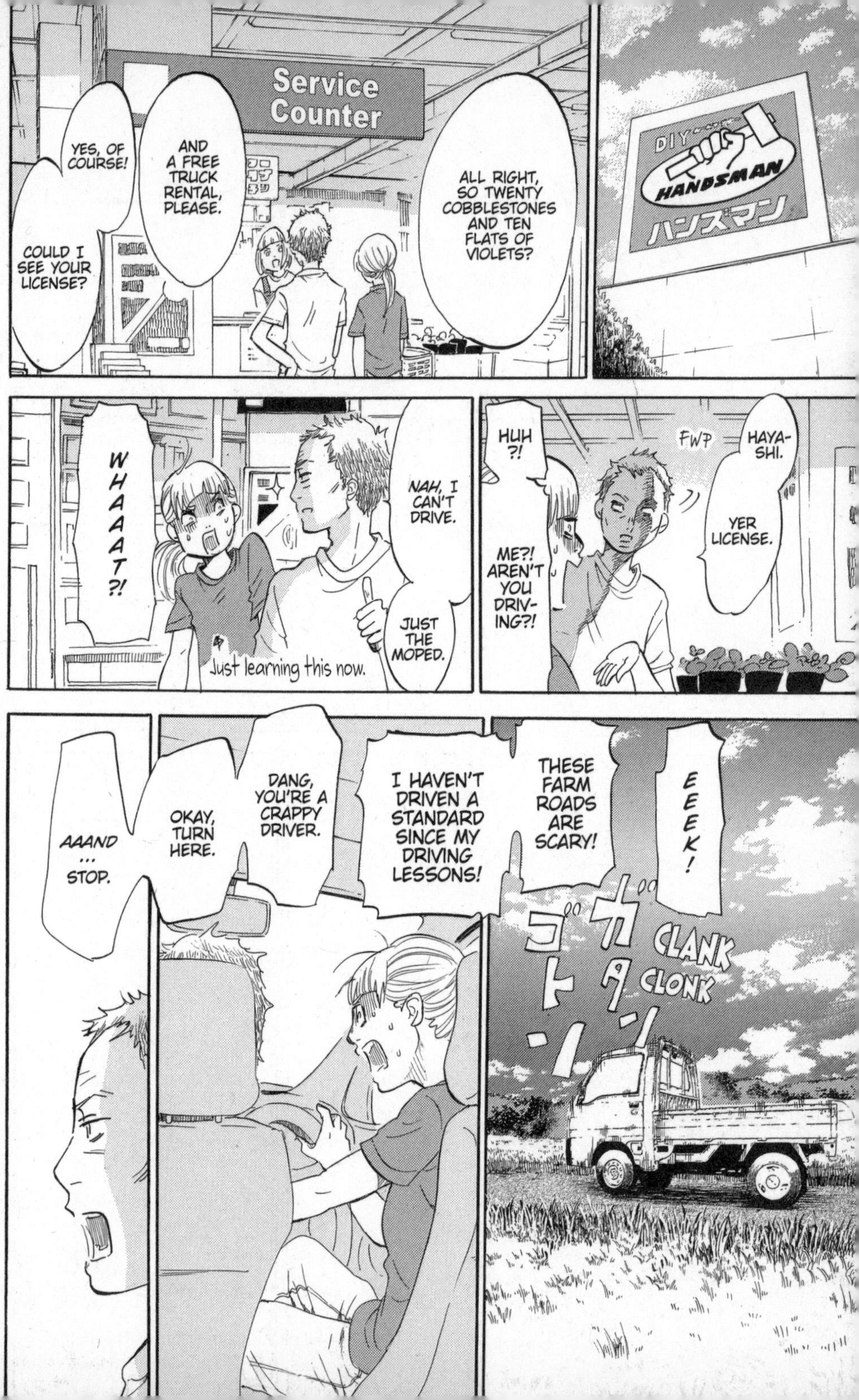
DIY
HANDSMAN
ハンズマン
Service Counter
ALL RIGHT, SO TWENTY COBBLESTONES AND TEN FLATS OF VIOLETS?
AND A FREE TRUCK RENTAL, PLEASE.
YES, OF COURSE!
COULD I SEE YOUR LICENSE?
HAYA-SHI.
FWP
YER LICENSE.
HUH?!
ME?! AREN'T YOU DRIVING?!
NAH, I CAN'T DRIVE.
JUST THE MOPED.
WHAAAAT?!
Just learning this now.
EEEEK!
THESE FARM ROADS ARE SCARY!
CLANK
CLONK
I HAVEN'T DRIVEN A STANDARD SINCE MY DRIVING LESSONS!
DANG, YOU'RE A CRAPPY DRIVER.
OKAY, TURN HERE.
AAAND ... STOP.

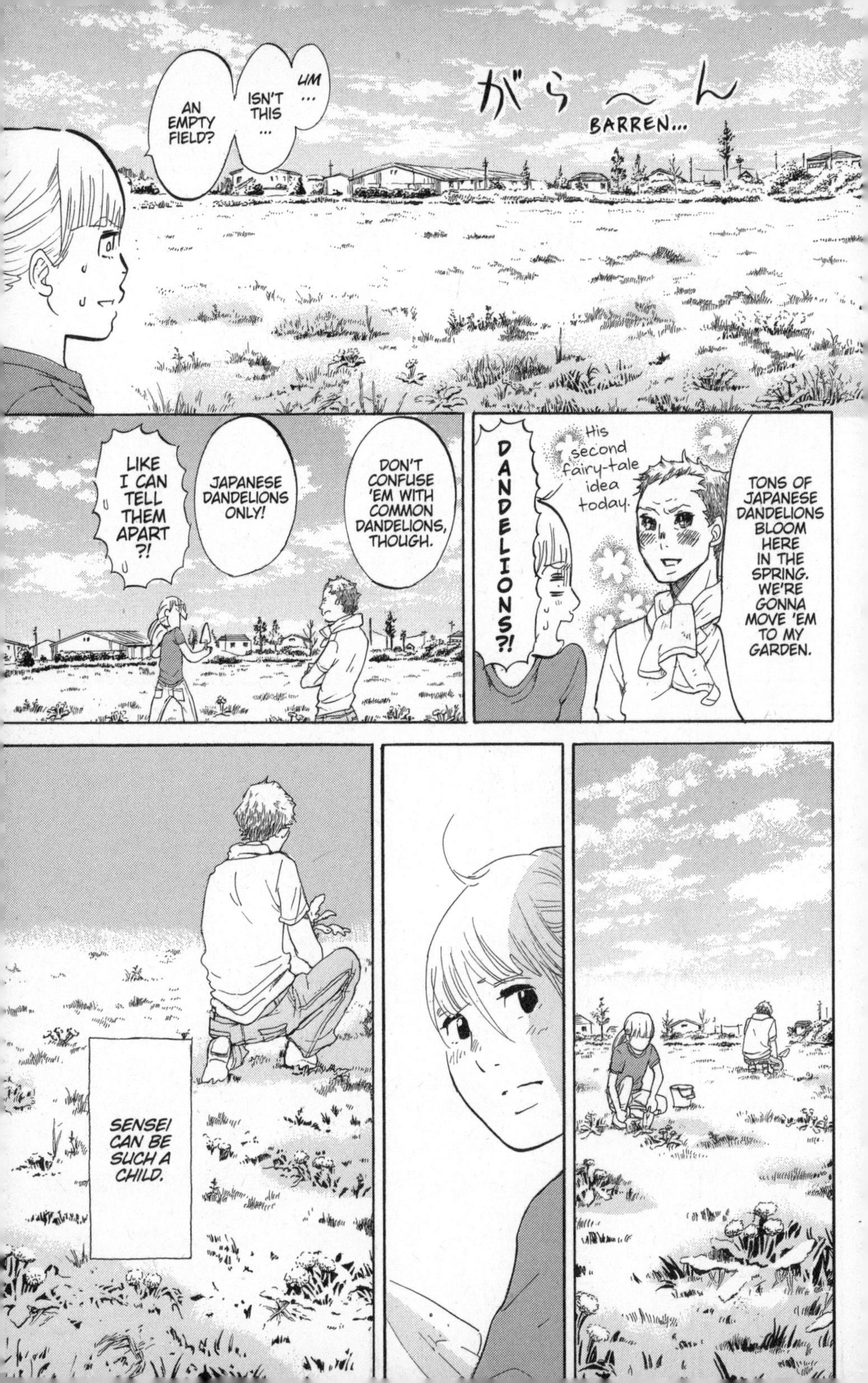
がら〜ん
BARREN...
UM...
ISN'T THIS...
AN EMPTY FIELD?
TONS OF JAPANESE DANDELIONS BLOOM HERE IN THE SPRING. WE'RE GONNA MOVE 'EM TO MY GARDEN.
His second fairy-tale idea today.
DANDELIONS?!
DON'T CONFUSE 'EM WITH COMMON DANDELIONS, THOUGH.
JAPANESE DANDELIONS ONLY!
LIKE I CAN TELL THEM APART?!
SENSEI CAN BE SUCH A CHILD.

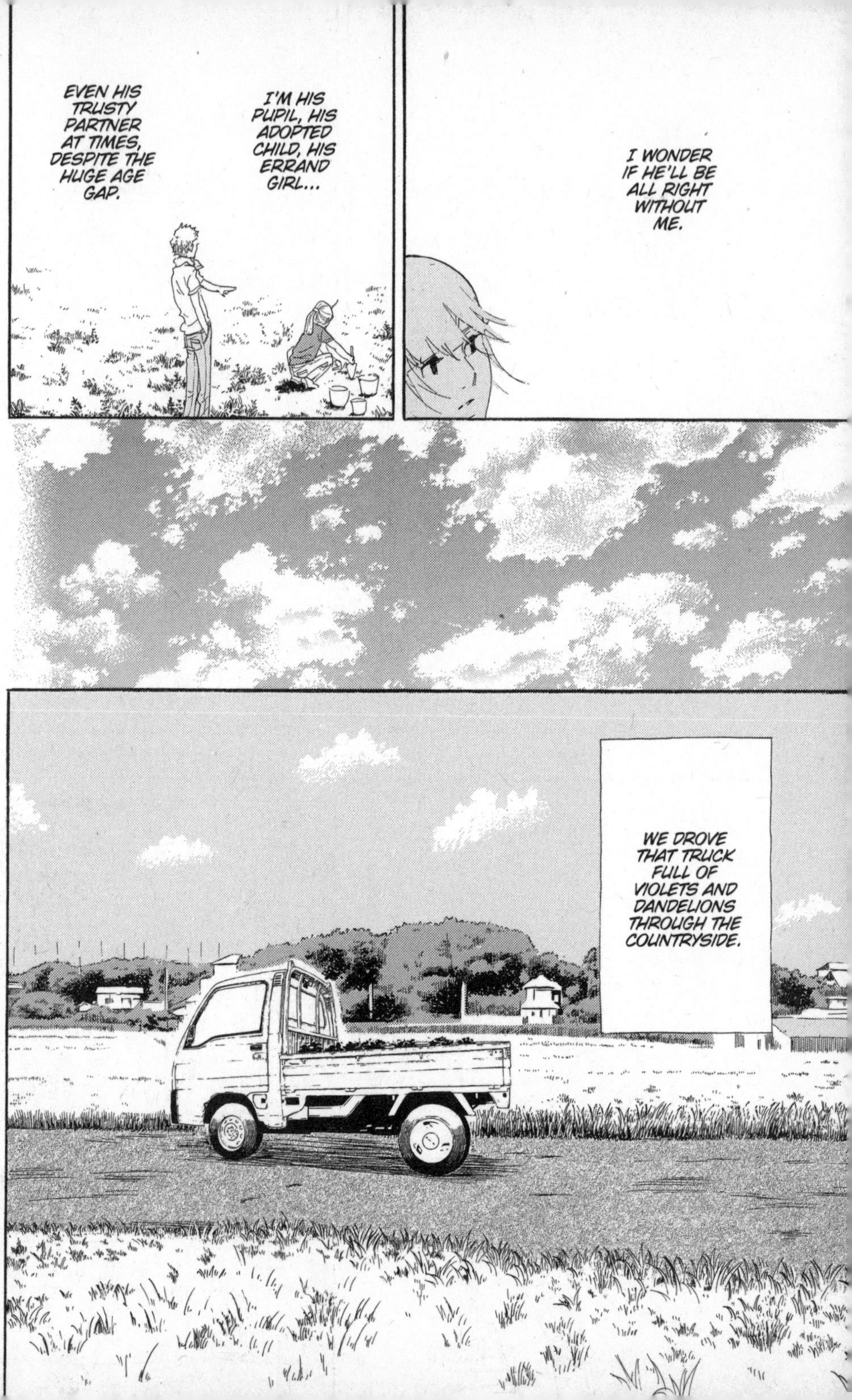
I WONDER IF HE'LL BE ALL RIGHT WITHOUT ME.
I'M HIS PUPIL, HIS ADOPTED CHILD, HIS ERRAND GIRL...
EVEN HIS TRUSTY PARTNER AT TIMES, DESPITE THE HUGE AGE GAP.
WE DROVE THAT TRUCK FULL OF VIOLETS AND DANDELIONS THROUGH THE COUNTRYSIDE.

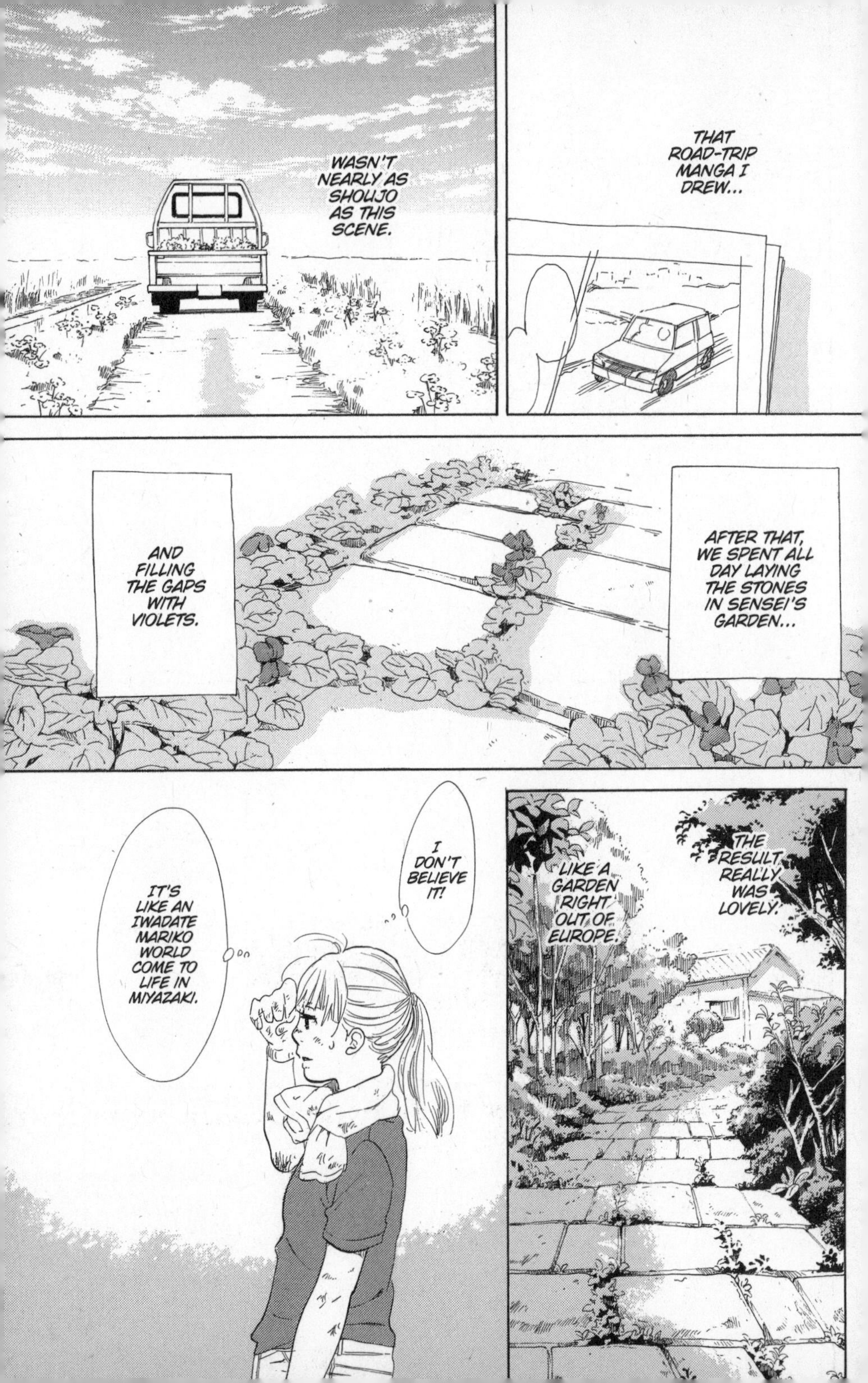
THAT ROAD-TRIP MANGA I DREW...
WASN'T NEARLY AS SHOUJO AS THIS SCENE.
AFTER THAT, WE SPENT ALL DAY LAYING THE STONES IN SENSEI'S GARDEN...
AND FILLING THE GAPS WITH VIOLETS.
THE RESULT REALLY WAS LOVELY.
LIKE A GARDEN RIGHT OUT OF EUROPE.
I DON'T BELIEVE IT!
IT'S LIKE AN IWADATE MARIKO WORLD COME TO LIFE IN MIYAZAKI.

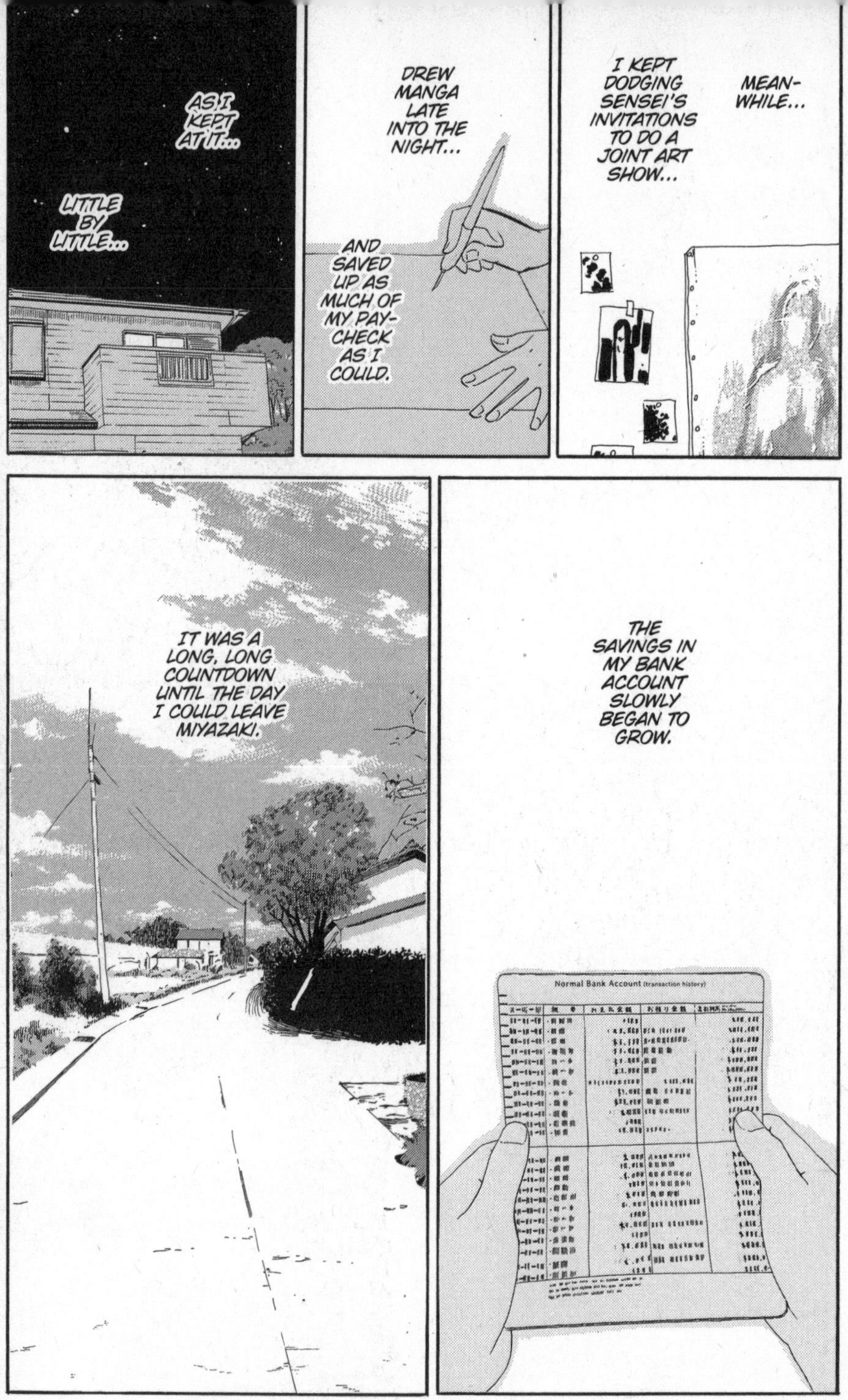
MEAN-WHILE...
I KEPT DODGING SENSEI'S INVITATIONS TO DO A JOINT ART SHOW...
DREW MANGA LATE INTO THE NIGHT...
AND SAVED UP AS MUCH OF MY PAY-CHECK AS I COULD.
AS I KEPT AT IT...
LITTLE BY LITTLE...
THE SAVINGS IN MY BANK ACCOUNT SLOWLY BEGAN TO GROW.
Normal Bank Account (transaction history)
IT WAS A LONG, LONG COUNTDOWN UNTIL THE DAY I COULD LEAVE MIYAZAKI.

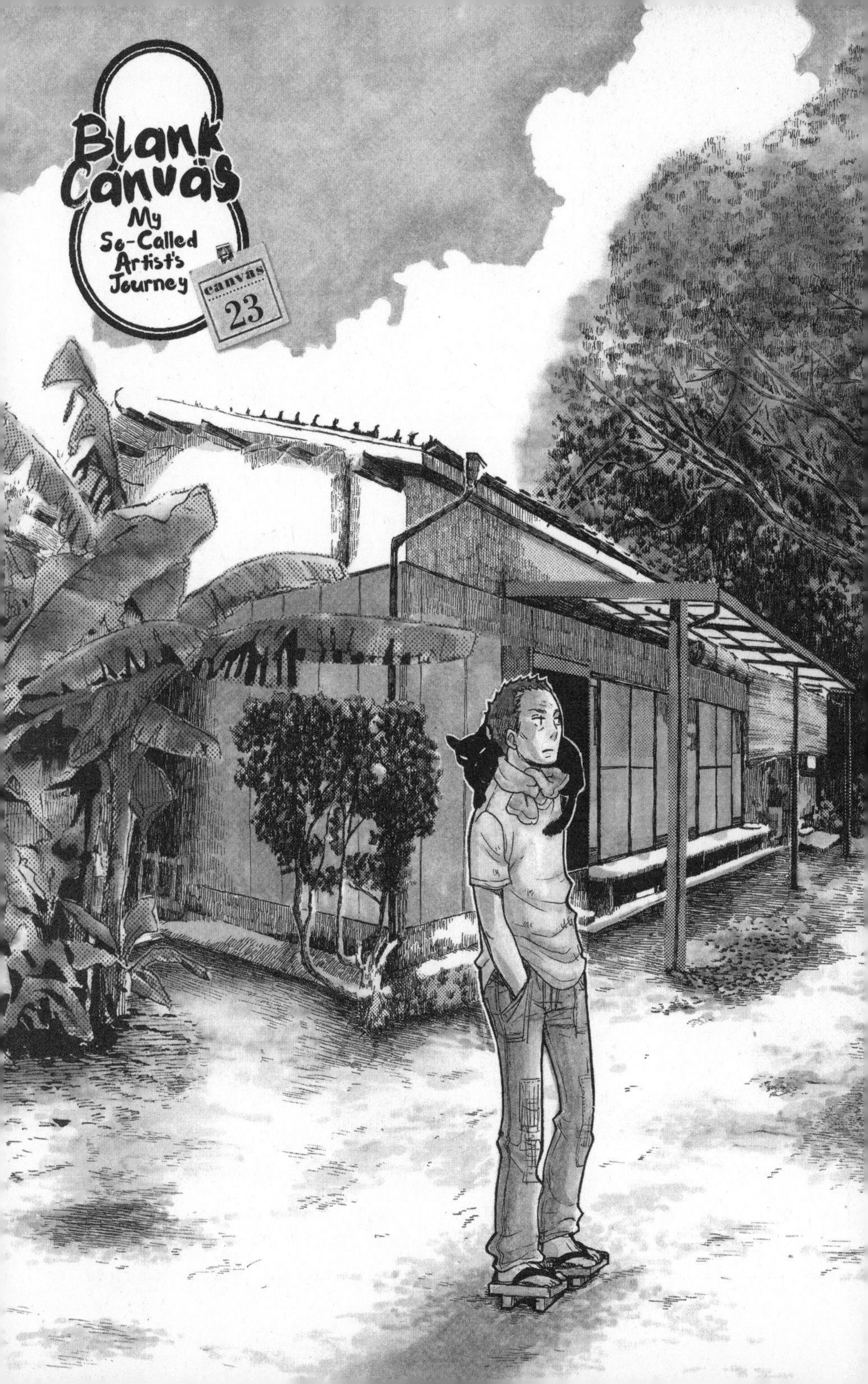
Blank Canvas
My So-Called Artist's Journey
canvas
23

Blank
Canvas
My So-Called
Artist's Journey

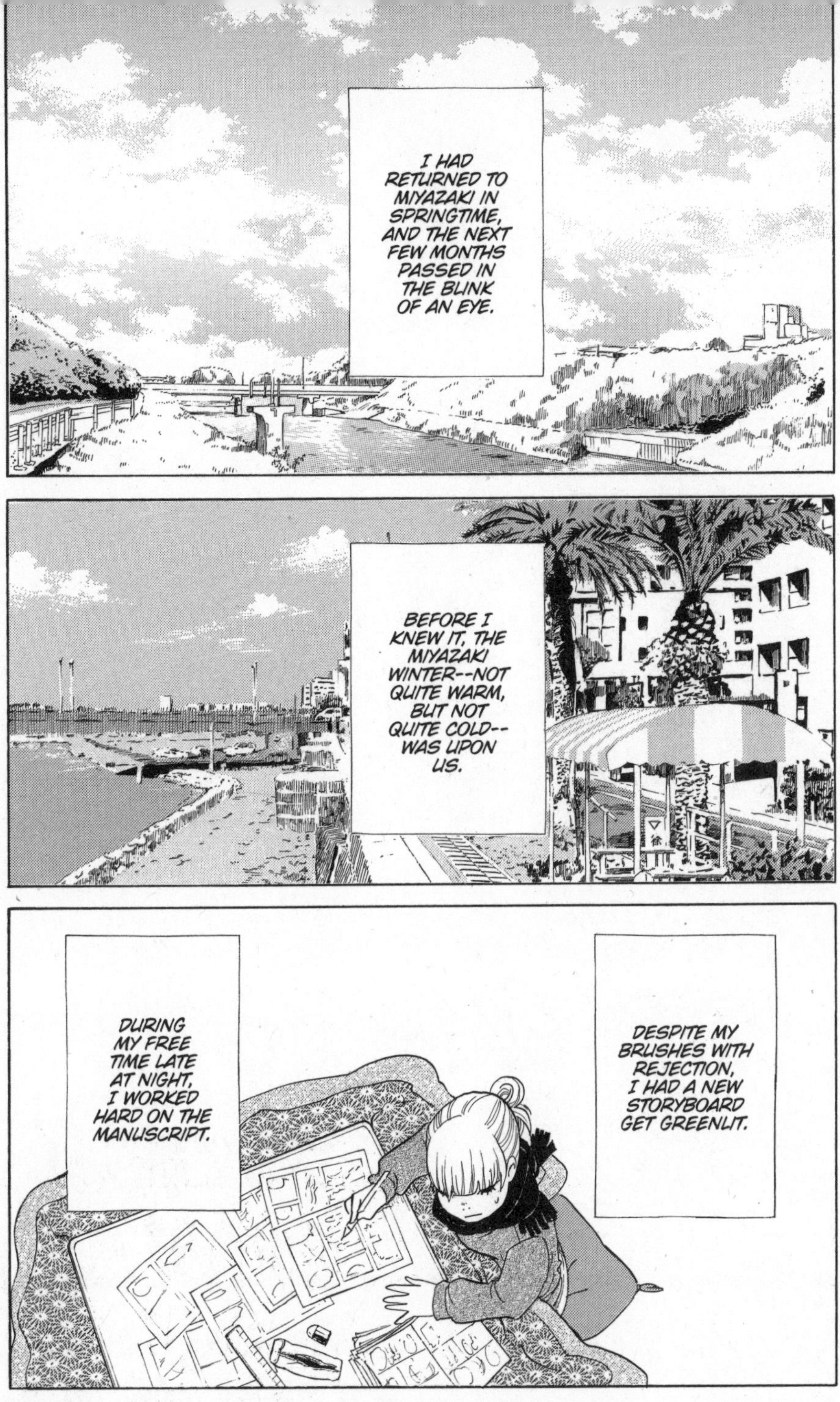
I HAD RETURNED TO MIYAZAKI IN SPRINGTIME, AND THE NEXT FEW MONTHS PASSED IN THE BLINK OF AN EYE.
BEFORE I KNEW IT, THE MIYAZAKI WINTER--NOT QUITE WARM, BUT NOT QUITE COLD--WAS UPON US.
DESPITE MY BRUSHES WITH REJECTION, I HAD A NEW STORYBOARD GET GREENLIT.
DURING MY FREE TIME LATE AT NIGHT, I WORKED HARD ON THE MANUSCRIPT.

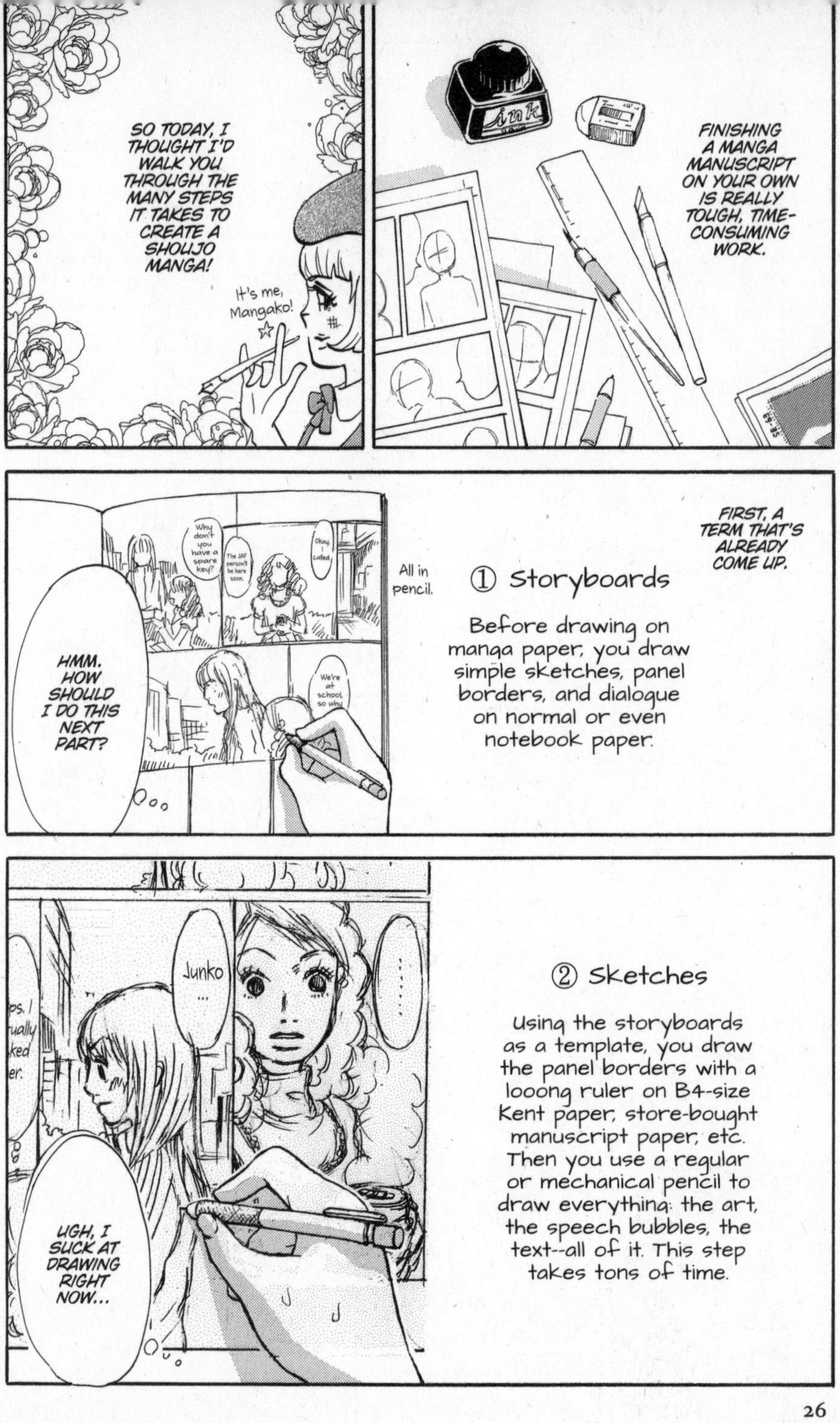
FINISHING A MANGA MANUSCRIPT ON YOUR OWN IS REALLY TOUGH, TIME-CONSUMING WORK.
SO TODAY, I THOUGHT I'D WALK YOU THROUGH THE MANY STEPS IT TAKES TO CREATE A SHOUJO MANGA!
It's me, Mangako! ☆
FIRST, A TERM THAT'S ALREADY COME UP.
① Storyboards
Before drawing on manga paper, you draw simple sketches, panel borders, and dialogue on normal or even notebook paper.
All in pencil.
Okay, I called.
The JAF person'll be here soon.
Why don't you have a spare key?
We're at school, so why
HMM. HOW SHOULD I DO THIS NEXT PART?
② Sketches
Using the storyboards as a template, you draw the panel borders with a looong ruler on B4-size Kent paper, store-bought manuscript paper, etc. Then you use a regular or mechanical pencil to draw everything: the art, the speech bubbles, the text--all of it. This step takes tons of time.
Junko...
UGH, I SUCK AT DRAWING RIGHT NOW...

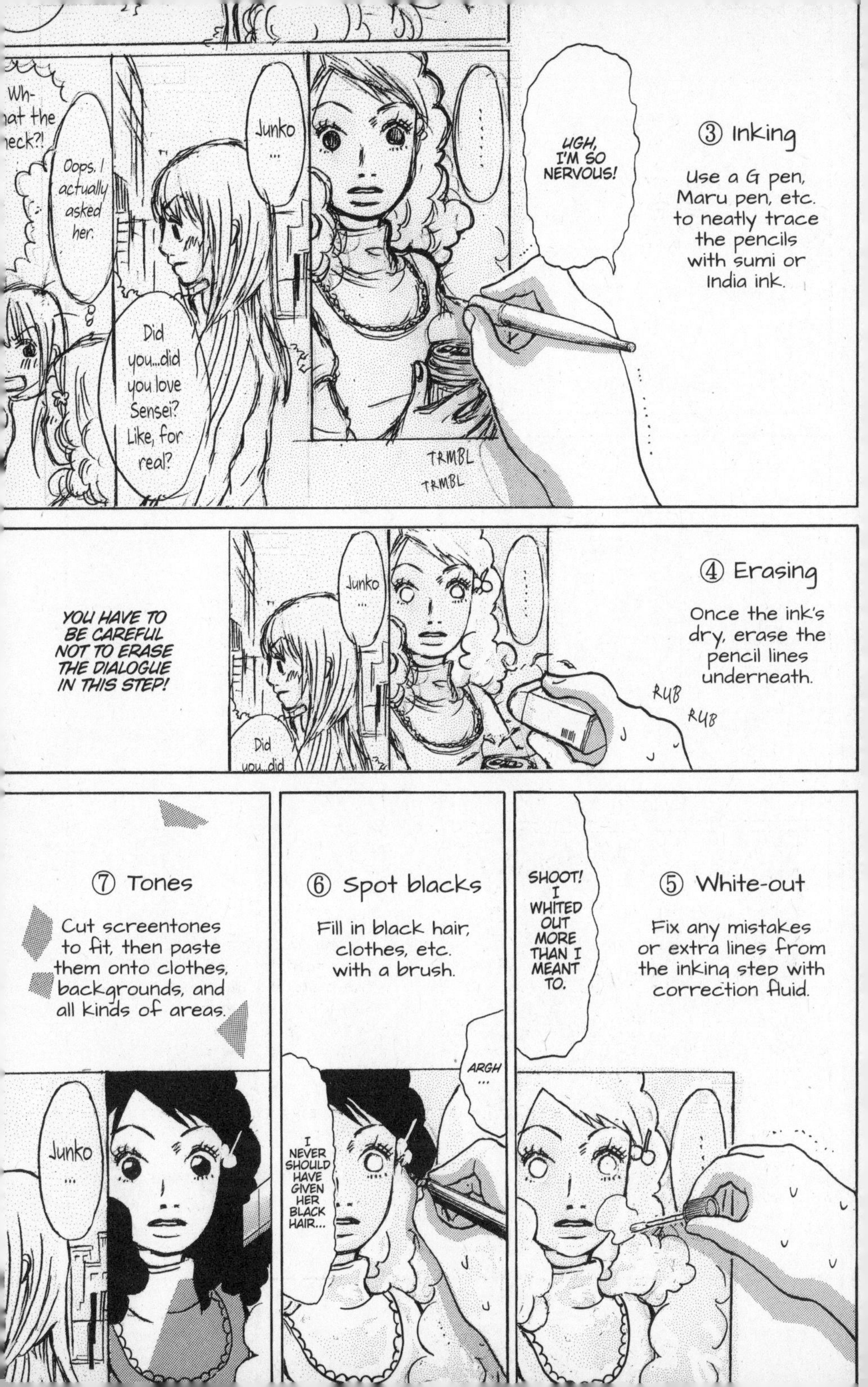

③ Inking
Use a G pen, Maru pen, etc. to neatly trace the pencils with sumi or India ink.
UGH, I'M SO NERVOUS!
......
Junko ...
Oops. I actually asked her.
Wh- at the eck?!
Did you...did you love Sensei? Like, for real?
TRMBL TRMBL
④ Erasing
Once the ink's dry, erase the pencil lines underneath.
RUB RUB
......
Junko ...
Did you...did
YOU HAVE TO BE CAREFUL NOT TO ERASE THE DIALOGUE IN THIS STEP!
⑤ White-out
Fix any mistakes or extra lines from the inking step with correction fluid.
SHOOT! I WHITED OUT MORE THAN I MEANT TO.
⑥ Spot blacks
Fill in black hair, clothes, etc. with a brush.
ARGH ...
I NEVER SHOULD HAVE GIVEN HER BLACK HAIR...
⑦ Tones
Cut screentones to fit, then paste them onto clothes, backgrounds, and all kinds of areas.
Junko ...

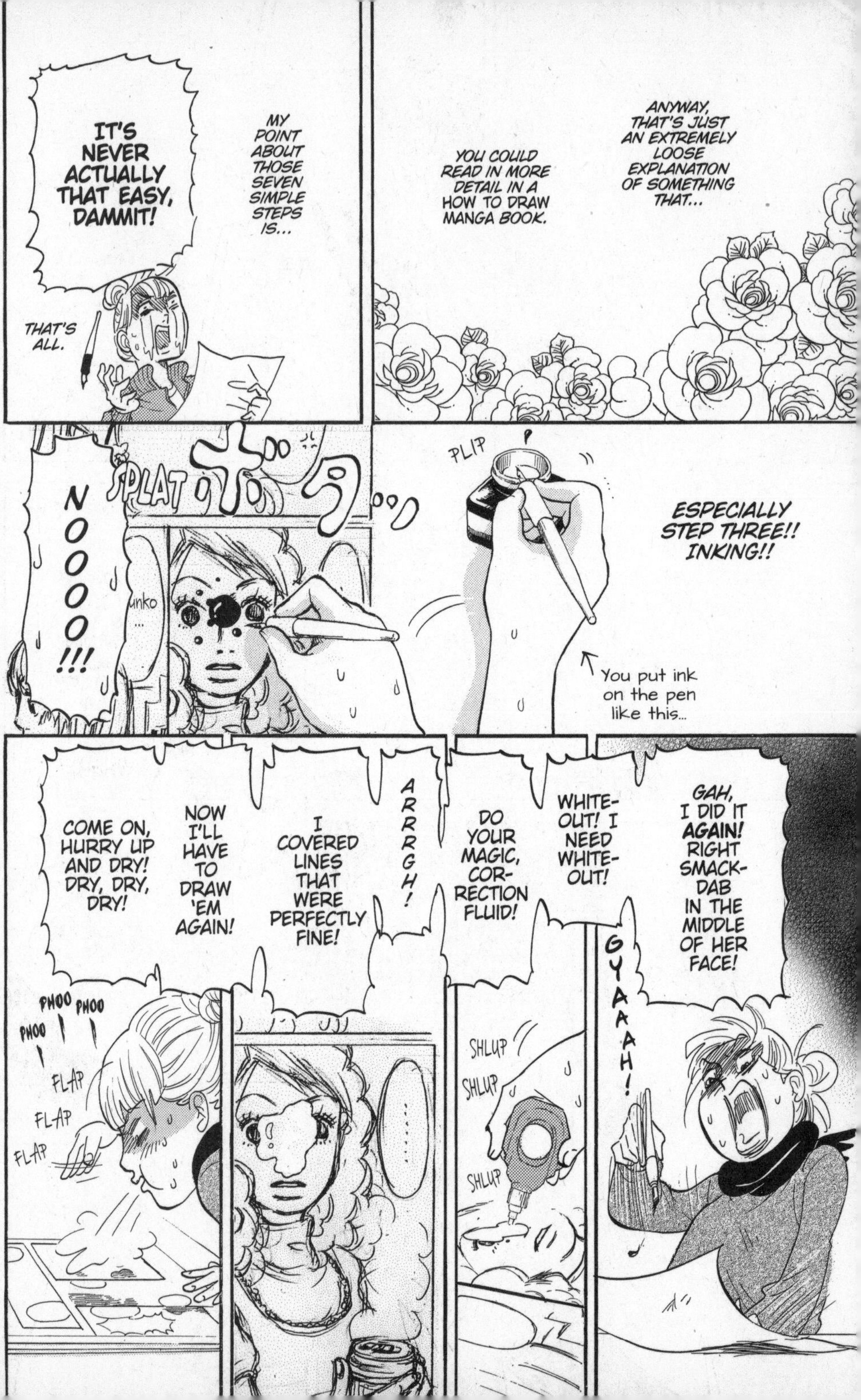
ANYWAY, THAT'S JUST AN EXTREMELY LOOSE EXPLANATION OF SOMETHING THAT...
YOU COULD READ IN MORE DETAIL IN A HOW TO DRAW MANGA BOOK.
MY POINT ABOUT THOSE SEVEN SIMPLE STEPS IS...
IT'S NEVER ACTUALLY THAT EASY, DAMMIT!
THAT'S ALL.
ESPECIALLY STEP THREE!! INKING!!
PLIP
You put ink on the pen like this...
SPLAT
NOOOOO!!!
GAH, I DID IT AGAIN! RIGHT SMACK-DAB IN THE MIDDLE OF HER FACE!
GYAAAH!
WHITE-OUT! I NEED WHITE-OUT!
DO YOUR MAGIC, COR-RECTION FLUID!
SHLUP
SHLUP
SHLUP
ARRRGH!
I COVERED LINES THAT WERE PERFECTLY FINE!
NOW I'LL HAVE TO DRAW 'EM AGAIN!
......
COME ON, HURRY UP AND DRY! DRY, DRY, DRY!
PHOO
PHOO
PHOO
FLAP
FLAP
FLAP

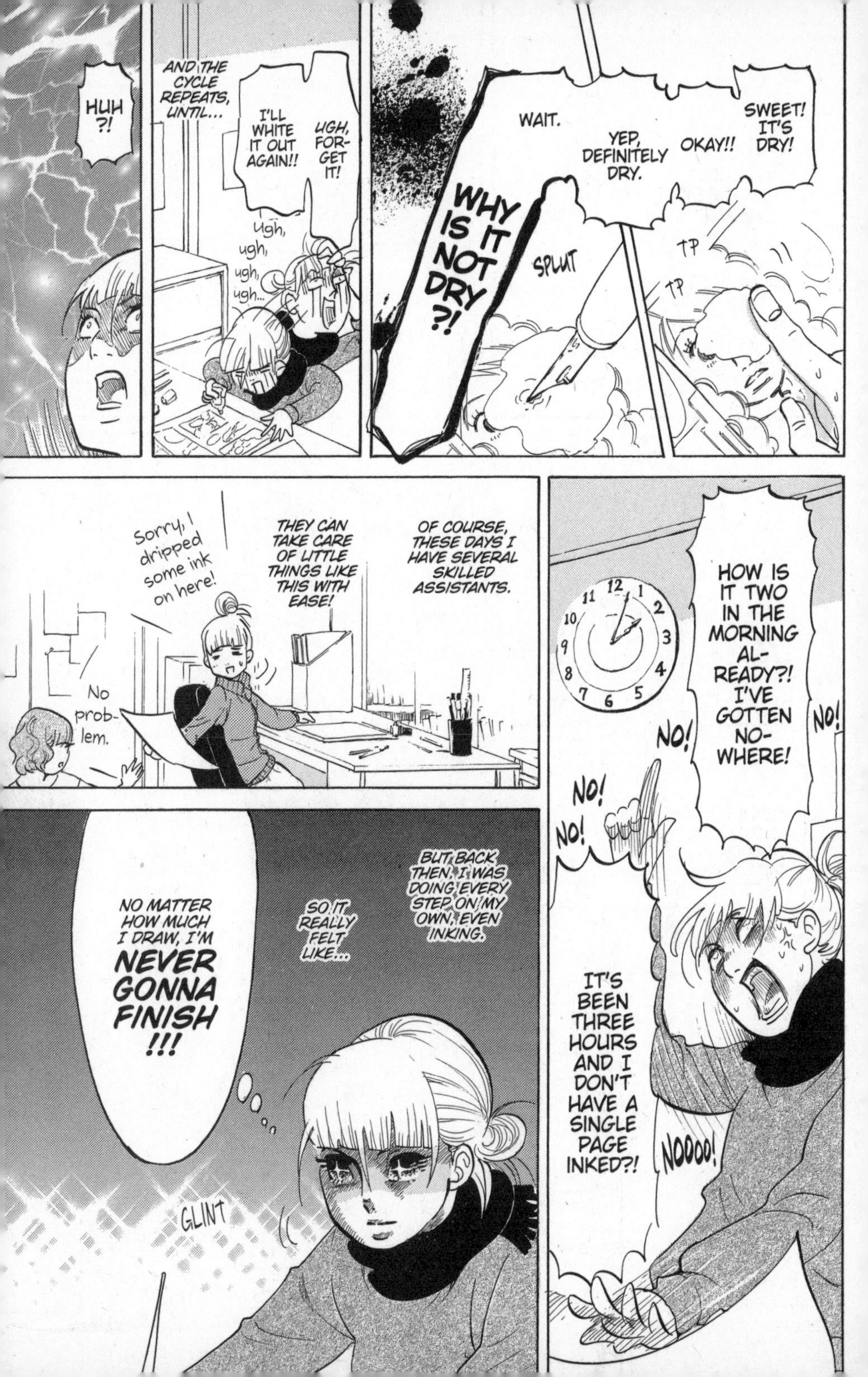
SWEET! IT'S DRY!
OKAY!!
YEP, DEFINITELY DRY.
WAIT.
TP
TP
WHY IS IT NOT DRY?!
SPLUT
AND THE CYCLE REPEATS, UNTIL...
UGH, FOR-GET IT!
I'LL WHITE IT OUT AGAIN!!
Ugh, ugh, ugh, ugh...
HUH?!
HOW IS IT TWO IN THE MORNING AL-READY?! I'VE GOTTEN NO-WHERE!
NO!
NO!
NO!
NO!
IT'S BEEN THREE HOURS AND I DON'T HAVE A SINGLE PAGE INKED?!
NOOOO!
OF COURSE, THESE DAYS I HAVE SEVERAL SKILLED ASSISTANTS.
THEY CAN TAKE CARE OF LITTLE THINGS LIKE THIS WITH EASE!
Sorry, I dripped some ink on here!
No prob-lem.
BUT BACK THEN, I WAS DOING EVERY STEP ON MY OWN, EVEN INKING.
SO IT REALLY FELT LIKE...
NO MATTER HOW MUCH I DRAW, I'M NEVER GONNA FINISH!!!
GLINT

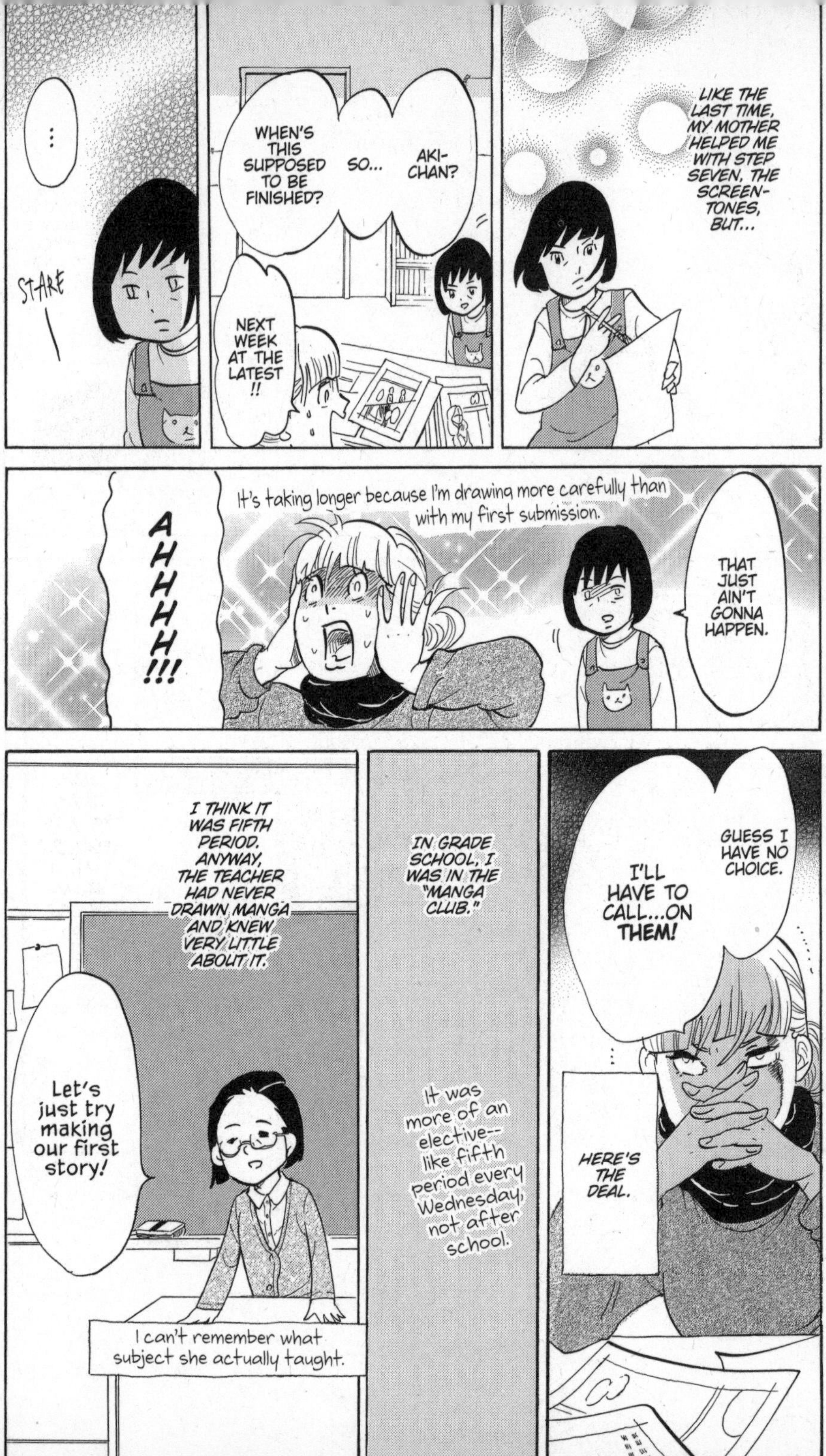
LIKE THE LAST TIME, MY MOTHER HELPED ME WITH STEP SEVEN, THE SCREEN-TONES, BUT...
AKI-CHAN?
SO...
WHEN'S THIS SUPPOSED TO BE FINISHED?
NEXT WEEK AT THE LATEST!!
...
STARE
THAT JUST AIN'T GONNA HAPPEN.
It's taking longer because I'm drawing more carefully than with my first submission.
AHHHHH!!!
GUESS I HAVE NO CHOICE.
I'LL HAVE TO CALL...ON THEM!
HERE'S THE DEAL.
IN GRADE SCHOOL, I WAS IN THE "MANGA CLUB."
It was more of an elective--like fifth period every Wednesday, not after school.
I THINK IT WAS FIFTH PERIOD. ANYWAY, THE TEACHER HAD NEVER DRAWN MANGA AND KNEW VERY LITTLE ABOUT IT.
Let's just try making our first story!
I can't remember what subject she actually taught.

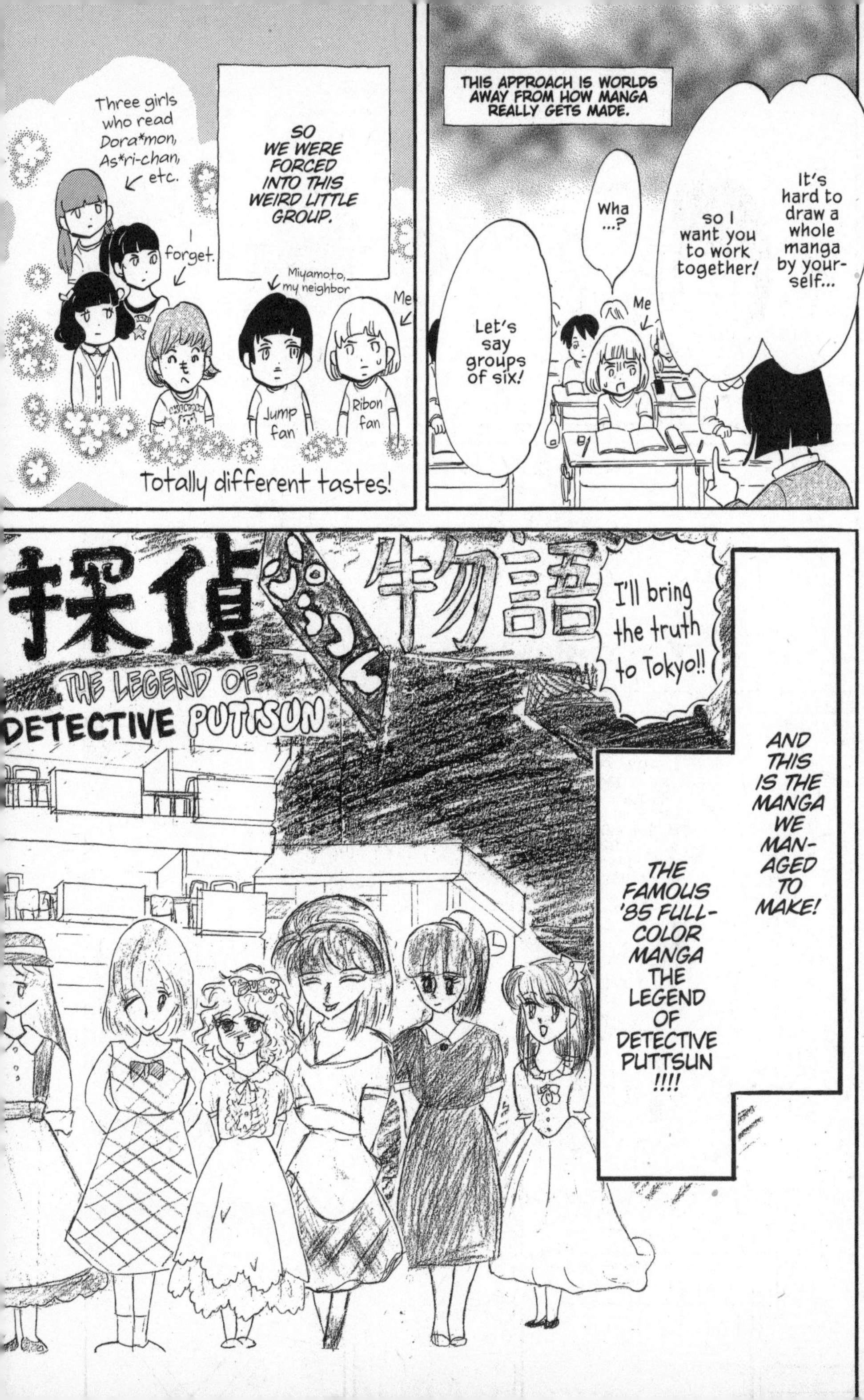
THIS APPROACH IS WORLDS AWAY FROM HOW MANGA REALLY GETS MADE.
It's hard to draw a whole manga by your-self...
so I want you to work together!
Wha ...?
Me
Let's say groups of six!
SO WE WERE FORCED INTO THIS WEIRD LITTLE GROUP.
Me
Ribon fan
Miyamoto, my neighbor
Jump fan
I forget.
Three girls who read Dora*mon, As*ri-chan, etc.
Totally different tastes!
AND THIS IS THE MANGA WE MAN-AGED TO MAKE!
THE FAMOUS '85 FULL-COLOR MANGA THE LEGEND OF DETECTIVE PUTTSUN !!!!
I'll bring the truth to Tokyo!!
探偵ぷっつん物語
THE LEGEND OF DETECTIVE PUTTSUN

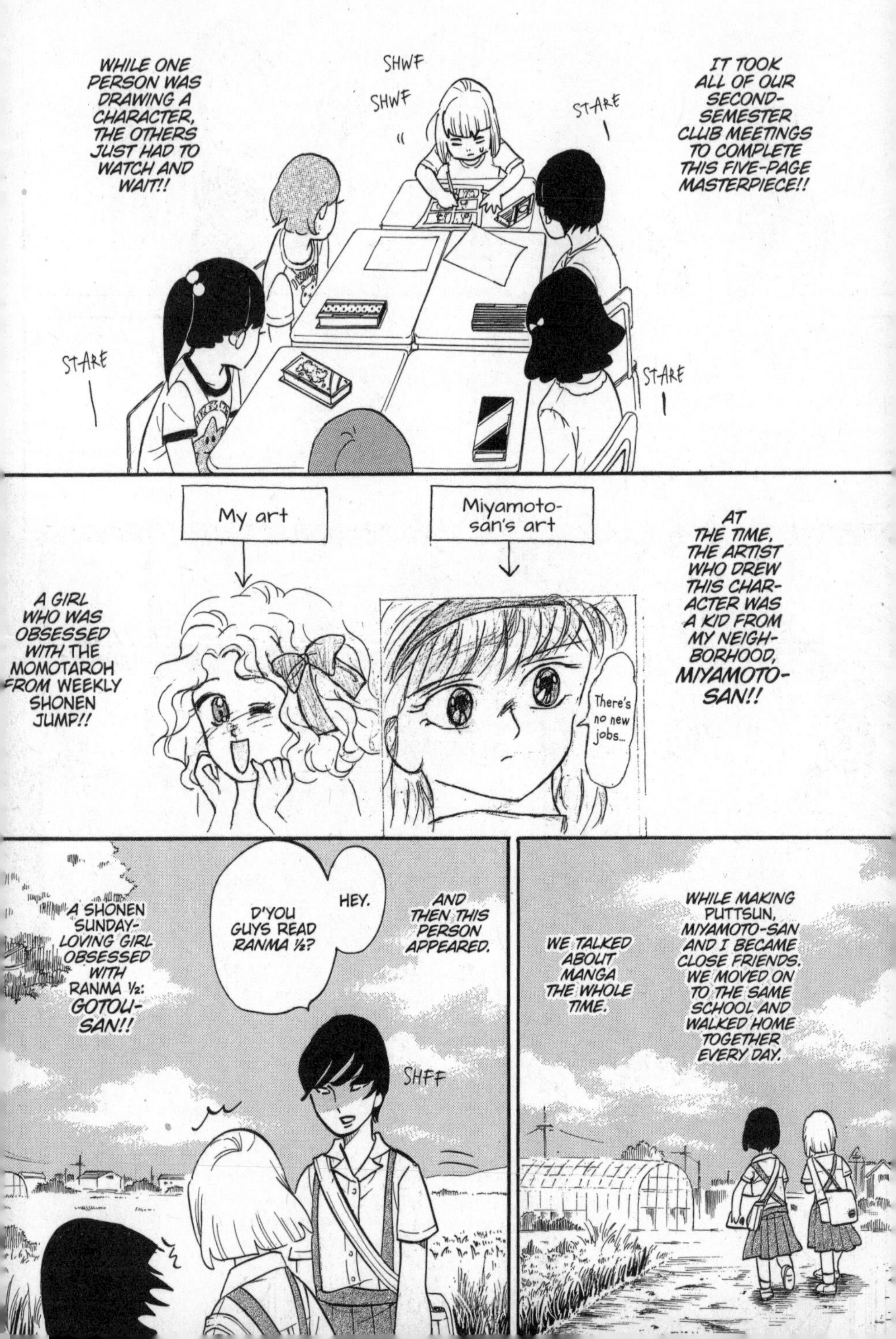
IT TOOK ALL OF OUR SECOND-SEMESTER CLUB MEETINGS TO COMPLETE THIS FIVE-PAGE MASTERPIECE!!
STARE
SHWF
SHWF
WHILE ONE PERSON WAS DRAWING A CHARACTER, THE OTHERS JUST HAD TO WATCH AND WAIT!!
STARE
STARE
AT THE TIME, THE ARTIST WHO DREW THIS CHARACTER WAS A KID FROM MY NEIGHBORHOOD, MIYAMOTO-SAN!!
Miyamoto-san's art
There's no new jobs...
My art
A GIRL WHO WAS OBSESSED WITH THE MOMOTAROH FROM WEEKLY SHONEN JUMP!!
WHILE MAKING PUTTSUN, MIYAMOTO-SAN AND I BECAME CLOSE FRIENDS. WE MOVED ON TO THE SAME SCHOOL AND WALKED HOME TOGETHER EVERY DAY.
WE TALKED ABOUT MANGA THE WHOLE TIME.
AND THEN THIS PERSON APPEARED.
HEY.
D'YOU GUYS READ RANMA ½?
SHFF
A SHONEN SUNDAY-LOVING GIRL OBSESSED WITH RANMA ½: GOTOU-SAN!!

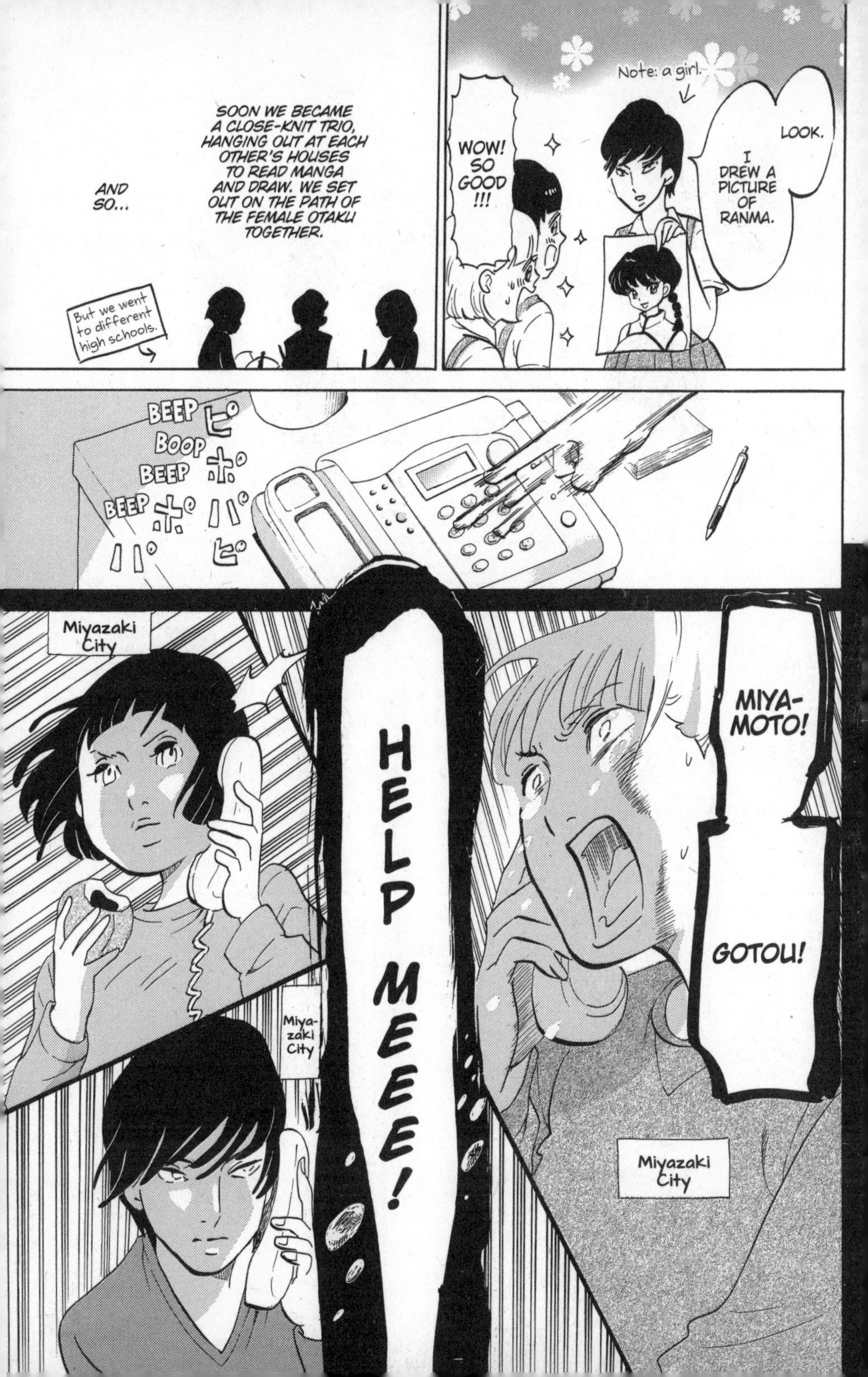
Note: a girl.
LOOK. I DREW A PICTURE OF RANMA.
WOW! SO GOOD!!!
SOON WE BECAME A CLOSE-KNIT TRIO, HANGING OUT AT EACH OTHER'S HOUSES TO READ MANGA AND DRAW. WE SET OUT ON THE PATH OF THE FEMALE OTAKU TOGETHER.
AND SO...
But we went to different high schools.
BEEP Boop BEEP BEEP
ピポパピ
ポパ
MIYA-MOTO!
GOTOU!
HELP MEEE!
Miyazaki City
Miyazaki City
Miya-zaki City

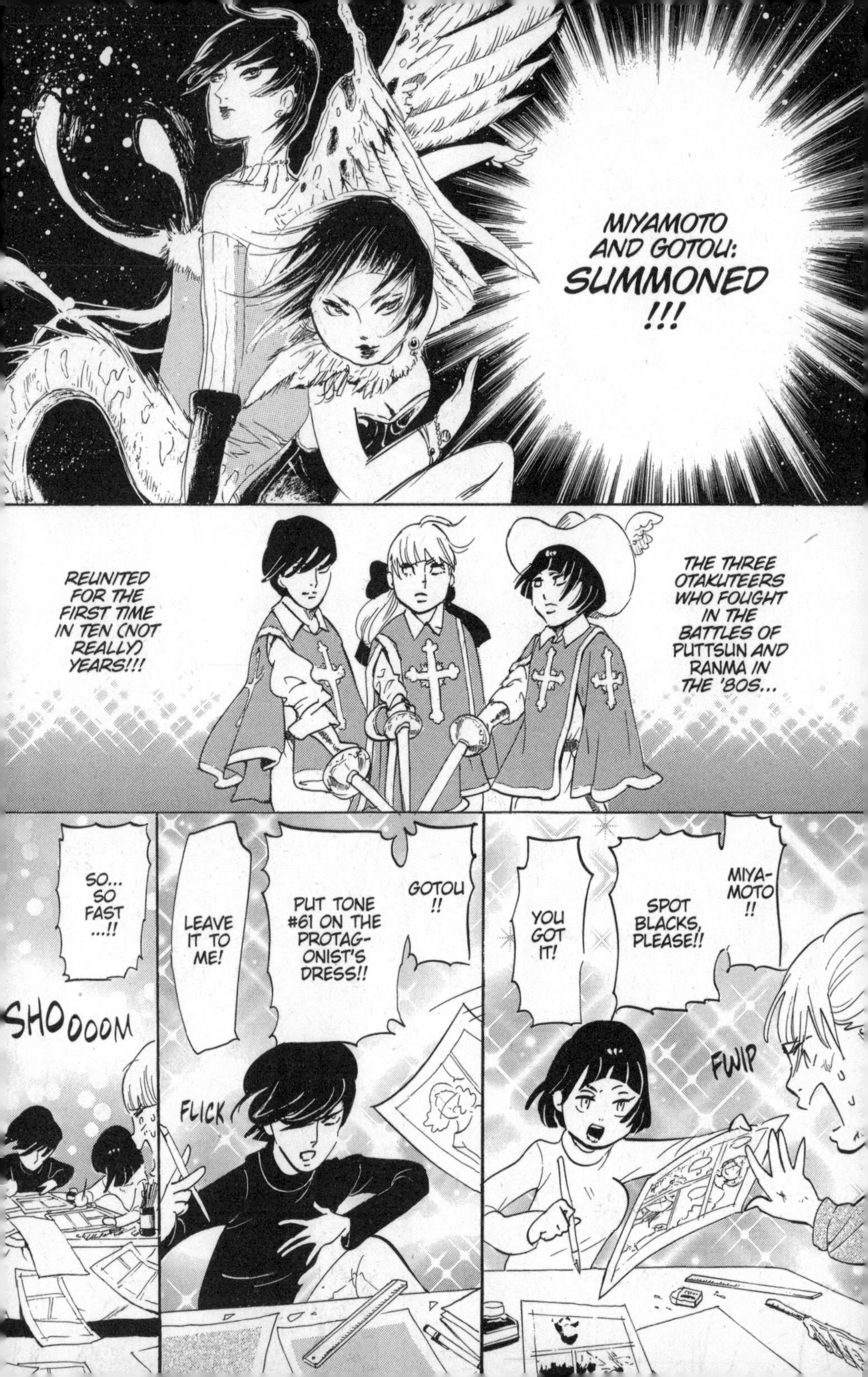
MIYAMOTO AND GOTOU: SUMMONED !!!
THE THREE OTAKUTEERS WHO FOUGHT IN THE BATTLES OF PUTTSUN AND RANMA IN THE '80S...
REUNITED FOR THE FIRST TIME IN TEN (NOT REALLY) YEARS!!!
MIYA-MOTO !!
SPOT BLACKS, PLEASE!!
YOU GOT IT!
FWIP
GOTOU !!
PUT TONE #61 ON THE PROTAG-ONIST'S DRESS!!
LEAVE IT TO ME!
FLICK
SO... SO FAST ...!!
SHOOOOM

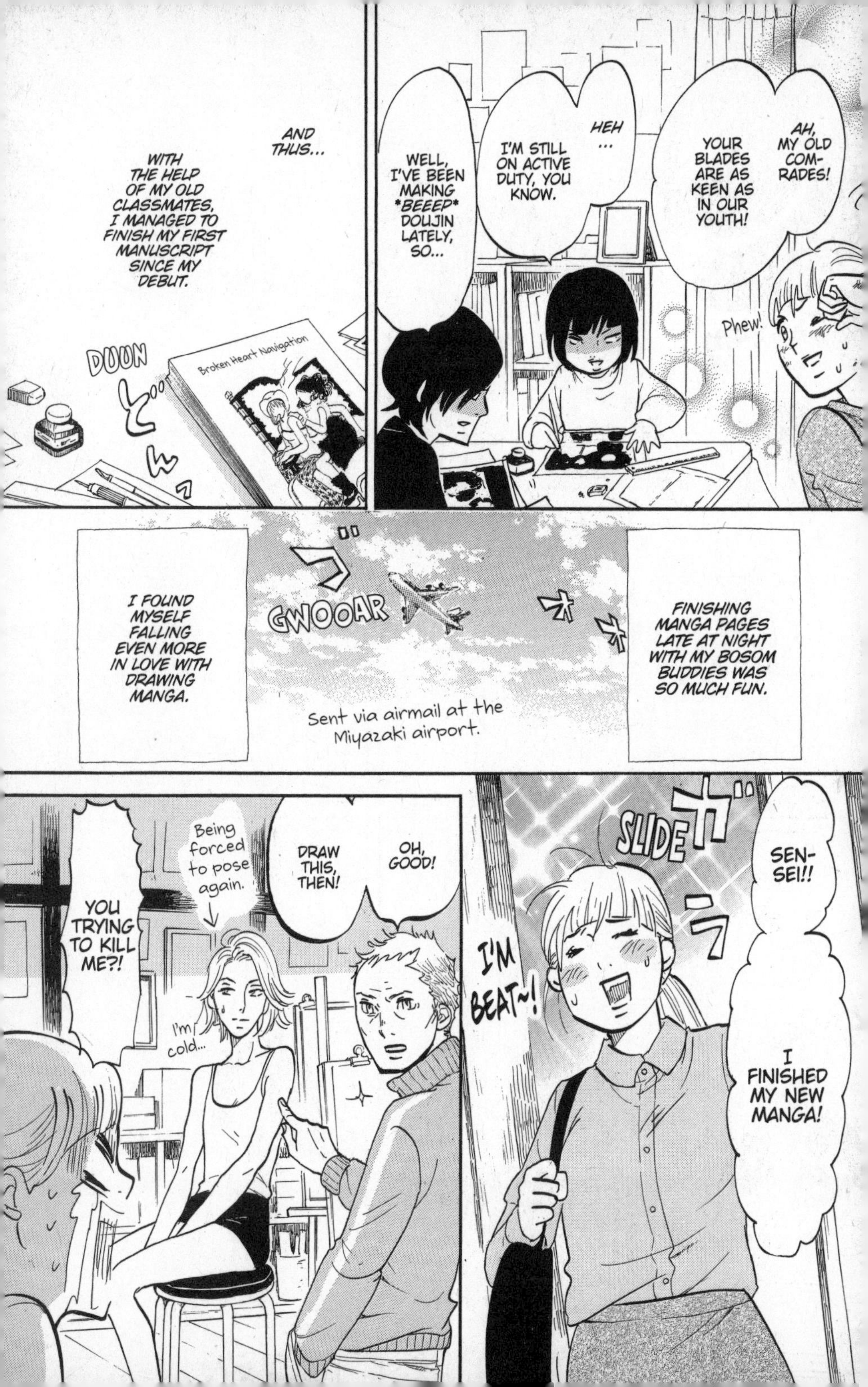
AH, MY OLD COM-RADES!
YOUR BLADES ARE AS KEEN AS IN OUR YOUTH!
Phew!
HEH...
I'M STILL ON ACTIVE DUTY, YOU KNOW.
WELL, I'VE BEEN MAKING *BEEEP* DOUJIN LATELY, SO...
AND THUS...
WITH THE HELP OF MY OLD CLASSMATES, I MANAGED TO FINISH MY FIRST MANUSCRIPT SINCE MY DEBUT.
Broken Heart Navigation
DUUN
FINISHING MANGA PAGES LATE AT NIGHT WITH MY BOSOM BUDDIES WAS SO MUCH FUN.
GWOOAR
Sent via airmail at the Miyazaki airport.
I FOUND MYSELF FALLING EVEN MORE IN LOVE WITH DRAWING MANGA.
SLIDE
SEN-SEI!!
I'M BEAT~!
I FINISHED MY NEW MANGA!
OH, GOOD!
DRAW THIS, THEN!
Being forced to pose again.
YOU TRYING TO KILL ME?!
I'm cold...

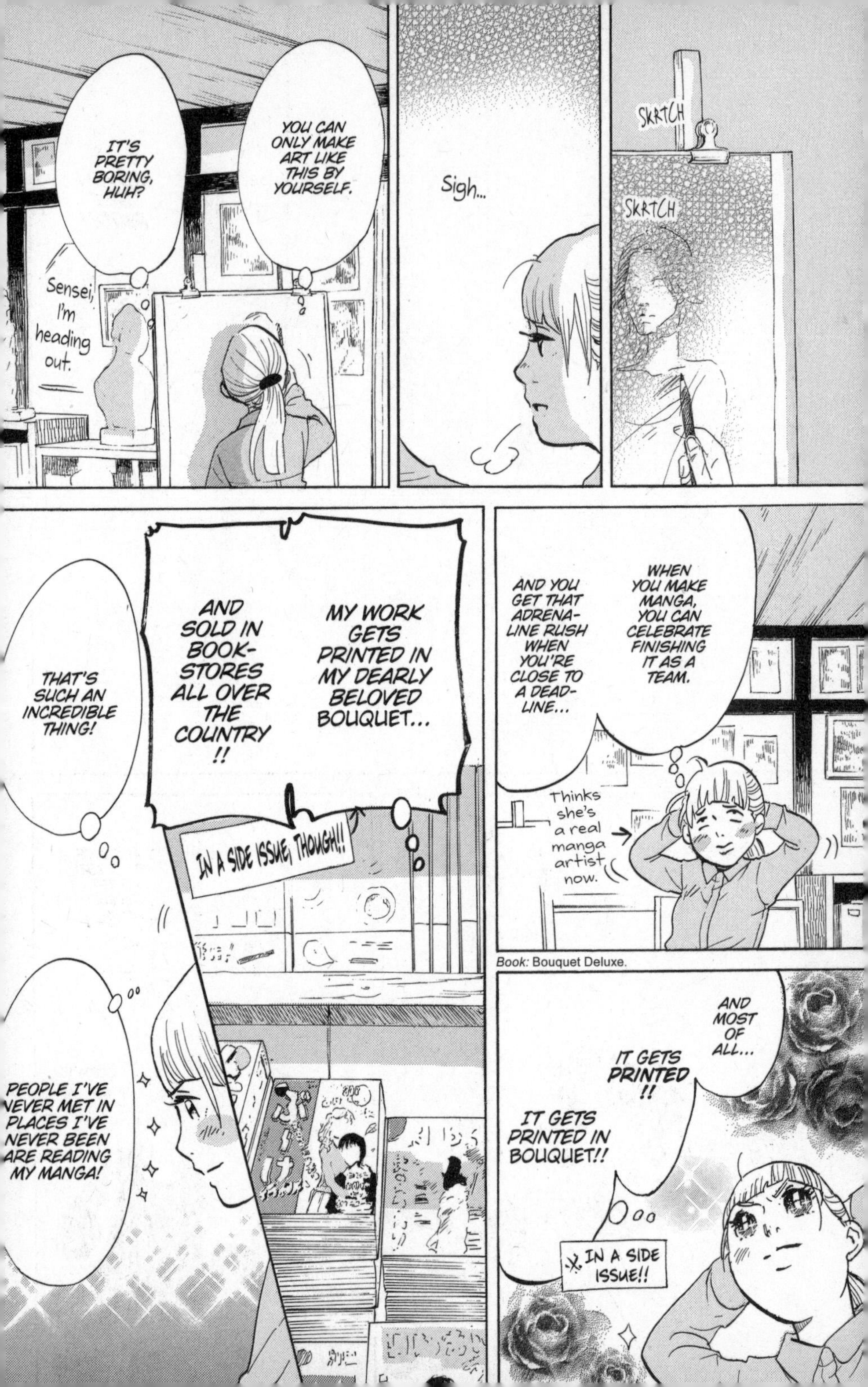
SKRTCH
SKRTCH
Sigh...
YOU CAN ONLY MAKE ART LIKE THIS BY YOURSELF.
IT'S PRETTY BORING, HUH?
Sensei, I'm heading out.
WHEN YOU MAKE MANGA, YOU CAN CELEBRATE FINISHING IT AS A TEAM.
AND YOU GET THAT ADRENA-LINE RUSH WHEN YOU'RE CLOSE TO A DEAD-LINE...
Thinks she's a real manga artist now.
AND MOST OF ALL...
IT GETS PRINTED!!
IT GETS PRINTED IN BOUQUET!!
※ IN A SIDE ISSUE!!
MY WORK GETS PRINTED IN MY DEARLY BELOVED BOUQUET...
AND SOLD IN BOOK-STORES ALL OVER THE COUNTRY!!
IN A SIDE ISSUE, THOUGH!!
THAT'S SUCH AN INCREDIBLE THING!
PEOPLE I'VE NEVER MET IN PLACES I'VE NEVER BEEN ARE READING MY MANGA!
Book: Bouquet Deluxe.

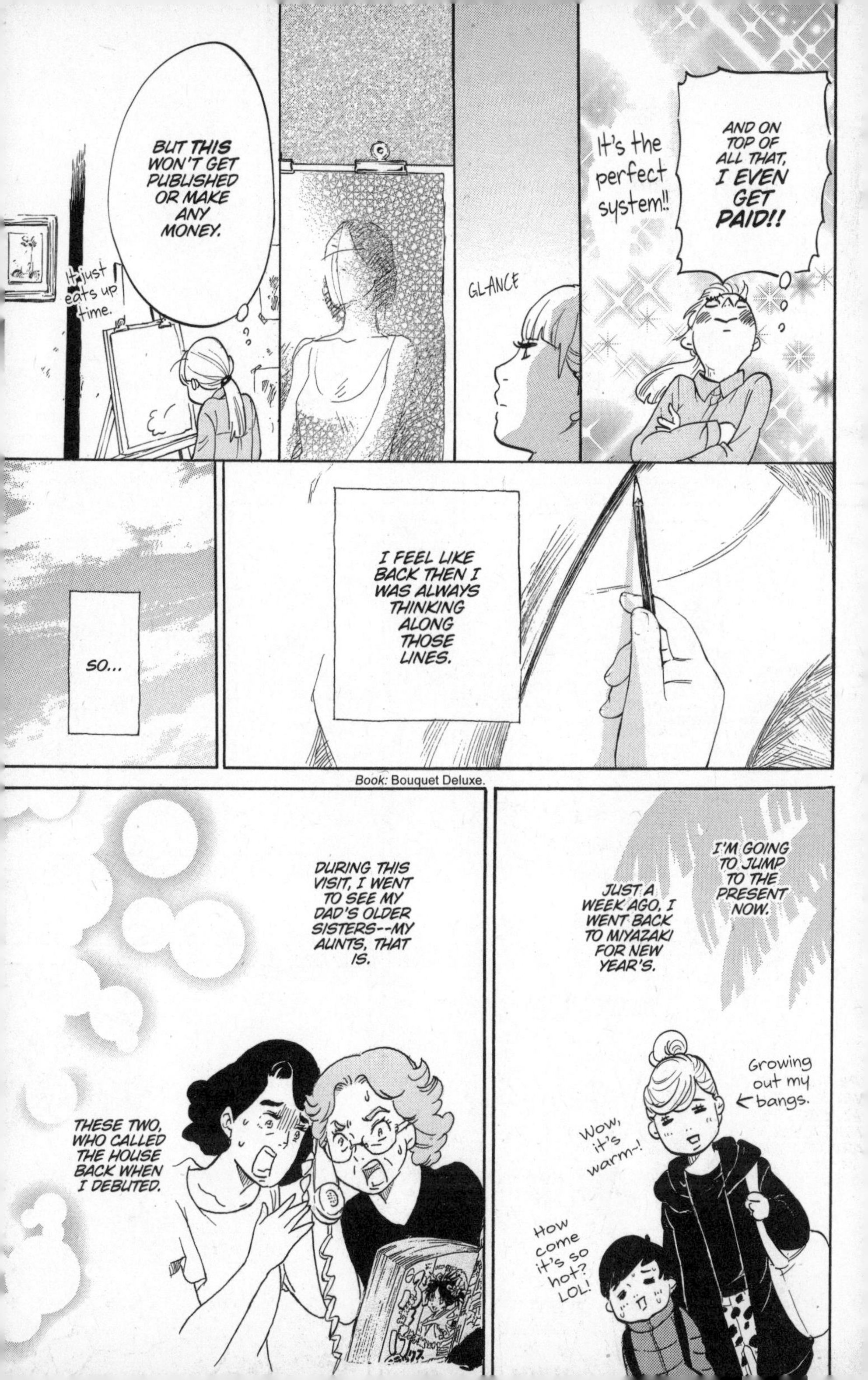
AND ON TOP OF ALL THAT, I EVEN GET PAID!!
It's the perfect system!!
GLANCE
BUT THIS WON'T GET PUBLISHED OR MAKE ANY MONEY.
It just eats up time.
I FEEL LIKE BACK THEN I WAS ALWAYS THINKING ALONG THOSE LINES.
SO...
Book: Bouquet Deluxe.
I'M GOING TO JUMP TO THE PRESENT NOW.
JUST A WEEK AGO, I WENT BACK TO MIYAZAKI FOR NEW YEAR'S.
Growing out my bangs.
Wow, it's warm~!
How come it's so hot? LOL!
DURING THIS VISIT, I WENT TO SEE MY DAD'S OLDER SISTERS--MY AUNTS, THAT IS.
THESE TWO, WHO CALLED THE HOUSE BACK WHEN I DEBUTED.

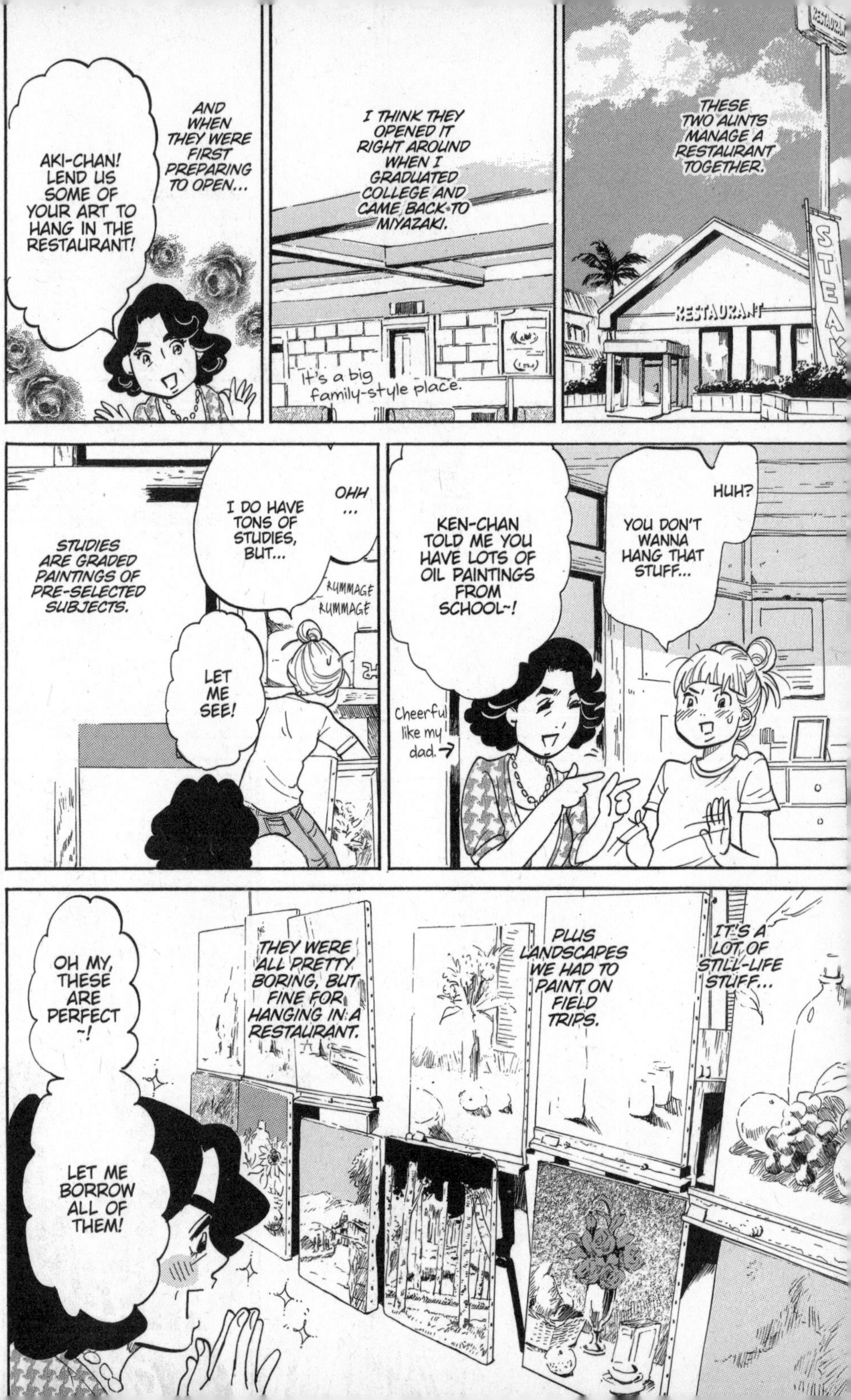

RESTAURANT
THESE TWO AUNTS MANAGE A RESTAURANT TOGETHER.
STEAK
RESTAURANT
I THINK THEY OPENED IT RIGHT AROUND WHEN I GRADUATED COLLEGE AND CAME BACK TO MIYAZAKI.
It's a big family-style place.
AND WHEN THEY WERE FIRST PREPARING TO OPEN...
AKI-CHAN! LEND US SOME OF YOUR ART TO HANG IN THE RESTAURANT!
HUH?
YOU DON'T WANNA HANG THAT STUFF...
KEN-CHAN TOLD ME YOU HAVE LOTS OF OIL PAINTINGS FROM SCHOOL~!
Cheerful like my dad.
OHH ...
I DO HAVE TONS OF STUDIES, BUT...
STUDIES ARE GRADED PAINTINGS OF PRE-SELECTED SUBJECTS.
RUMMAGE RUMMAGE
LET ME SEE!
IT'S A LOT OF STILL-LIFE STUFF...
PLUS LANDSCAPES WE HAD TO PAINT ON FIELD TRIPS.
THEY WERE ALL PRETTY BORING, BUT FINE FOR HANGING IN A RESTAURANT.
OH MY, THESE ARE PERFECT~!
LET ME BORROW ALL OF THEM!

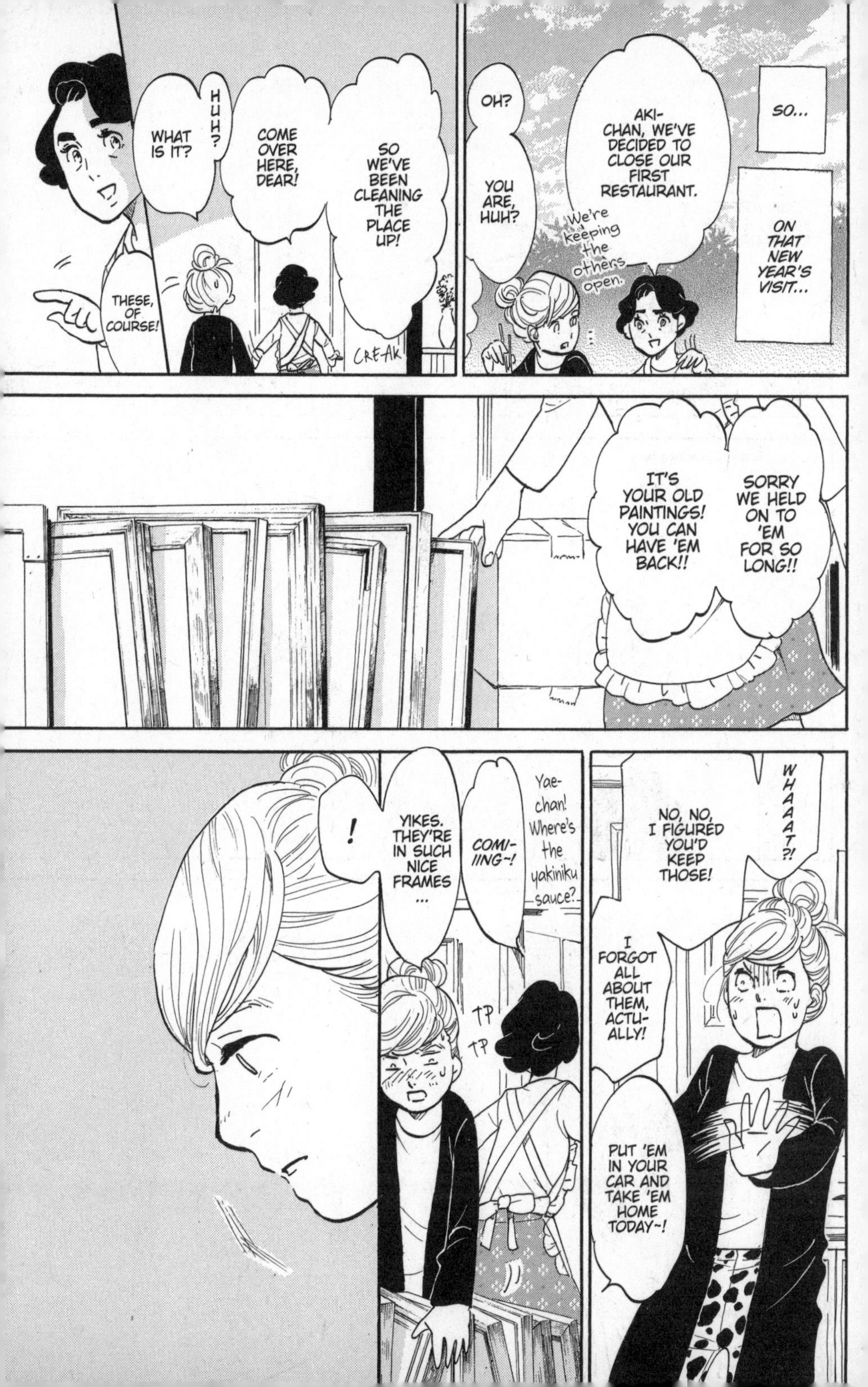
SO...
ON THAT NEW YEAR'S VISIT...
AKI-CHAN, WE'VE DECIDED TO CLOSE OUR FIRST RESTAURANT.
We're keeping the others open.
OH? YOU ARE, HUH?
SO WE'VE BEEN CLEANING THE PLACE UP!
COME OVER HERE, DEAR!
HUH?
WHAT IS IT?
THESE, OF COURSE!
CREAK
SORRY WE HELD ON TO 'EM FOR SO LONG!!
IT'S YOUR OLD PAINTINGS! YOU CAN HAVE 'EM BACK!!
WHAAAAT?!
NO, NO, I FIGURED YOU'D KEEP THOSE!
I FORGOT ALL ABOUT THEM, ACTUALLY!
PUT 'EM IN YOUR CAR AND TAKE 'EM HOME TODAY~!
Yae-chan! Where's the yakiniku sauce?
COMI-IING~!
YIKES. THEY'RE IN SUCH NICE FRAMES...
TP
TP
!

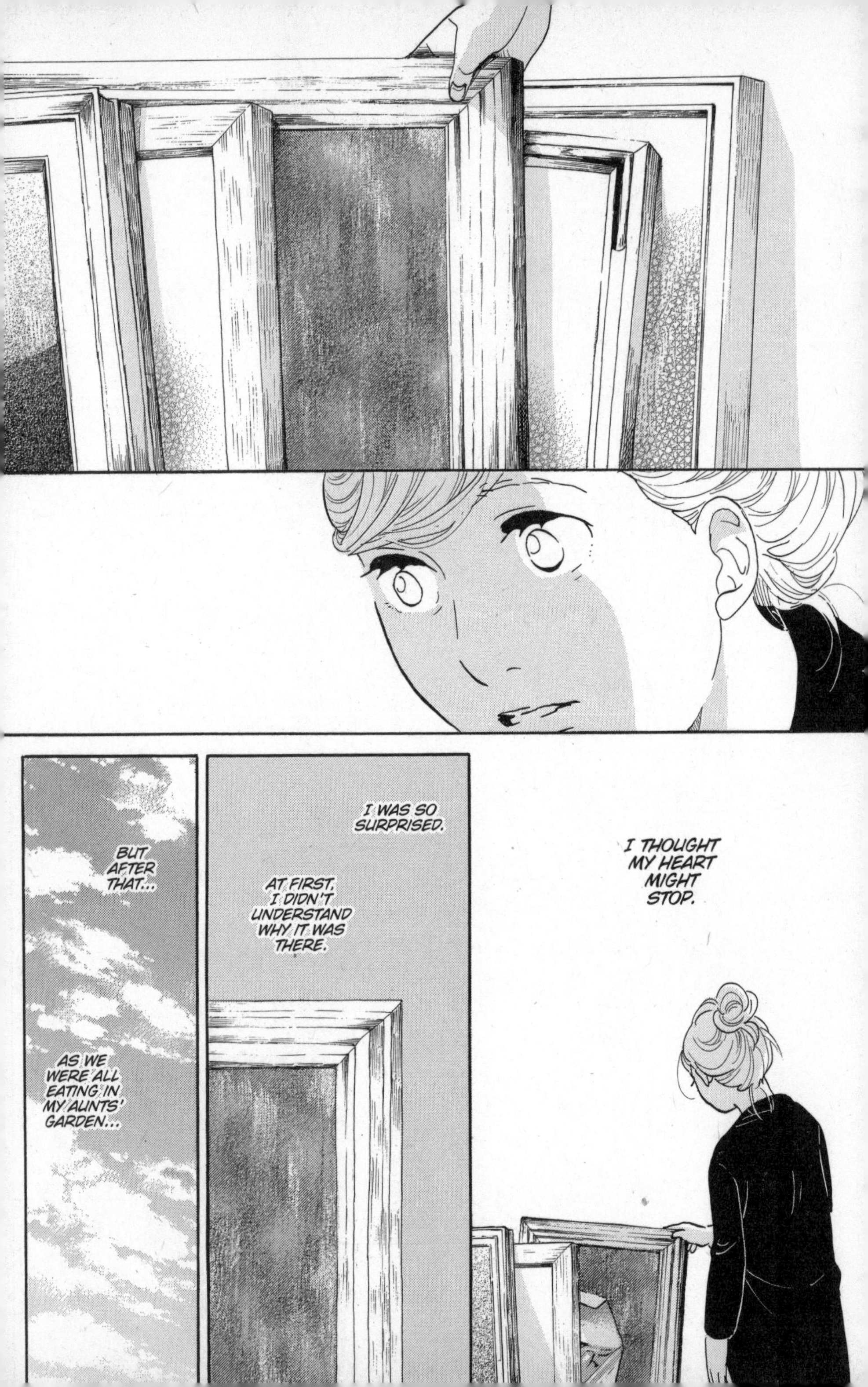
I THOUGHT MY HEART MIGHT STOP.
I WAS SO SURPRISED.
AT FIRST, I DIDN'T UNDERSTAND WHY IT WAS THERE.
BUT AFTER THAT...
AS WE WERE ALL EATING IN MY AUNTS' GARDEN...

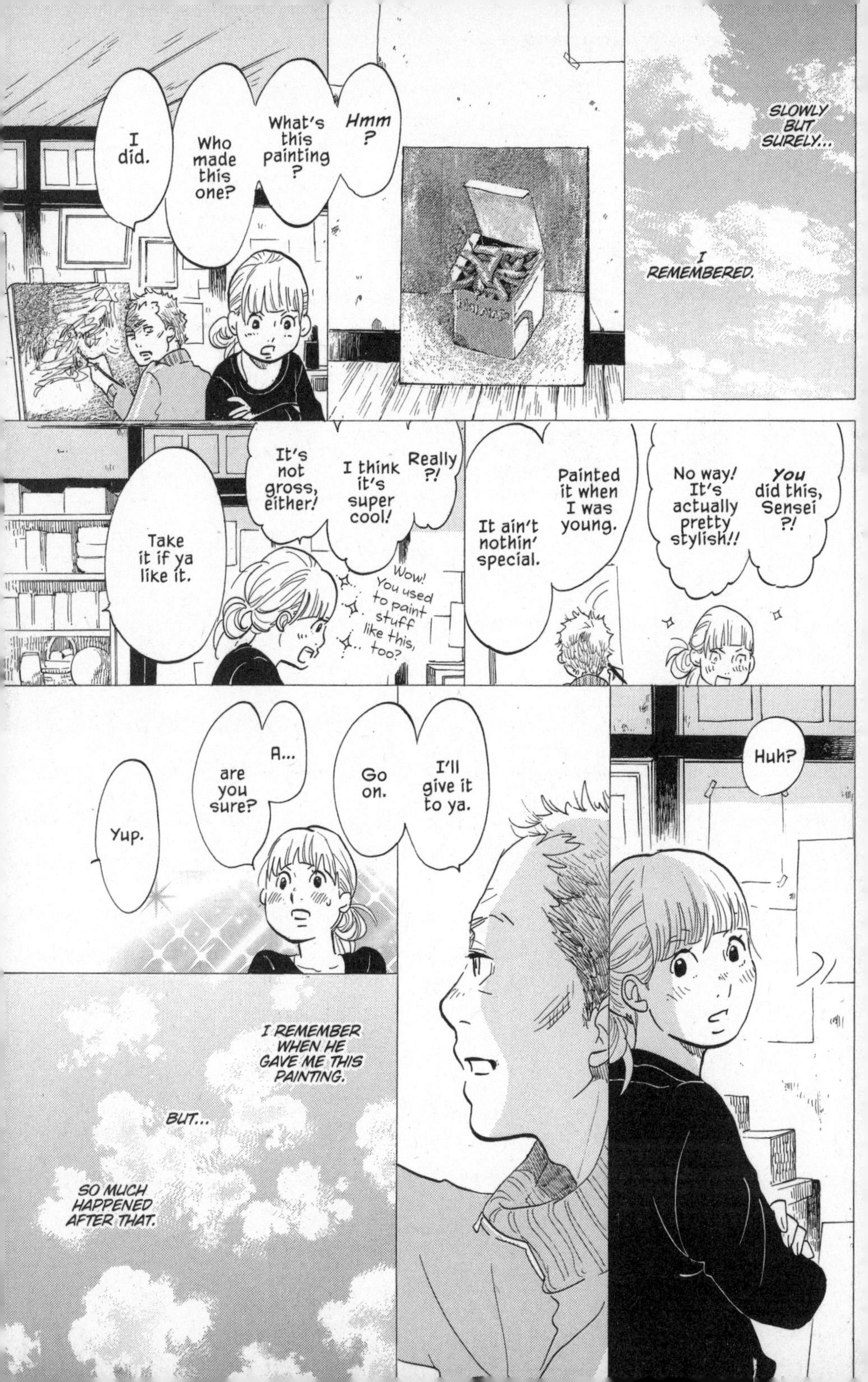
SLOWLY BUT SURELY...
I REMEMBERED.
Hmm?
What's this painting?
Who made this one?
I did.
You did this, Sensei?!
No way! It's actually pretty stylish!!
Painted it when I was young.
It ain't nothin' special.
Really?!
I think it's super cool!
It's not gross, either!
Wow! You used to paint stuff like this, too?
Take it if ya like it.
Huh?
I'll give it to ya.
Go on.
A... are you sure?
Yup.
I REMEMBER WHEN HE GAVE ME THIS PAINTING.
BUT...
SO MUCH HAPPENED AFTER THAT.

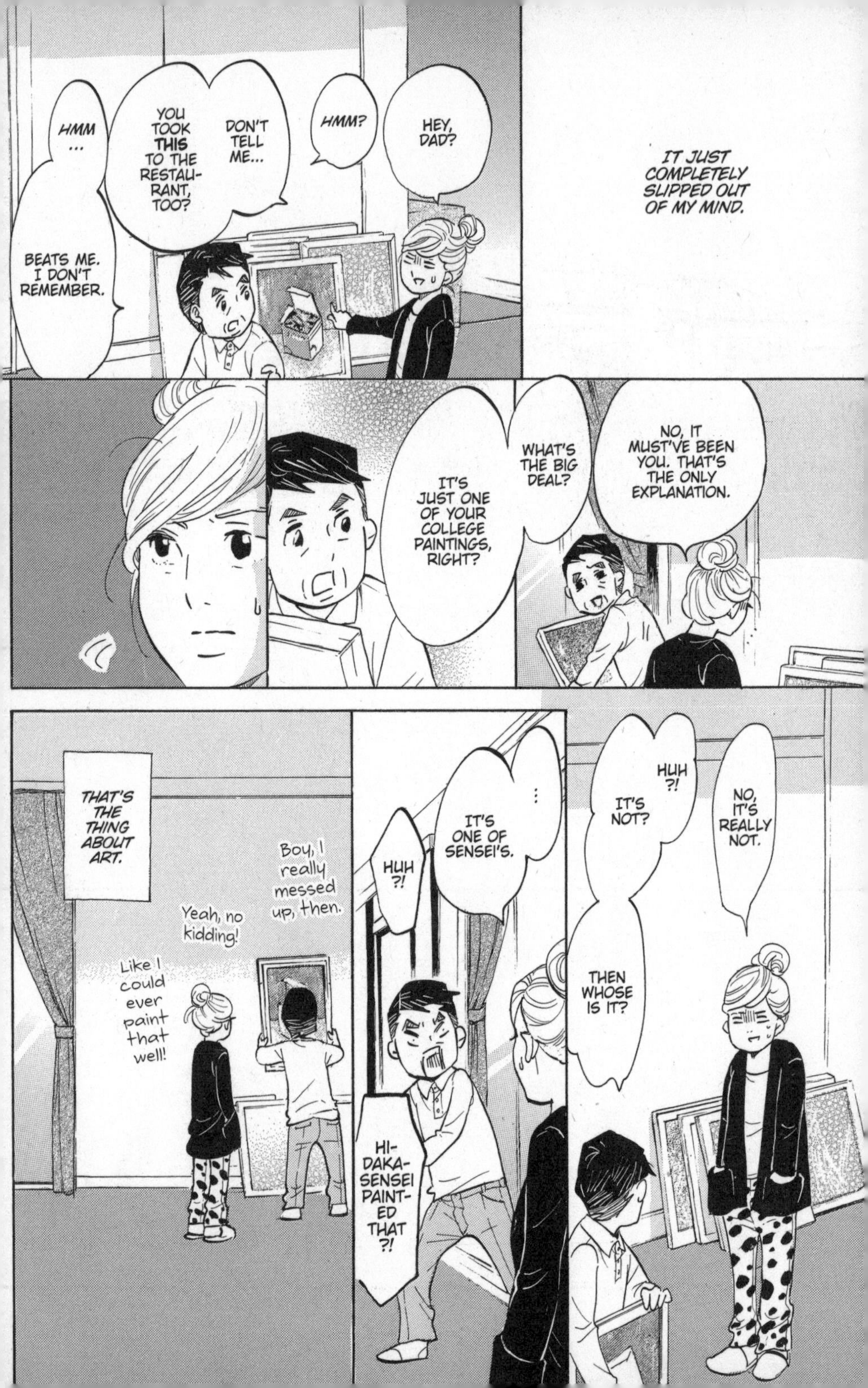
IT JUST COMPLETELY SLIPPED OUT OF MY MIND.
HEY, DAD?
HMM?
DON'T TELL ME...
YOU TOOK **THIS** TO THE RESTAURANT, TOO?
HMM ...
BEATS ME. I DON'T REMEMBER.
NO, IT MUST'VE BEEN YOU. THAT'S THE ONLY EXPLANATION.
WHAT'S THE BIG DEAL?
IT'S JUST ONE OF YOUR COLLEGE PAINTINGS, RIGHT?
NO, IT'S REALLY NOT.
HUH ?!
IT'S NOT?
THEN WHOSE IS IT?
...
IT'S ONE OF SENSEI'S.
HUH ?!
HI-DAKA-SENSEI PAINT-ED THAT ?!
THAT'S THE THING ABOUT ART.
Boy, I really messed up, then.
Yeah, no kidding!
Like I could ever paint that well!

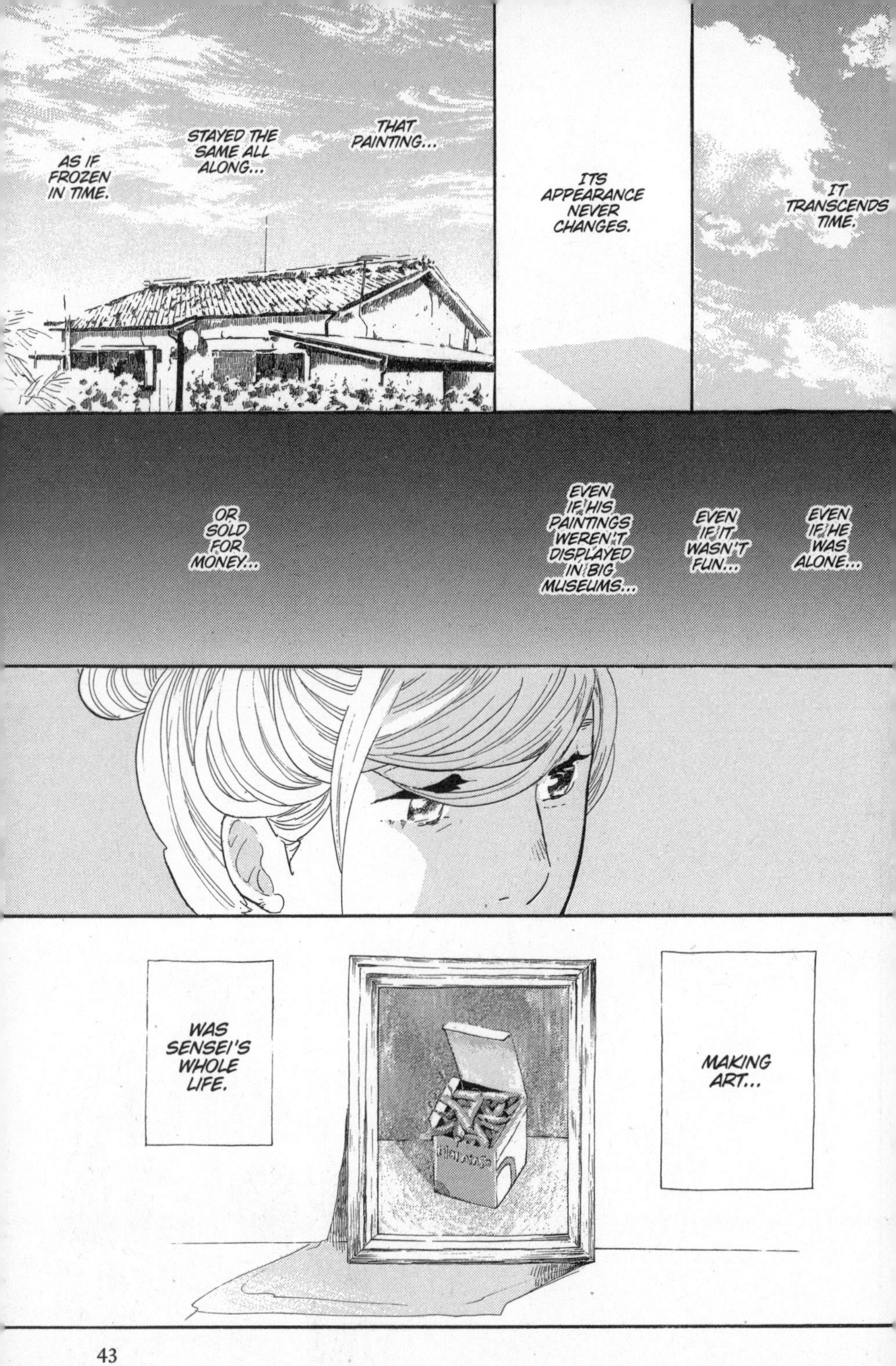
IT TRANSCENDS TIME.
ITS APPEARANCE NEVER CHANGES.
THAT PAINTING...
STAYED THE SAME ALL ALONG...
AS IF FROZEN IN TIME.
EVEN IF HE WAS ALONE...
EVEN IF IT WASN'T FUN...
EVEN IF HIS PAINTINGS WEREN'T DISPLAYED IN BIG MUSEUMS...
OR SOLD FOR MONEY...
MAKING ART...
WAS SENSEI'S WHOLE LIFE.

Blank Canvas

My So-Called Artist's Journey

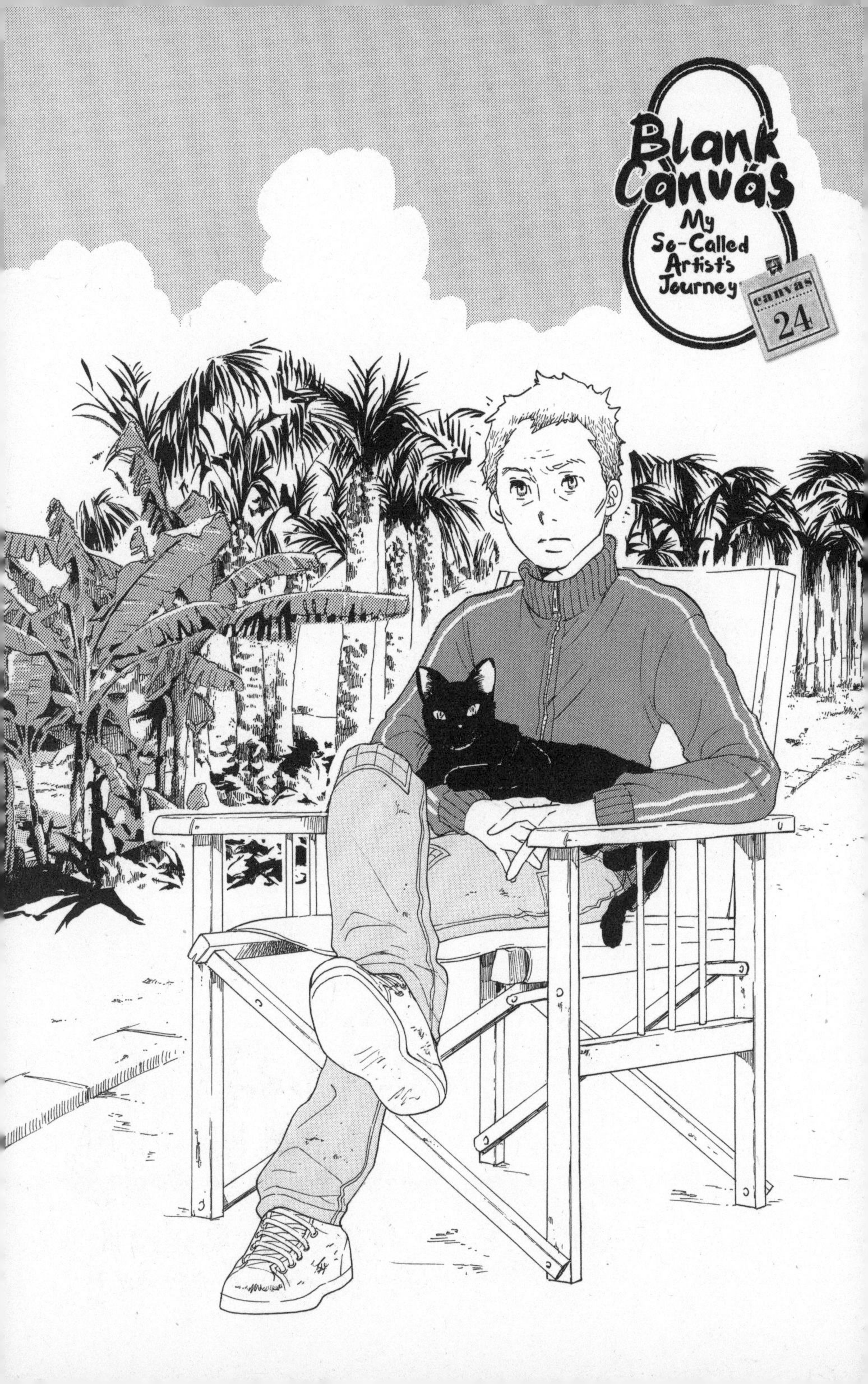
Blank Canvas
My So-Called Artist's Journey
canvas
24

IN AUGUST 1999...
I RECEIVED MY FIRST-EVER MANUSCRIPT FEE.
Normal Bank Account (transaction history)
Magazine: Bouquet.
WHOA ...
HANG ON.
I REALLY GET THIS MUCH MONEY?
THE FIRST TIME I'D RECEIVED A NEWCOMER DEBUT "PRIZE," BUT THIS WAS THE REAL THING.
A MANGA MANUSCRIPT FEE.
AT THE TIME, NEW SHOUJO MANGA ARTISTS WERE PAID FIVE THOUSAND YEN PER PAGE.
※ Seinen magazines etc. paid a bit better due to assistant fees.
Broken Heart Navigation
MY ONE-SHOT WAS 24 PAGES, SO 24 X 5000 = 120,000 YEN!!

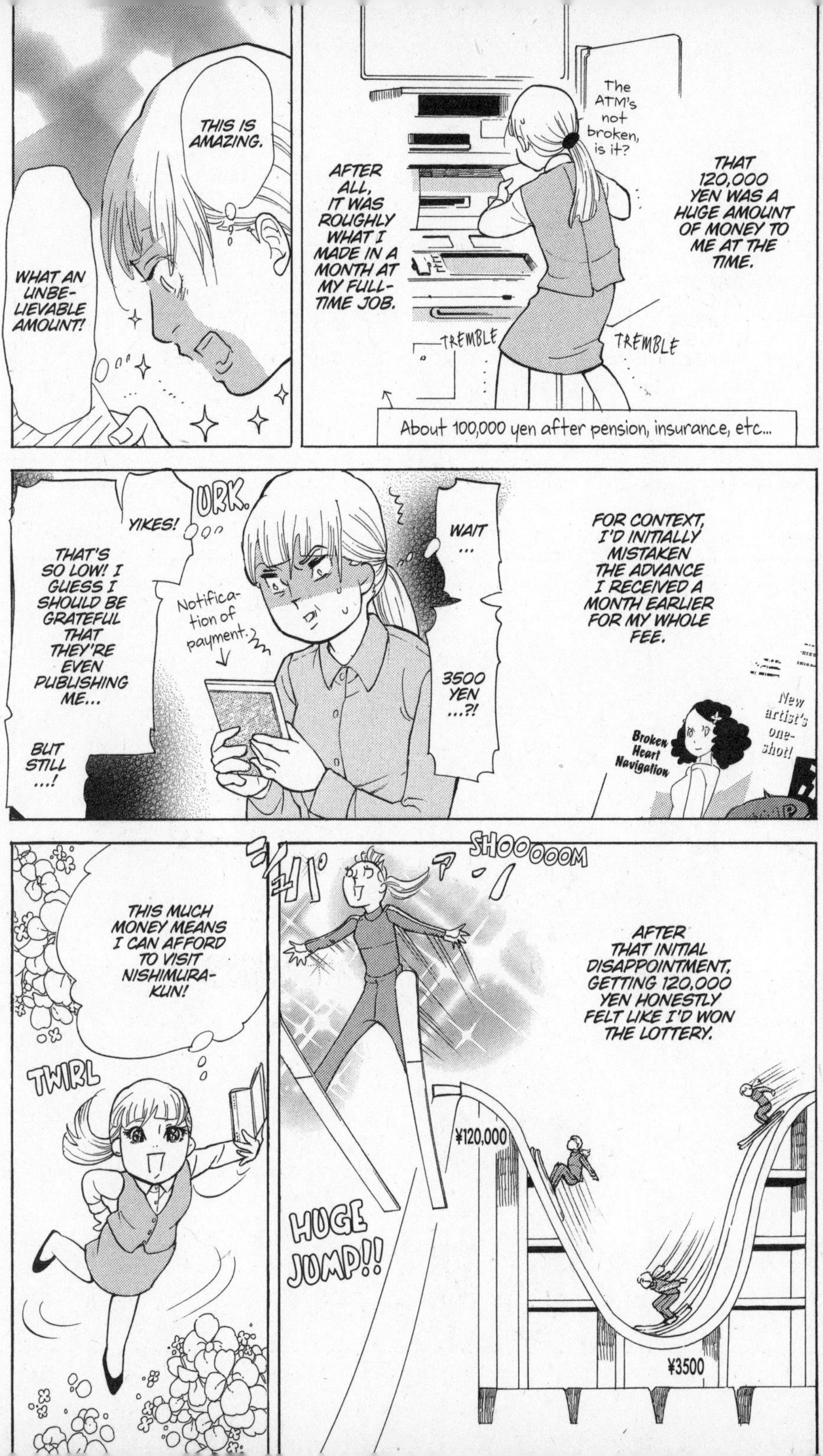
THAT 120,000 YEN WAS A HUGE AMOUNT OF MONEY TO ME AT THE TIME.
The ATM's not broken, is it?
AFTER ALL, IT WAS ROUGHLY WHAT I MADE IN A MONTH AT MY FULL-TIME JOB.
TREMBLE
TREMBLE
About 100,000 yen after pension, insurance, etc...
THIS IS AMAZING.
WHAT AN UNBELIEVABLE AMOUNT!
FOR CONTEXT, I'D INITIALLY MISTAKEN THE ADVANCE I RECEIVED A MONTH EARLIER FOR MY WHOLE FEE.
New artist's one-shot!
Broken Heart Navigation
WAIT ...
3500 YEN ...?!
URK.
Notification of payment.
YIKES!
THAT'S SO LOW! I GUESS I SHOULD BE GRATEFUL THAT THEY'RE EVEN PUBLISHING ME...
BUT STILL ...!
SHOOOOOM
AFTER THAT INITIAL DISAPPOINTMENT, GETTING 120,000 YEN HONESTLY FELT LIKE I'D WON THE LOTTERY.
¥120,000
¥3500
HUGE JUMP!!
THIS MUCH MONEY MEANS I CAN AFFORD TO VISIT NISHIMURA-KUN!
TWIRL

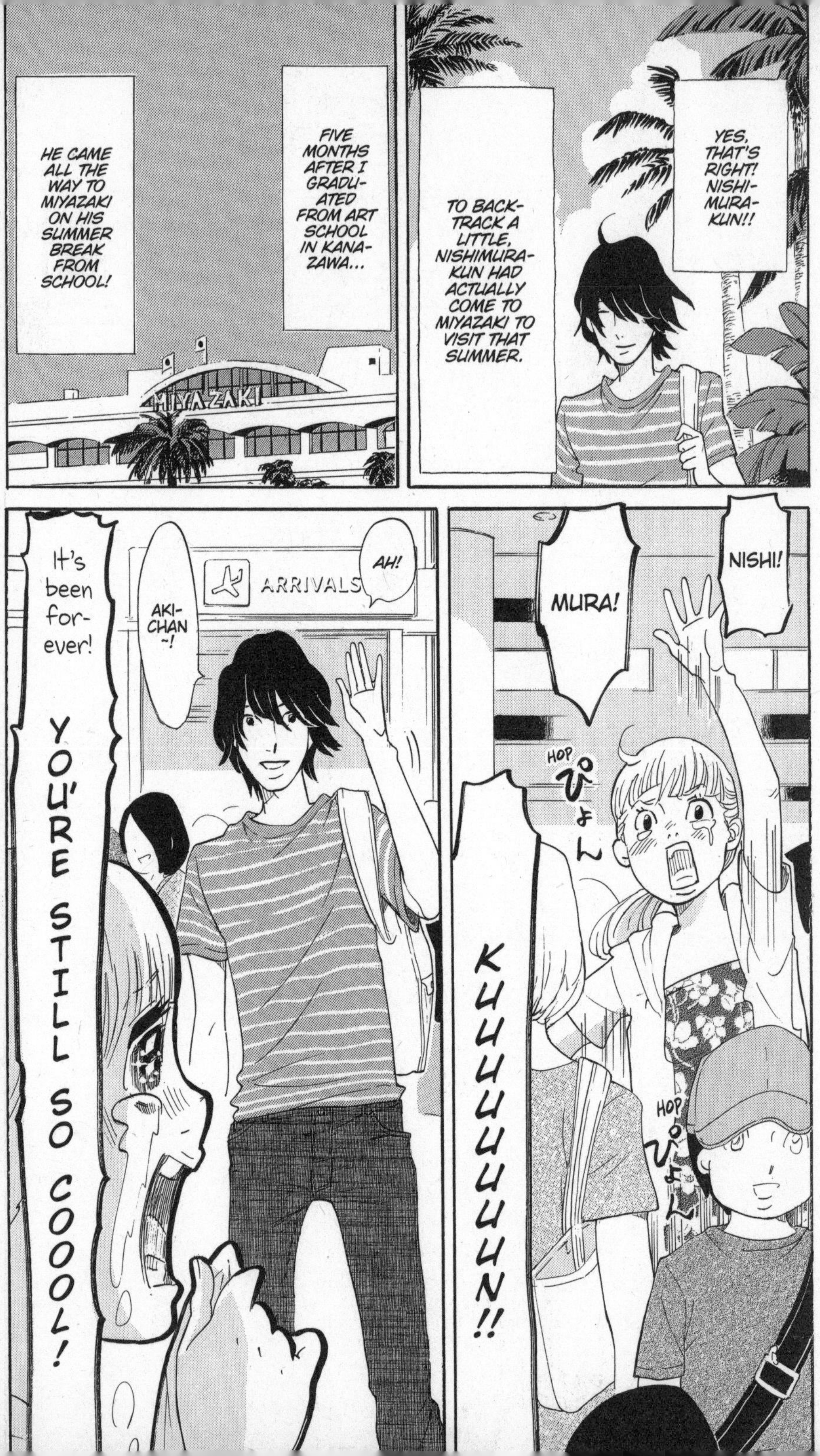
YES, THAT'S RIGHT! NISHIMURA-KUN!!
TO BACKTRACK A LITTLE, NISHIMURA-KUN HAD ACTUALLY COME TO MIYAZAKI TO VISIT THAT SUMMER.
FIVE MONTHS AFTER I GRADUATED FROM ART SCHOOL IN KANAZAWA...
HE CAME ALL THE WAY TO MIYAZAKI ON HIS SUMMER BREAK FROM SCHOOL!
MIYAZAKI
NISHI!
MURA!
HOP
ぴょん
KUUUUUUUUUUN!!
HOP
ぴょん
AH!
ARRIVALS
AKI-CHAN~!
It's been forever!
YOU'RE STILL SO COOOOL!

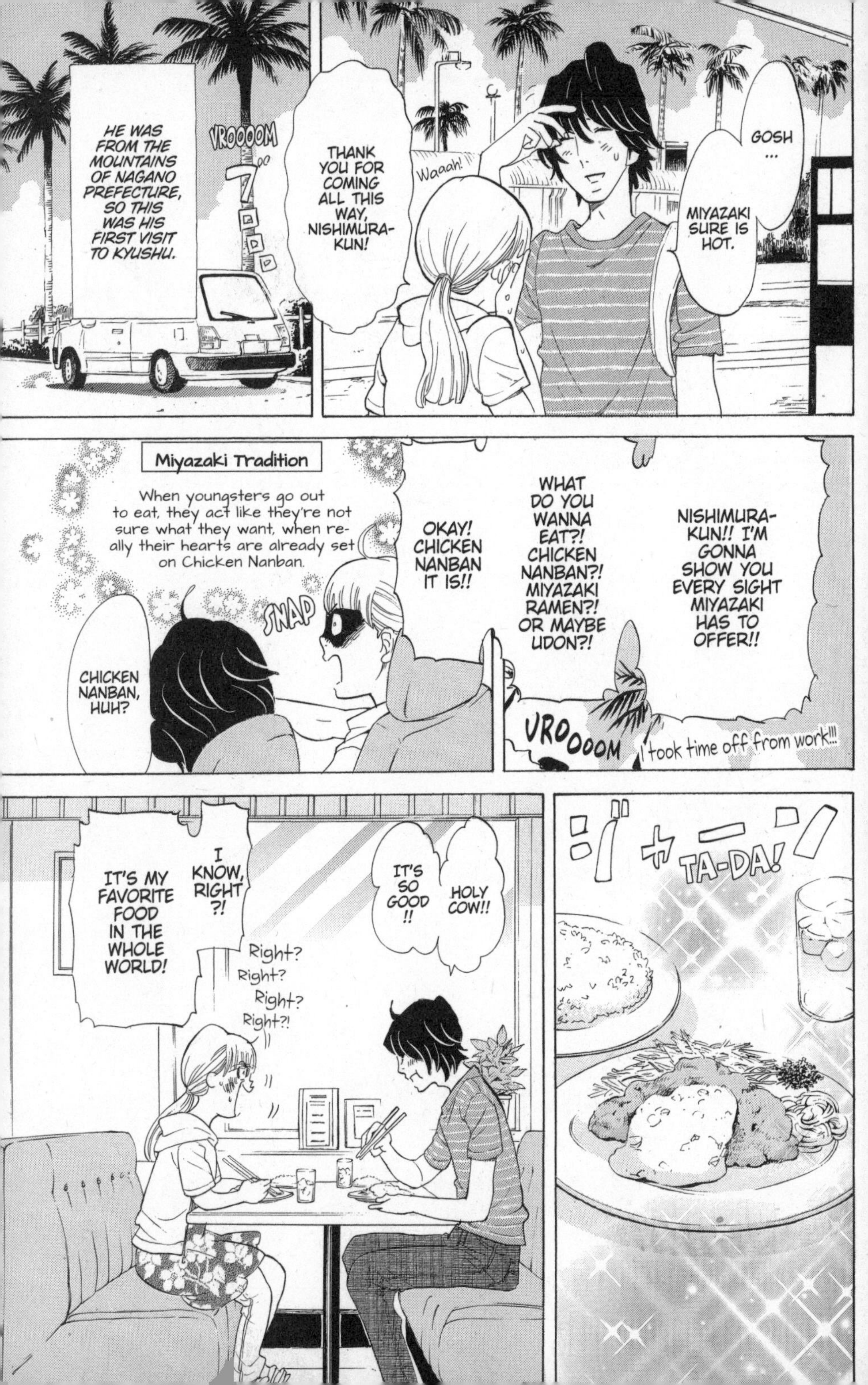
GOSH ...
MIYAZAKI SURE IS HOT.
Waaah!
THANK YOU FOR COMING ALL THIS WAY, NISHIMURA-KUN!
VROOOOM
HE WAS FROM THE MOUNTAINS OF NAGANO PREFECTURE, SO THIS WAS HIS FIRST VISIT TO KYUSHU.
NISHIMURA-KUN!! I'M GONNA SHOW YOU EVERY SIGHT MIYAZAKI HAS TO OFFER!!
I took time off from work!!!
VROOOOOM
WHAT DO YOU WANNA EAT?! CHICKEN NANBAN?! MIYAZAKI RAMEN?! OR MAYBE UDON?!
OKAY! CHICKEN NANBAN IT IS!!
SNAP
CHICKEN NANBAN, HUH?
Miyazaki Tradition
When youngsters go out to eat, they act like they're not sure what they want, when really their hearts are already set on Chicken Nanban.
TA-DA!
HOLY COW!!
IT'S SO GOOD!!
I KNOW, RIGHT?!
IT'S MY FAVORITE FOOD IN THE WHOLE WORLD!
Right?
Right?
Right?
Right?!

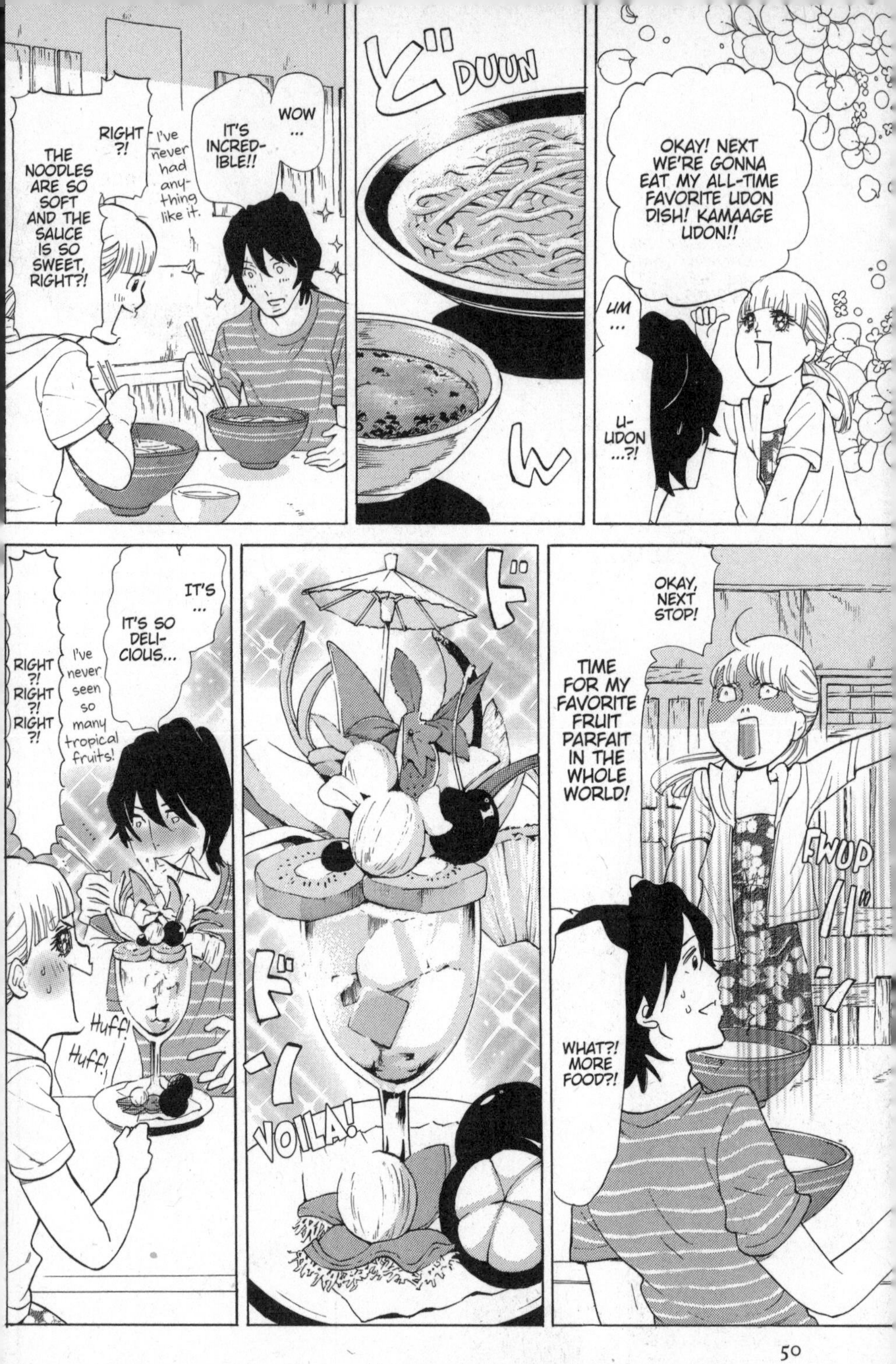
OKAY! NEXT WE'RE GONNA EAT MY ALL-TIME FAVORITE UDON DISH! KAMAAGE UDON!!
UM ...
U-UDON ...?!
DUUN
WOW ...
IT'S INCREDIBLE!!
I've never had anything like it.
RIGHT ?!
THE NOODLES ARE SO SOFT AND THE SAUCE IS SO SWEET, RIGHT?!
OKAY, NEXT STOP!
TIME FOR MY FAVORITE FRUIT PARFAIT IN THE WHOLE WORLD!
FWUP
WHAT?! MORE FOOD?!
VOILA!
IT'S ...
IT'S SO DELICIOUS...
I've never seen so many tropical fruits!
RIGHT ?! RIGHT ?! RIGHT ?!
Huff! Huff!

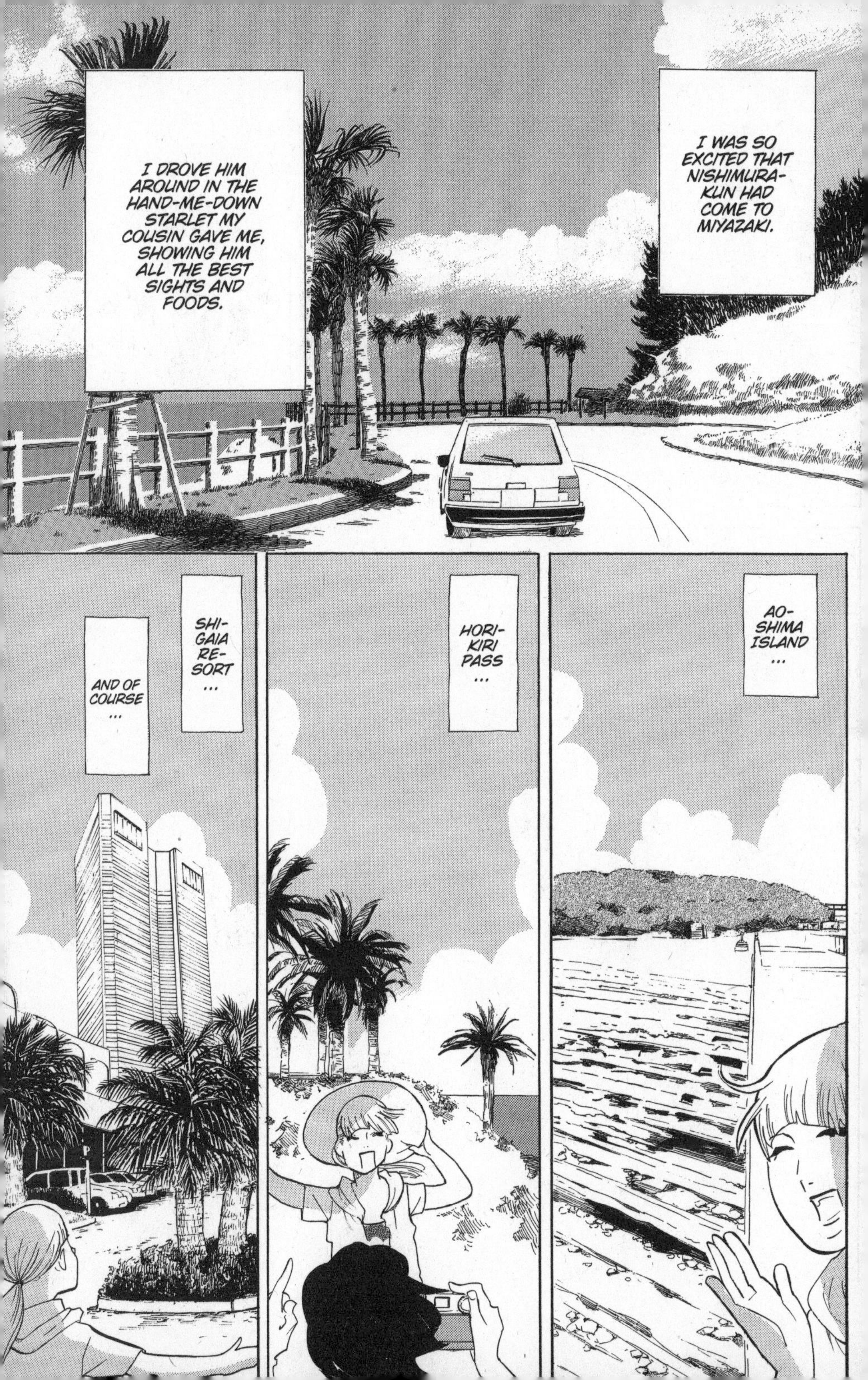
I WAS SO EXCITED THAT NISHIMURA-KUN HAD COME TO MIYAZAKI.
I DROVE HIM AROUND IN THE HAND-ME-DOWN STARLET MY COUSIN GAVE ME, SHOWING HIM ALL THE BEST SIGHTS AND FOODS.
AO-SHIMA ISLAND ...
HORI-KIRI PASS ...
SHI-GAIA RE-SORT ...
AND OF COURSE ...

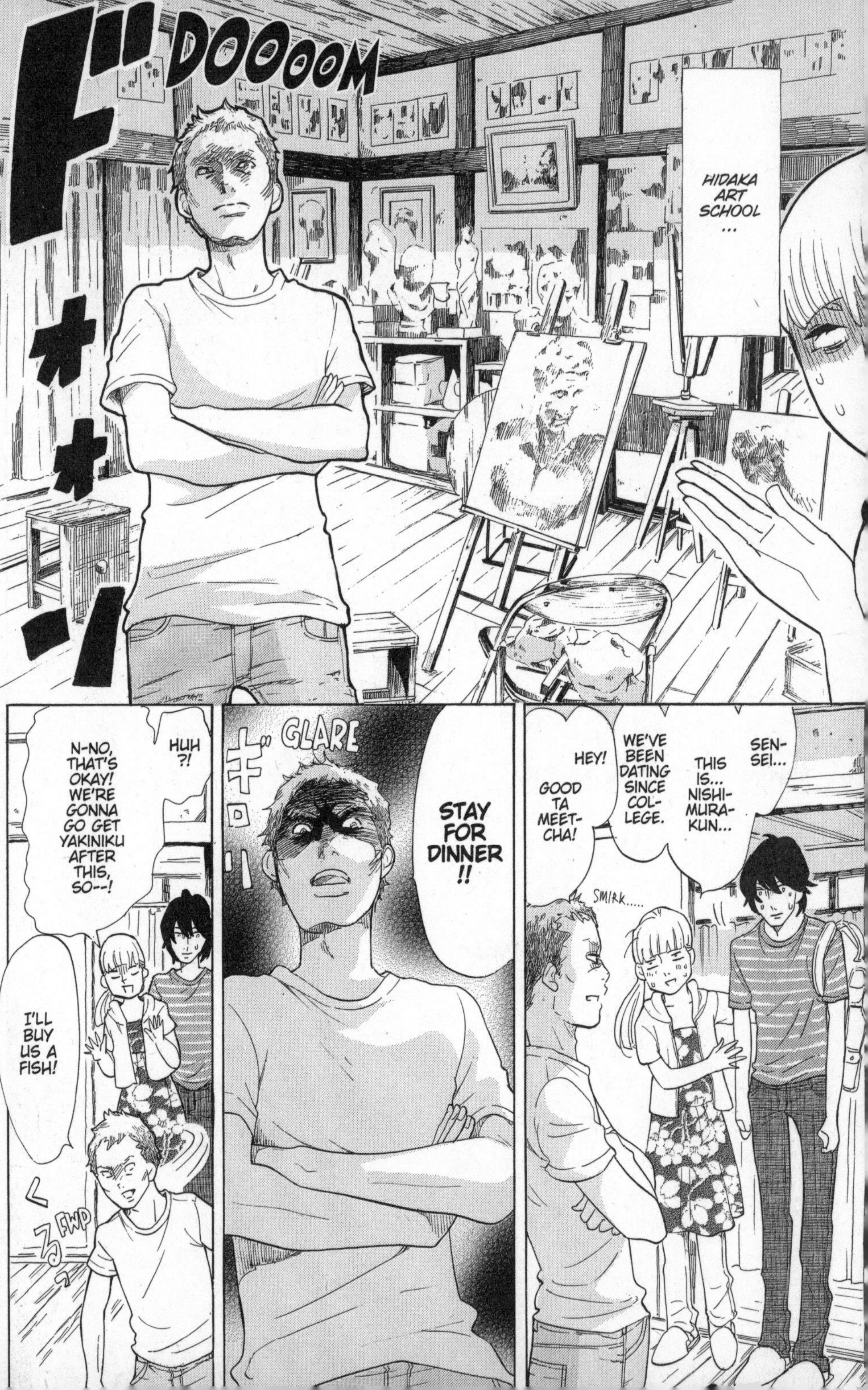
DOOOOM
HIDAKA ART SCHOOL ...
SEN-SEI...
THIS IS... NISHIMURA-KUN...
WE'VE BEEN DATING SINCE COL-LEGE.
HEY!
GOOD TA MEET-CHA!
SMIRK.....
GLARE
STAY FOR DINNER!!
HUH?!
N-NO, THAT'S OKAY! WE'RE GONNA GO GET YAKINIKU AFTER THIS, SO--!
I'LL BUY US A FISH!
FWP

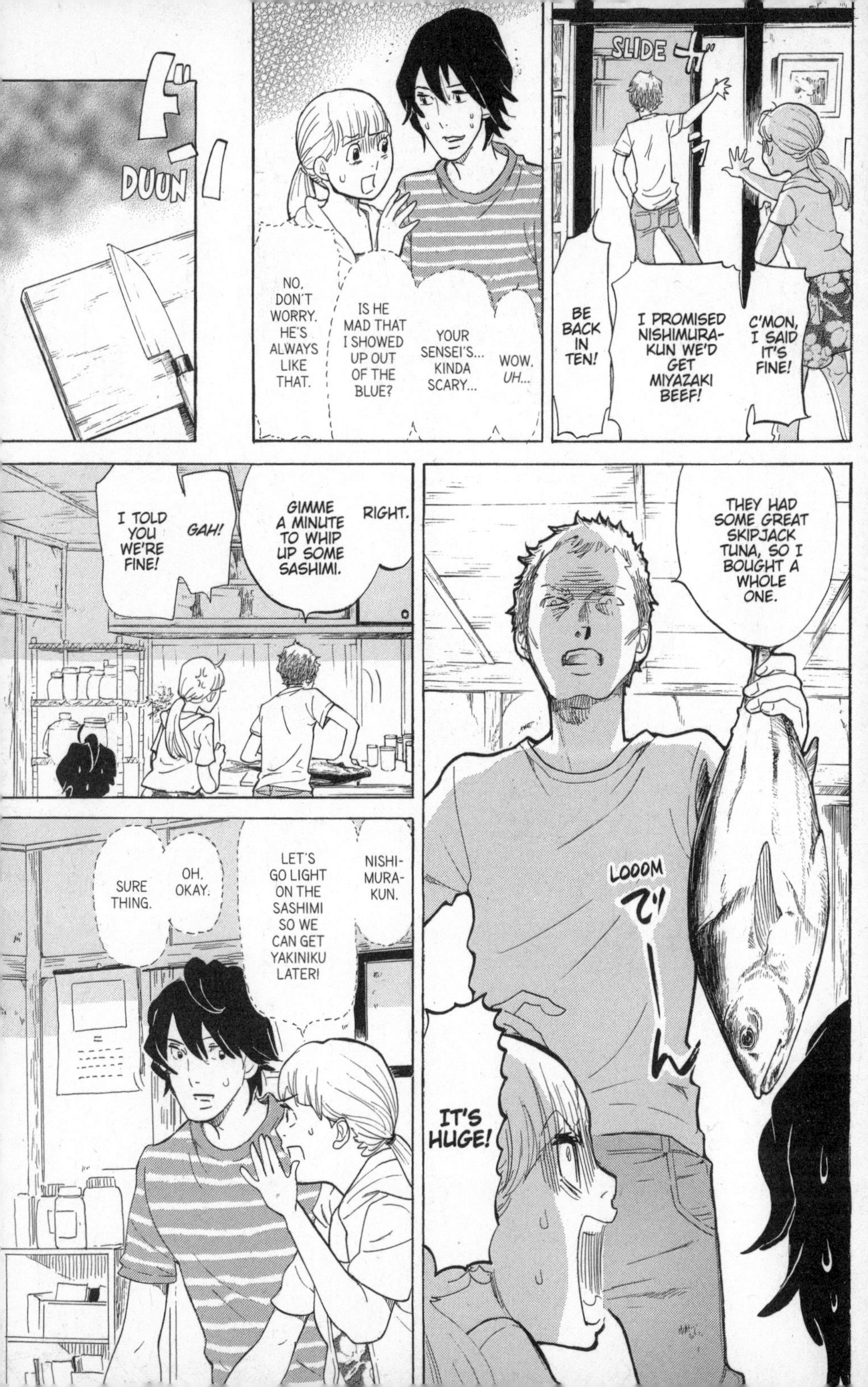
SLIDE
C'MON, I SAID IT'S FINE!
I PROMISED NISHIMURA-KUN WE'D GET MIYAZAKI BEEF!
BE BACK IN TEN!
WOW, UH...
YOUR SENSEI'S... KINDA SCARY...
IS HE MAD THAT I SHOWED UP OUT OF THE BLUE?
NO, DON'T WORRY. HE'S ALWAYS LIKE THAT.
DUUN
THEY HAD SOME GREAT SKIPJACK TUNA, SO I BOUGHT A WHOLE ONE.
LOOOM
IT'S HUGE!
RIGHT.
GIMME A MINUTE TO WHIP UP SOME SASHIMI.
GAH!
I TOLD YOU WE'RE FINE!
NISHIMURA-KUN.
LET'S GO LIGHT ON THE SASHIMI SO WE CAN GET YAKINIKU LATER!
OH, OKAY.
SURE THING.

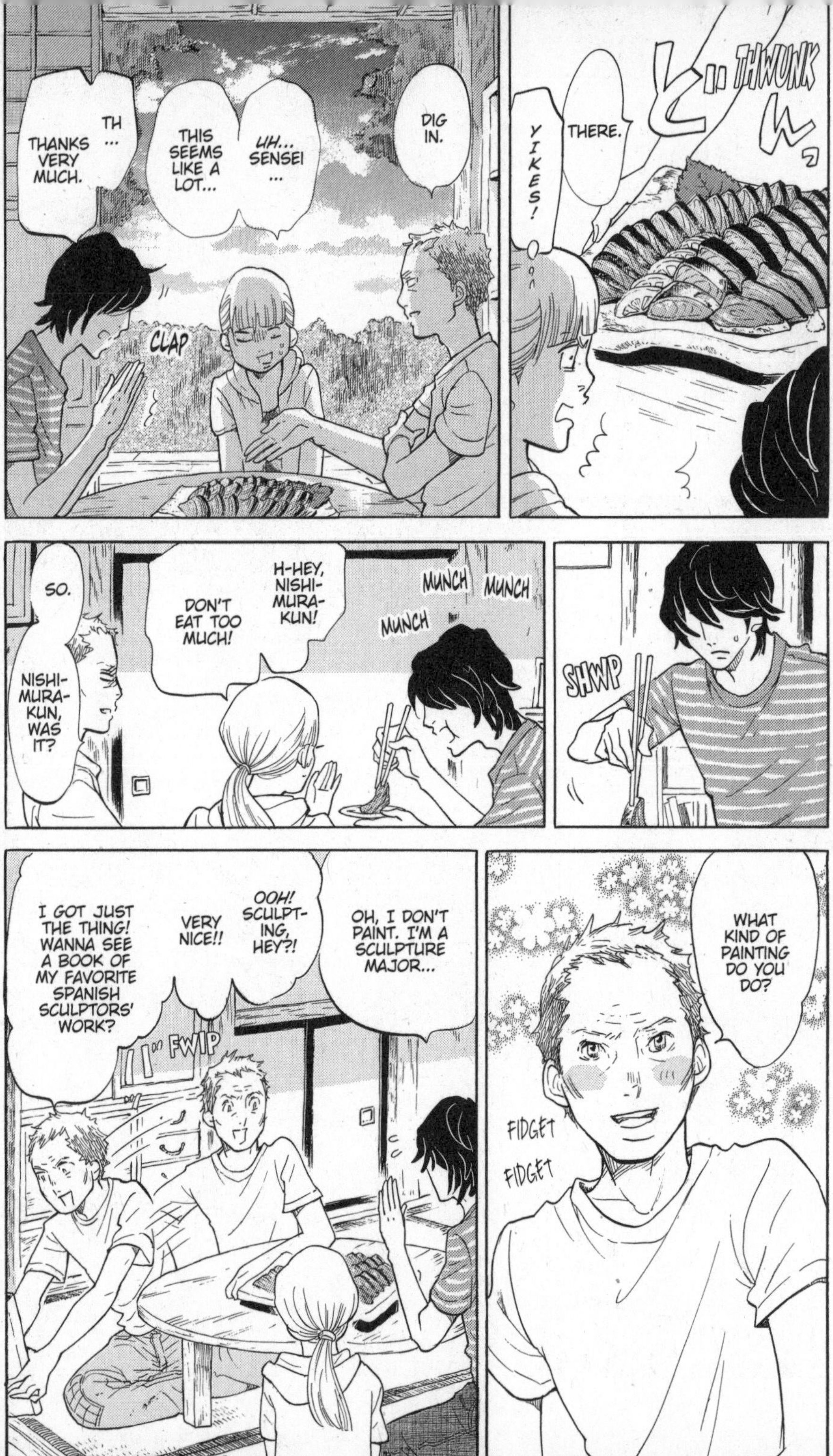
THWUNK
THERE.
YIKES!
DIG IN.
UH... SENSEI...
THIS SEEMS LIKE A LOT...
TH...
THANKS VERY MUCH.
CLAP
SHWP
MUNCH MUNCH
MUNCH
H-HEY, NISHIMURA-KUN!
DON'T EAT TOO MUCH!
SO.
NISHIMURA-KUN, WAS IT?
WHAT KIND OF PAINTING DO YOU DO?
FIDGET
FIDGET
OH, I DON'T PAINT. I'M A SCULPTURE MAJOR...
OOH! SCULPTING, HEY?!
VERY NICE!!
I GOT JUST THE THING! WANNA SEE A BOOK OF MY FAVORITE SPANISH SCULPTORS' WORK?
FWIP

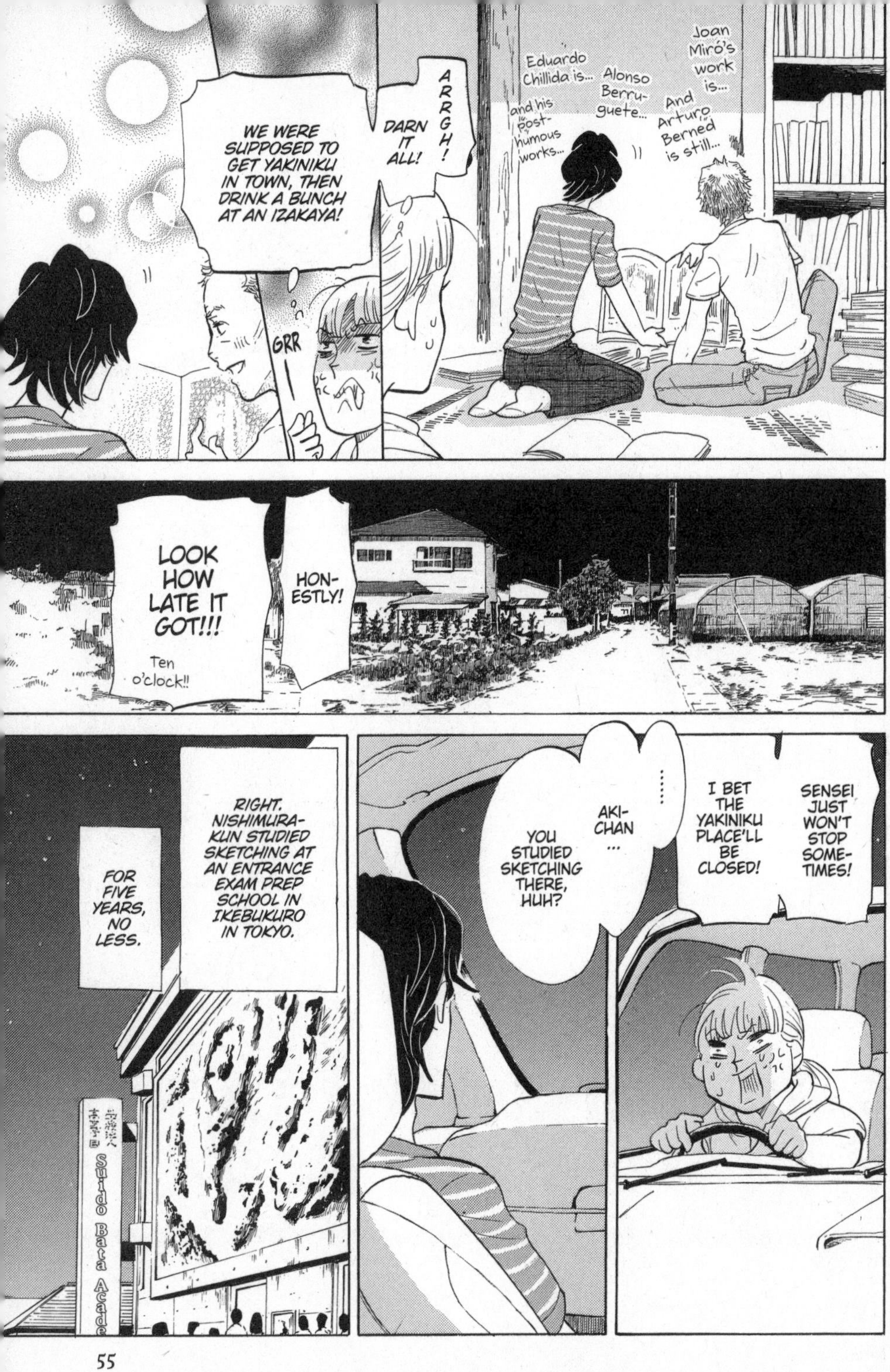

Joan Miró's work is...
And Arturo Berned is still...
Alonso Berruguete...
Eduardo Chillida is...
and his posthumous works...
ARRGH!
DARN IT ALL!
WE WERE SUPPOSED TO GET YAKINIKU IN TOWN, THEN DRINK A BUNCH AT AN IZAKAYA!
GRR
HONESTLY!
LOOK HOW LATE IT GOT!!!
Ten o'clock!!
SENSEI JUST WON'T STOP SOMETIMES!
I BET THE YAKINIKU PLACE'LL BE CLOSED!
......
AKI-CHAN...
YOU STUDIED SKETCHING THERE, HUH?
RIGHT. NISHIMURA-KUN STUDIED SKETCHING AT AN ENTRANCE EXAM PREP SCHOOL IN IKEBUKURO IN TOKYO.
FOR FIVE YEARS, NO LESS.
Suido Bata Acade

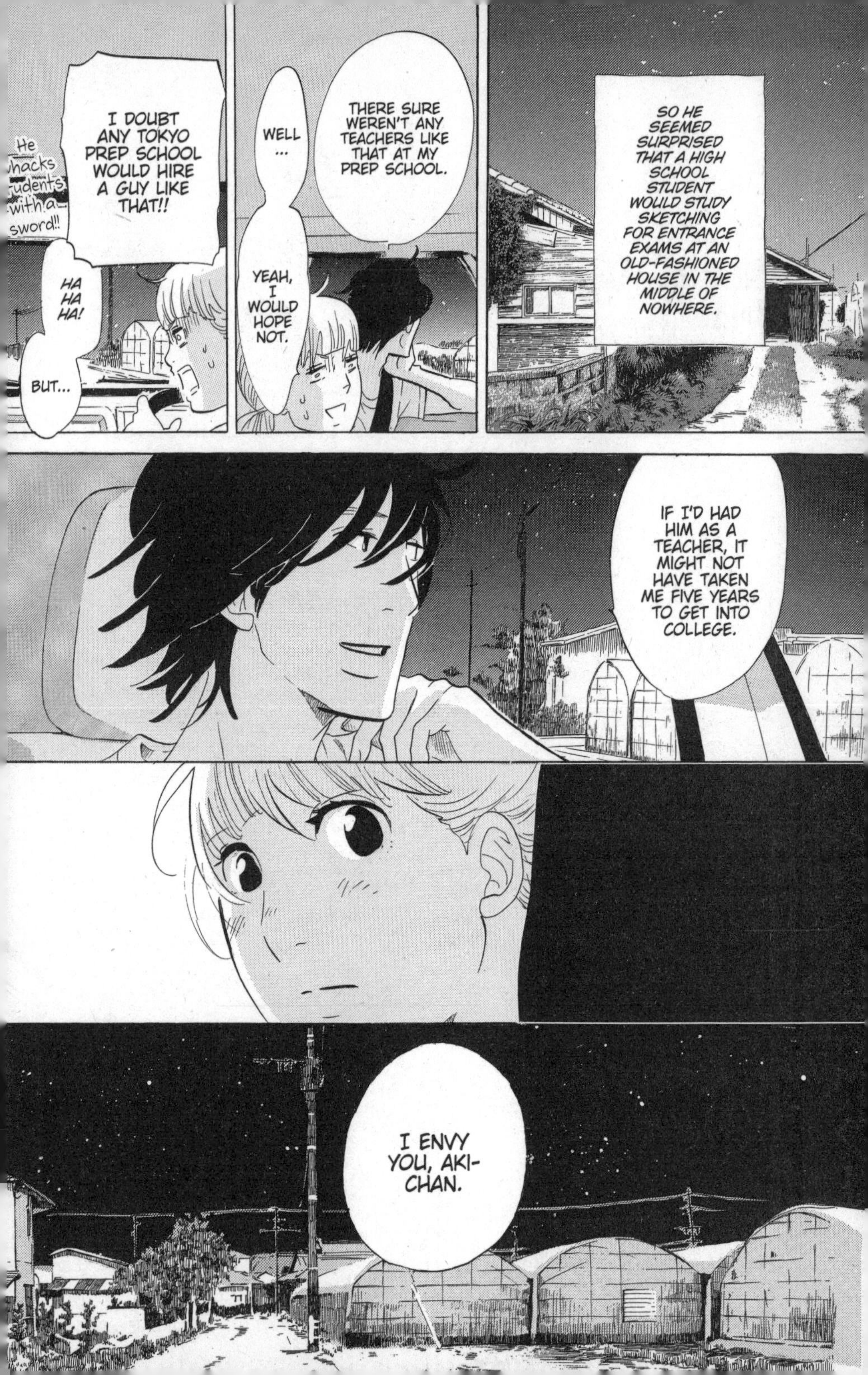
SO HE SEEMED SURPRISED THAT A HIGH SCHOOL STUDENT WOULD STUDY SKETCHING FOR ENTRANCE EXAMS AT AN OLD-FASHIONED HOUSE IN THE MIDDLE OF NOWHERE.
THERE SURE WEREN'T ANY TEACHERS LIKE THAT AT MY PREP SCHOOL.
WELL ...
YEAH, I WOULD HOPE NOT.
I DOUBT ANY TOKYO PREP SCHOOL WOULD HIRE A GUY LIKE THAT!!
He whacks students with a sword!!
HA HA HA!
BUT...
IF I'D HAD HIM AS A TEACHER, IT MIGHT NOT HAVE TAKEN ME FIVE YEARS TO GET INTO COLLEGE.
I ENVY YOU, AKI-CHAN.

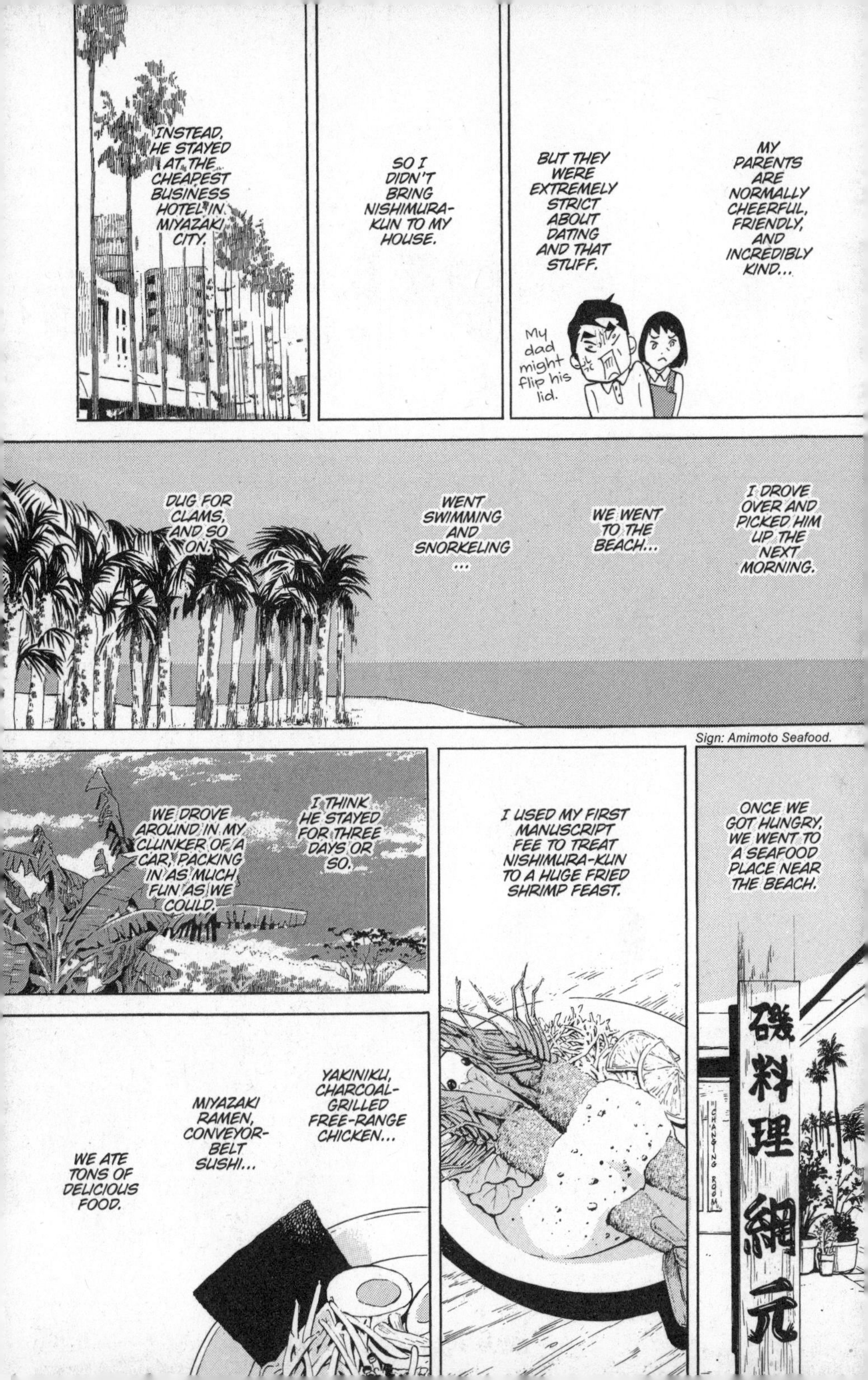
MY PARENTS ARE NORMALLY CHEERFUL, FRIENDLY, AND INCREDIBLY KIND...
BUT THEY WERE EXTREMELY STRICT ABOUT DATING AND THAT STUFF.
My dad might flip his lid.
SO I DIDN'T BRING NISHIMURA-KUN TO MY HOUSE.
INSTEAD, HE STAYED AT THE CHEAPEST BUSINESS HOTEL IN MIYAZAKI CITY.
I DROVE OVER AND PICKED HIM UP THE NEXT MORNING.
WE WENT TO THE BEACH...
WENT SWIMMING AND SNORKELING...
DUG FOR CLAMS, AND SO ON.
Sign: Amimoto Seafood.
ONCE WE GOT HUNGRY, WE WENT TO A SEAFOOD PLACE NEAR THE BEACH.
磯料理 網元
CHANGING ROOM
I USED MY FIRST MANUSCRIPT FEE TO TREAT NISHIMURA-KUN TO A HUGE FRIED SHRIMP FEAST.
I THINK HE STAYED FOR THREE DAYS OR SO.
WE DROVE AROUND IN MY CLUNKER OF A CAR, PACKING IN AS MUCH FUN AS WE COULD.
YAKINIKU, CHARCOAL-GRILLED FREE-RANGE CHICKEN...
MIYAZAKI RAMEN, CONVEYOR-BELT SUSHI...
WE ATE TONS OF DELICIOUS FOOD.

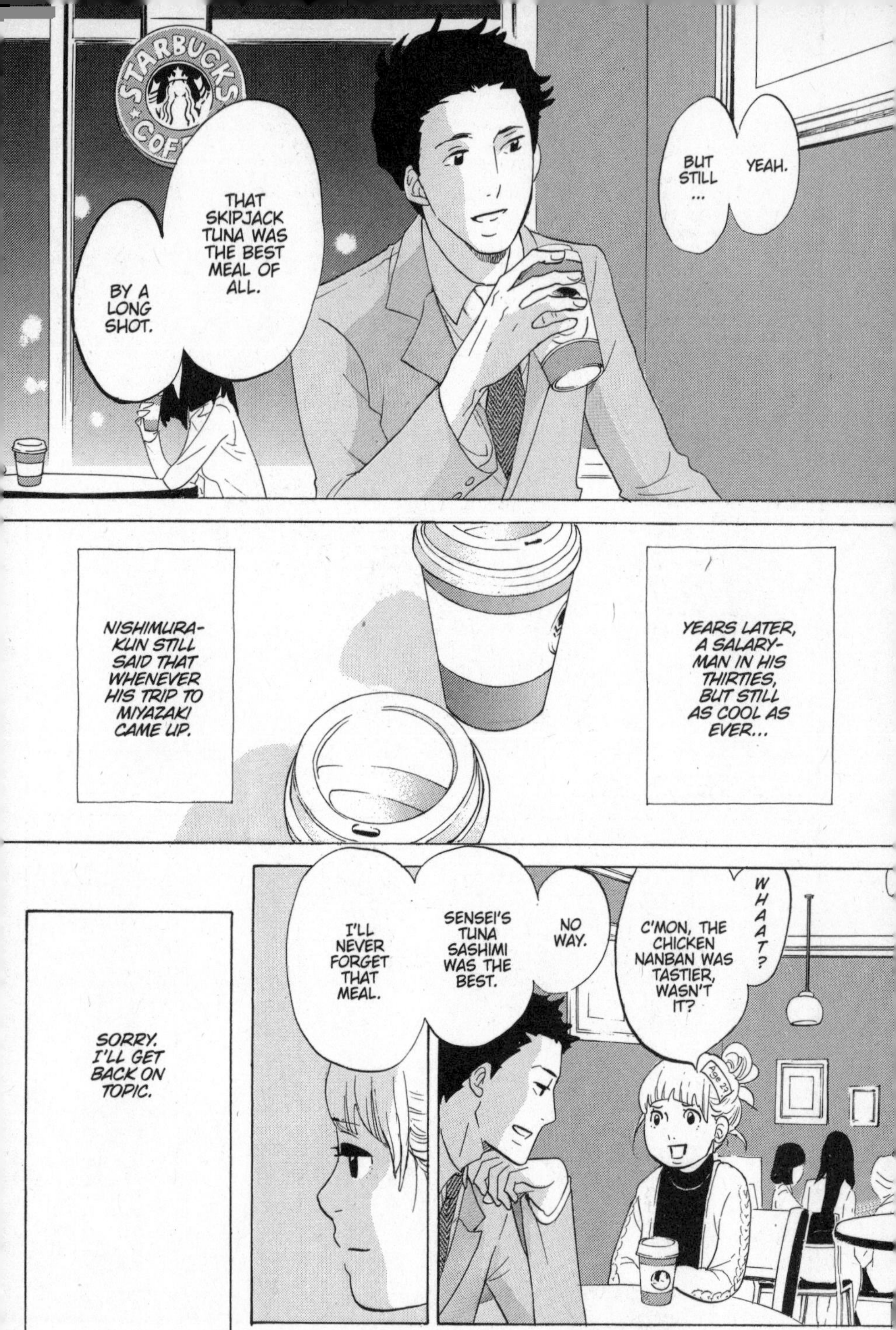
STARBUCKS COFFEE
YEAH.
BUT STILL ...
THAT SKIPJACK TUNA WAS THE BEST MEAL OF ALL.
BY A LONG SHOT.
YEARS LATER, A SALARYMAN IN HIS THIRTIES, BUT STILL AS COOL AS EVER...
NISHIMURA-KUN STILL SAID THAT WHENEVER HIS TRIP TO MIYAZAKI CAME UP.
WHAAAT?
C'MON, THE CHICKEN NANBAN WAS TASTIER, WASN'T IT?
Age 27
NO WAY.
SENSEI'S TUNA SASHIMI WAS THE BEST.
I'LL NEVER FORGET THAT MEAL.
SORRY. I'LL GET BACK ON TOPIC.

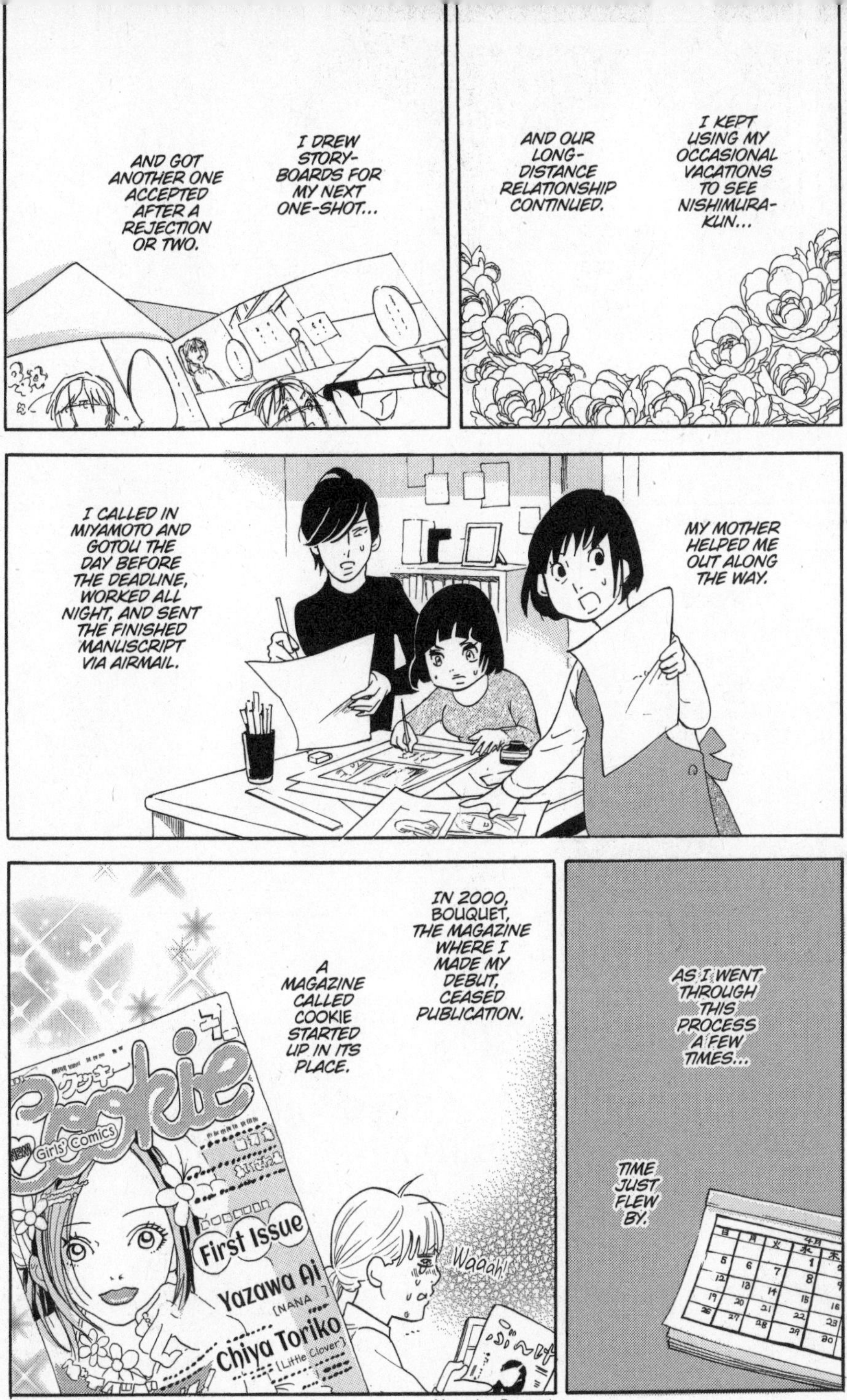
I KEPT USING MY OCCASIONAL VACATIONS TO SEE NISHIMURA-KUN...
AND OUR LONG-DISTANCE RELATIONSHIP CONTINUED.
I DREW STORY-BOARDS FOR MY NEXT ONE-SHOT...
AND GOT ANOTHER ONE ACCEPTED AFTER A REJECTION OR TWO.
MY MOTHER HELPED ME OUT ALONG THE WAY.
I CALLED IN MIYAMOTO AND GOTOU THE DAY BEFORE THE DEADLINE, WORKED ALL NIGHT, AND SENT THE FINISHED MANUSCRIPT VIA AIRMAIL.
AS I WENT THROUGH THIS PROCESS A FEW TIMES...
TIME JUST FLEW BY.
IN 2000, BOUQUET, THE MAGAZINE WHERE I MADE MY DEBUT, CEASED PUBLICATION.
A MAGAZINE CALLED COOKIE STARTED UP IN ITS PLACE.
Cookie
NEW
Girls' Comics
First Issue
Yazawa Ai
[NANA]
Chiya Toriko
[Little Clover]
Waaah!

Magazine: Bouquet.

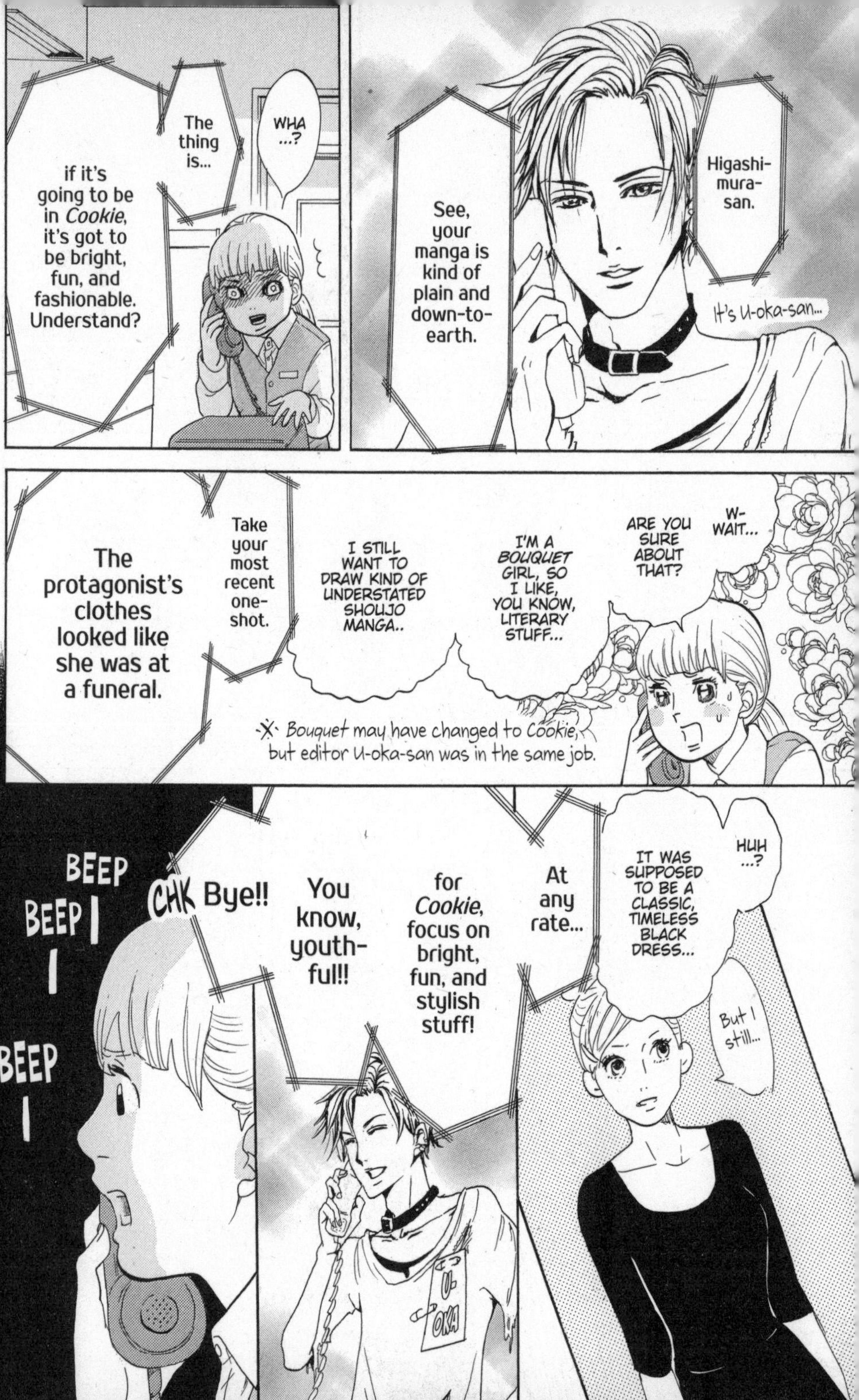
Higashi-mura-san.
See, your manga is kind of plain and down-to-earth.
It's U-oka-san...
WHA ...?
The thing is...
if it's going to be in *Cookie*, it's got to be bright, fun, and fashionable. Understand?
W-WAIT...
ARE YOU SURE ABOUT THAT?
I'M A *BOUQUET* GIRL, SO I LIKE, YOU KNOW, LITERARY STUFF...
I STILL WANT TO DRAW KIND OF UNDERSTATED SHOUJO MANGA..
Take your most recent one-shot.
The protagonist's clothes looked like she was at a funeral.
※ *Bouquet* may have changed to *Cookie*, but editor U-oka-san was in the same job.
HUH ...?
IT WAS SUPPOSED TO BE A CLASSIC, TIMELESS BLACK DRESS...
But I still...
At any rate...
for *Cookie*, focus on bright, fun, and stylish stuff!
You know, youth-ful!!
U-OKA
CHK Bye!!
BEEP
BEEP
BEEP

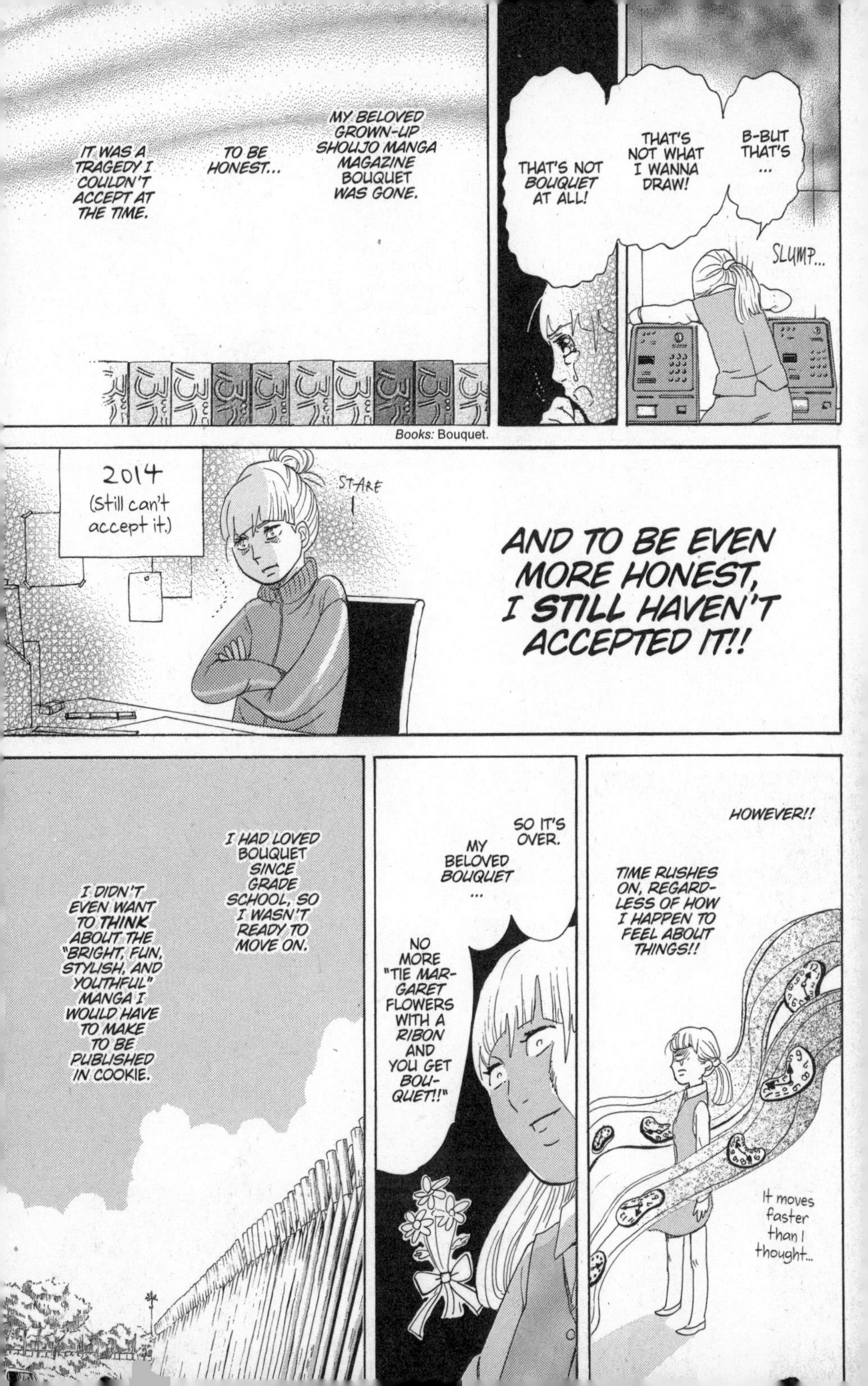
B-BUT THAT'S ...
THAT'S NOT WHAT I WANNA DRAW!
THAT'S NOT BOUQUET AT ALL!
SLUMP...
MY BELOVED GROWN-UP SHOUJO MANGA MAGAZINE BOUQUET WAS GONE.
TO BE HONEST...
IT WAS A TRAGEDY I COULDN'T ACCEPT AT THE TIME.
Books: Bouquet.
AND TO BE EVEN MORE HONEST, I STILL HAVEN'T ACCEPTED IT!!
STARE
2014 (Still can't accept it.)
HOWEVER!!
TIME RUSHES ON, REGARDLESS OF HOW I HAPPEN TO FEEL ABOUT THINGS!!
It moves faster than I thought...
SO IT'S OVER.
MY BELOVED BOUQUET ...
NO MORE "TIE MARGARET FLOWERS WITH A RIBON AND YOU GET BOUQUET!!"
I HAD LOVED BOUQUET SINCE GRADE SCHOOL, SO I WASN'T READY TO MOVE ON.
I DIDN'T EVEN WANT TO THINK ABOUT THE "BRIGHT, FUN, STYLISH, AND YOUTHFUL" MANGA I WOULD HAVE TO MAKE TO BE PUBLISHED IN COOKIE.

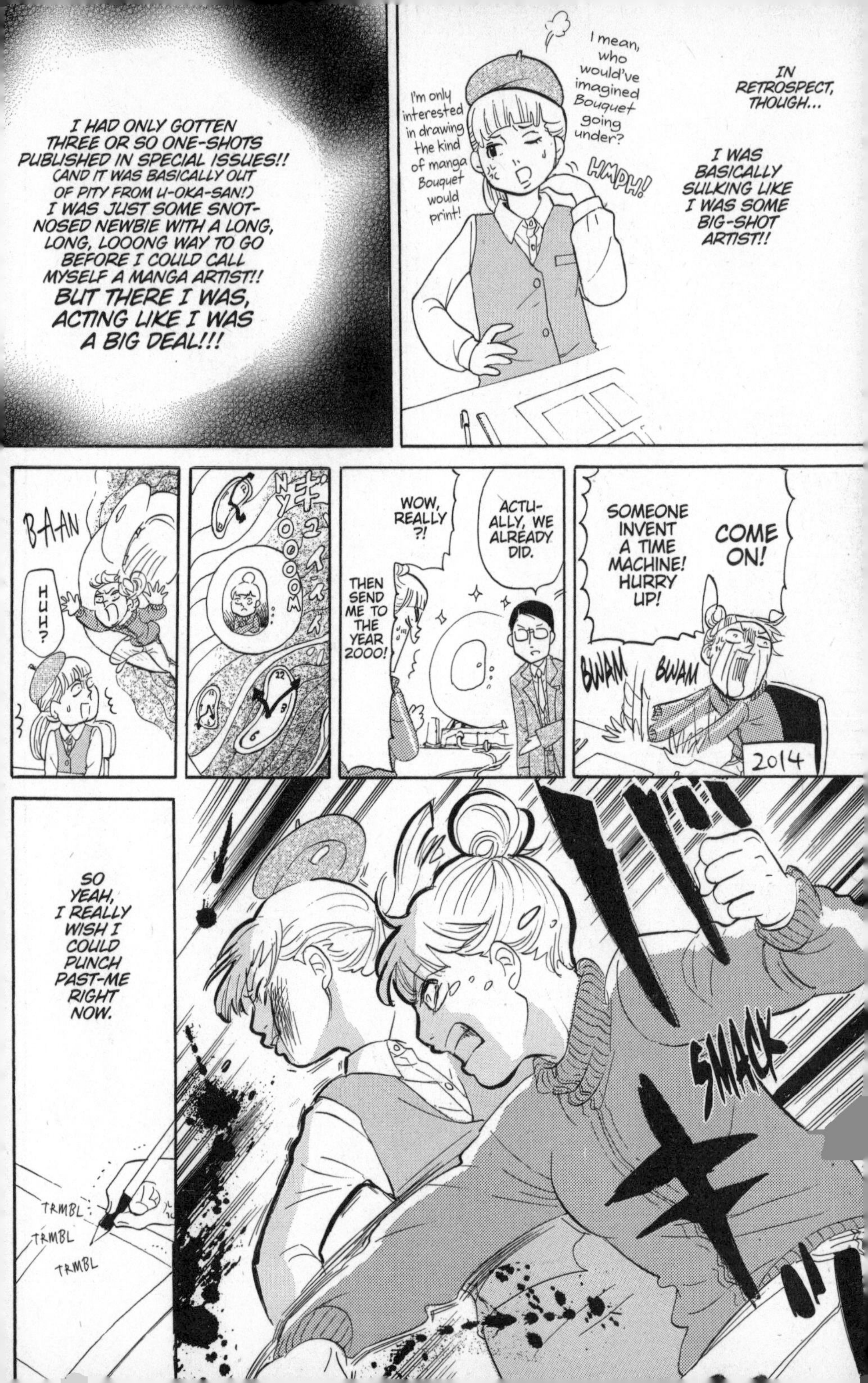
IN RETROSPECT, THOUGH...
I mean, who would've imagined Bouquet going under?
I'm only interested in drawing the kind of manga Bouquet would print!
HMPH!
I WAS BASICALLY SULKING LIKE I WAS SOME BIG-SHOT ARTIST!!
I HAD ONLY GOTTEN THREE OR SO ONE-SHOTS PUBLISHED IN SPECIAL ISSUES!! (AND IT WAS BASICALLY OUT OF PITY FROM U-OKA-SAN!) I WAS JUST SOME SNOT-NOSED NEWBIE WITH A LONG, LONG, LOOONG WAY TO GO BEFORE I COULD CALL MYSELF A MANGA ARTIST!! BUT THERE I WAS, ACTING LIKE I WAS A BIG DEAL!!!
COME ON!
SOMEONE INVENT A TIME MACHINE! HURRY UP!
BWAM
BWAM
2014
ACTU-ALLY, WE ALREADY DID.
WOW, REALLY ?!
THEN SEND ME TO THE YEAR 2000!
NYOOOOOOM
BAAN
HUH?
SMACK
SO YEAH, I REALLY WISH I COULD PUNCH PAST-ME RIGHT NOW.
TRMBL
TRMBL
TRMBL

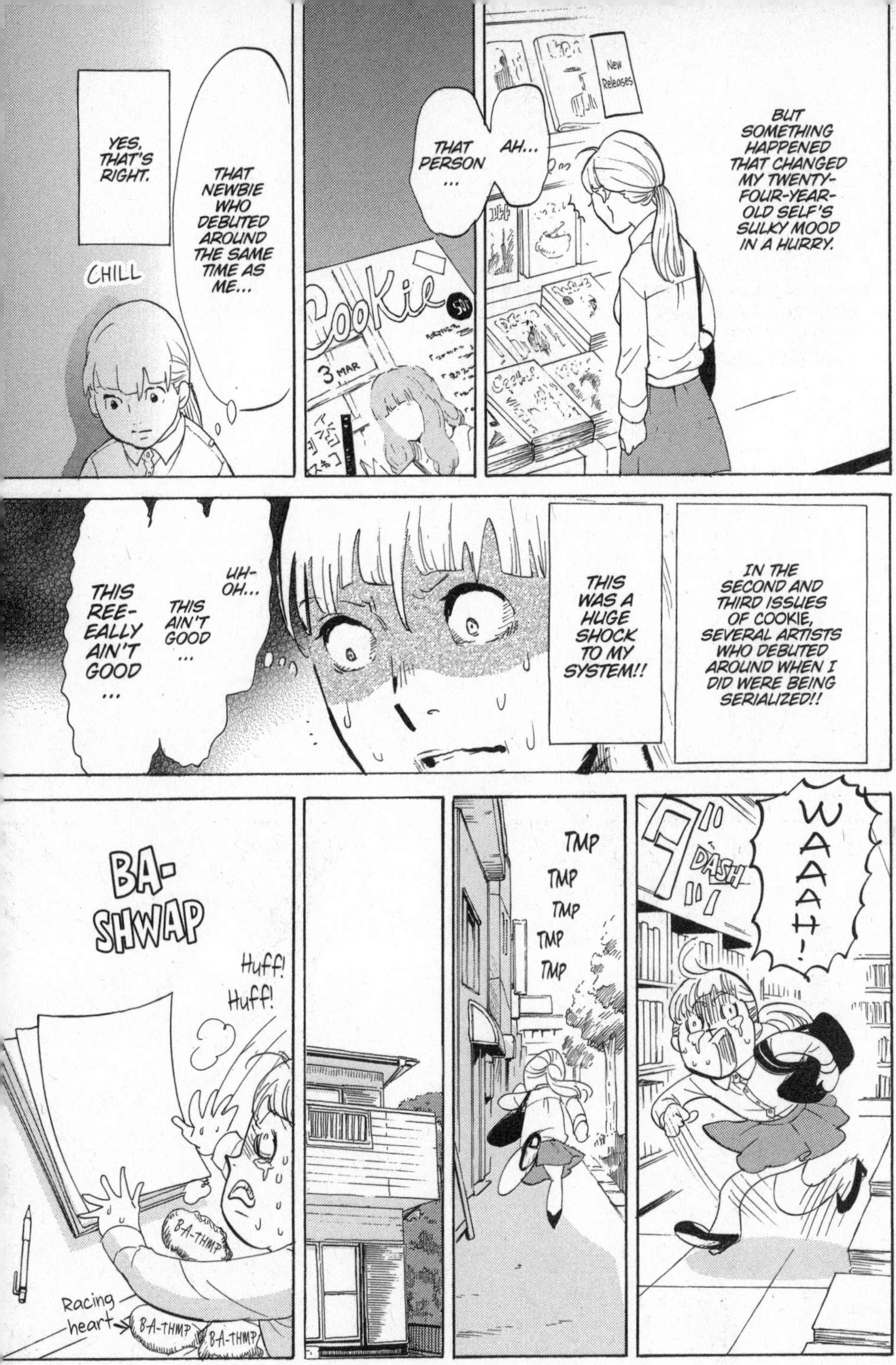

New Releases
BUT SOMETHING HAPPENED THAT CHANGED MY TWENTY-FOUR-YEAR-OLD SELF'S SULKY MOOD IN A HURRY.
AH... THAT PERSON...
Cookie
3 MAR
THAT NEWBIE WHO DEBUTED AROUND THE SAME TIME AS ME...
YES, THAT'S RIGHT.
CHILL
IN THE SECOND AND THIRD ISSUES OF COOKIE, SEVERAL ARTISTS WHO DEBUTED AROUND WHEN I DID WERE BEING SERIALIZED!!
THIS WAS A HUGE SHOCK TO MY SYSTEM!!
UH-OH... THIS AIN'T GOOD... THIS REE-EALLY AIN'T GOOD...
WAAAH!
DASH
TMP
TMP
TMP
TMP
TMP
BA-SHWAP
Huff! Huff!
B-A-THMP
Racing heart
B-A-THMP
B-A-THMP

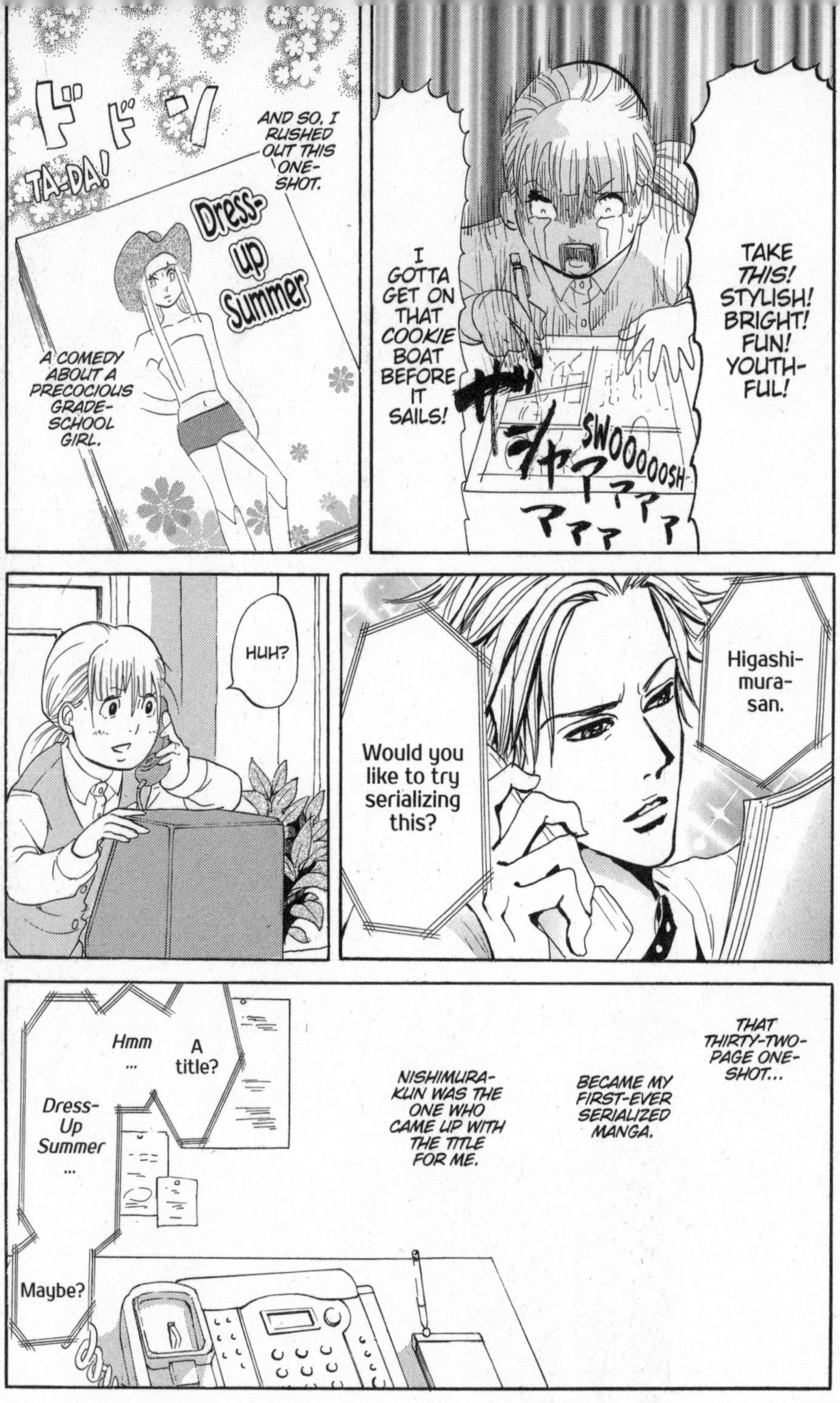

TAKE THIS! STYLISH! BRIGHT! FUN! YOUTHFUL!
I GOTTA GET ON THAT COOKIE BOAT BEFORE IT SAILS!
ザ
シャアアアアアアア
SWOOOOOOSH
AND SO, I RUSHED OUT THIS ONE-SHOT.
ドドーン
TA-DA!
Dress-up Summer
A COMEDY ABOUT A PRECOCIOUS GRADE-SCHOOL GIRL.
Higashimura-san.
Would you like to try serializing this?
HUH?
THAT THIRTY-TWO-PAGE ONE-SHOT...
BECAME MY FIRST-EVER SERIALIZED MANGA.
NISHIMURA-KUN WAS THE ONE WHO CAME UP WITH THE TITLE FOR ME.
A title?
Hmm...
Dress-Up Summer...
Maybe?

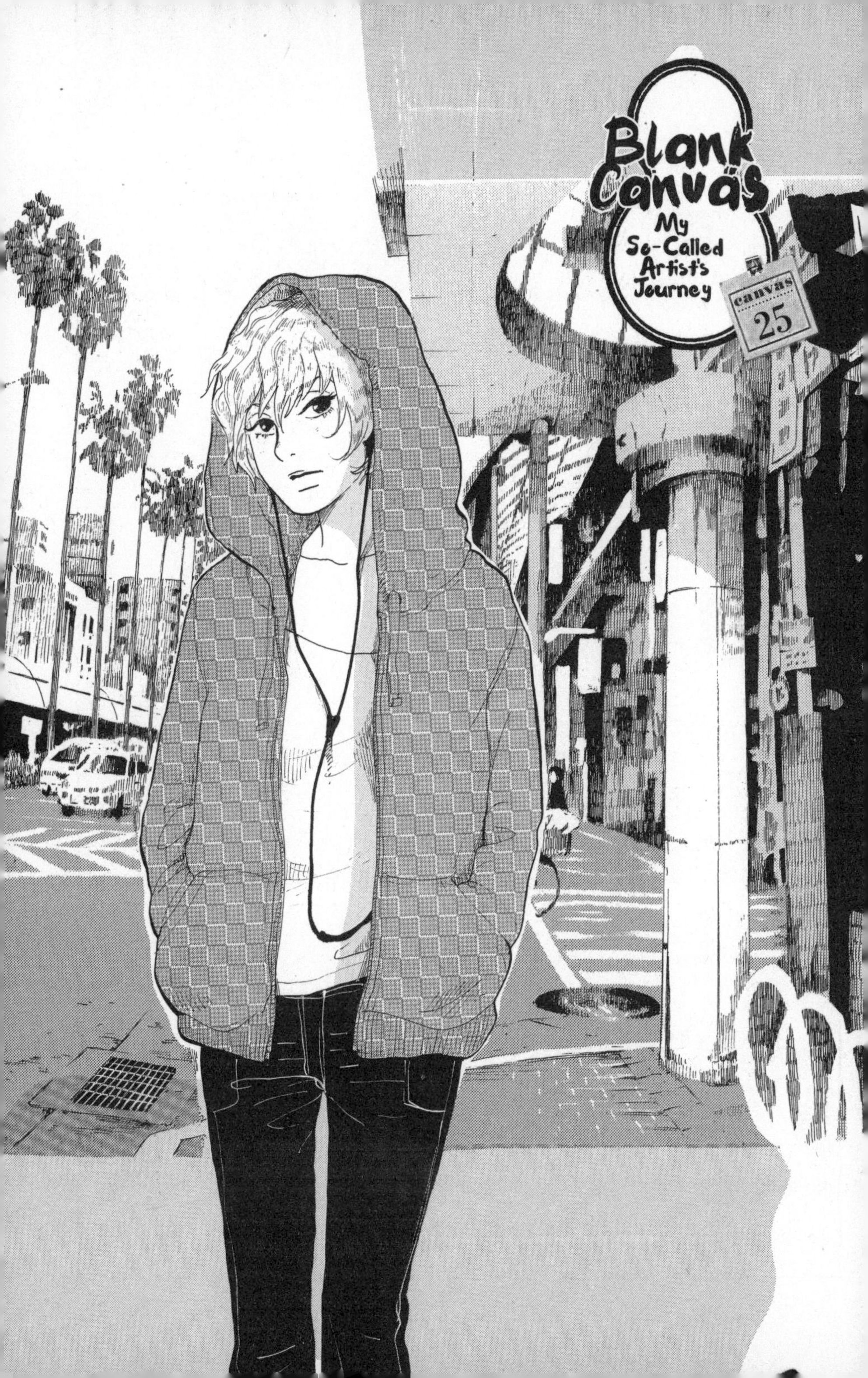
Blank Canvas
My So-Called Artist's Journey
canvas
25

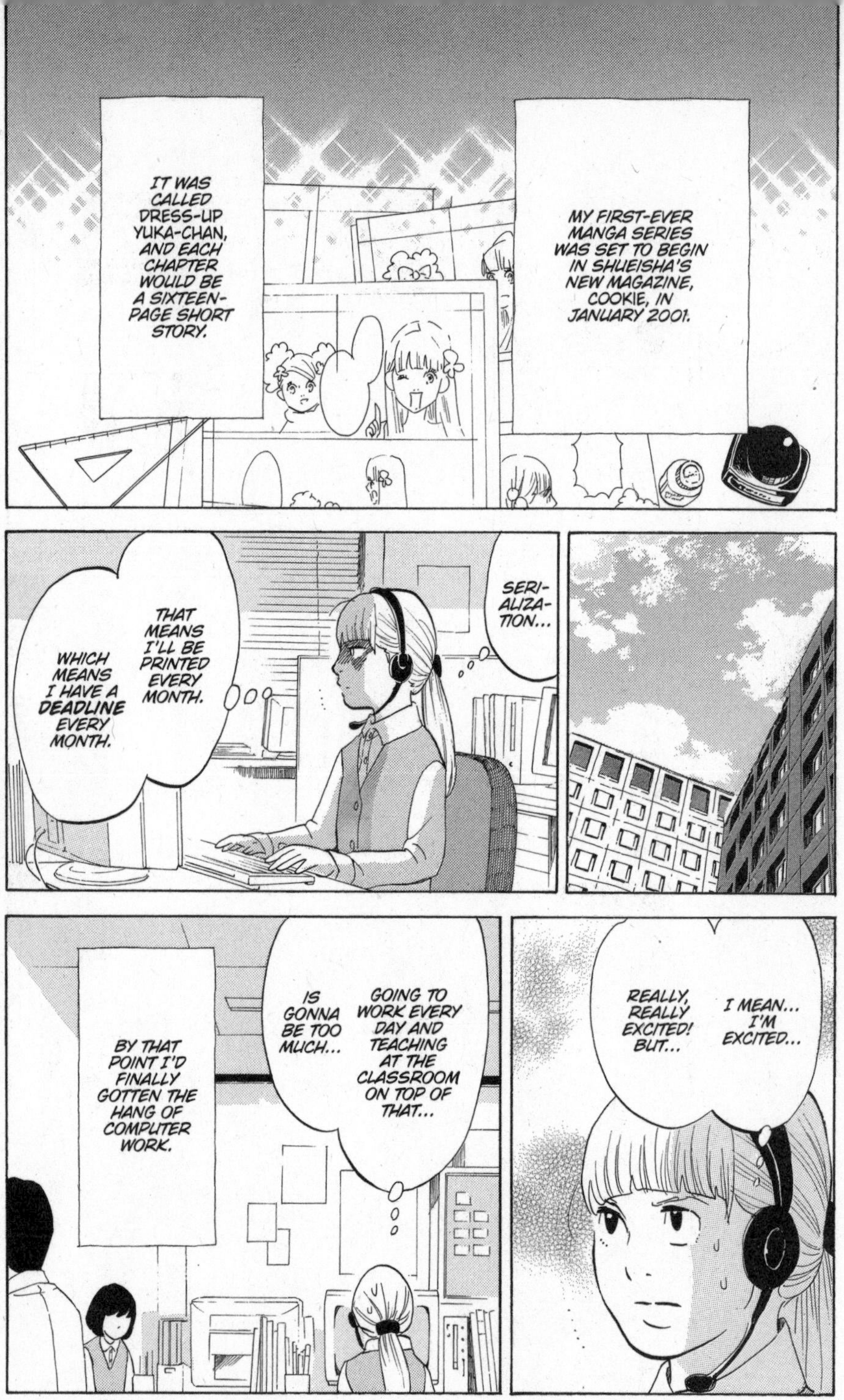
MY FIRST-EVER MANGA SERIES WAS SET TO BEGIN IN SHUEISHA'S NEW MAGAZINE, COOKIE, IN JANUARY 2001.
IT WAS CALLED DRESS-UP YUKA-CHAN, AND EACH CHAPTER WOULD BE A SIXTEEN-PAGE SHORT STORY.
SERI-ALIZATION...
THAT MEANS I'LL BE PRINTED EVERY MONTH.
WHICH MEANS I HAVE A DEADLINE EVERY MONTH.
I MEAN... I'M EXCITED...
REALLY, REALLY EXCITED! BUT...
GOING TO WORK EVERY DAY AND TEACHING AT THE CLASSROOM ON TOP OF THAT...
IS GONNA BE TOO MUCH...
BY THAT POINT I'D FINALLY GOTTEN THE HANG OF COMPUTER WORK.

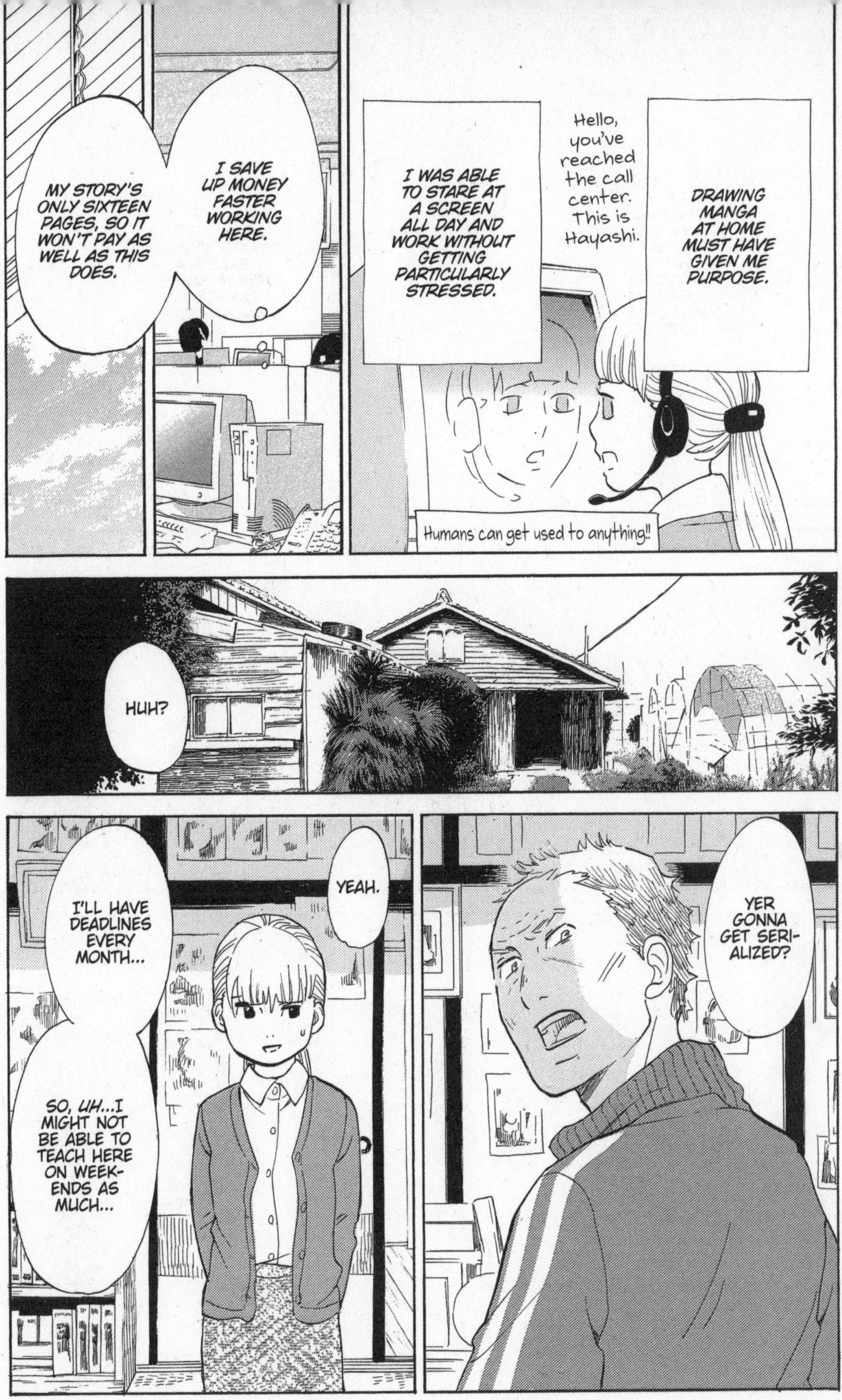
DRAWING MANGA AT HOME MUST HAVE GIVEN ME PURPOSE.
Hello, you've reached the call center. This is Hayashi.
I WAS ABLE TO STARE AT A SCREEN ALL DAY AND WORK WITHOUT GETTING PARTICULARLY STRESSED.
Humans can get used to anything!!
I SAVE UP MONEY FASTER WORKING HERE.
MY STORY'S ONLY SIXTEEN PAGES, SO IT WON'T PAY AS WELL AS THIS DOES.
HUH?
YER GONNA GET SERIALIZED?
YEAH.
I'LL HAVE DEADLINES EVERY MONTH...
SO, UH...I MIGHT NOT BE ABLE TO TEACH HERE ON WEEKENDS AS MUCH...

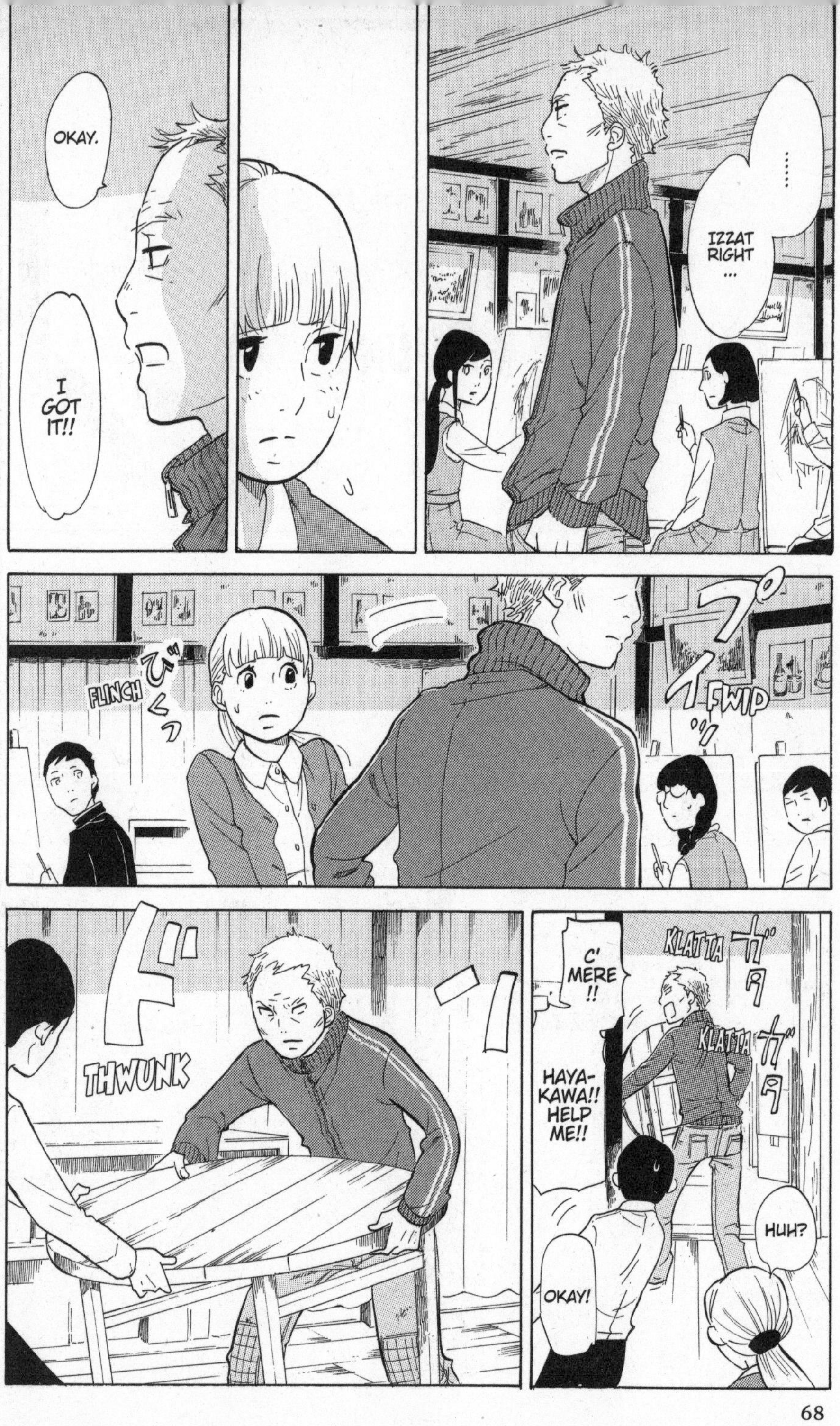
……
IZZAT RIGHT ...
OKAY.
I GOT IT!!
プイ
FWIP
びくっ
FLINCH
KLATTA
ガタ
C' MERE!!
KLATTA
ガタ
HAYA-KAWA!! HELP ME!!
HUH?
OKAY!
THWUNK

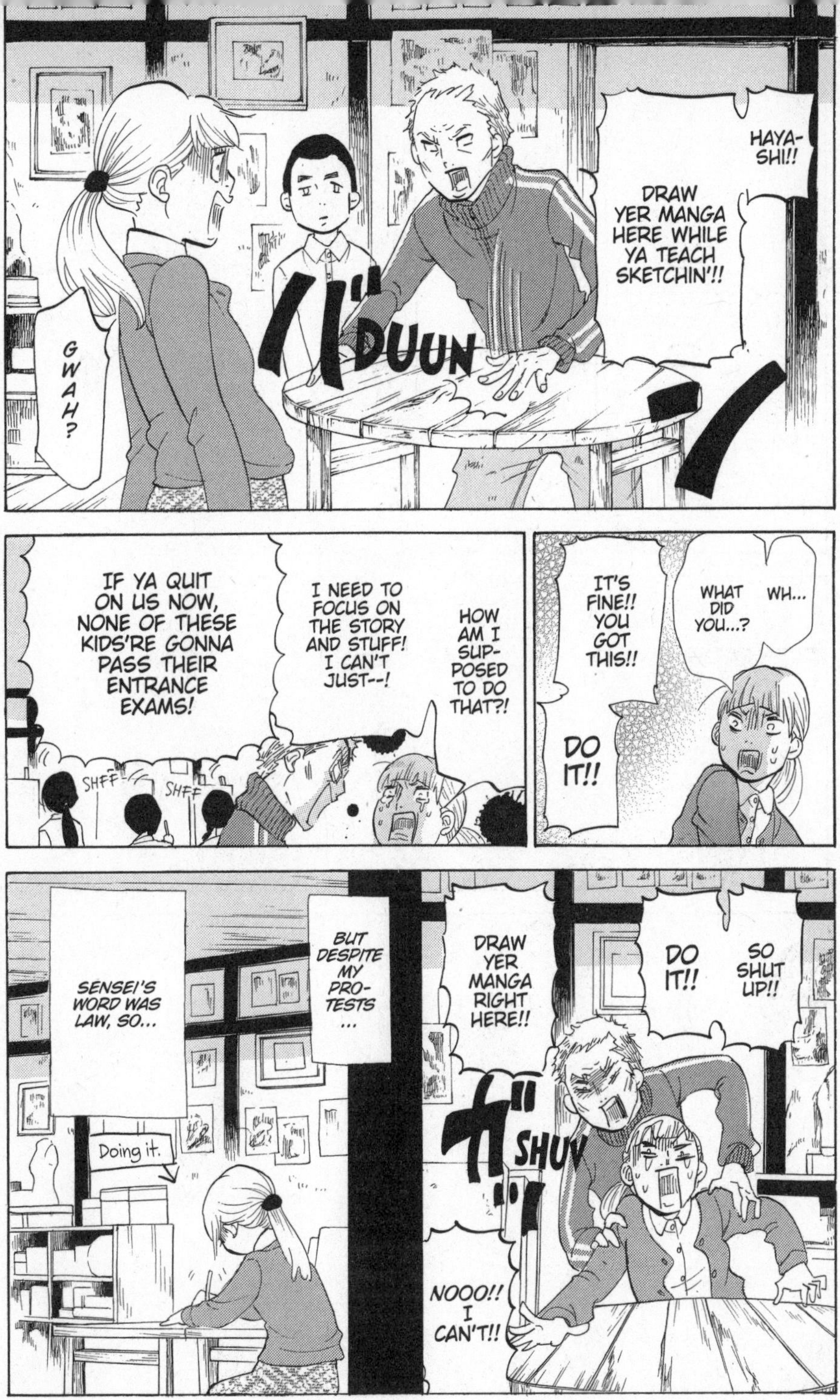
HAYA-SHI!!
DRAW YER MANGA HERE WHILE YA TEACH SKETCHIN'!!
DUUN
GWAH?
WH...
WHAT DID YOU...?
IT'S FINE!! YOU GOT THIS!!
DO IT!!
HOW AM I SUP-POSED TO DO THAT?!
I NEED TO FOCUS ON THE STORY AND STUFF! I CAN'T JUST--!
IF YA QUIT ON US NOW, NONE OF THESE KIDS'RE GONNA PASS THEIR ENTRANCE EXAMS!
SHFF
SHFF
SO SHUT UP!!
DO IT!!
DRAW YER MANGA RIGHT HERE!!
SHUV
NOOO!! I CAN'T!!
BUT DESPITE MY PRO-TESTS...
SENSEI'S WORD WAS LAW, SO...
Doing it.

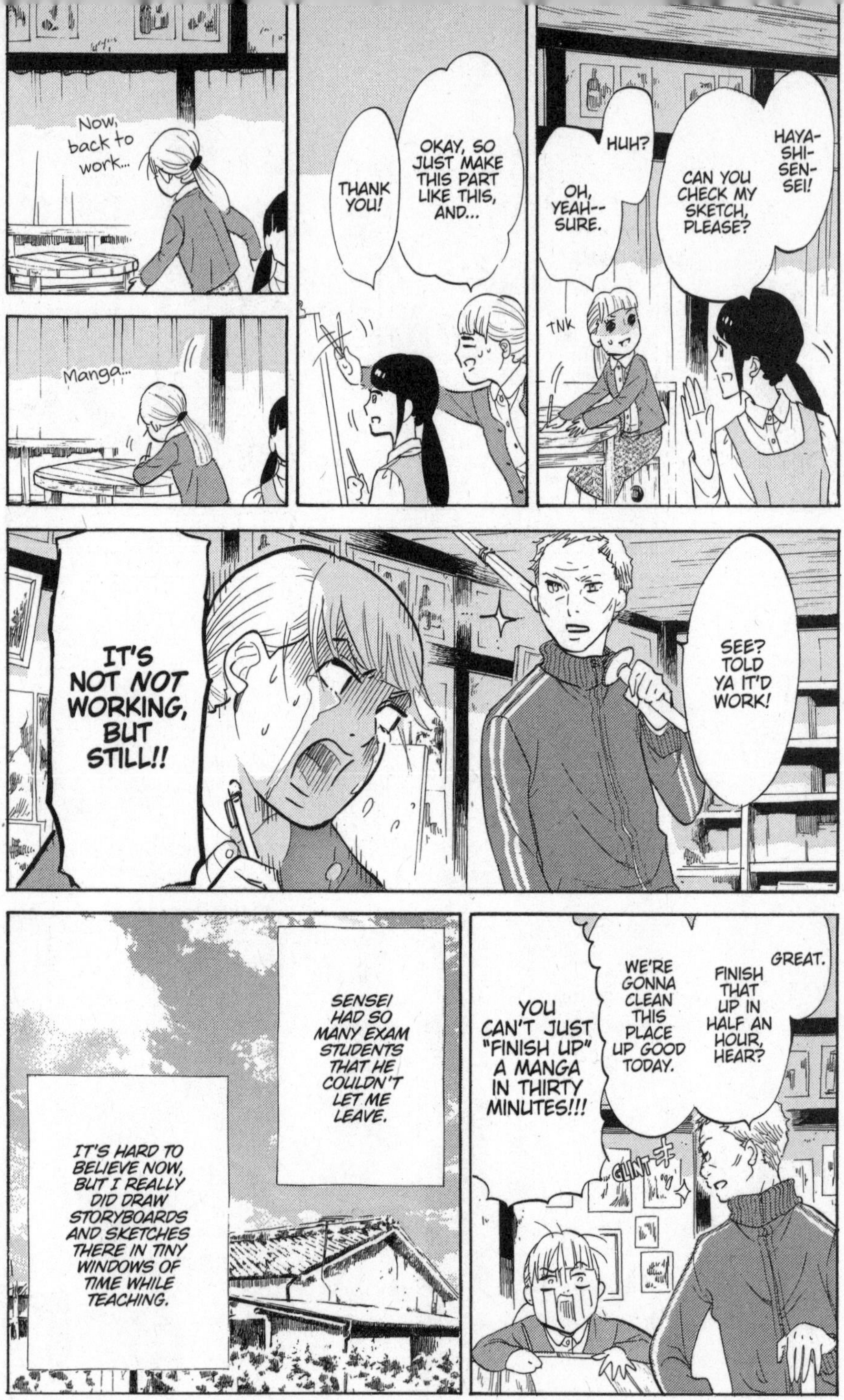
HAYA-SHI-SEN-SEI!
CAN YOU CHECK MY SKETCH, PLEASE?
HUH?
OH, YEAH-- SURE.
TNK
OKAY, SO JUST MAKE THIS PART LIKE THIS, AND...
THANK YOU!
Now, back to work...
Manga...
SEE? TOLD YA IT'D WORK!
IT'S NOT *NOT* WORKING, BUT STILL!!
GREAT.
FINISH THAT UP IN HALF AN HOUR, HEAR?
WE'RE GONNA CLEAN THIS PLACE UP GOOD TODAY.
YOU CAN'T JUST "FINISH UP" A MANGA IN THIRTY MINUTES!!!
GLINT
SENSEI HAD SO MANY EXAM STUDENTS THAT HE COULDN'T LET ME LEAVE.
IT'S HARD TO BELIEVE NOW, BUT I REALLY DID DRAW STORYBOARDS AND SKETCHES THERE IN TINY WINDOWS OF TIME WHILE TEACHING.

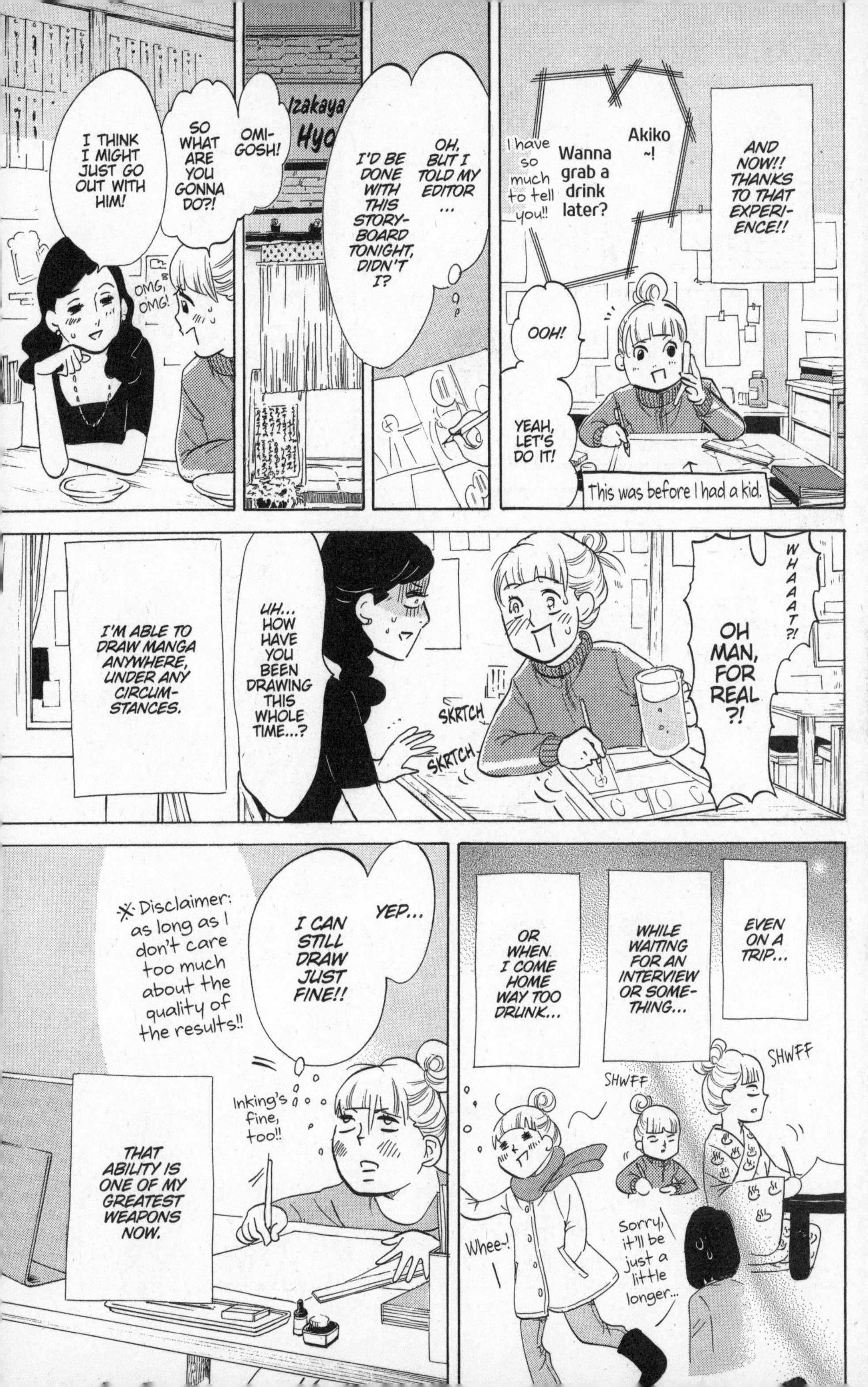
AND NOW!! THANKS TO THAT EXPERIENCE!!
Akiko ~!
Wanna grab a drink later?
I have so much to tell you!!
OOH!
YEAH, LET'S DO IT!
This was before I had a kid.
OH, BUT I TOLD MY EDITOR ...
I'D BE DONE WITH THIS STORYBOARD TONIGHT, DIDN'T I?
Izakaya Hyo
OMI-GOSH!
SO WHAT ARE YOU GONNA DO?!
I THINK I MIGHT JUST GO OUT WITH HIM!
OMG, OMG!
WHAAAAT?!
OH MAN, FOR REAL?!
SKRTCH
SKRTCH
UH... HOW HAVE YOU BEEN DRAWING THIS WHOLE TIME...?
I'M ABLE TO DRAW MANGA ANYWHERE, UNDER ANY CIRCUMSTANCES.
EVEN ON A TRIP...
WHILE WAITING FOR AN INTERVIEW OR SOME-THING...
OR WHEN I COME HOME WAY TOO DRUNK...
SHWFF
SHWFF
Sorry, it'll be just a little longer...
Whee~!
YEP...
I CAN STILL DRAW JUST FINE!!
※ Disclaimer: as long as I don't care too much about the quality of the results!!
Inking's fine, too!!
THAT ABILITY IS ONE OF MY GREATEST WEAPONS NOW.

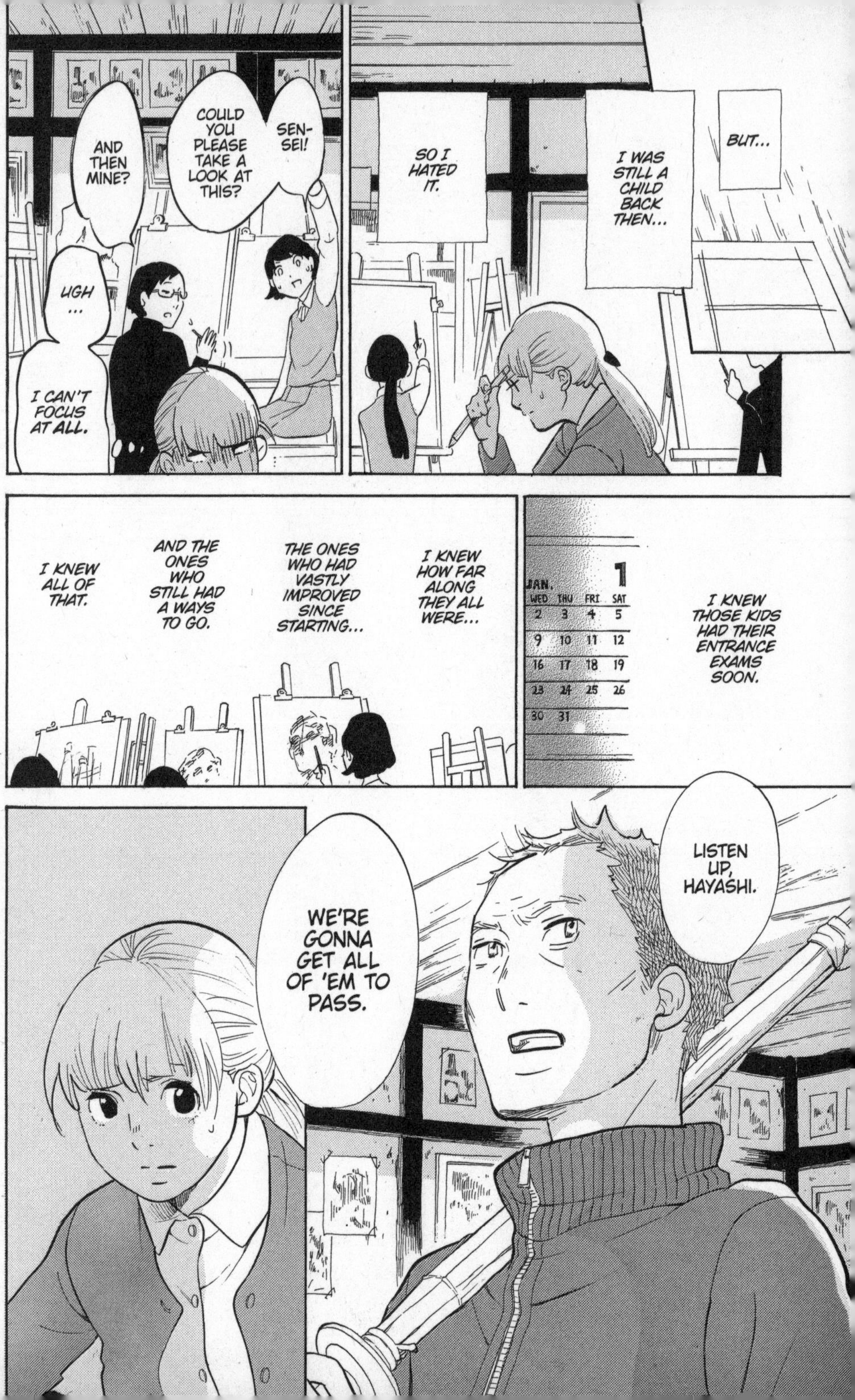
I WAS STILL A CHILD BACK THEN...
SO I HATED IT.
BUT...
SEN-SEI!
COULD YOU PLEASE TAKE A LOOK AT THIS?
AND THEN MINE?
UGH...
I CAN'T FOCUS AT ALL.
I KNEW THOSE KIDS HAD THEIR ENTRANCE EXAMS SOON.
JAN. 1
WED THU FRI SAT
2 3 4 5
9 10 11 12
16 17 18 19
23 24 25 26
30 31
I KNEW HOW FAR ALONG THEY ALL WERE...
THE ONES WHO HAD VASTLY IMPROVED SINCE STARTING...
AND THE ONES WHO STILL HAD A WAYS TO GO.
I KNEW ALL OF THAT.
LISTEN UP, HAYASHI.
WE'RE GONNA GET ALL OF 'EM TO PASS.

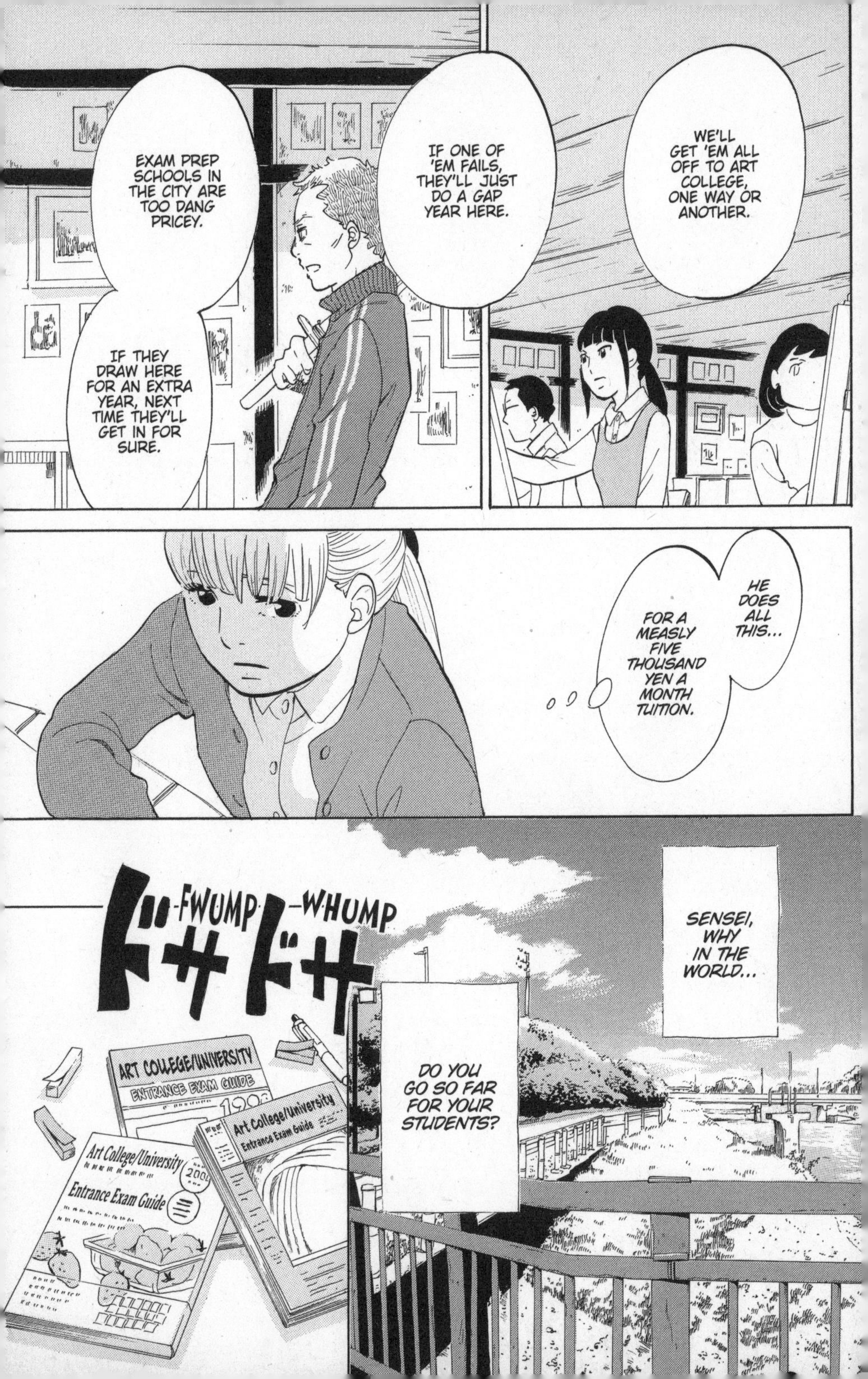
WE'LL GET 'EM ALL OFF TO ART COLLEGE, ONE WAY OR ANOTHER.
IF ONE OF 'EM FAILS, THEY'LL JUST DO A GAP YEAR HERE.
EXAM PREP SCHOOLS IN THE CITY ARE TOO DANG PRICEY.
IF THEY DRAW HERE FOR AN EXTRA YEAR, NEXT TIME THEY'LL GET IN FOR SURE.
HE DOES ALL THIS...
FOR A MEASLY FIVE THOUSAND YEN A MONTH TUITION.
SENSEI, WHY IN THE WORLD...
DO YOU GO SO FAR FOR YOUR STUDENTS?
-FWUMP -WHUMP
ART COLLEGE/UNIVERSITY ENTRANCE EXAM GUIDE
Art College/University Entrance Exam Guide
Art College/University Entrance Exam Guide

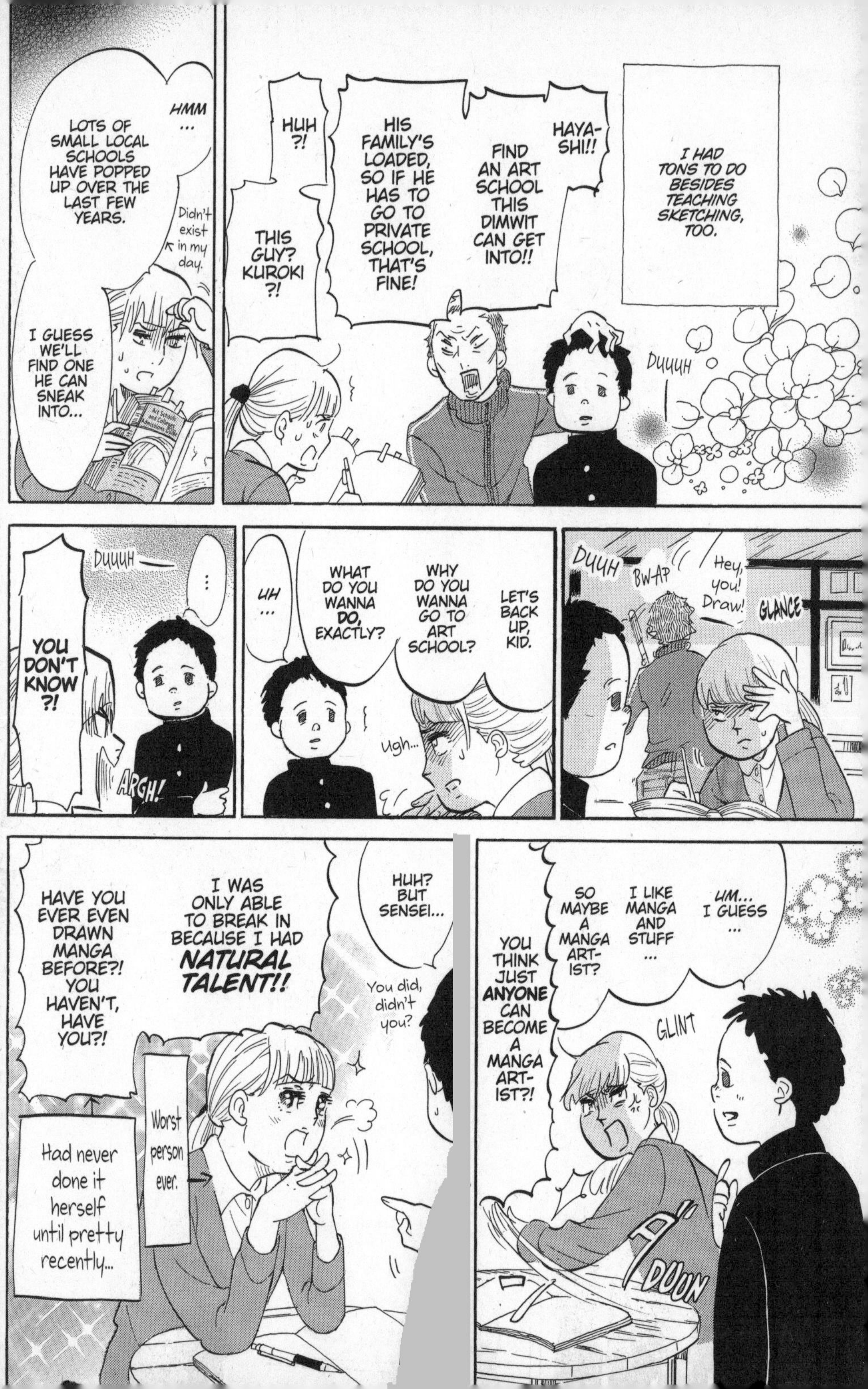

I HAD TONS TO DO BESIDES TEACHING SKETCHING, TOO.
DUUUH
HAYA-SHI!!
FIND AN ART SCHOOL THIS DIMWIT CAN GET INTO!!
HIS FAMILY'S LOADED, SO IF HE HAS TO GO TO PRIVATE SCHOOL, THAT'S FINE!
HUH?!
THIS GUY? KUROKI?!
HMM...
LOTS OF SMALL LOCAL SCHOOLS HAVE POPPED UP OVER THE LAST FEW YEARS.
Didn't exist in my day.
I GUESS WE'LL FIND ONE HE CAN SNEAK INTO...
Hey, you! Draw!
BW-AP
DUUH
GLANCE
LET'S BACK UP, KID.
WHY DO YOU WANNA GO TO ART SCHOOL?
WHAT DO YOU WANNA DO, EXACTLY?
UH...
Ugh...
...
DUUUH
YOU DON'T KNOW?!
ARGH!
UM... I GUESS...
I LIKE MANGA AND STUFF...
SO MAYBE A MANGA ART-IST?
YOU THINK JUST ANYONE CAN BECOME A MANGA ART-IST?!
GLINT
DUUN
HUH? BUT SENSEI...
You did, didn't you?
I WAS ONLY ABLE TO BREAK IN BECAUSE I HAD NATURAL TALENT!!
HAVE YOU EVER EVEN DRAWN MANGA BEFORE?! YOU HAVEN'T, HAVE YOU?!
Worst person ever.
Had never done it herself until pretty recently...

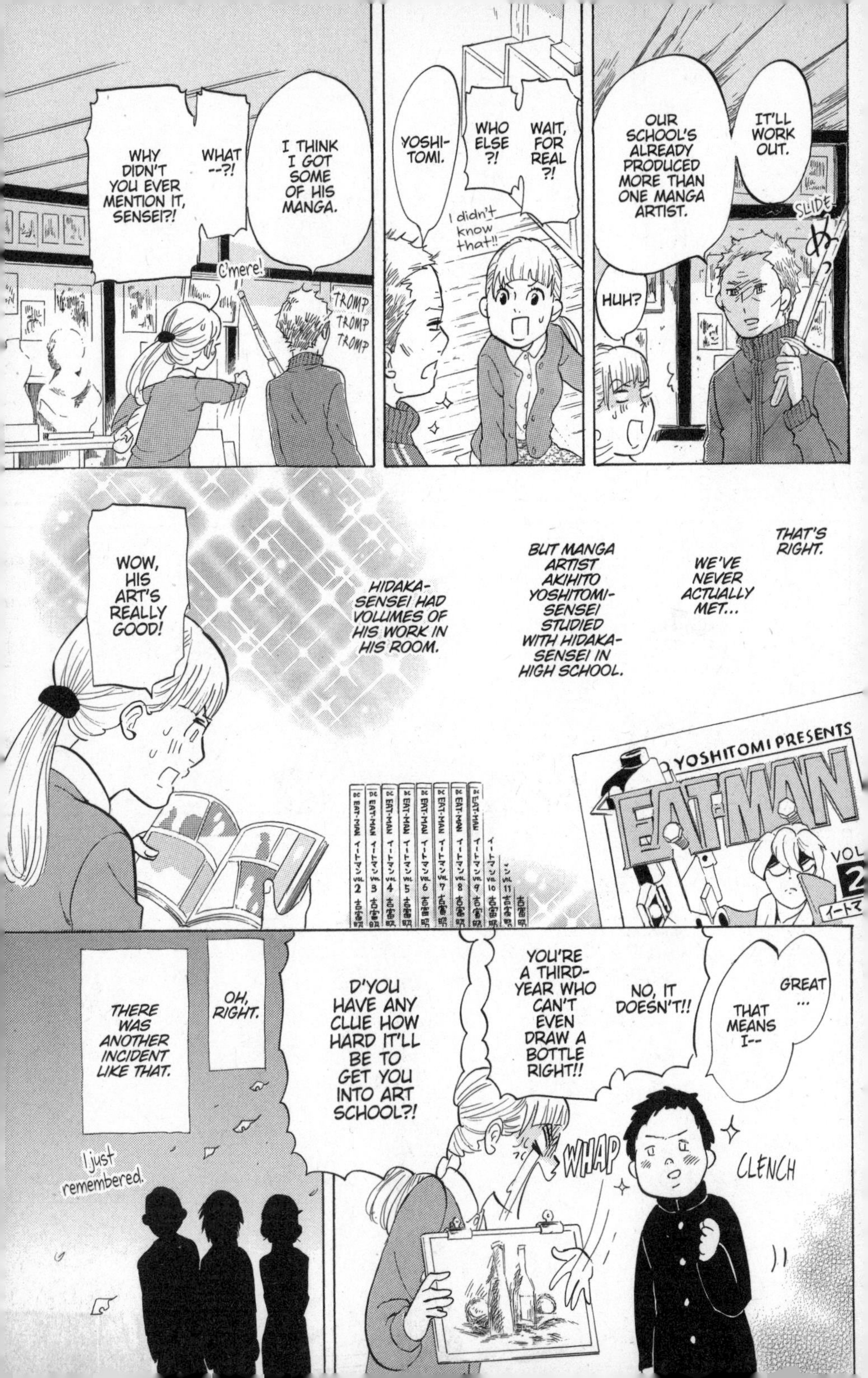
IT'LL WORK OUT.
OUR SCHOOL'S ALREADY PRODUCED MORE THAN ONE MANGA ARTIST.
SLIDE
HUH?
WAIT, FOR REAL?!
WHO ELSE?!
YOSHI-TOMI.
I didn't know that!!
I THINK I GOT SOME OF HIS MANGA.
WHAT--?!
WHY DIDN'T YOU EVER MENTION IT, SENSEI?!
C'mere!
TROMP TROMP TROMP
THAT'S RIGHT.
WE'VE NEVER ACTUALLY MET...
BUT MANGA ARTIST AKIHITO YOSHITOMI-SENSEI STUDIED WITH HIDAKA-SENSEI IN HIGH SCHOOL.
HIDAKA-SENSEI HAD VOLUMES OF HIS WORK IN HIS ROOM.
WOW, HIS ART'S REALLY GOOD!
YOSHITOMI PRESENTS
EAT-MAN
VOL 2
GREAT...
THAT MEANS I--
NO, IT DOESN'T!!
YOU'RE A THIRD-YEAR WHO CAN'T EVEN DRAW A BOTTLE RIGHT!!
WHAP
CLENCH
D'YOU HAVE ANY CLUE HOW HARD IT'LL BE TO GET YOU INTO ART SCHOOL?!
OH, RIGHT.
THERE WAS ANOTHER INCIDENT LIKE THAT.
I just remembered.

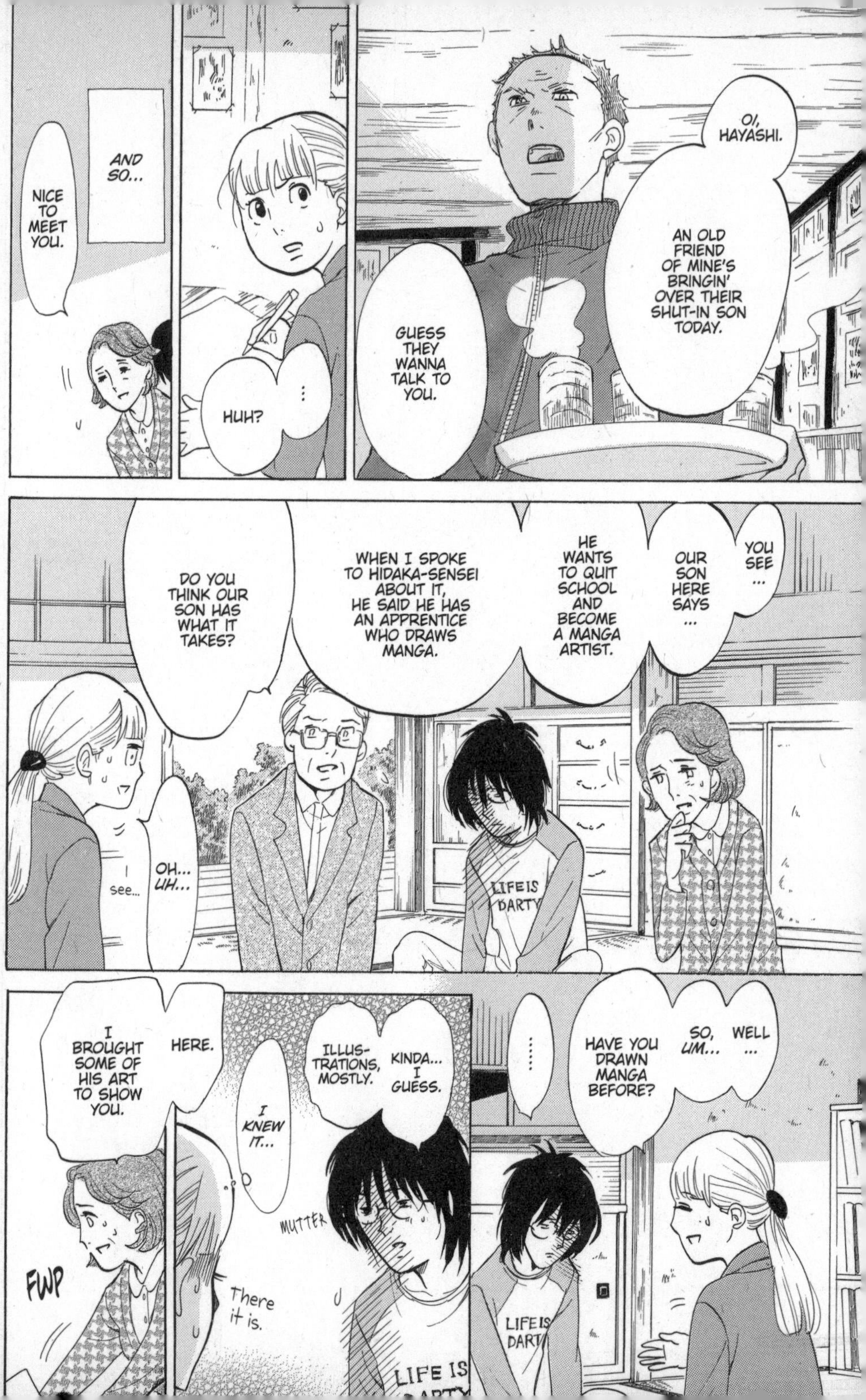
OI, HAYASHI.
AN OLD FRIEND OF MINE'S BRINGIN' OVER THEIR SHUT-IN SON TODAY.
GUESS THEY WANNA TALK TO YOU.
...
HUH?
AND SO...
NICE TO MEET YOU.
YOU SEE...
OUR SON HERE SAYS...
HE WANTS TO QUIT SCHOOL AND BECOME A MANGA ARTIST.
WHEN I SPOKE TO HIDAKA-SENSEI ABOUT IT, HE SAID HE HAS AN APPRENTICE WHO DRAWS MANGA.
DO YOU THINK OUR SON HAS WHAT IT TAKES?
LIFE IS DARTY
OH... UH...
I see...
WELL...
SO, UM...
HAVE YOU DRAWN MANGA BEFORE?
......
KINDA... I GUESS.
ILLUS-TRATIONS, MOSTLY.
I KNEW IT...
MUTTER
HERE.
I BROUGHT SOME OF HIS ART TO SHOW YOU.
There it is.
FWP

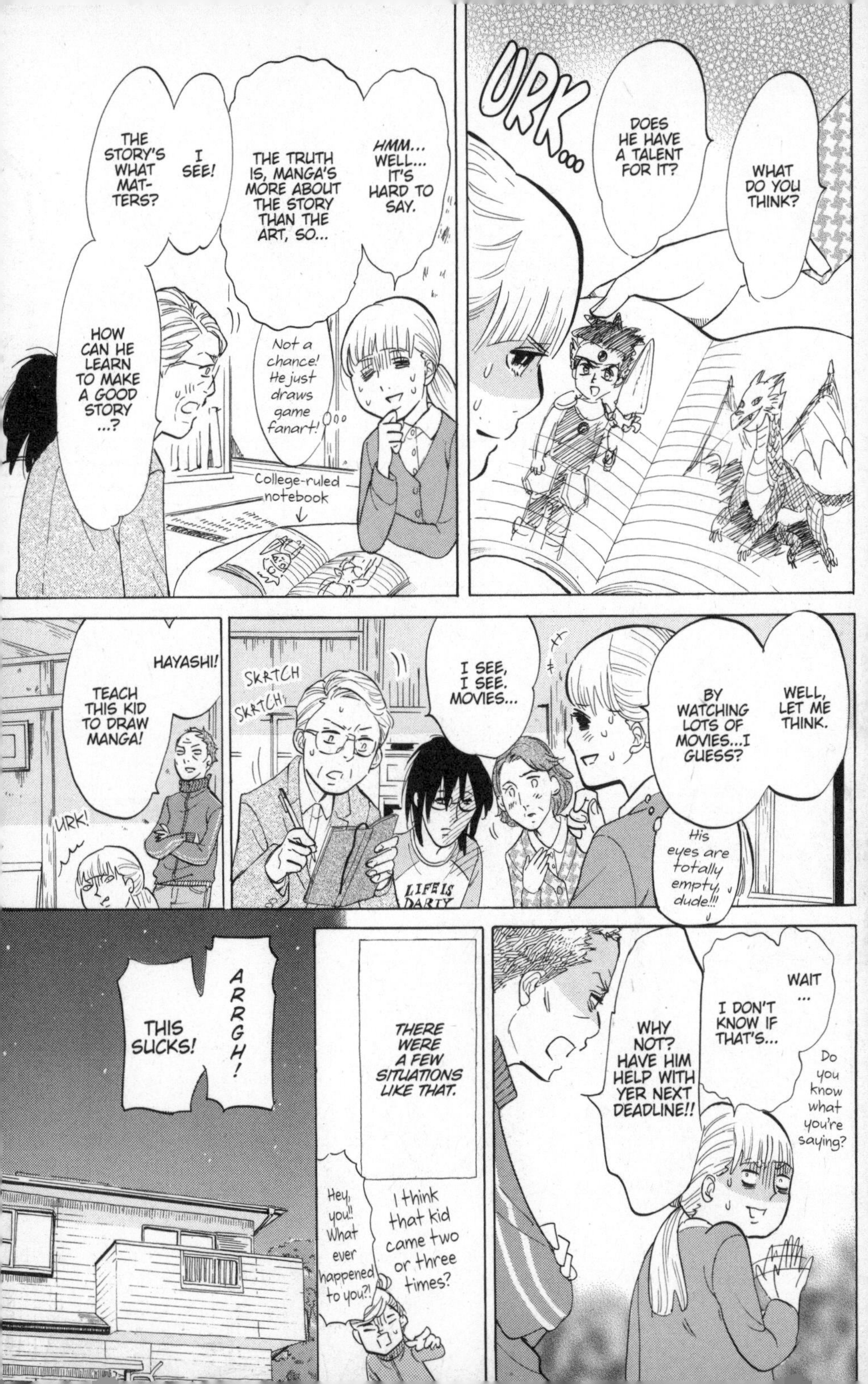

WHAT DO YOU THINK?
DOES HE HAVE A TALENT FOR IT?
URKooo
HMM... WELL... IT'S HARD TO SAY.
THE TRUTH IS, MANGA'S MORE ABOUT THE STORY THAN THE ART, SO...
I SEE!
THE STORY'S WHAT MAT-TERS?
HOW CAN HE LEARN TO MAKE A GOOD STORY ...?
Not a chance! He just draws game fanart!
College-ruled notebook
WELL, LET ME THINK.
BY WATCHING LOTS OF MOVIES...I GUESS?
His eyes are totally empty, dude!!!
I SEE, I SEE. MOVIES...
SKRTCH
SKRTCH
LIFE IS DARTY
HAYASHI!
TEACH THIS KID TO DRAW MANGA!
URK!
WAIT ...
I DON'T KNOW IF THAT'S...
Do you know what you're saying?
WHY NOT? HAVE HIM HELP WITH YER NEXT DEADLINE!!
THERE WERE A FEW SITUATIONS LIKE THAT.
I think that kid came two or three times?
Hey, you!! What ever happened to you?!
ARRGH!
THIS SUCKS!

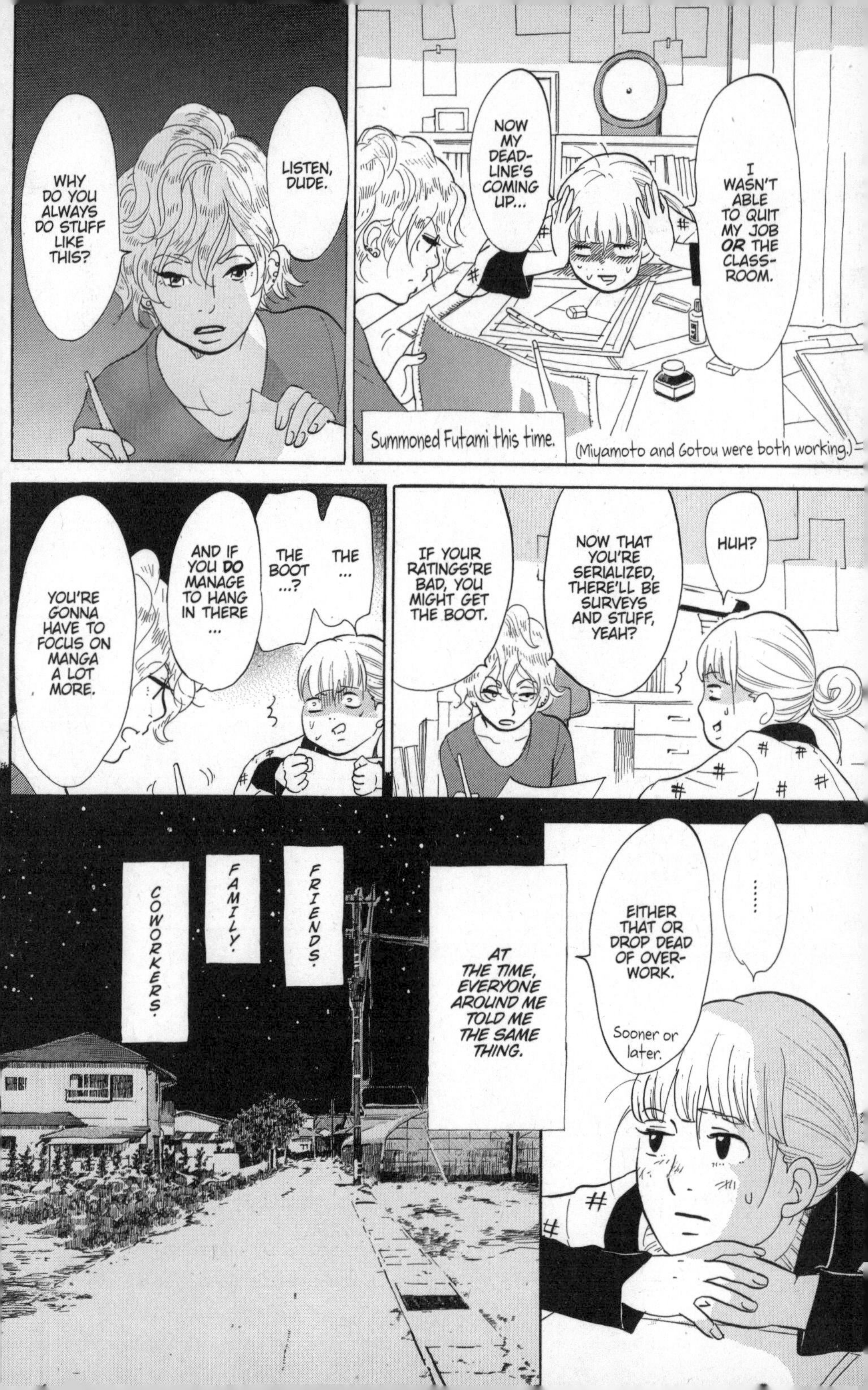
I WASN'T ABLE TO QUIT MY JOB OR THE CLASSROOM.
NOW MY DEADLINE'S COMING UP...
Summoned Futami this time.
(Miyamoto and Gotou were both working.)
LISTEN, DUDE.
WHY DO YOU ALWAYS DO STUFF LIKE THIS?
HUH?
NOW THAT YOU'RE SERIALIZED, THERE'LL BE SURVEYS AND STUFF, YEAH?
IF YOUR RATINGS'RE BAD, YOU MIGHT GET THE BOOT.
THE ...
THE BOOT ...?
AND IF YOU DO MANAGE TO HANG IN THERE ...
YOU'RE GONNA HAVE TO FOCUS ON MANGA A LOT MORE.
......
EITHER THAT OR DROP DEAD OF OVERWORK.
Sooner or later.
AT THE TIME, EVERYONE AROUND ME TOLD ME THE SAME THING.
FRIENDS.
FAMILY.
COWORKERS.

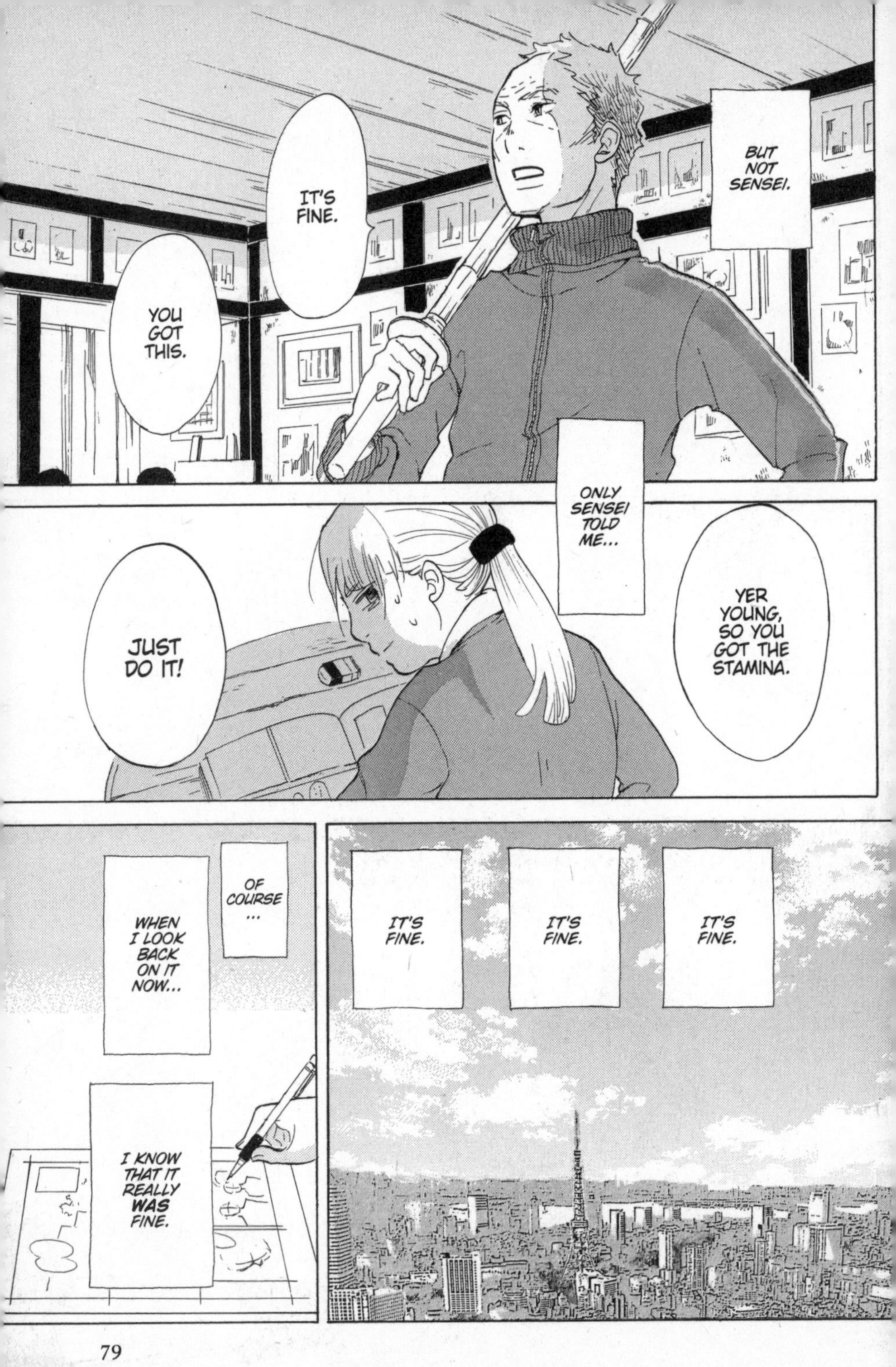
BUT NOT SENSEI.
IT'S FINE.
YOU GOT THIS.
ONLY SENSEI TOLD ME...
YER YOUNG, SO YOU GOT THE STAMINA.
JUST DO IT!
IT'S FINE.
IT'S FINE.
IT'S FINE.
OF COURSE...
WHEN I LOOK BACK ON IT NOW...
I KNOW THAT IT REALLY WAS FINE.

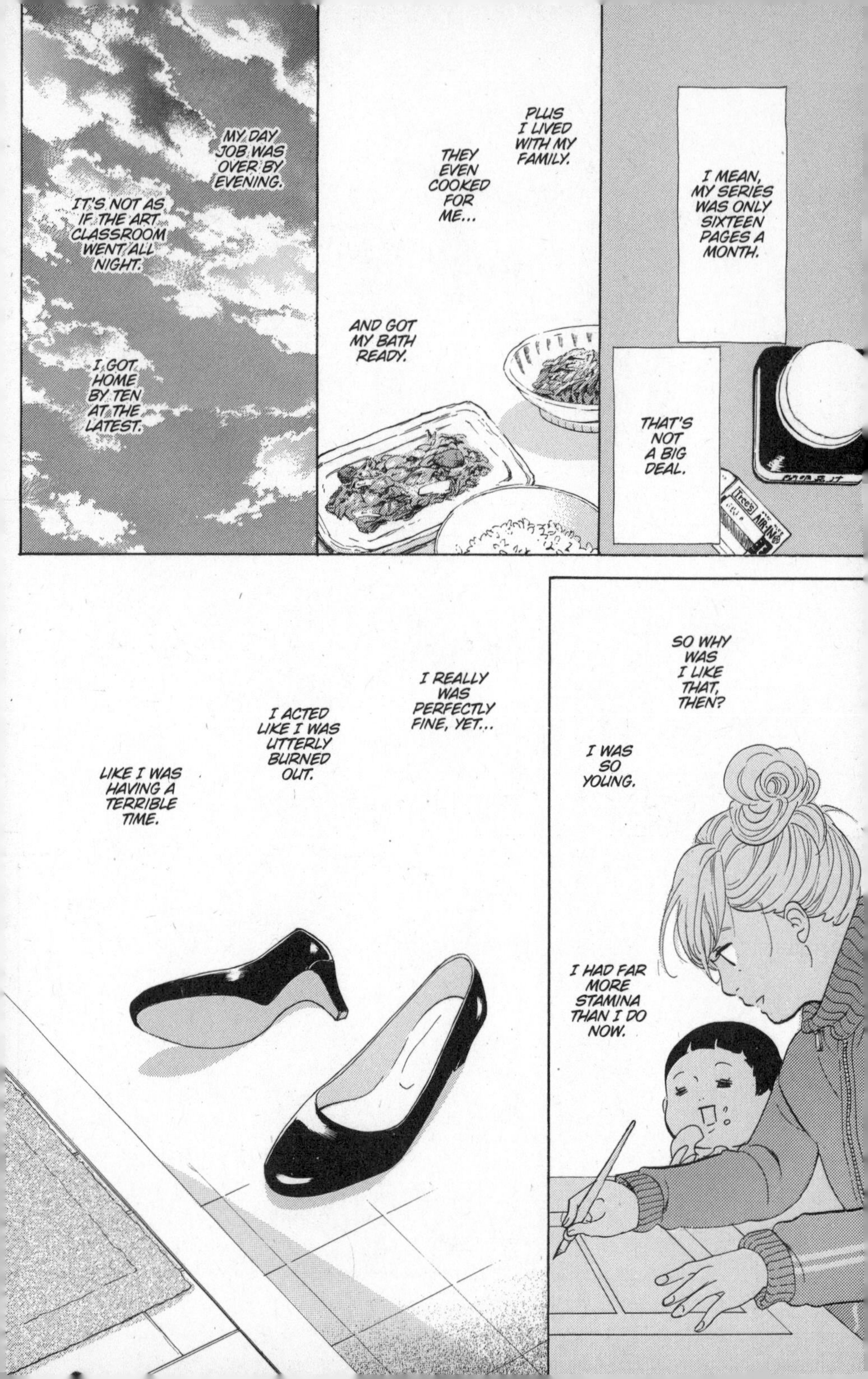
I MEAN, MY SERIES WAS ONLY SIXTEEN PAGES A MONTH.
THAT'S NOT A BIG DEAL.
PLUS I LIVED WITH MY FAMILY.
THEY EVEN COOKED FOR ME...
AND GOT MY BATH READY.
MY DAY JOB WAS OVER BY EVENING.
IT'S NOT AS IF THE ART CLASSROOM WENT ALL NIGHT.
I GOT HOME BY TEN AT THE LATEST.
SO WHY WAS I LIKE THAT, THEN?
I WAS SO YOUNG.
I HAD FAR MORE STAMINA THAN I DO NOW.
I REALLY WAS PERFECTLY FINE, YET...
I ACTED LIKE I WAS UTTERLY BURNED OUT.
LIKE I WAS HAVING A TERRIBLE TIME.

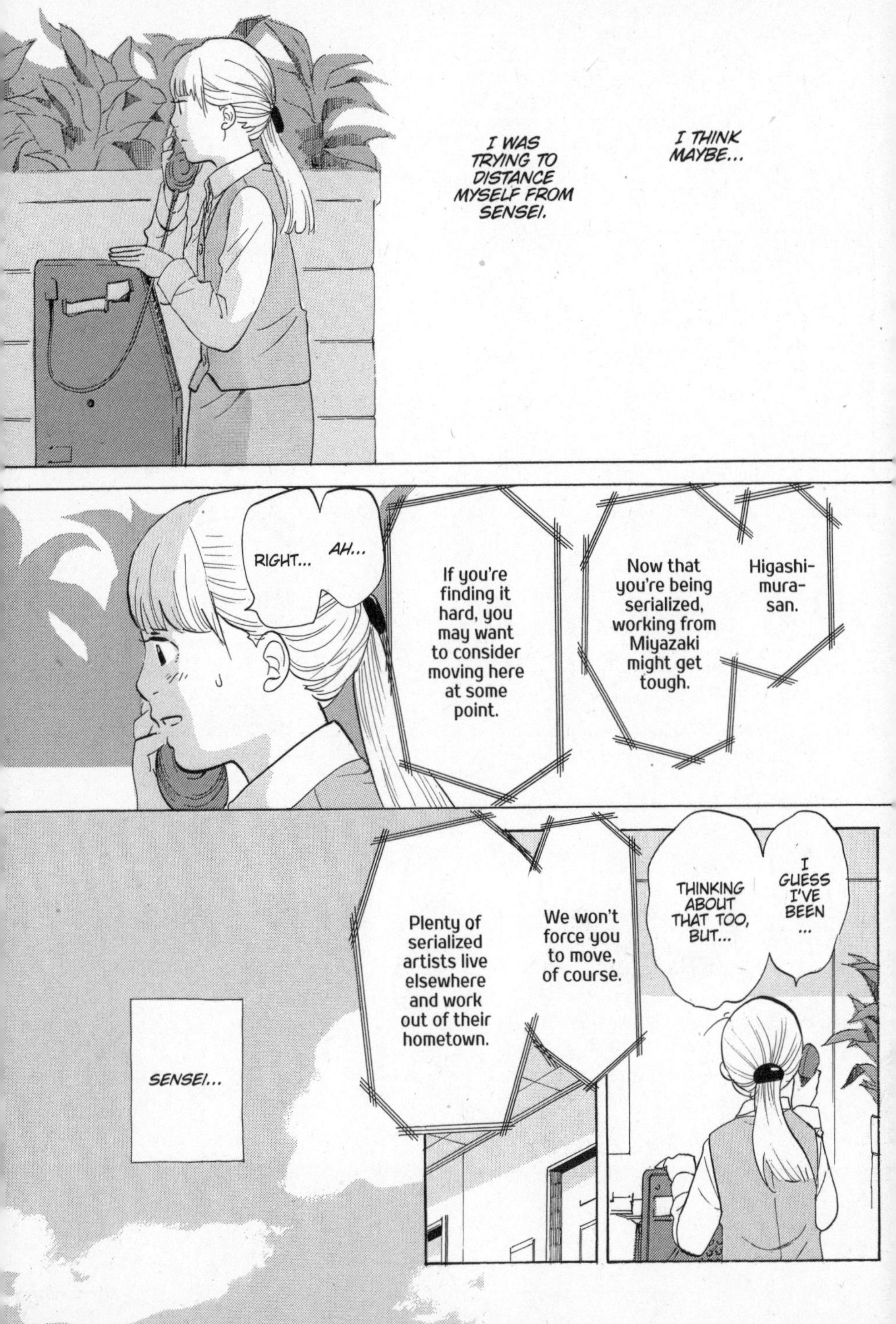
I THINK MAYBE...
I WAS TRYING TO DISTANCE MYSELF FROM SENSEI.
Higashi-mura-san.
Now that you're being serialized, working from Miyazaki might get tough.
If you're finding it hard, you may want to consider moving here at some point.
AH...
RIGHT...
I GUESS I'VE BEEN ...
THINKING ABOUT THAT TOO, BUT...
We won't force you to move, of course.
Plenty of serialized artists live elsewhere and work out of their hometown.
SENSEI...

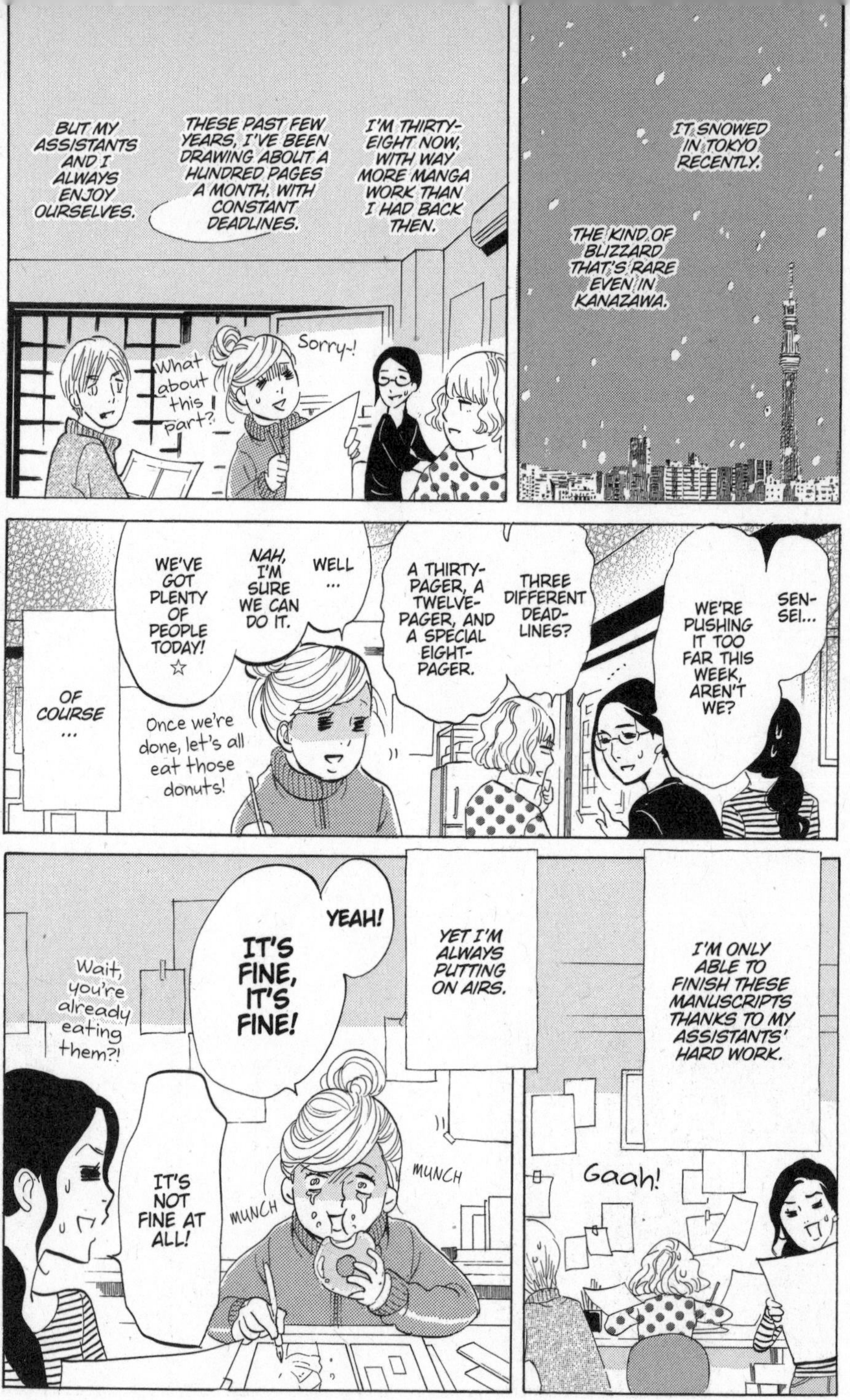
IT SNOWED IN TOKYO RECENTLY.
THE KIND OF BLIZZARD THAT'S RARE EVEN IN KANAZAWA.
I'M THIRTY-EIGHT NOW, WITH WAY MORE MANGA WORK THAN I HAD BACK THEN.
THESE PAST FEW YEARS, I'VE BEEN DRAWING ABOUT A HUNDRED PAGES A MONTH, WITH CONSTANT DEADLINES.
BUT MY ASSISTANTS AND I ALWAYS ENJOY OURSELVES.
Sorry~!
What about this part?
SEN-SEI...
WE'RE PUSHING IT TOO FAR THIS WEEK, AREN'T WE?
THREE DIFFERENT DEAD-LINES?
A THIRTY-PAGER, A TWELVE-PAGER, AND A SPECIAL EIGHT-PAGER.
WELL...
NAH, I'M SURE WE CAN DO IT.
WE'VE GOT PLENTY OF PEOPLE TODAY! ☆
Once we're done, let's all eat those donuts!
OF COURSE...
I'M ONLY ABLE TO FINISH THESE MANUSCRIPTS THANKS TO MY ASSISTANTS' HARD WORK.
Gaah!
YET I'M ALWAYS PUTTING ON AIRS.
YEAH!
IT'S FINE, IT'S FINE!
Wait, you're already eating them?!
MUNCH
MUNCH
IT'S NOT FINE AT ALL!

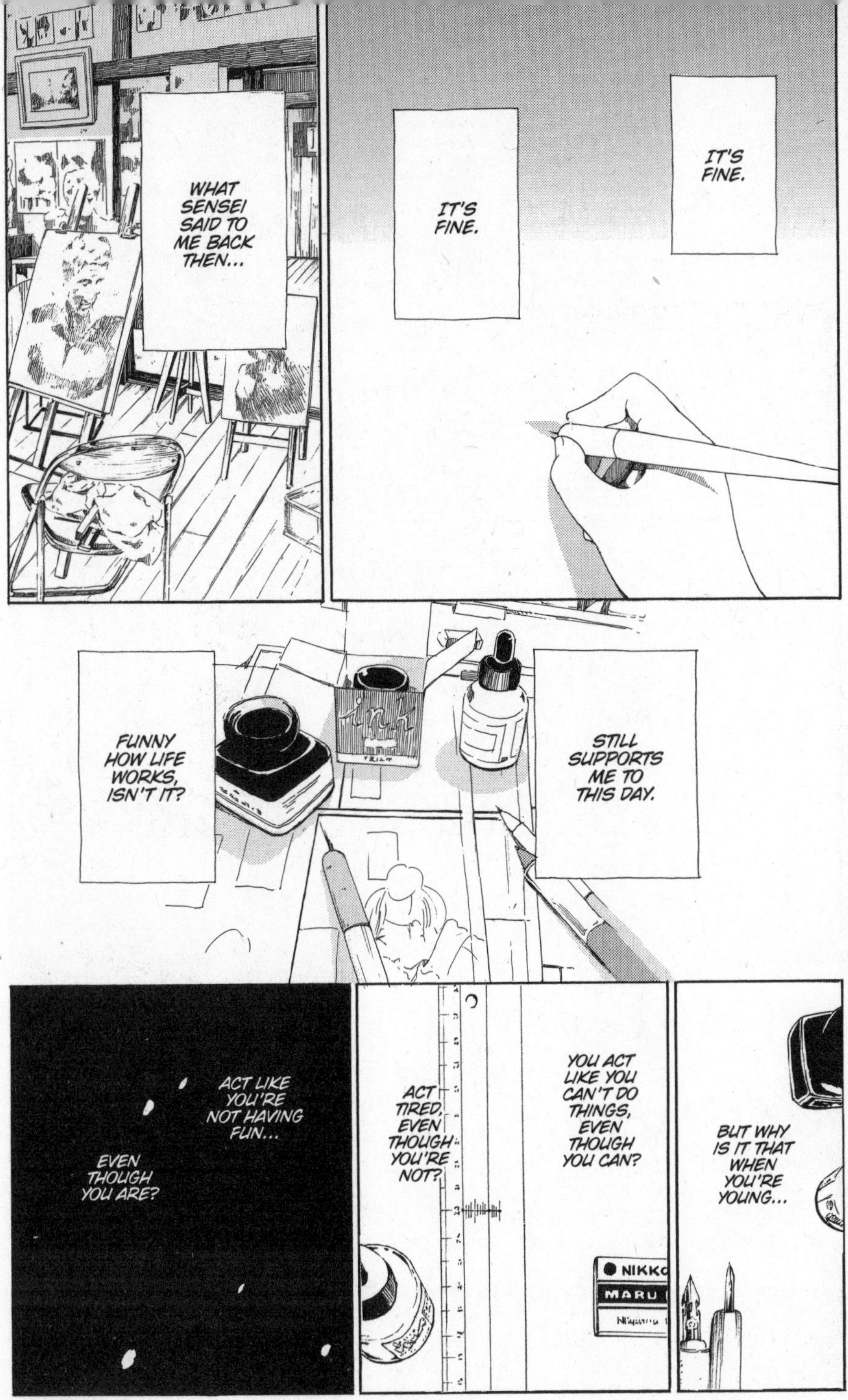
IT'S FINE.
IT'S FINE.
WHAT SENSEI SAID TO ME BACK THEN...
STILL SUPPORTS ME TO THIS DAY.
FUNNY HOW LIFE WORKS, ISN'T IT?
BUT WHY IS IT THAT WHEN YOU'RE YOUNG...
YOU ACT LIKE YOU CAN'T DO THINGS, EVEN THOUGH YOU CAN?
NIKKO
MARU
ACT TIRED, EVEN THOUGH YOU'RE NOT?
ACT LIKE YOU'RE NOT HAVING FUN...
EVEN THOUGH YOU ARE?

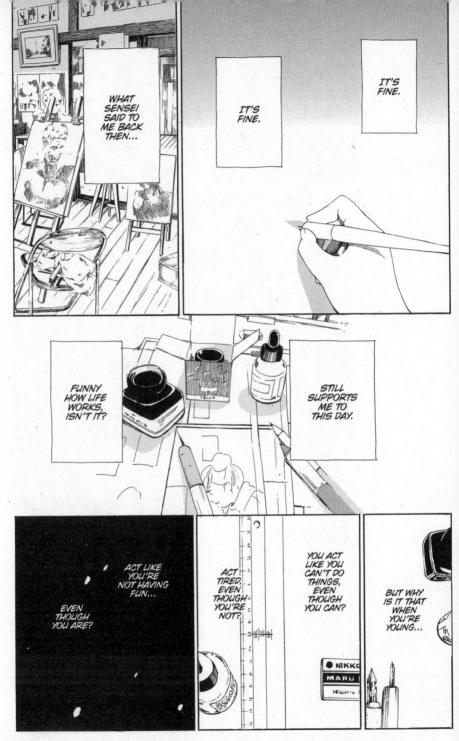

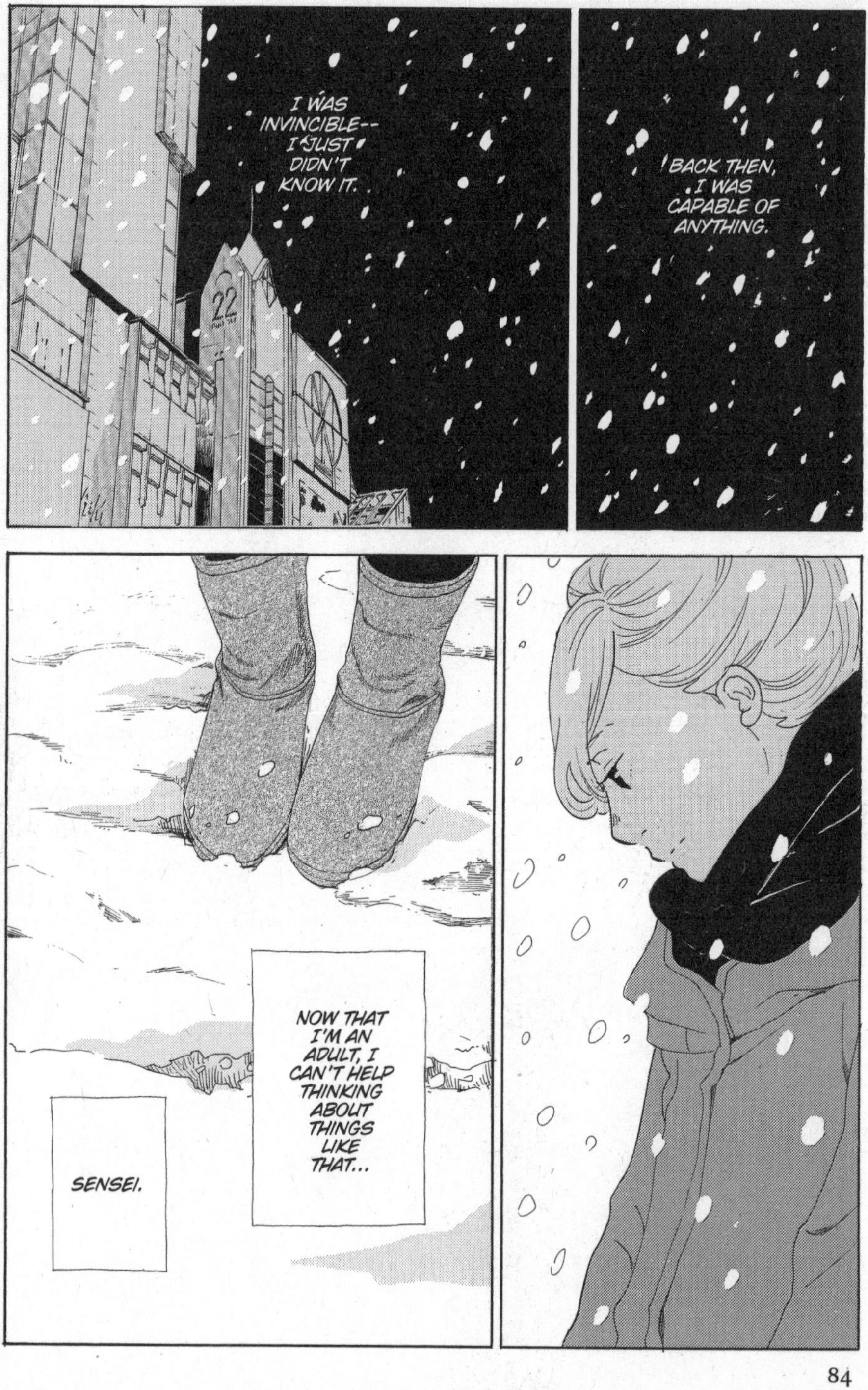
BACK THEN, I WAS CAPABLE OF ANYTHING.
I WAS INVINCIBLE-- I JUST DIDN'T KNOW IT.
NOW THAT I'M AN ADULT, I CAN'T HELP THINKING ABOUT THINGS LIKE THAT...
SENSEI.

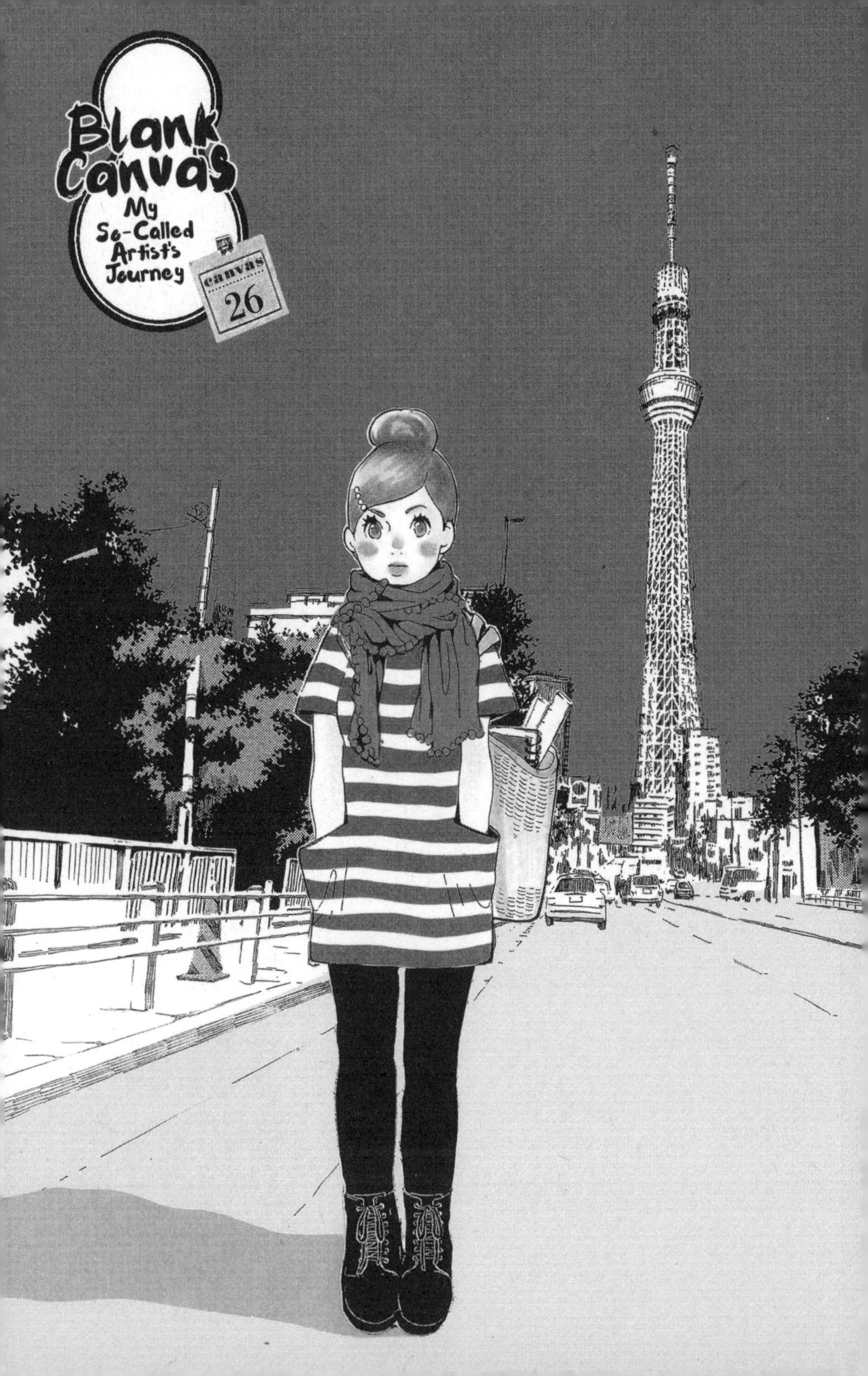
Blank Canvas
My So-Called Artist's Journey
canvas
26

Blank Canvas

My So-Called Artist's Journey

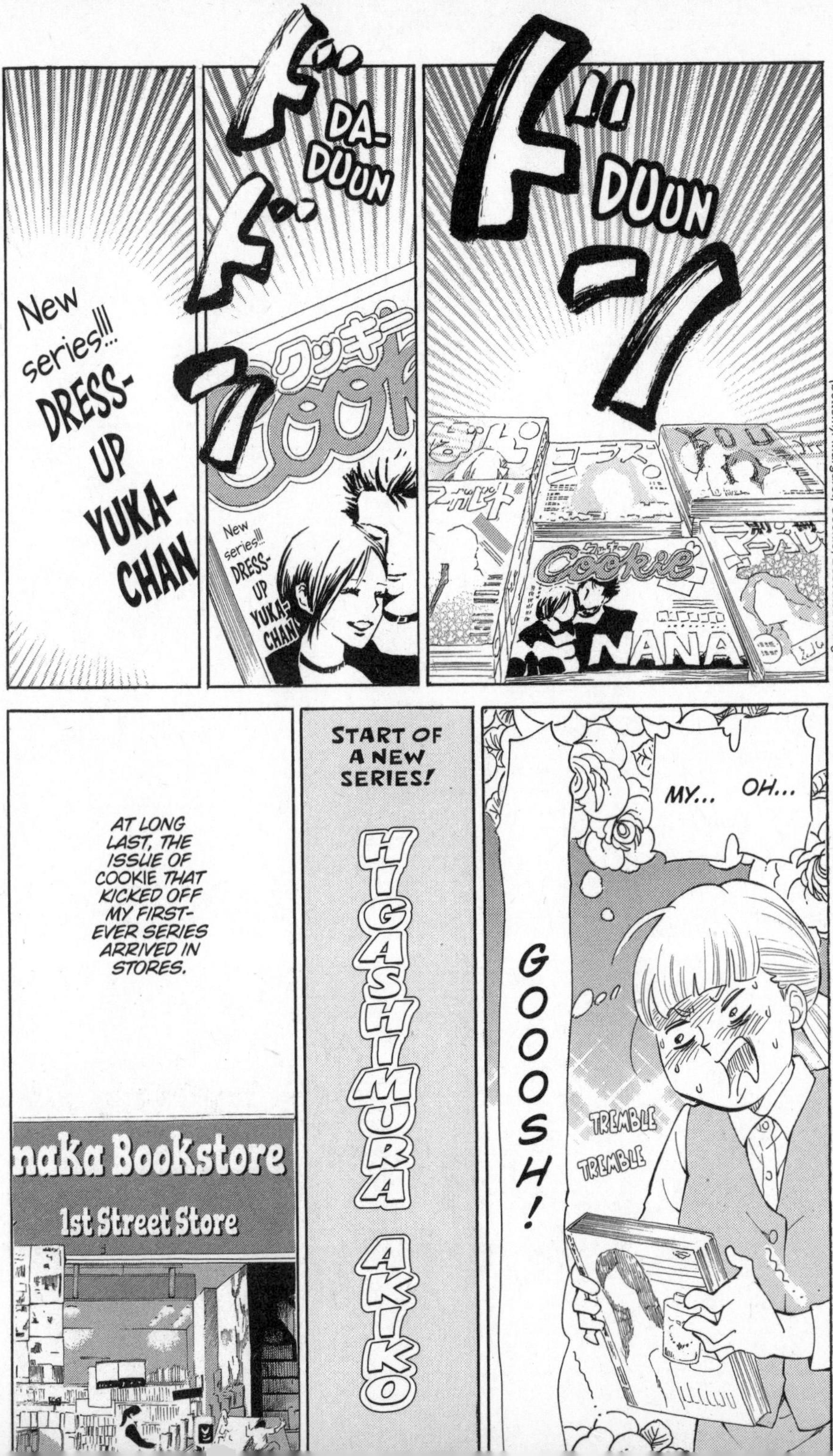
DUUN
NANA
DA-DUUN
New series!!! DRESS-UP YUKA-CHAN
New series!!!... DRESS-UP YUKA-CHAN
MY... OH...
GOOOOSH!
TREMBLE
TREMBLE
START OF A NEW SERIES!
HIGASHIMURA AKIKO
AT LONG LAST, THE ISSUE OF COOKIE THAT KICKED OFF MY FIRST-EVER SERIES ARRIVED IN STORES.
naka Bookstore
1st Street Store

Magazines (top): Ribon, Chorus, YOU. (bottom): Margaret, Cookie, Bessatsu Margaret.

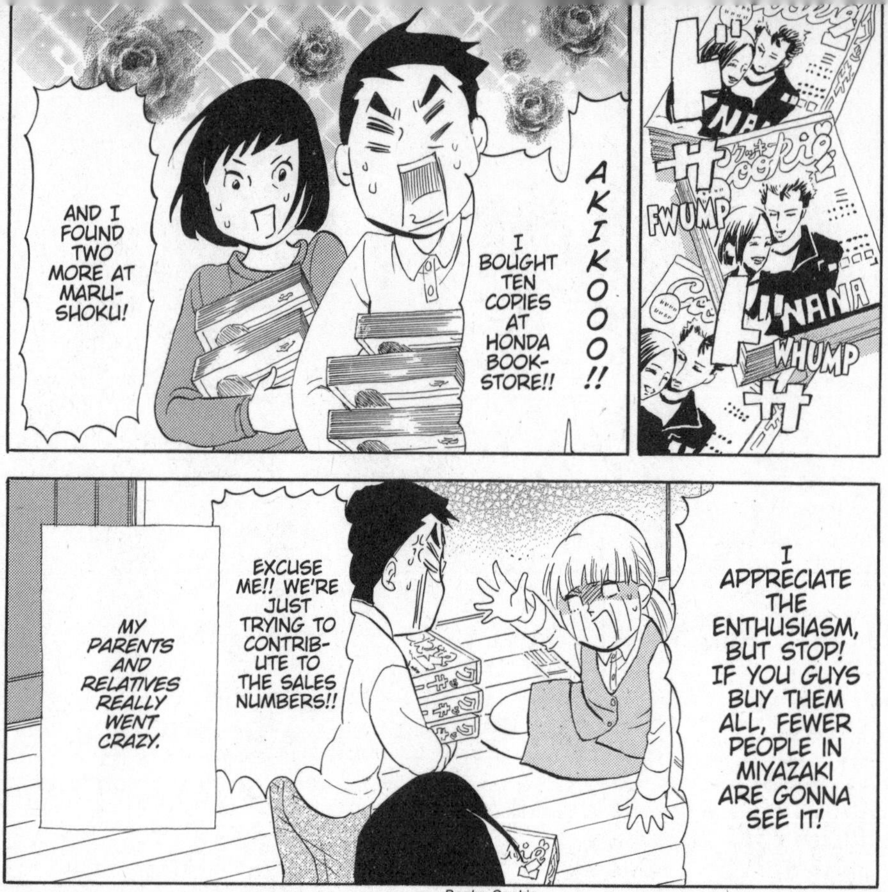
FWUMP
WHUMP
AKIKOOOO!!
I BOUGHT TEN COPIES AT HONDA BOOKSTORE!!
AND I FOUND TWO MORE AT MARU-SHOKU!
I APPRECIATE THE ENTHUSIASM, BUT STOP! IF YOU GUYS BUY THEM ALL, FEWER PEOPLE IN MIYAZAKI ARE GONNA SEE IT!
EXCUSE ME!! WE'RE JUST TRYING TO CONTRIBUTE TO THE SALES NUMBERS!!
MY PARENTS AND RELATIVES REALLY WENT CRAZY.

Books: Cookie.

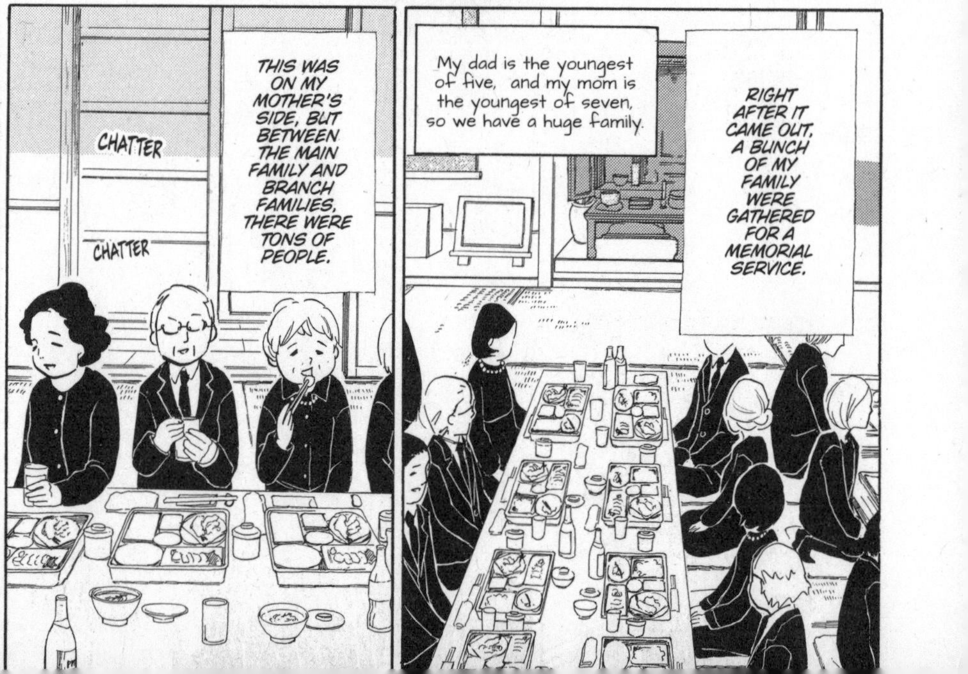
RIGHT AFTER IT CAME OUT, A BUNCH OF MY FAMILY WERE GATHERED FOR A MEMORIAL SERVICE.
My dad is the youngest of five, and my mom is the youngest of seven, so we have a huge family.
THIS WAS ON MY MOTHER'S SIDE, BUT BETWEEN THE MAIN FAMILY AND BRANCH FAMILIES, THERE WERE TONS OF PEOPLE.
CHATTER
CHATTER

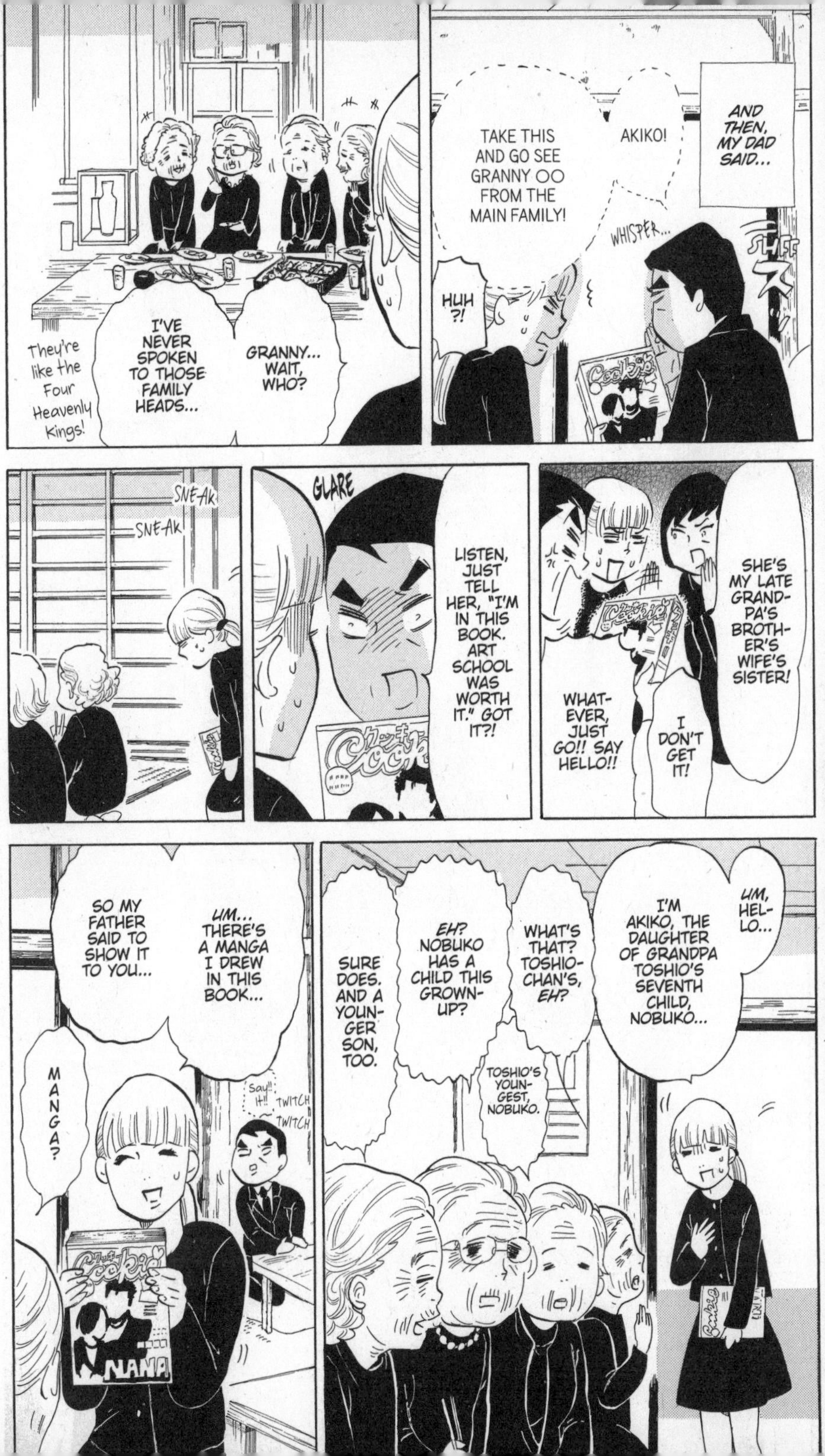
AND THEN, MY DAD SAID...
AKIKO!
TAKE THIS AND GO SEE GRANNY OO FROM THE MAIN FAMILY!
WHISPER...
SHFF
HUH?!
GRANNY... WAIT, WHO?
I'VE NEVER SPOKEN TO THOSE FAMILY HEADS...
They're like the Four Heavenly Kings!
SHE'S MY LATE GRANDPA'S BROTHER'S WIFE'S SISTER!
I DON'T GET IT!
WHATEVER, JUST GO!! SAY HELLO!!
GLARE
LISTEN, JUST TELL HER, "I'M IN THIS BOOK. ART SCHOOL WAS WORTH IT." GOT IT?!
SNE-AK
SNE-AK
UM, HELLO...
I'M AKIKO, THE DAUGHTER OF GRANDPA TOSHIO'S SEVENTH CHILD, NOBUKO...
WHAT'S THAT? TOSHIO-CHAN'S, EH?
EH? NOBUKO HAS A CHILD THIS GROWN-UP?
SURE DOES. AND A YOUNGER SON, TOO.
TOSHIO'S YOUNGEST, NOBUKO.
UM... THERE'S A MANGA I DREW IN THIS BOOK...
SO MY FATHER SAID TO SHOW IT TO YOU...
Say!! It!!
TWITCH
TWITCH
MANGA?

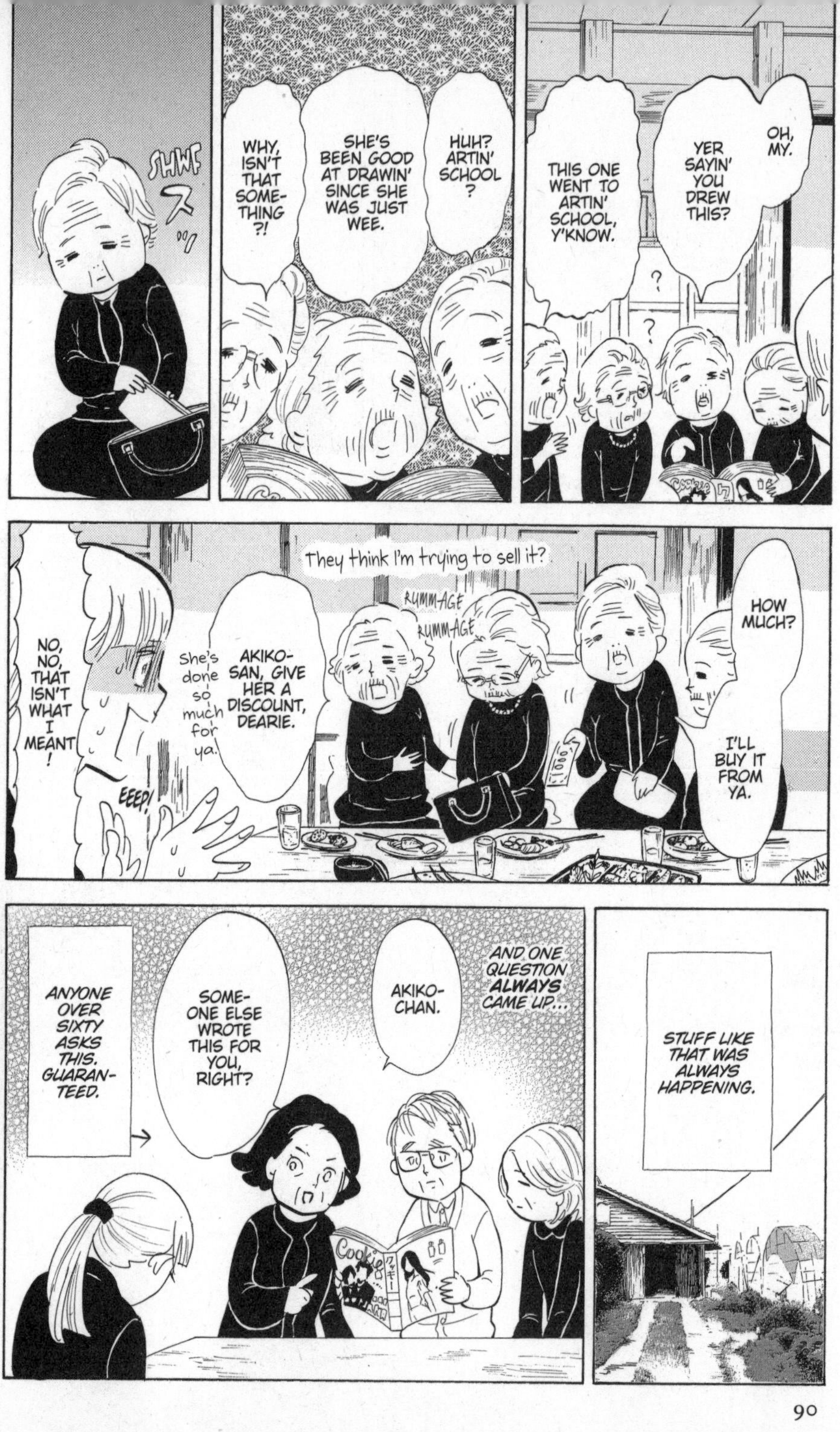
OH, MY.
YER SAYIN' YOU DREW THIS?
THIS ONE WENT TO ARTIN' SCHOOL, Y'KNOW.
HUH? ARTIN' SCHOOL?
SHE'S BEEN GOOD AT DRAWIN' SINCE SHE WAS JUST WEE.
WHY, ISN'T THAT SOME-THING?!
SHWF
HOW MUCH?
I'LL BUY IT FROM YA.
They think I'm trying to sell it?
RUMMAGE
RUMMAGE
AKIKO-SAN, GIVE HER A DISCOUNT, DEARIE.
She's done so much for ya.
NO, NO, THAT ISN'T WHAT I MEANT!
EEEP!
STUFF LIKE THAT WAS ALWAYS HAPPENING.
AND ONE QUESTION ALWAYS CAME UP...
AKIKO-CHAN.
SOME-ONE ELSE WROTE THIS FOR YOU, RIGHT?
ANYONE OVER SIXTY ASKS THIS. GUARAN-TEED.
Cookie

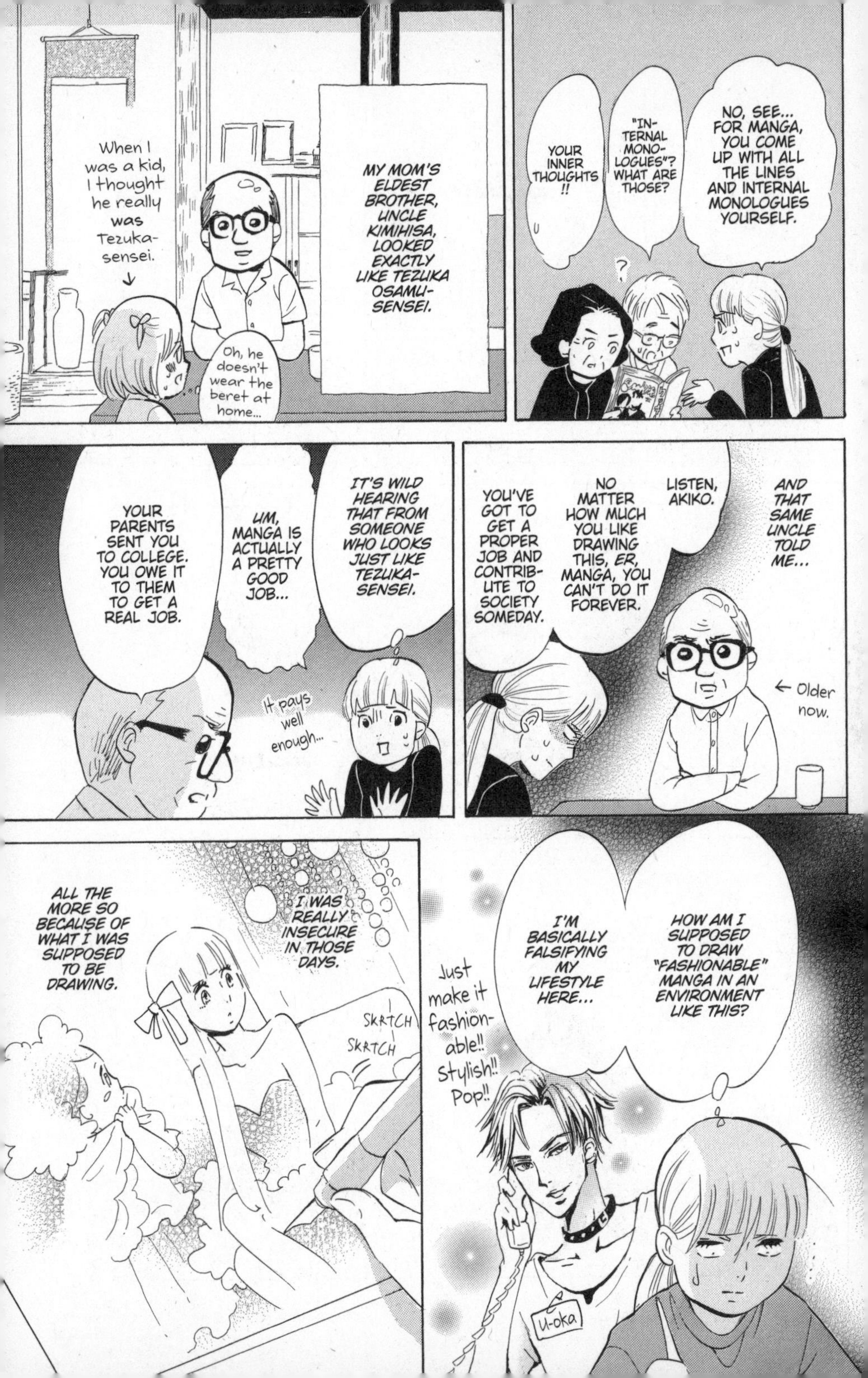
NO, SEE... FOR MANGA, YOU COME UP WITH ALL THE LINES AND INTERNAL MONOLOGUES YOURSELF.
"INTERNAL MONOLOGUES"? WHAT ARE THOSE?
YOUR INNER THOUGHTS!!
?
MY MOM'S ELDEST BROTHER, UNCLE KIMIHISA, LOOKED EXACTLY LIKE TEZUKA OSAMU-SENSEI.
When I was a kid, I thought he really was Tezuka-sensei.
Oh, he doesn't wear the beret at home...
AND THAT SAME UNCLE TOLD ME...
LISTEN, AKIKO.
NO MATTER HOW MUCH YOU LIKE DRAWING THIS, ER, MANGA, YOU CAN'T DO IT FOREVER.
YOU'VE GOT TO GET A PROPER JOB AND CONTRIBUTE TO SOCIETY SOMEDAY.
← Older now.
IT'S WILD HEARING THAT FROM SOMEONE WHO LOOKS JUST LIKE TEZUKA-SENSEI.
UM, MANGA IS ACTUALLY A PRETTY GOOD JOB...
YOUR PARENTS SENT YOU TO COLLEGE. YOU OWE IT TO THEM TO GET A REAL JOB.
It pays well enough...
HOW AM I SUPPOSED TO DRAW "FASHIONABLE" MANGA IN AN ENVIRONMENT LIKE THIS?
I'M BASICALLY FALSIFYING MY LIFESTYLE HERE...
Just make it fashionable!! Stylish!! Pop!!
U-oka
I WAS REALLY INSECURE IN THOSE DAYS.
ALL THE MORE SO BECAUSE OF WHAT I WAS SUPPOSED TO BE DRAWING.
SKRTCH
SKRTCH

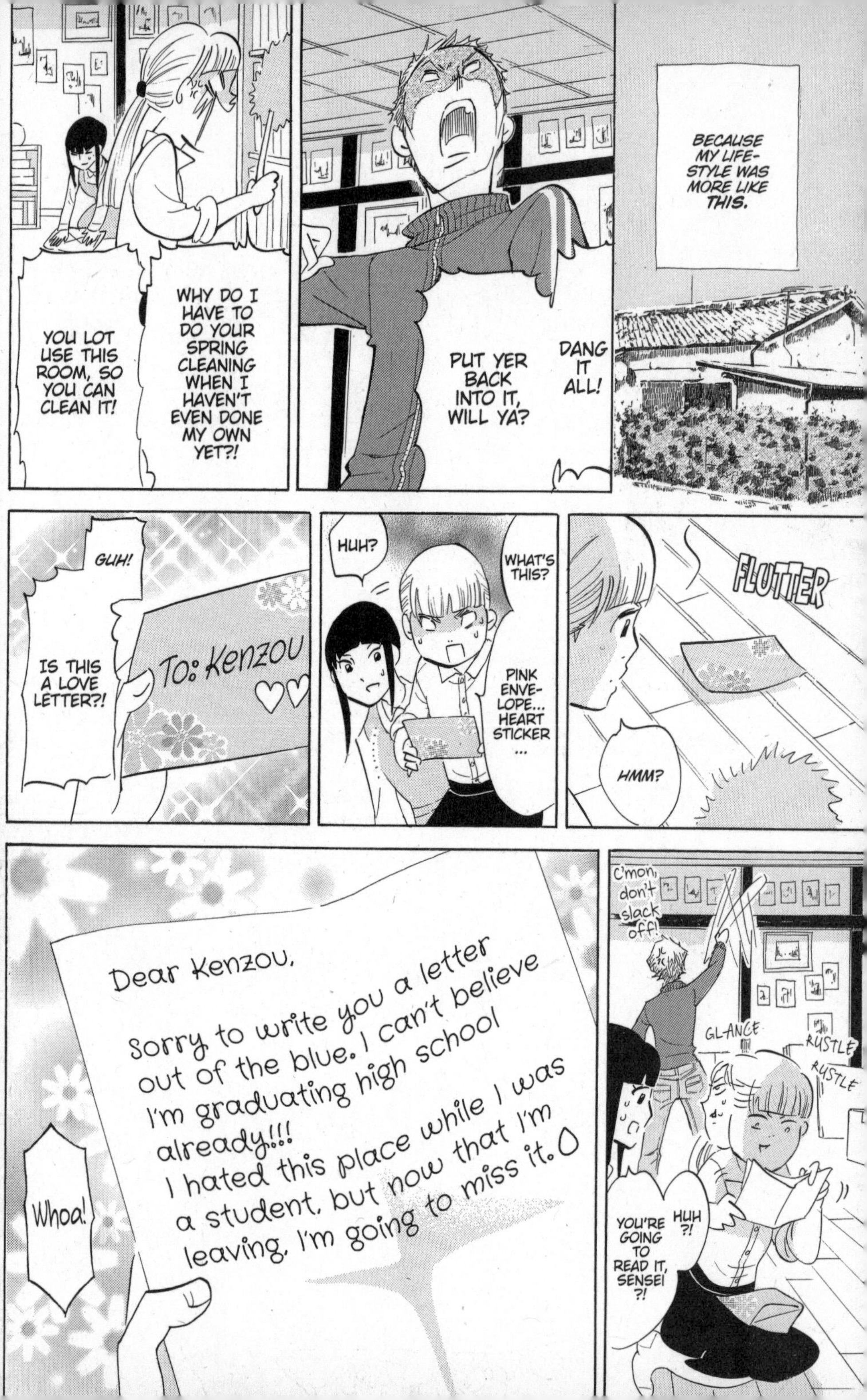
BECAUSE MY LIFE-STYLE WAS MORE LIKE THIS.
DANG IT ALL!
PUT YER BACK INTO IT, WILL YA?
WHY DO I HAVE TO DO YOUR SPRING CLEANING WHEN I HAVEN'T EVEN DONE MY OWN YET?!
YOU LOT USE THIS ROOM, SO YOU CAN CLEAN IT!
FLUTTER
HMM?
WHAT'S THIS?
HUH?
PINK ENVELOPE... HEART STICKER ...
GUH!
To: Kenzou
IS THIS A LOVE LETTER?!
C'mon, don't slack off!
GLANCE
RUSTLE
RUSTLE
HUH?!
YOU'RE GOING TO READ IT, SENSEI?!
Dear Kenzou,
Sorry to write you a letter out of the blue. I can't believe I'm graduating high school already!!!
I hated this place while I was a student, but now that I'm leaving, I'm going to miss it.
Whoa!

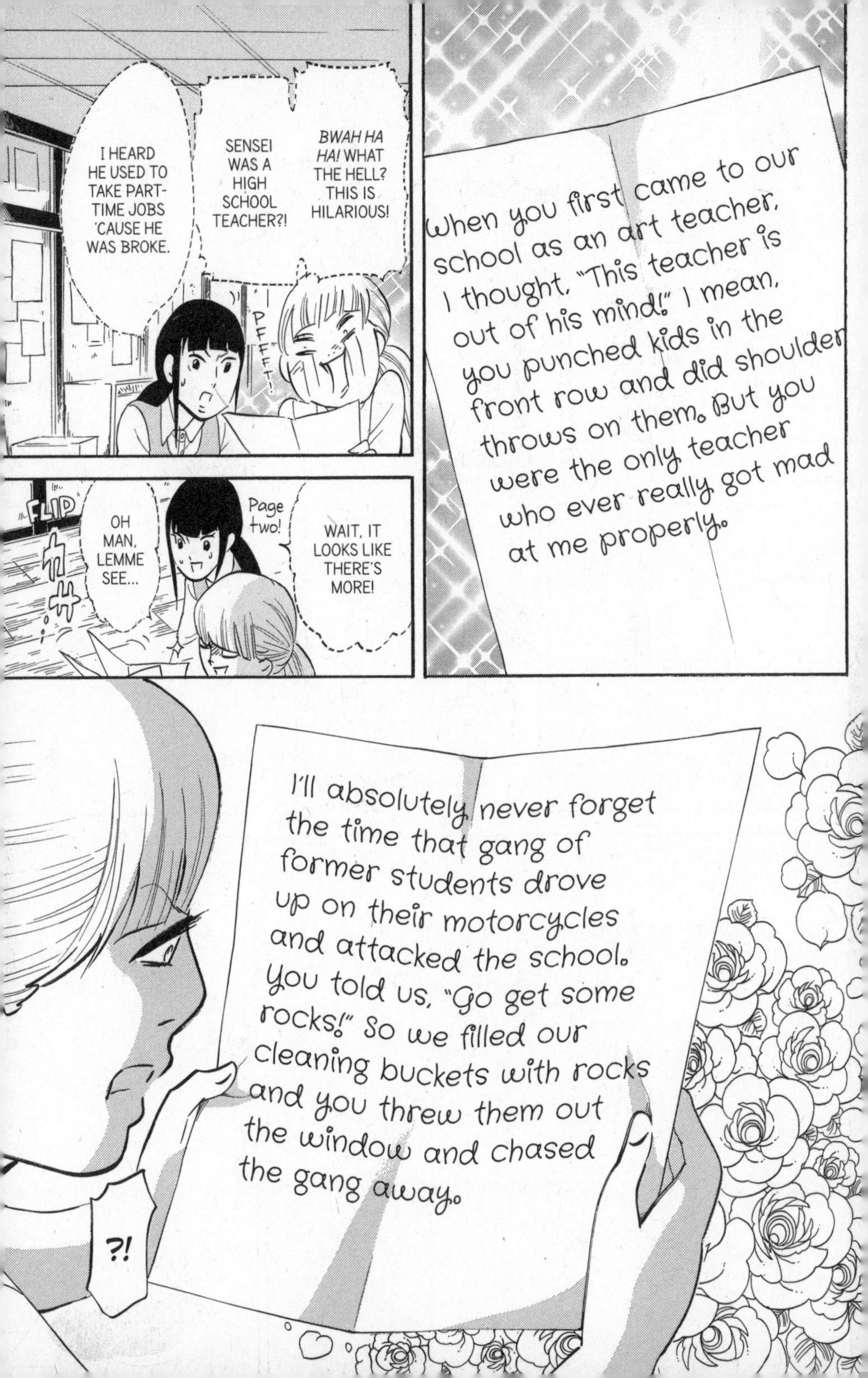
When you first came to our school as an art teacher, I thought, "This teacher is out of his mind!" I mean, you punched kids in the front row and did shoulder throws on them. But you were the only teacher who ever really got mad at me properly.
BWAH HA HA! WHAT THE HELL? THIS IS HILARIOUS!
SENSEI WAS A HIGH SCHOOL TEACHER?!
I HEARD HE USED TO TAKE PART-TIME JOBS 'CAUSE HE WAS BROKE.
PFFFT!
WAIT, IT LOOKS LIKE THERE'S MORE!
Page two!
OH MAN, LEMME SEE...
FLIP
I'll absolutely never forget the time that gang of former students drove up on their motorcycles and attacked the school. You told us, "Go get some rocks!" So we filled our cleaning buckets with rocks and you threw them out the window and chased the gang away.
?!

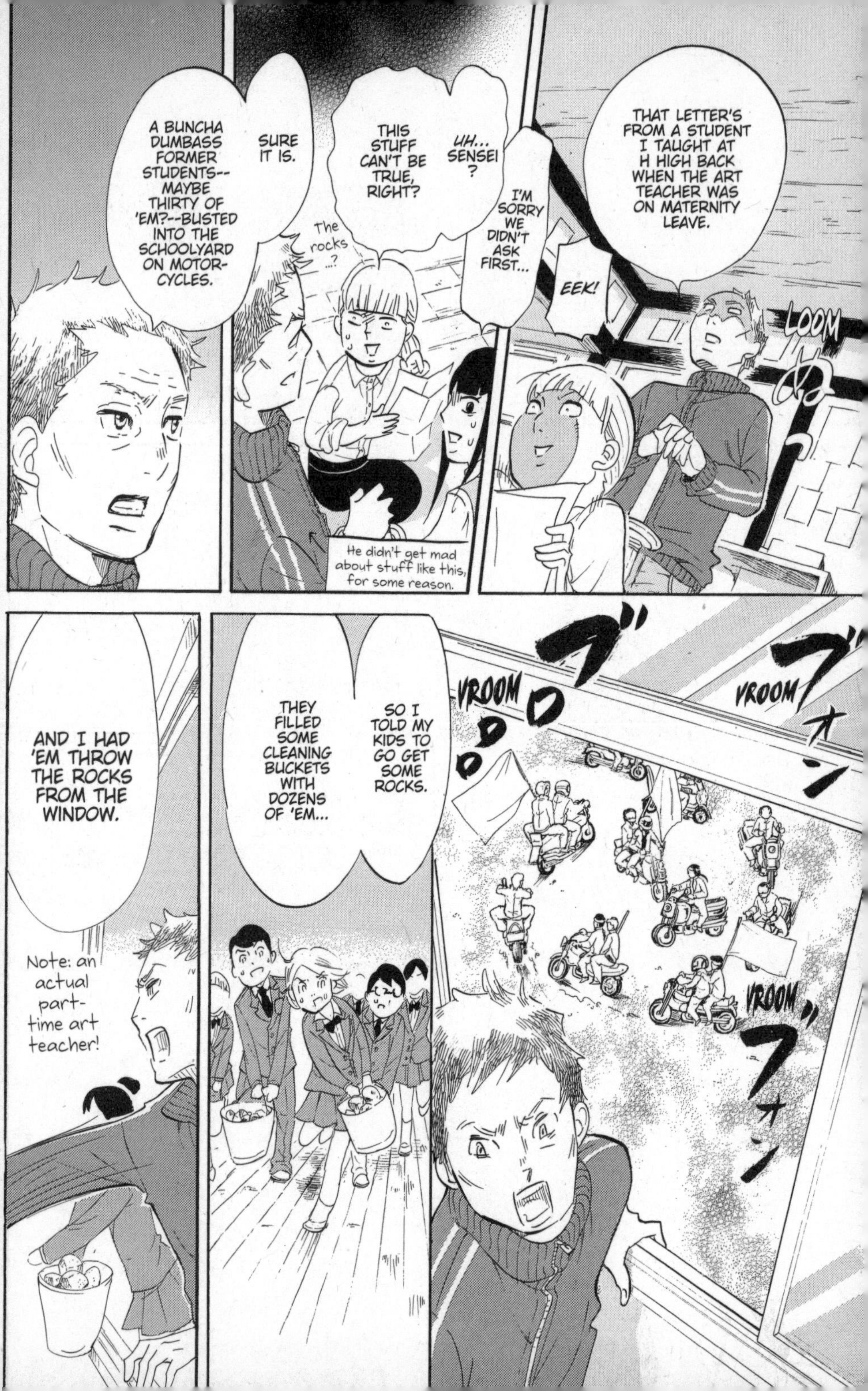
THAT LETTER'S FROM A STUDENT I TAUGHT AT H HIGH BACK WHEN THE ART TEACHER WAS ON MATERNITY LEAVE.
LOOM
EEK!
I'M SORRY WE DIDN'T ASK FIRST...
UH... SENSEI?
THIS STUFF CAN'T BE TRUE, RIGHT?
The rocks ...?
He didn't get mad about stuff like this, for some reason.
SURE IT IS.
A BUNCHA DUMBASS FORMER STUDENTS--MAYBE THIRTY OF 'EM?--BUSTED INTO THE SCHOOLYARD ON MOTORCYCLES.
VROOM
VROOM
VROOM
SO I TOLD MY KIDS TO GO GET SOME ROCKS.
THEY FILLED SOME CLEANING BUCKETS WITH DOZENS OF 'EM...
AND I HAD 'EM THROW THE ROCKS FROM THE WINDOW.
Note: an actual part-time art teacher!

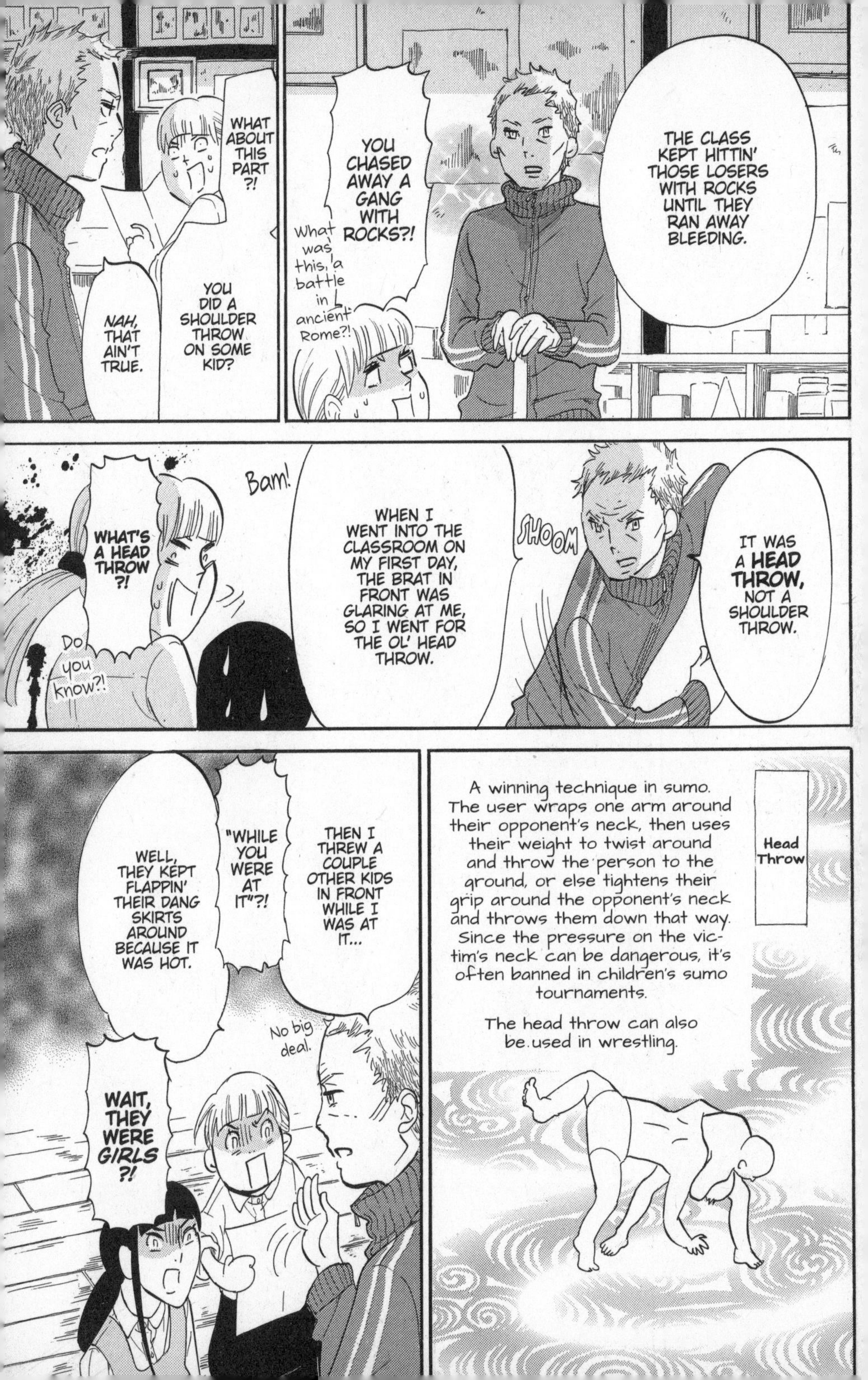
THE CLASS KEPT HITTIN' THOSE LOSERS WITH ROCKS UNTIL THEY RAN AWAY BLEEDING.
YOU CHASED AWAY A GANG WITH ROCKS?!
What was this, a battle in ancient Rome?!
WHAT ABOUT THIS PART?!
YOU DID A SHOULDER THROW ON SOME KID?
NAH, THAT AIN'T TRUE.
IT WAS A **HEAD THROW,** NOT A SHOULDER THROW.
SHOOM
WHEN I WENT INTO THE CLASSROOM ON MY FIRST DAY, THE BRAT IN FRONT WAS GLARING AT ME, SO I WENT FOR THE OL' HEAD THROW.
Bam!
WHAT'S A HEAD THROW?!
Do you know?!
Head Throw
A winning technique in sumo. The user wraps one arm around their opponent's neck, then uses their weight to twist around and throw the person to the ground, or else tightens their grip around the opponent's neck and throws them down that way. Since the pressure on the victim's neck can be dangerous, it's often banned in children's sumo tournaments.
The head throw can also be used in wrestling.
THEN I THREW A COUPLE OTHER KIDS IN FRONT WHILE I WAS AT IT...
"WHILE YOU WERE AT IT"?!
WELL, THEY KEPT FLAPPIN' THEIR DANG SKIRTS AROUND BECAUSE IT WAS HOT.
No big deal.
WAIT, THEY WERE *GIRLS*?!

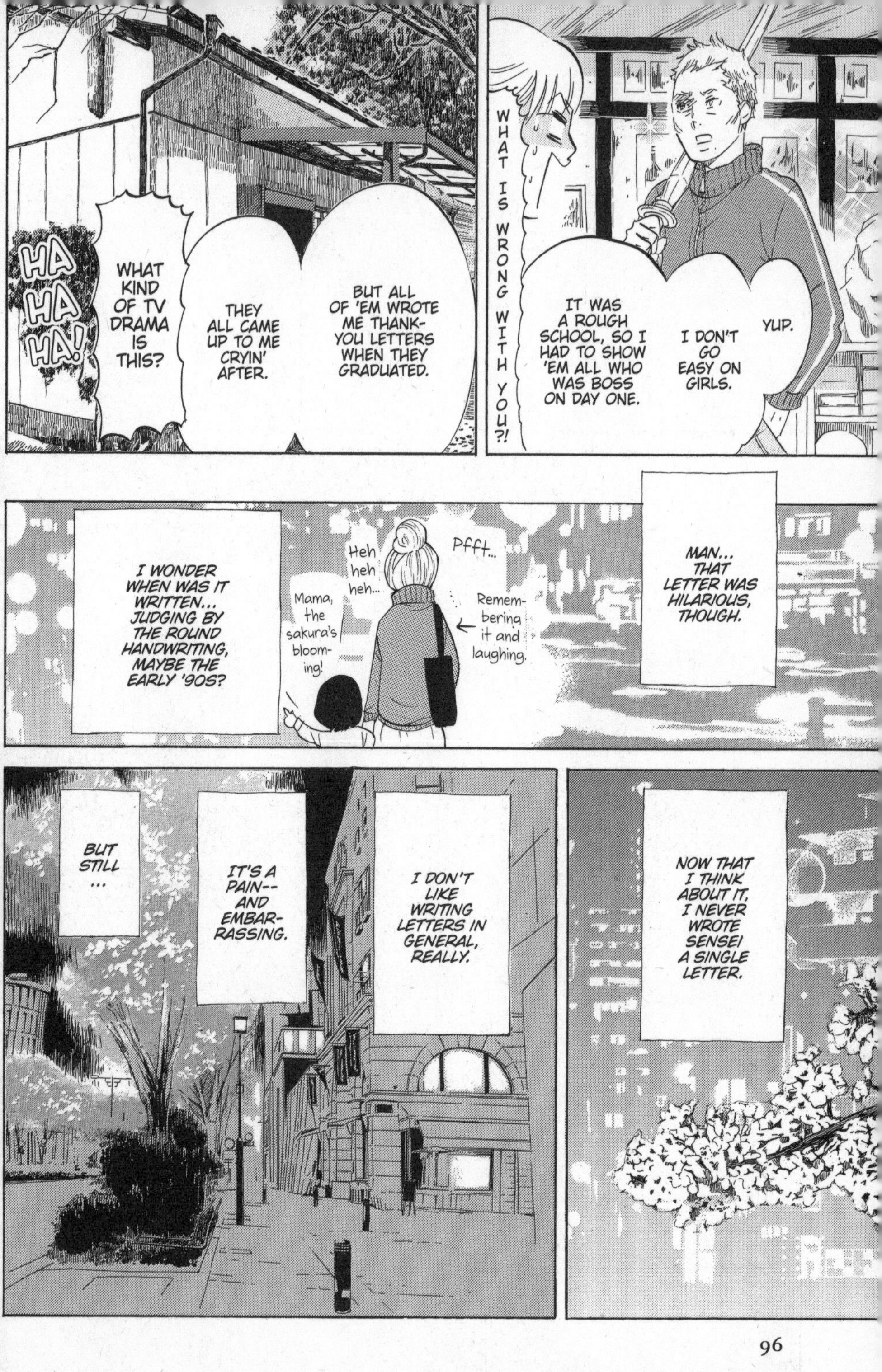
YUP.
I DON'T GO EASY ON GIRLS.
IT WAS A ROUGH SCHOOL, SO I HAD TO SHOW 'EM ALL WHO WAS BOSS ON DAY ONE.
WHAT IS WRONG WITH YOU?!
BUT ALL OF 'EM WROTE ME THANK-YOU LETTERS WHEN THEY GRADUATED.
THEY ALL CAME UP TO ME CRYIN' AFTER.
WHAT KIND OF TV DRAMA IS THIS?
HA HA HA!
MAN... THAT LETTER WAS HILARIOUS, THOUGH.
Pfft...
Remembering it and laughing.
Heh heh heh...
Mama, the sakura's blooming!
I WONDER WHEN WAS IT WRITTEN... JUDGING BY THE ROUND HANDWRITING, MAYBE THE EARLY '90S?
NOW THAT I THINK ABOUT IT, I NEVER WROTE SENSEI A SINGLE LETTER.
I DON'T LIKE WRITING LETTERS IN GENERAL, REALLY.
IT'S A PAIN--AND EMBARRASSING.
BUT STILL...

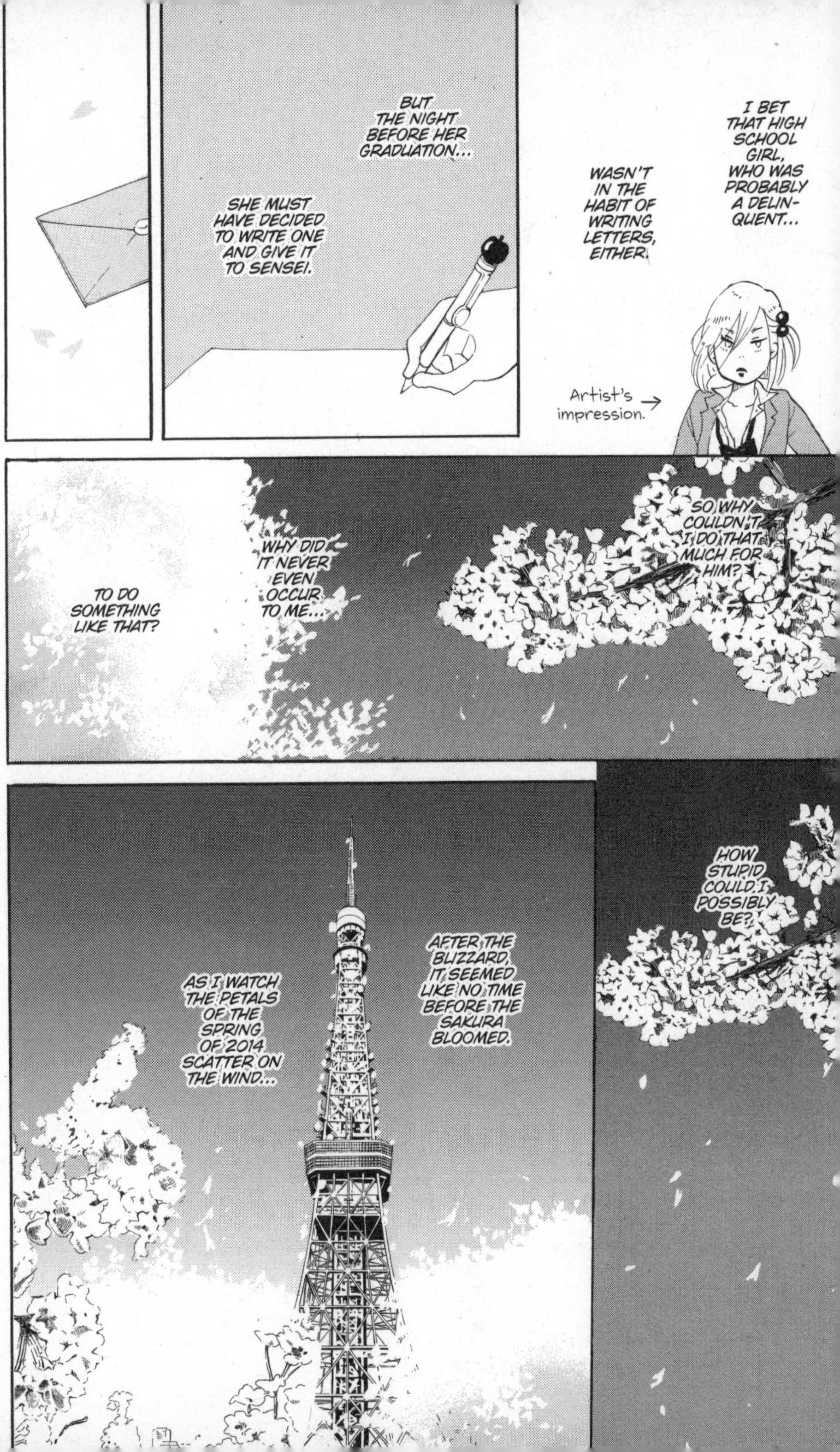
I BET THAT HIGH SCHOOL GIRL, WHO WAS PROBABLY A DELINQUENT...
WASN'T IN THE HABIT OF WRITING LETTERS, EITHER.
Artist's impression.
BUT THE NIGHT BEFORE HER GRADUATION...
SHE MUST HAVE DECIDED TO WRITE ONE AND GIVE IT TO SENSEI.
SO WHY COULDN'T I DO THAT MUCH FOR HIM?
WHY DID IT NEVER EVEN OCCUR TO ME...
TO DO SOMETHING LIKE THAT?
HOW STUPID COULD I POSSIBLY BE?
AFTER THE BLIZZARD, IT SEEMED LIKE NO TIME BEFORE THE SAKURA BLOOMED.
AS I WATCH THE PETALS OF THE SPRING OF 2014 SCATTER ON THE WIND...

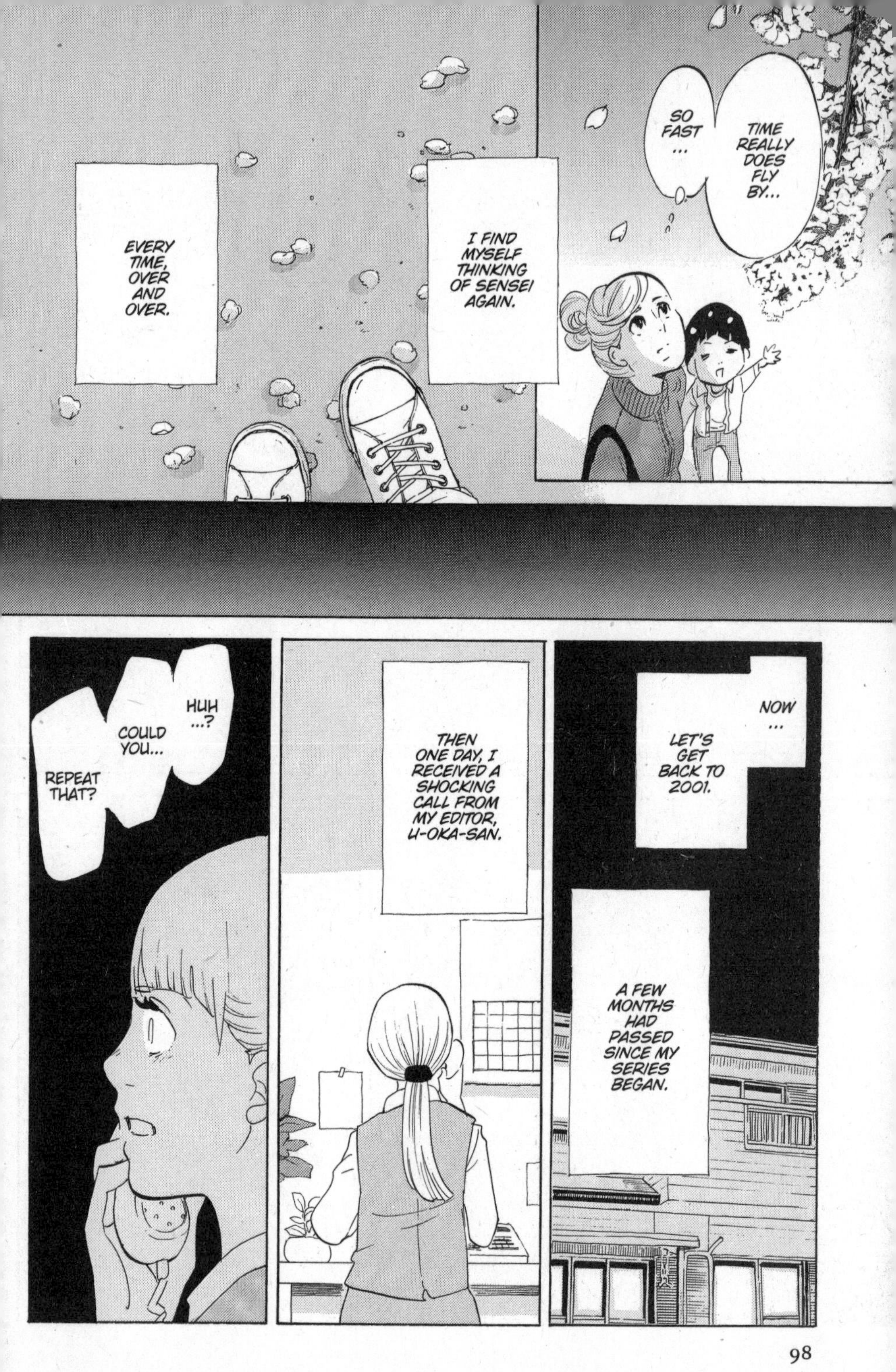
TIME REALLY DOES FLY BY...
SO FAST...
I FIND MYSELF THINKING OF SENSEI AGAIN.
EVERY TIME, OVER AND OVER.
NOW...
LET'S GET BACK TO 2001.
A FEW MONTHS HAD PASSED SINCE MY SERIES BEGAN.
THEN ONE DAY, I RECEIVED A SHOCKING CALL FROM MY EDITOR, U-OKA-SAN.
HUH...?
COULD YOU...
REPEAT THAT?

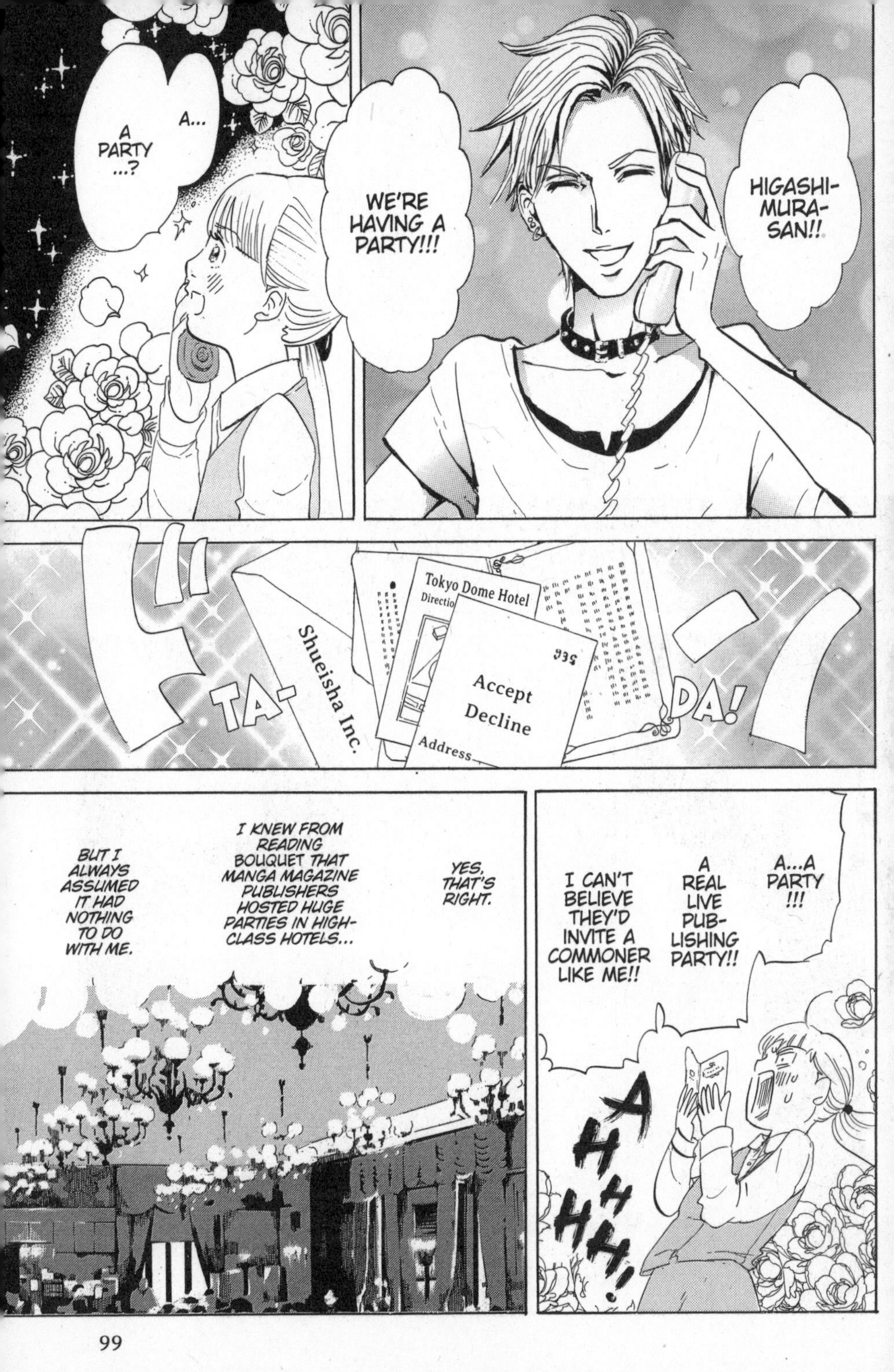
HIGASHI-MURA-SAN!!
WE'RE HAVING A PARTY!!!
A...
A PARTY...?
TA-DA!
Tokyo Dome Hotel
Shueisha Inc.
Accept
Decline
Address
A...A PARTY!!!
A REAL LIVE PUBLISHING PARTY!!
I CAN'T BELIEVE THEY'D INVITE A COMMONER LIKE ME!!
AHHHHH!
YES, THAT'S RIGHT.
I KNEW FROM READING BOUQUET THAT MANGA MAGAZINE PUBLISHERS HOSTED HUGE PARTIES IN HIGH-CLASS HOTELS...
BUT I ALWAYS ASSUMED IT HAD NOTHING TO DO WITH ME.

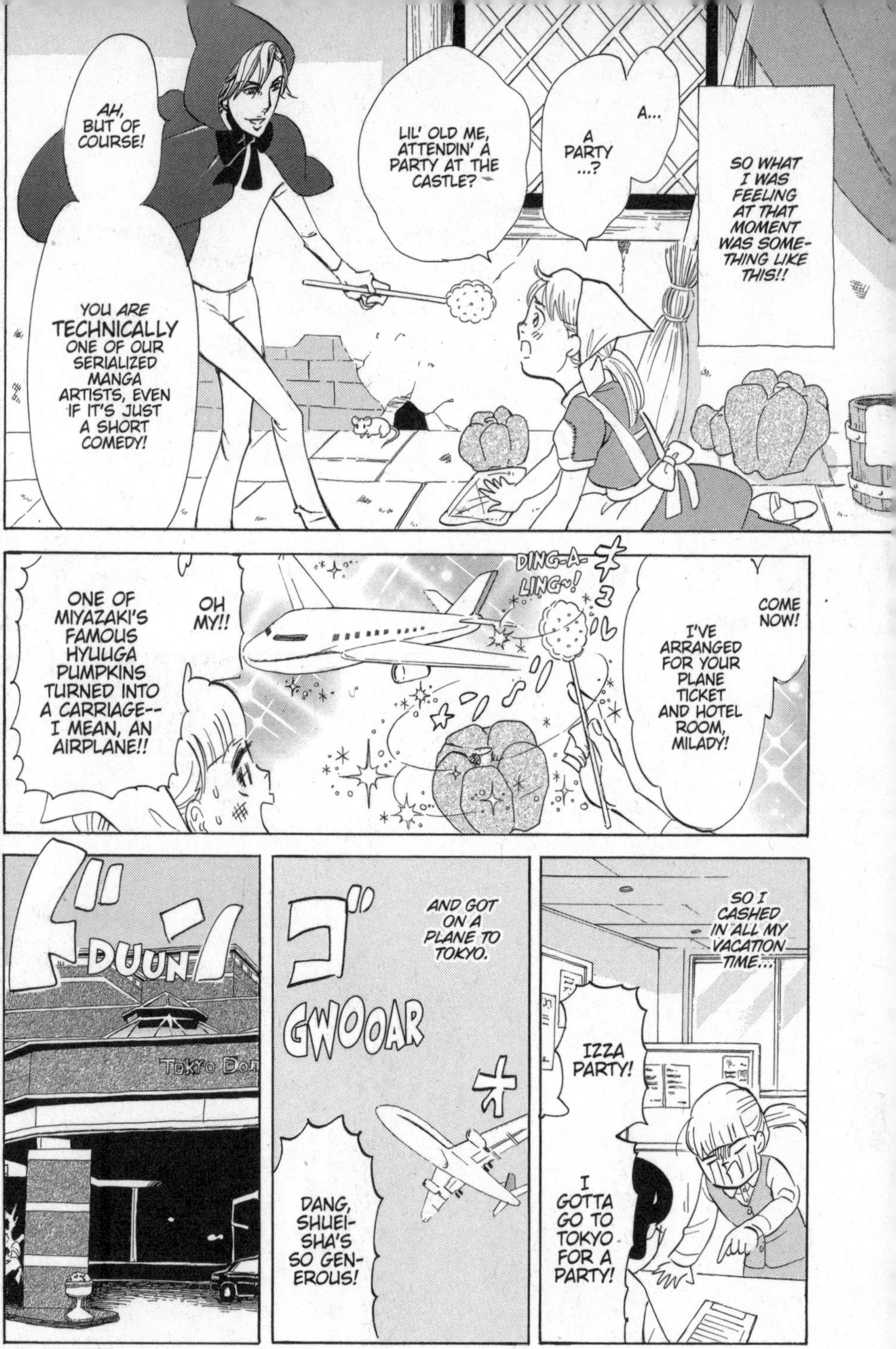
SO WHAT I WAS FEELING AT THAT MOMENT WAS SOME-THING LIKE THIS!!
A... A PARTY ...?
LIL' OLD ME, ATTENDIN' A PARTY AT THE CASTLE?
AH, BUT OF COURSE!
YOU ARE TECHNICALLY ONE OF OUR SERIALIZED MANGA ARTISTS, EVEN IF IT'S JUST A SHORT COMEDY!
COME NOW!
I'VE ARRANGED FOR YOUR PLANE TICKET AND HOTEL ROOM, MILADY!
DING-A-LING~!
OH MY!!
ONE OF MIYAZAKI'S FAMOUS HYUUGA PUMPKINS TURNED INTO A CARRIAGE-- I MEAN, AN AIRPLANE!!
SO I CASHED IN ALL MY VACATION TIME...
IZZA PARTY!
I GOTTA GO TO TOKYO FOR A PARTY!
AND GOT ON A PLANE TO TOKYO.
GWOOAR
DANG, SHUEI-SHA'S SO GEN-EROUS!
DUUN

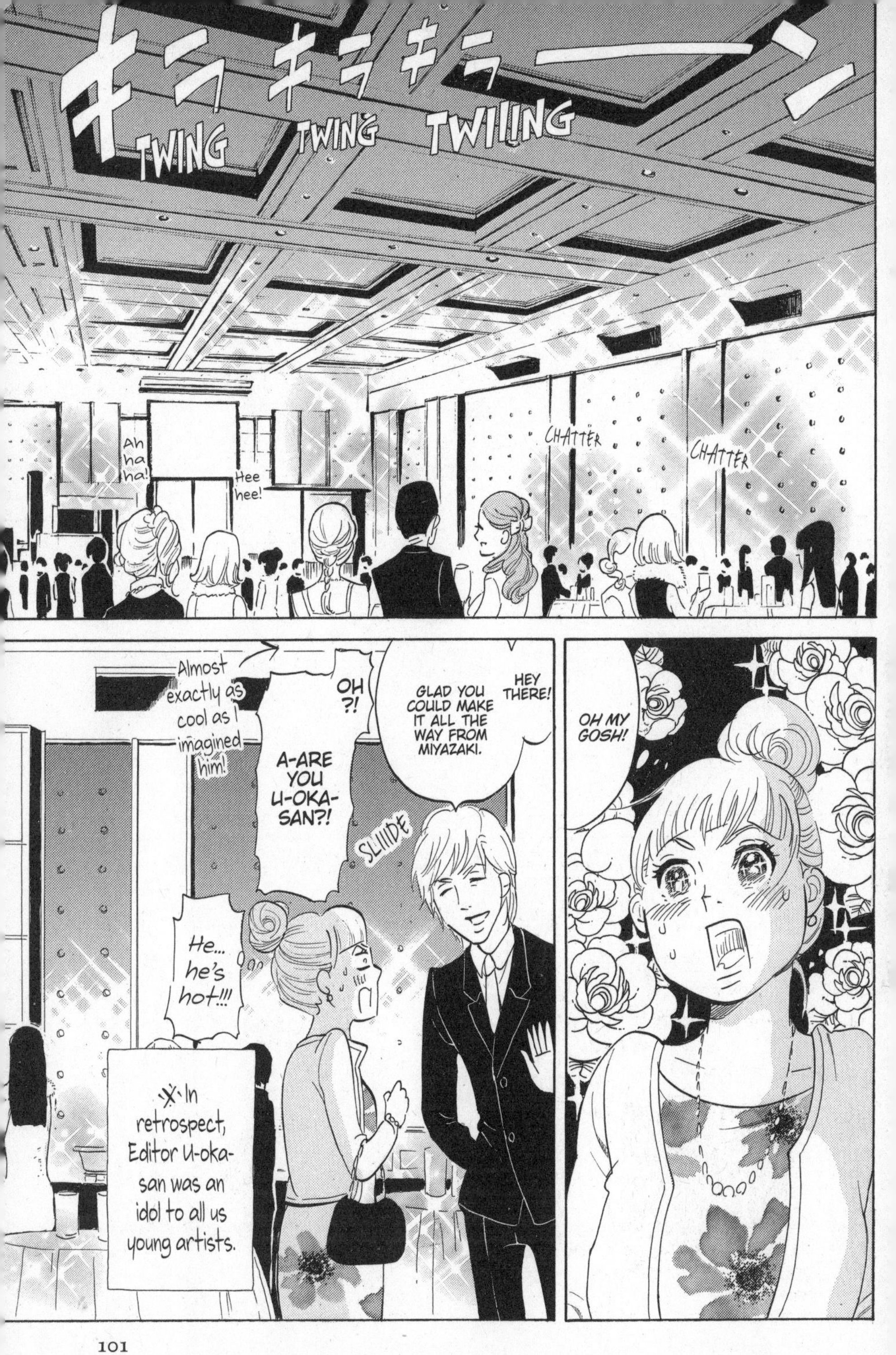

キラキラキラーン
TWING TWING TWILING
CHATTER
CHATTER
Hee hee!
Ah ha ha!
OH MY GOSH!
HEY THERE!
GLAD YOU COULD MAKE IT ALL THE WAY FROM MIYAZAKI.
OH ?!
A-ARE YOU U-OKA-SAN?!
SLIIDE
Almost exactly as cool as I imagined him!
He... he's hot!!!
※In retrospect, Editor U-oka-san was an idol to all us young artists.

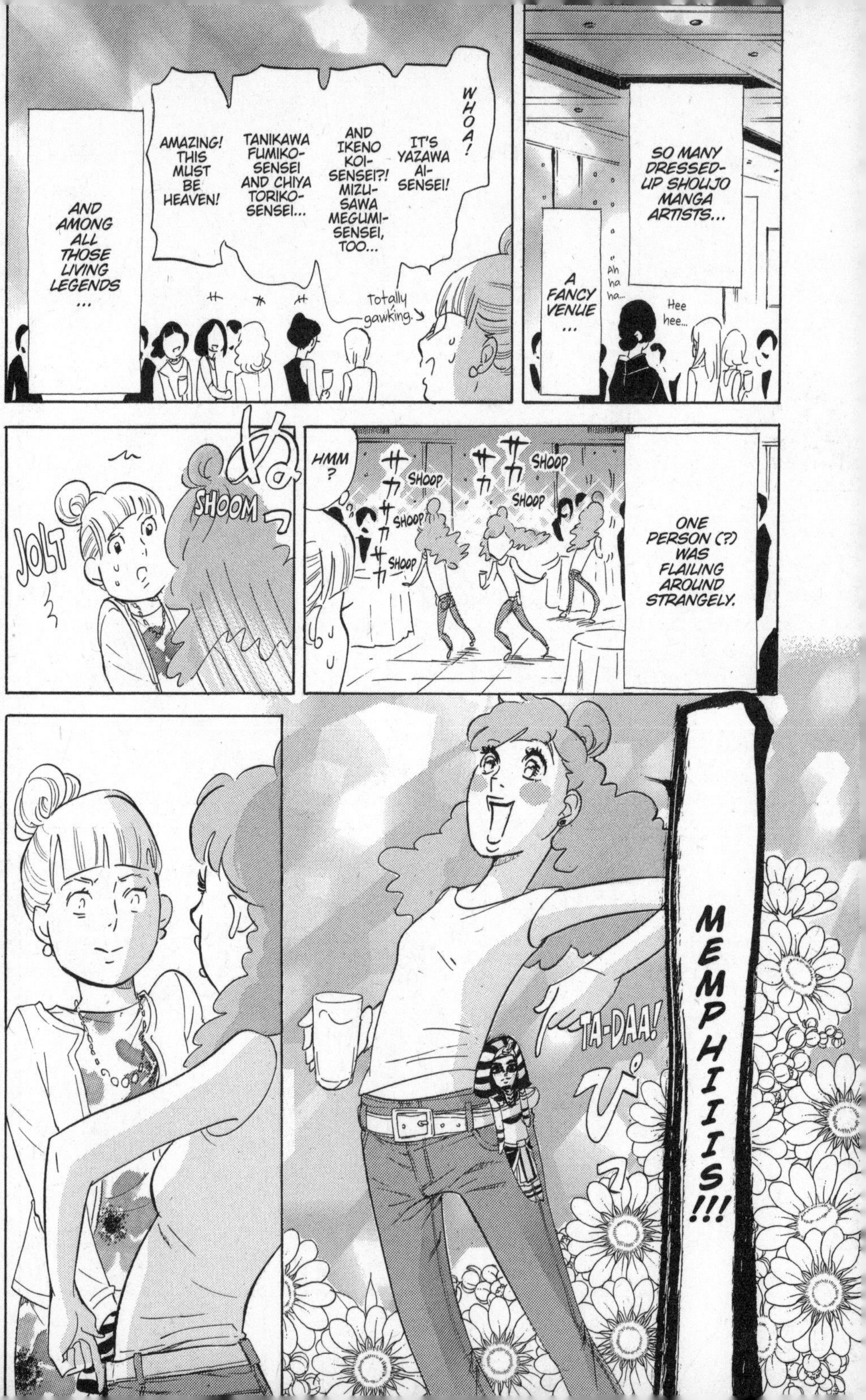
SO MANY DRESSED-UP SHOUJO MANGA ARTISTS...
A FANCY VENUE...
Ah ha ha...
Hee hee...
WHOA!
IT'S YAZAWA AI-SENSEI!
AND IKENO KOI-SENSEI?! MIZUSAWA MEGUMI-SENSEI, TOO...
TANIKAWA FUMIKO-SENSEI AND CHIYA TORIKO-SENSEI...
AMAZING! THIS MUST BE HEAVEN!
Totally gawking.
AND AMONG ALL THOSE LIVING LEGENDS...
ONE PERSON (?) WAS FLAILING AROUND STRANGELY.
SHOOP
SHOOP
SHOOP
SHOOP
SHOOP
HMM?
SHOOM
JOLT
MEMPHIIIS!!!
TA-DAA!

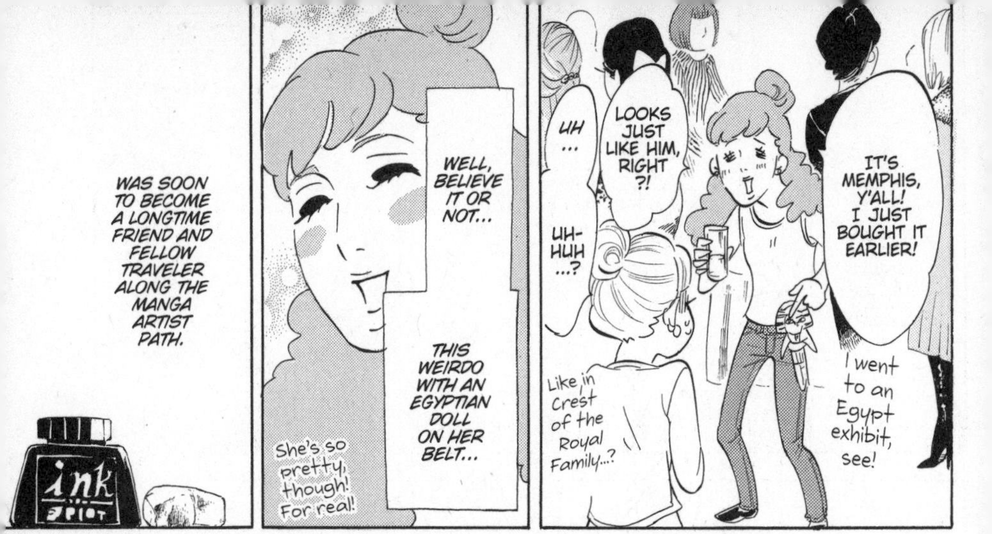
IT'S MEMPHIS, Y'ALL! I JUST BOUGHT IT EARLIER!
I went to an Egypt exhibit, see!
LOOKS JUST LIKE HIM, RIGHT?!
UH...
UH-HUH...?
Like in Crest of the Royal Family...?
WELL, BELIEVE IT OR NOT...
THIS WEIRDO WITH AN EGYPTIAN DOLL ON HER BELT...
She's so pretty, though! For real!
WAS SOON TO BECOME A LONGTIME FRIEND AND FELLOW TRAVELER ALONG THE MANGA ARTIST PATH.
ink

*Translator's note: -han is a Kansai dialect variation of -san.

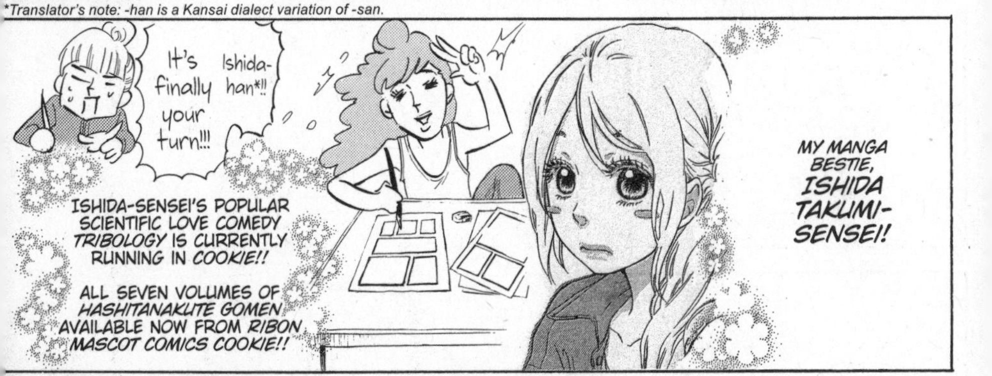
MY MANGA BESTIE, ISHIDA TAKUMI-SENSEI!
Ishida-han*!!
It's finally your turn!!!
ISHIDA-SENSEI'S POPULAR SCIENTIFIC LOVE COMEDY TRIBOLOGY IS CURRENTLY RUNNING IN COOKIE!!
ALL SEVEN VOLUMES OF HASHITANAKUTE GOMEN AVAILABLE NOW FROM RIBON MASCOT COMICS COOKIE!!

※ THIS INFORMATION IS AS OF JULY 2014.

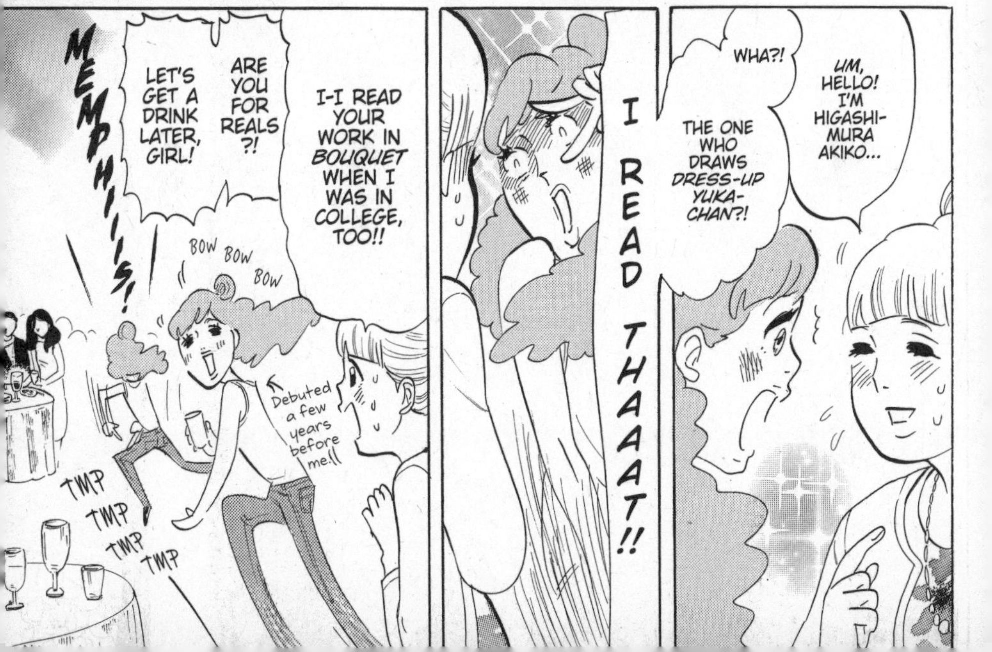
UM, HELLO! I'M HIGASHIMURA AKIKO...
WHA?!
THE ONE WHO DRAWS DRESS-UP YUKA-CHAN?!
I READ THAAAAT!!
I-I READ YOUR WORK IN BOUQUET WHEN I WAS IN COLLEGE, TOO!!
ARE YOU FOR REALS?!
LET'S GET A DRINK LATER, GIRL!
MEMPHIIIS!
BOW BOW BOW
Debuted a few years before me.
TMP TMP TMP TMP

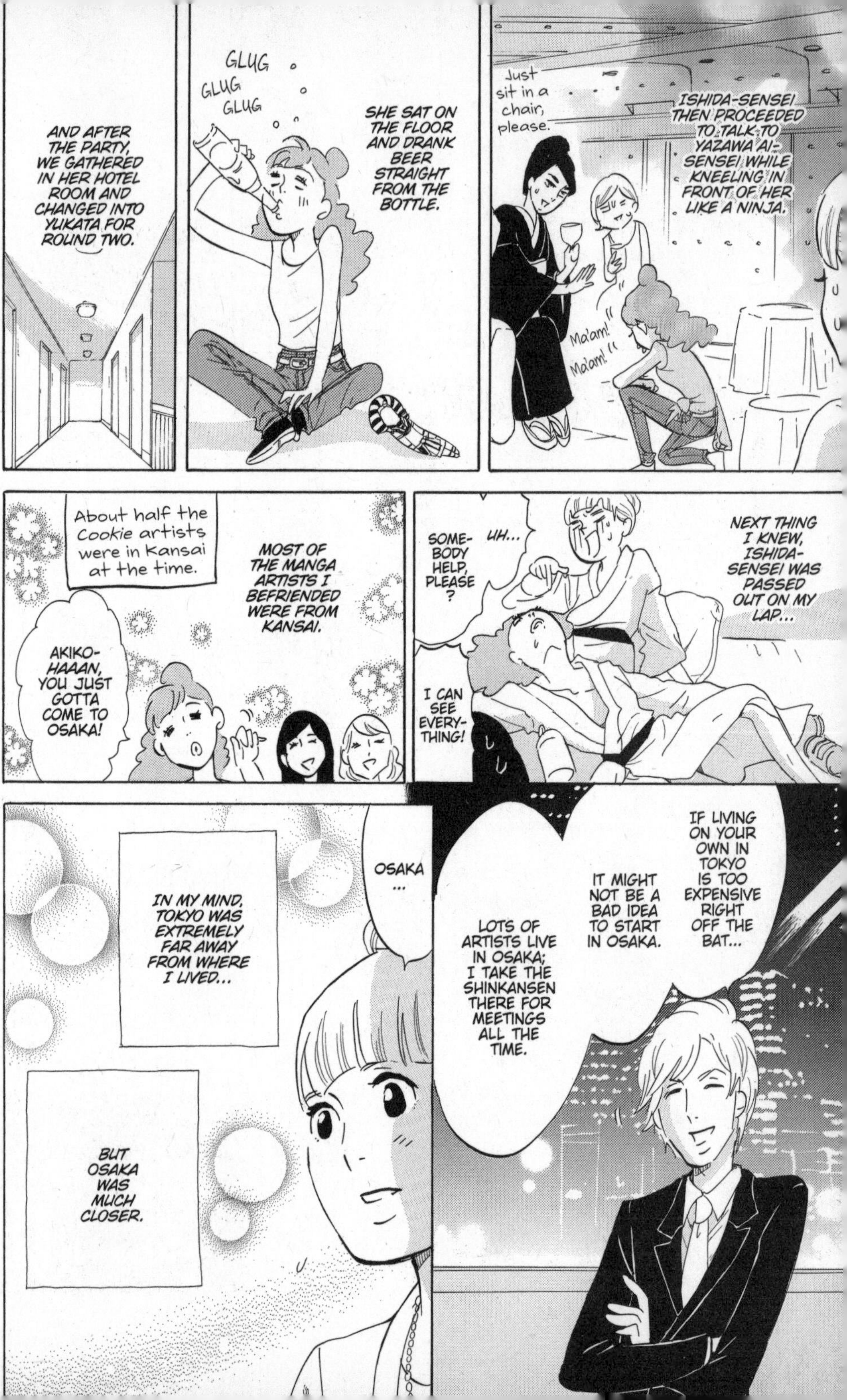
ISHIDA-SENSEI THEN PROCEEDED TO TALK TO YAZAWA AI-SENSEI WHILE KNEELING IN FRONT OF HER LIKE A NINJA.
Just sit in a chair, please.
Ma'am! Ma'am!
GLUG GLUG GLUG
SHE SAT ON THE FLOOR AND DRANK BEER STRAIGHT FROM THE BOTTLE.
AND AFTER THE PARTY, WE GATHERED IN HER HOTEL ROOM AND CHANGED INTO YUKATA FOR ROUND TWO.
NEXT THING I KNEW, ISHIDA-SENSEI WAS PASSED OUT ON MY LAP...
UH...
SOMEBODY HELP, PLEASE?
I CAN SEE EVERYTHING!
About half the Cookie artists were in Kansai at the time.
MOST OF THE MANGA ARTISTS I BEFRIENDED WERE FROM KANSAI.
AKIKO-HAAAN, YOU JUST GOTTA COME TO OSAKA!
IF LIVING ON YOUR OWN IN TOKYO IS TOO EXPENSIVE RIGHT OFF THE BAT...
IT MIGHT NOT BE A BAD IDEA TO START IN OSAKA.
LOTS OF ARTISTS LIVE IN OSAKA; I TAKE THE SHINKANSEN THERE FOR MEETINGS ALL THE TIME.
OSAKA...
IN MY MIND, TOKYO WAS EXTREMELY FAR AWAY FROM WHERE I LIVED...
BUT OSAKA WAS MUCH CLOSER.

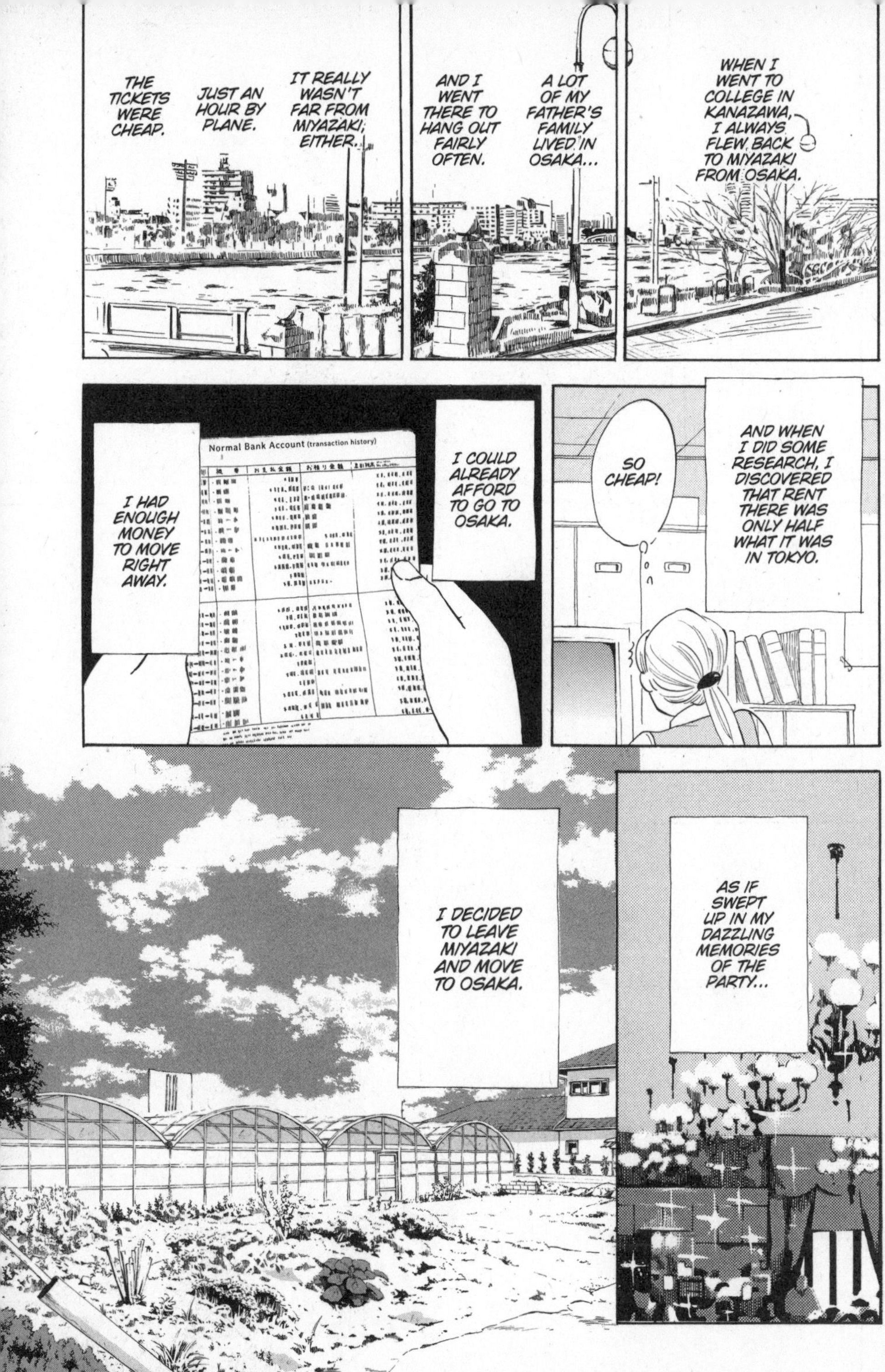
WHEN I WENT TO COLLEGE IN KANAZAWA, I ALWAYS FLEW BACK TO MIYAZAKI FROM OSAKA.
A LOT OF MY FATHER'S FAMILY LIVED IN OSAKA...
AND I WENT THERE TO HANG OUT FAIRLY OFTEN.
IT REALLY WASN'T FAR FROM MIYAZAKI, EITHER.
JUST AN HOUR BY PLANE.
THE TICKETS WERE CHEAP.
AND WHEN I DID SOME RESEARCH, I DISCOVERED THAT RENT THERE WAS ONLY HALF WHAT IT WAS IN TOKYO.
SO CHEAP!
I COULD ALREADY AFFORD TO GO TO OSAKA.
Normal Bank Account (transaction history)
I HAD ENOUGH MONEY TO MOVE RIGHT AWAY.
AS IF SWEPT UP IN MY DAZZLING MEMORIES OF THE PARTY...
I DECIDED TO LEAVE MIYAZAKI AND MOVE TO OSAKA.

Blank
Canvas
My So-Called
Artist's Journey

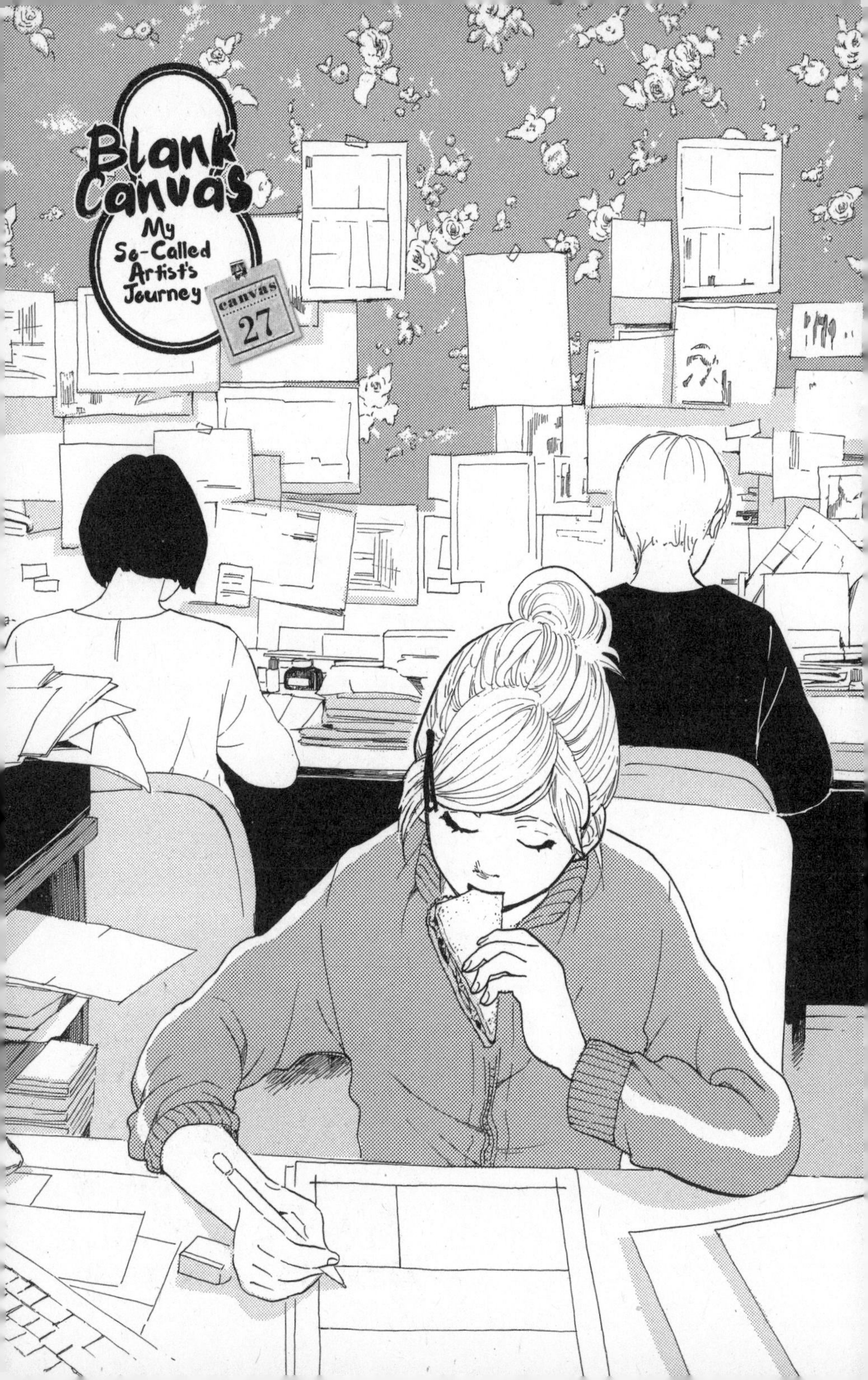
Blank Canvas
My So-Called Artist's Journey
canvas
27

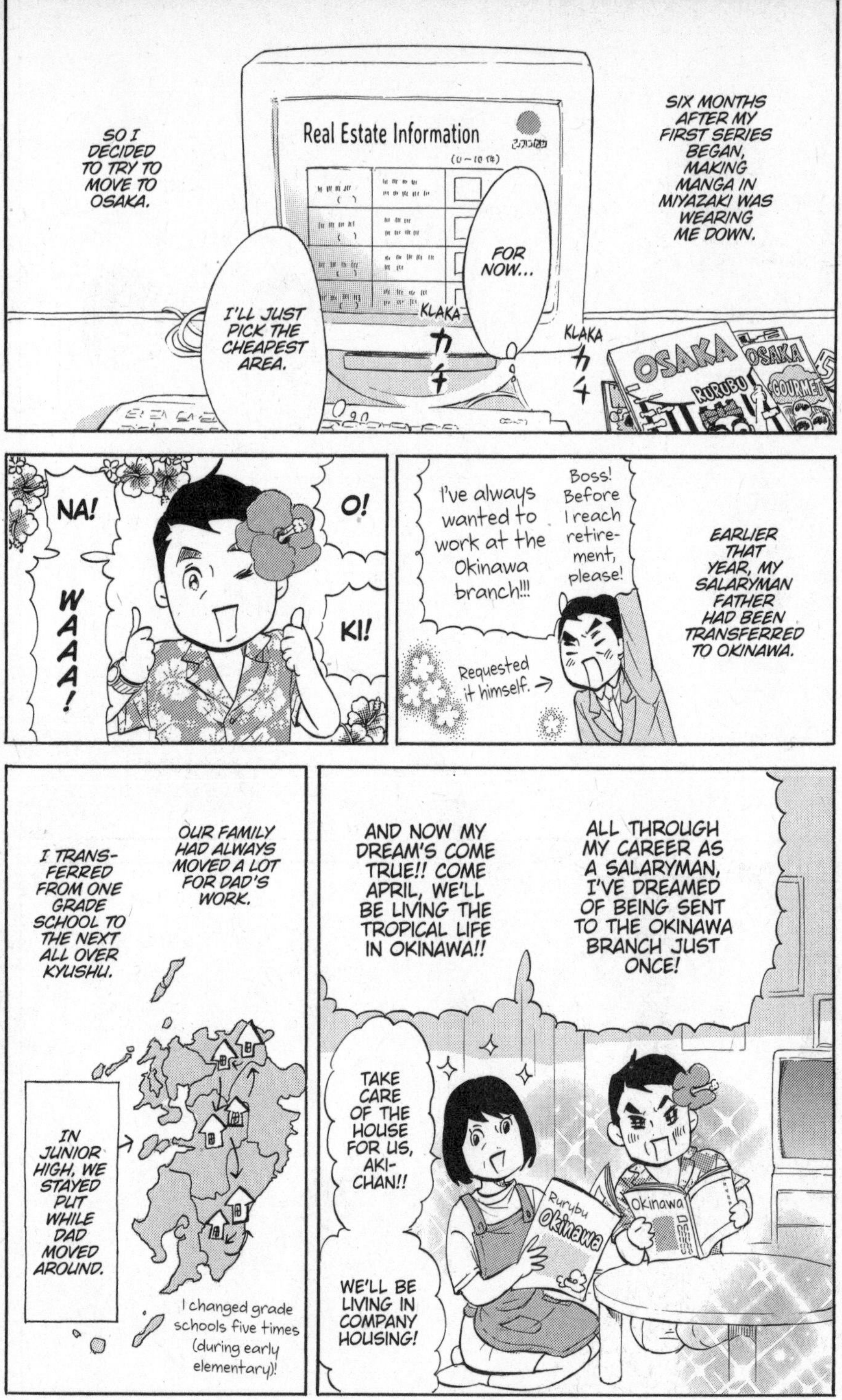
SIX MONTHS AFTER MY FIRST SERIES BEGAN, MAKING MANGA IN MIYAZAKI WAS WEARING ME DOWN.
SO I DECIDED TO TRY TO MOVE TO OSAKA.
Real Estate Information
FOR NOW...
I'LL JUST PICK THE CHEAPEST AREA.
KLAKA
KLAKA
OSAKA
RURUBU
OSAKA
GOURMET
EARLIER THAT YEAR, MY SALARYMAN FATHER HAD BEEN TRANSFERRED TO OKINAWA.
Boss! Before I reach retire-ment, please!
I've always wanted to work at the Okinawa branch!!!
Requested it himself. →
O!
KI!
NA!
WAAAA!
ALL THROUGH MY CAREER AS A SALARYMAN, I'VE DREAMED OF BEING SENT TO THE OKINAWA BRANCH JUST ONCE!
AND NOW MY DREAM'S COME TRUE!! COME APRIL, WE'LL BE LIVING THE TROPICAL LIFE IN OKINAWA!!
TAKE CARE OF THE HOUSE FOR US, AKI-CHAN!!
WE'LL BE LIVING IN COMPANY HOUSING!
Rurybu Okinawa
Okinawa
OUR FAMILY HAD ALWAYS MOVED A LOT FOR DAD'S WORK.
I TRANS-FERRED FROM ONE GRADE SCHOOL TO THE NEXT ALL OVER KYUSHU.
IN JUNIOR HIGH, WE STAYED PUT WHILE DAD MOVED AROUND.
I changed grade schools five times (during early elementary)!

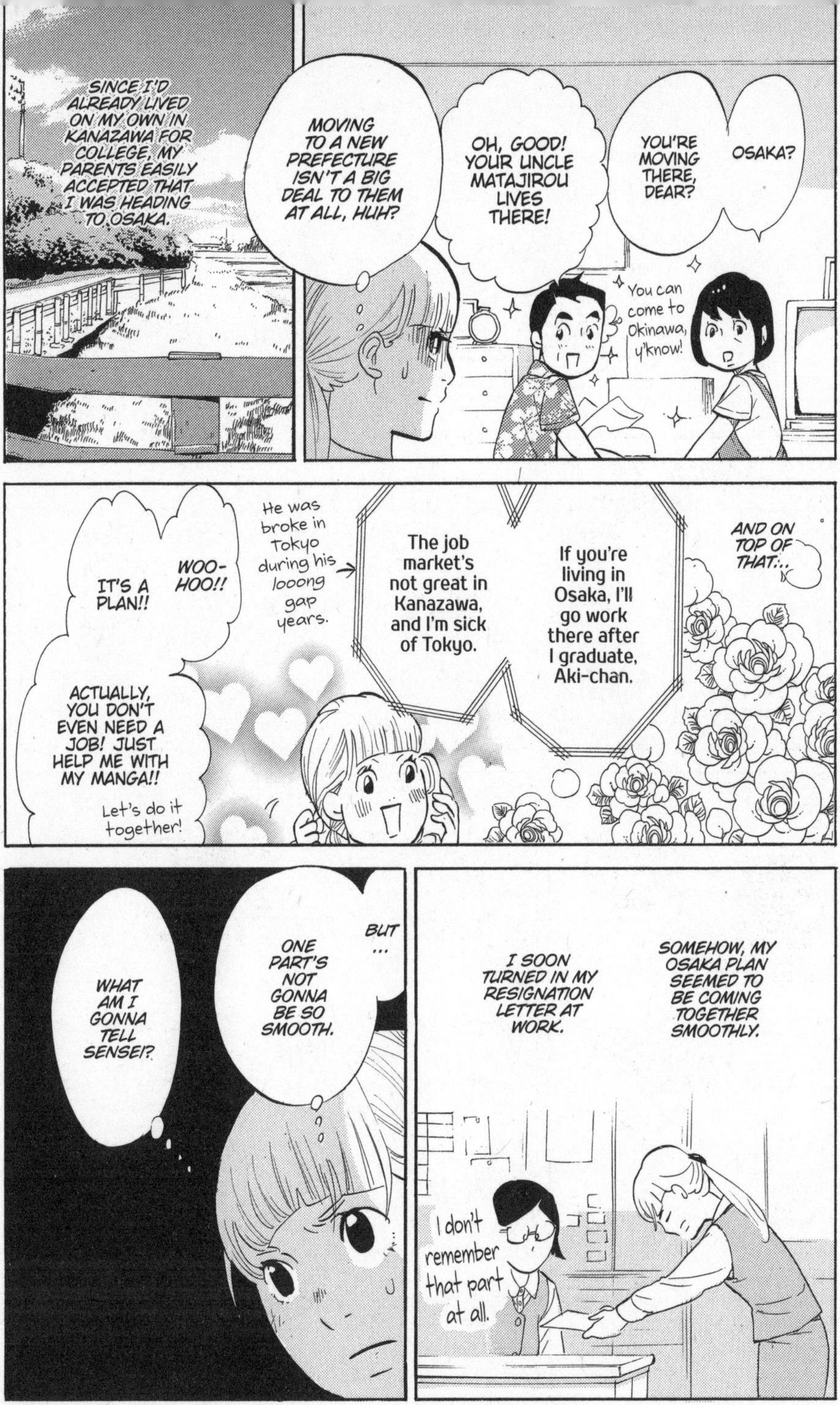

OSAKA?
YOU'RE MOVING THERE, DEAR?
You can come to Okinawa, y'know!
OH, GOOD! YOUR UNCLE MATAJIROU LIVES THERE!
MOVING TO A NEW PREFECTURE ISN'T A BIG DEAL TO THEM AT ALL, HUH?
SINCE I'D ALREADY LIVED ON MY OWN IN KANAZAWA FOR COLLEGE, MY PARENTS EASILY ACCEPTED THAT I WAS HEADING TO OSAKA.
AND ON TOP OF THAT...
If you're living in Osaka, I'll go work there after I graduate, Aki-chan.
The job market's not great in Kanazawa, and I'm sick of Tokyo.
He was broke in Tokyo during his looong gap years.
WOO-HOO!!
IT'S A PLAN!!
ACTUALLY, YOU DON'T EVEN NEED A JOB! JUST HELP ME WITH MY MANGA!!
Let's do it together!
SOMEHOW, MY OSAKA PLAN SEEMED TO BE COMING TOGETHER SMOOTHLY.
I SOON TURNED IN MY RESIGNATION LETTER AT WORK.
I don't remember that part at all.
BUT...
ONE PART'S NOT GONNA BE SO SMOOTH.
WHAT AM I GONNA TELL SENSEI!?

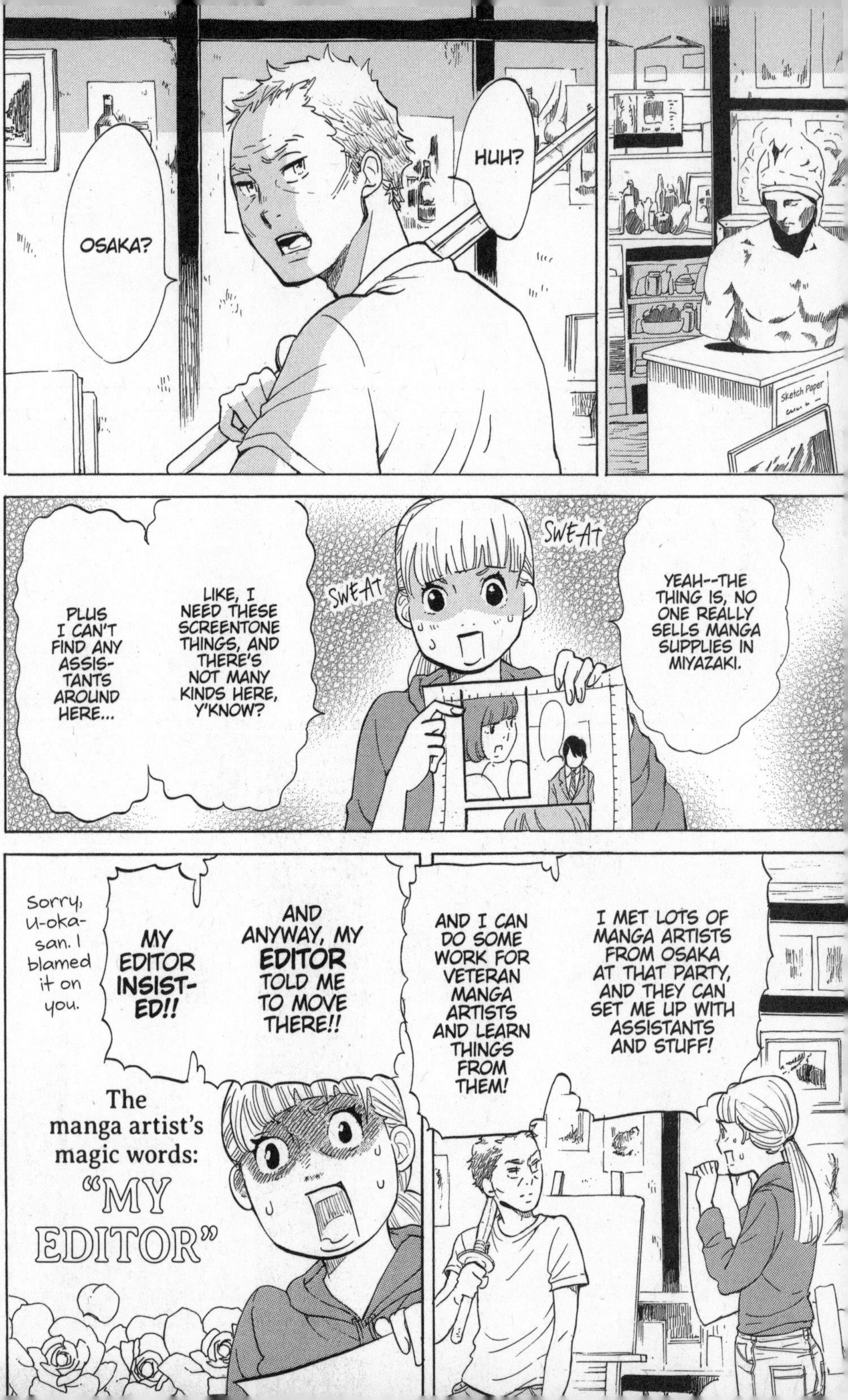
Sketch Paper
HUH?
OSAKA?
YEAH--THE THING IS, NO ONE REALLY SELLS MANGA SUPPLIES IN MIYAZAKI.
SWEAT
SWEAT
LIKE, I NEED THESE SCREENTONE THINGS, AND THERE'S NOT MANY KINDS HERE, Y'KNOW?
PLUS I CAN'T FIND ANY ASSIS-TANTS AROUND HERE...
I MET LOTS OF MANGA ARTISTS FROM OSAKA AT THAT PARTY, AND THEY CAN SET ME UP WITH ASSISTANTS AND STUFF!
AND I CAN DO SOME WORK FOR VETERAN MANGA ARTISTS AND LEARN THINGS FROM THEM!
AND ANYWAY, MY EDITOR TOLD ME TO MOVE THERE!!
MY EDITOR INSIST-ED!!
Sorry, U-oka-san. I blamed it on you.
The manga artist's magic words: "MY EDITOR"

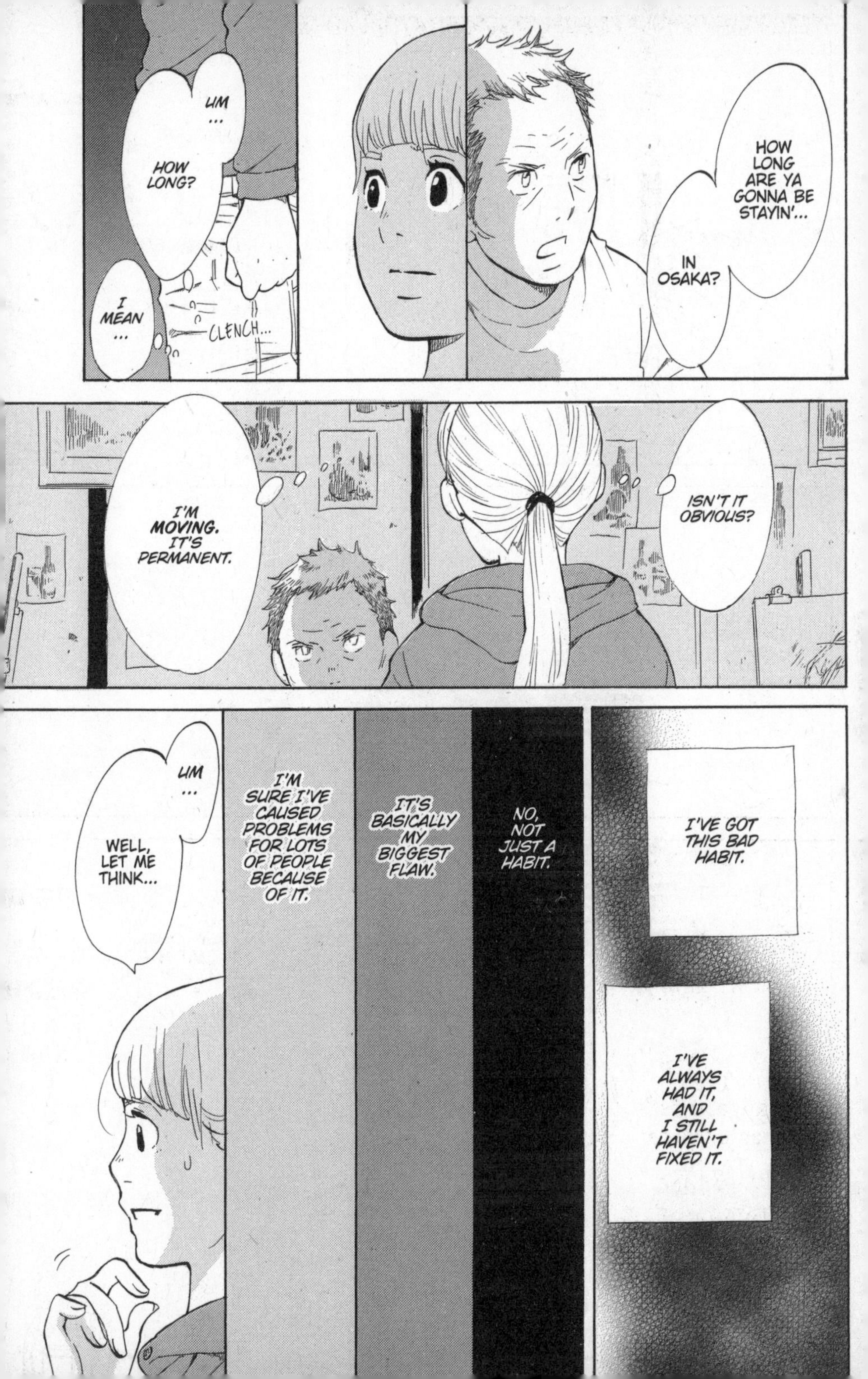
HOW LONG ARE YA GONNA BE STAYIN'...
IN OSAKA?
UM ... HOW LONG?
I MEAN ...
CLENCH...
ISN'T IT OBVIOUS?
I'M MOVING. IT'S PERMANENT.
I'VE GOT THIS BAD HABIT.
I'VE ALWAYS HAD IT, AND I STILL HAVEN'T FIXED IT.
NO, NOT JUST A HABIT.
IT'S BASICALLY MY BIGGEST FLAW.
I'M SURE I'VE CAUSED PROBLEMS FOR LOTS OF PEOPLE BECAUSE OF IT.
UM ...
WELL, LET ME THINK...

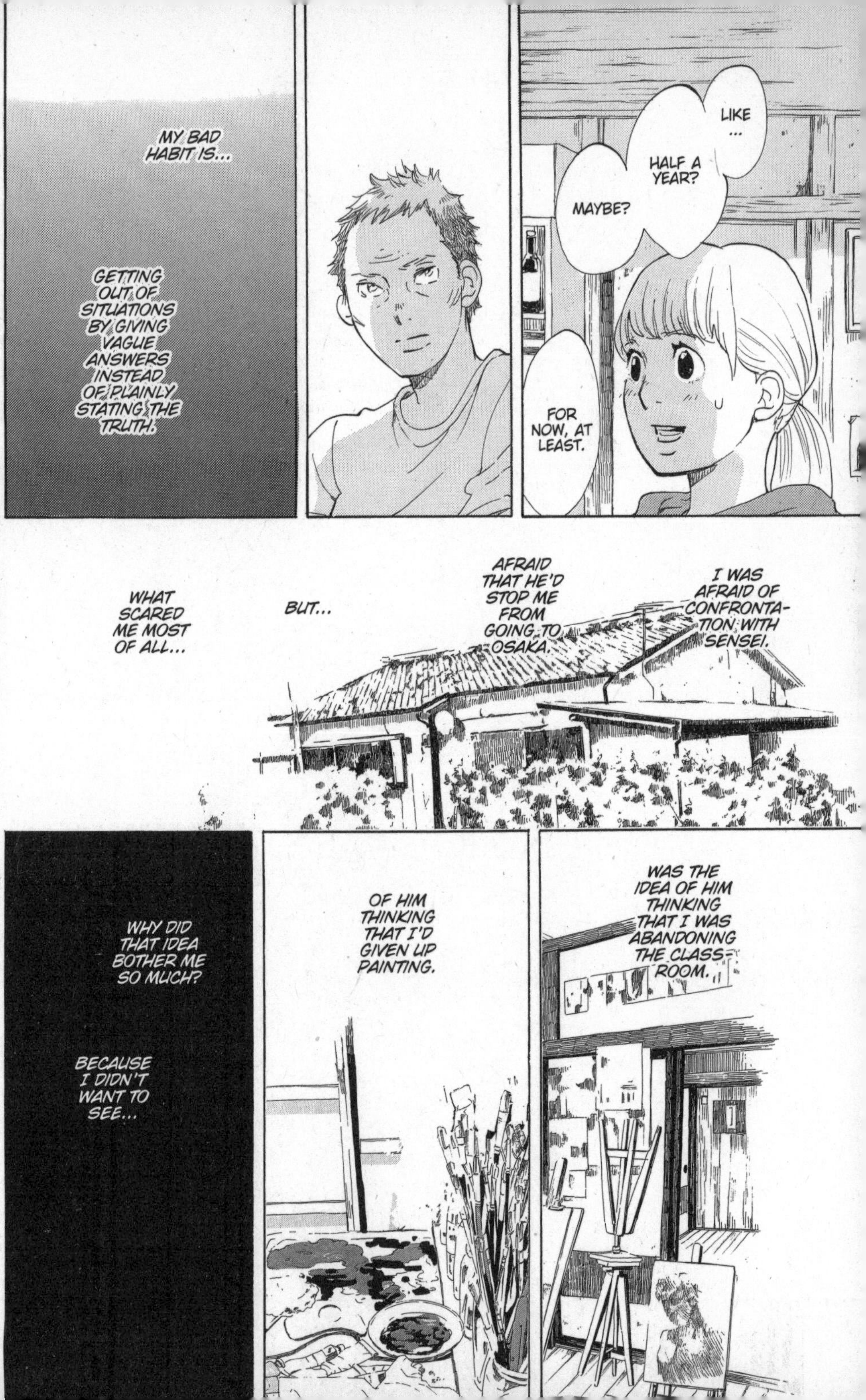
LIKE...
HALF A YEAR?
MAYBE?
FOR NOW, AT LEAST.
MY BAD HABIT IS...
GETTING OUT OF SITUATIONS BY GIVING VAGUE ANSWERS INSTEAD OF PLAINLY STATING THE TRUTH.
I WAS AFRAID OF CONFRONTATION WITH SENSEI.
AFRAID THAT HE'D STOP ME FROM GOING TO OSAKA.
BUT...
WHAT SCARED ME MOST OF ALL...
WAS THE IDEA OF HIM THINKING THAT I WAS ABANDONING THE CLASSROOM.
OF HIM THINKING THAT I'D GIVEN UP PAINTING.
WHY DID THAT IDEA BOTHER ME SO MUCH?
BECAUSE I DIDN'T WANT TO SEE...

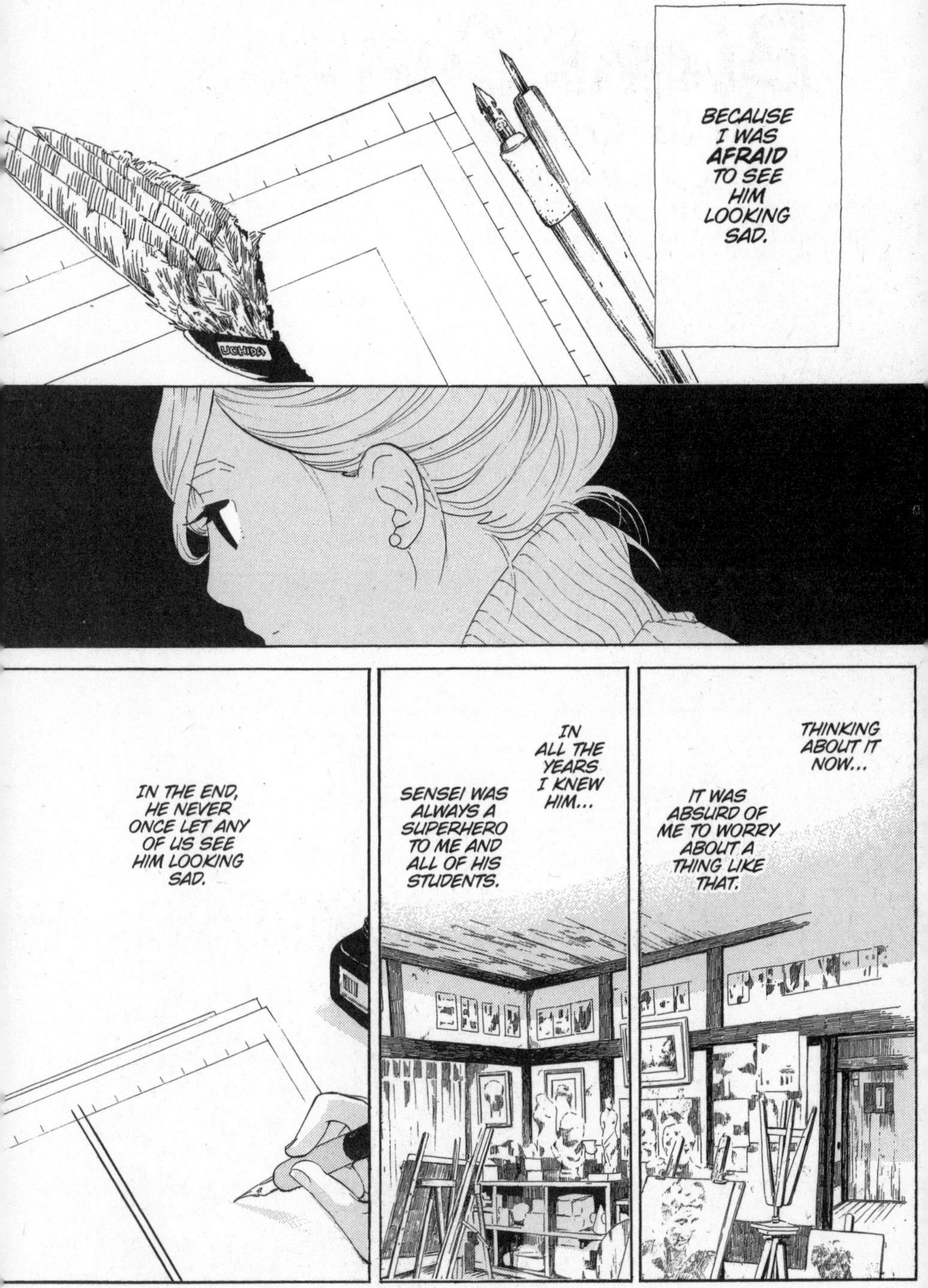
BECAUSE I WAS AFRAID TO SEE HIM LOOKING SAD.
UCHIDA
THINKING ABOUT IT NOW...
IT WAS ABSURD OF ME TO WORRY ABOUT A THING LIKE THAT.
IN ALL THE YEARS I KNEW HIM...
SENSEI WAS ALWAYS A SUPERHERO TO ME AND ALL OF HIS STUDENTS.
IN THE END, HE NEVER ONCE LET ANY OF US SEE HIM LOOKING SAD.

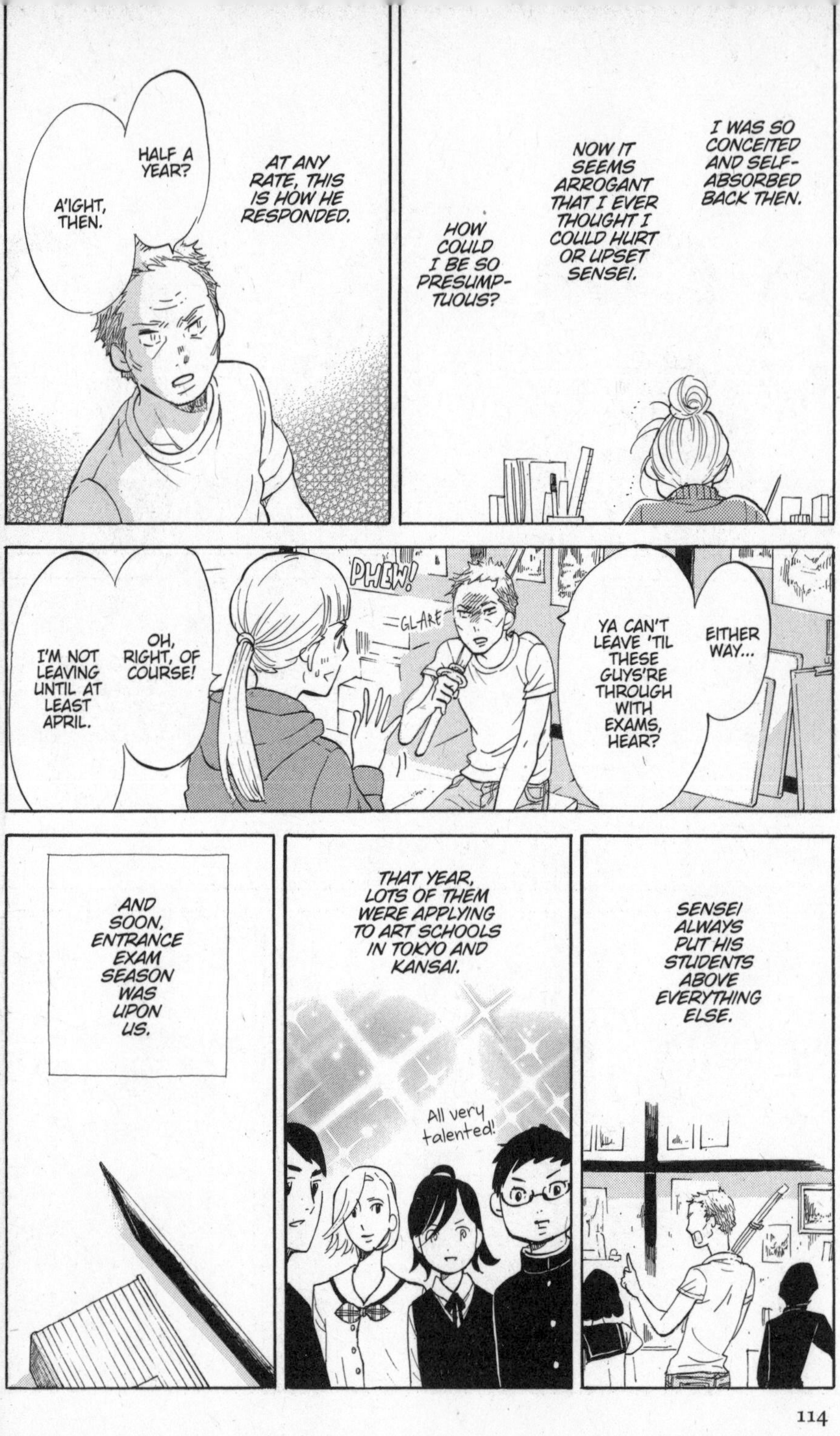
I WAS SO CONCEITED AND SELF-ABSORBED BACK THEN.
NOW IT SEEMS ARROGANT THAT I EVER THOUGHT I COULD HURT OR UPSET SENSEI.
HOW COULD I BE SO PRESUMP-TUOUS?
AT ANY RATE, THIS IS HOW HE RESPONDED.
HALF A YEAR?
A'IGHT, THEN.
EITHER WAY...
YA CAN'T LEAVE 'TIL THESE GUYS'RE THROUGH WITH EXAMS, HEAR?
GLARE
PHEW!
OH, RIGHT, OF COURSE!
I'M NOT LEAVING UNTIL AT LEAST APRIL.
SENSEI ALWAYS PUT HIS STUDENTS ABOVE EVERYTHING ELSE.
THAT YEAR, LOTS OF THEM WERE APPLYING TO ART SCHOOLS IN TOKYO AND KANSAI.
All very talented!
AND SOON, ENTRANCE EXAM SEASON WAS UPON US.

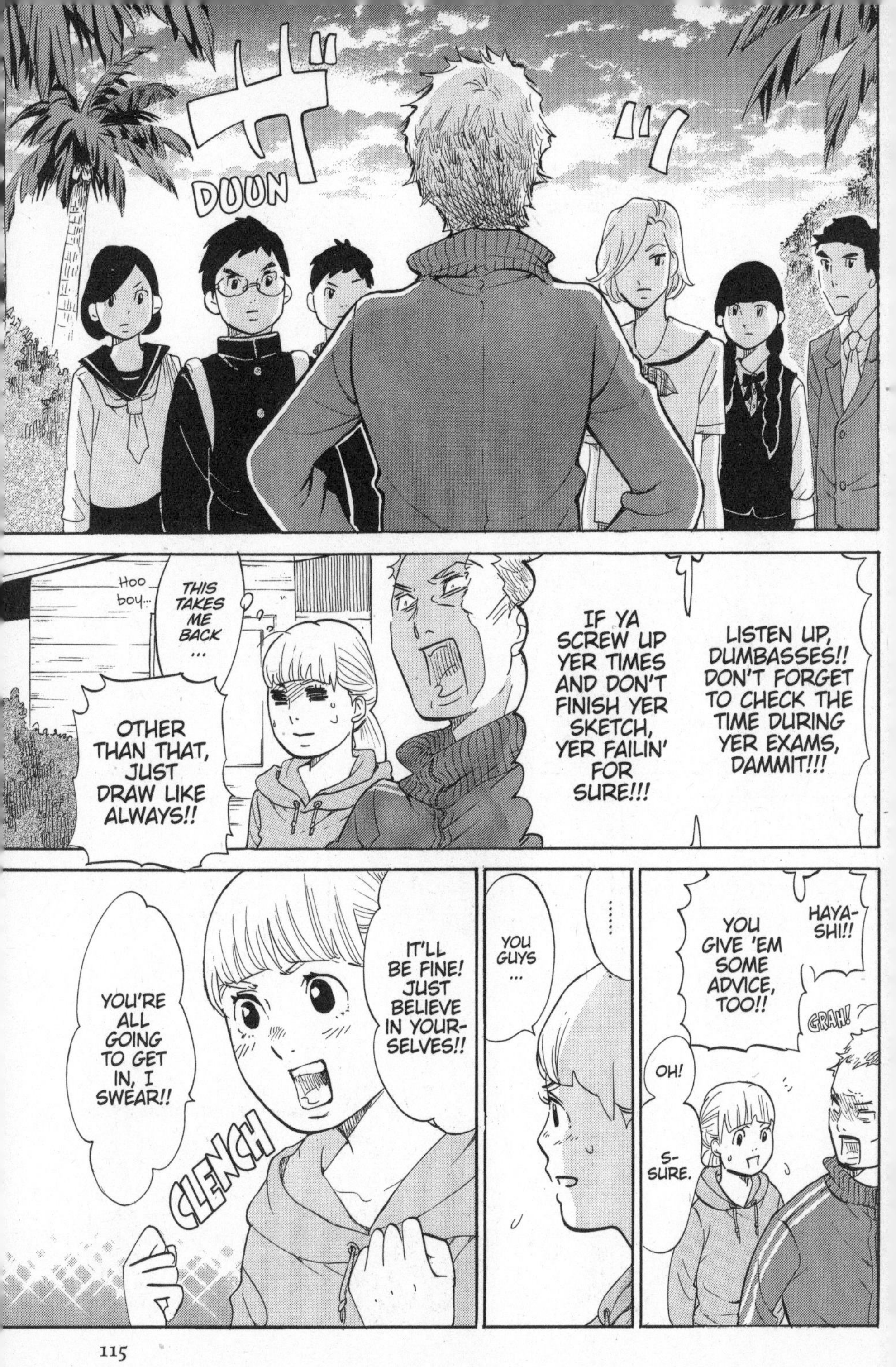
DUUN
LISTEN UP, DUMBASSES!! DON'T FORGET TO CHECK THE TIME DURING YER EXAMS, DAMMIT!!!
IF YA SCREW UP YER TIMES AND DON'T FINISH YER SKETCH, YER FAILIN' FOR SURE!!!
THIS TAKES ME BACK ...
Hoo boy...
OTHER THAN THAT, JUST DRAW LIKE ALWAYS!!
HAYA-SHI!!
YOU GIVE 'EM SOME ADVICE, TOO!!
GRAH!
OH!
S-SURE.
......
YOU GUYS ...
IT'LL BE FINE! JUST BELIEVE IN YOUR-SELVES!!
YOU'RE ALL GOING TO GET IN, I SWEAR!!
CLENCH

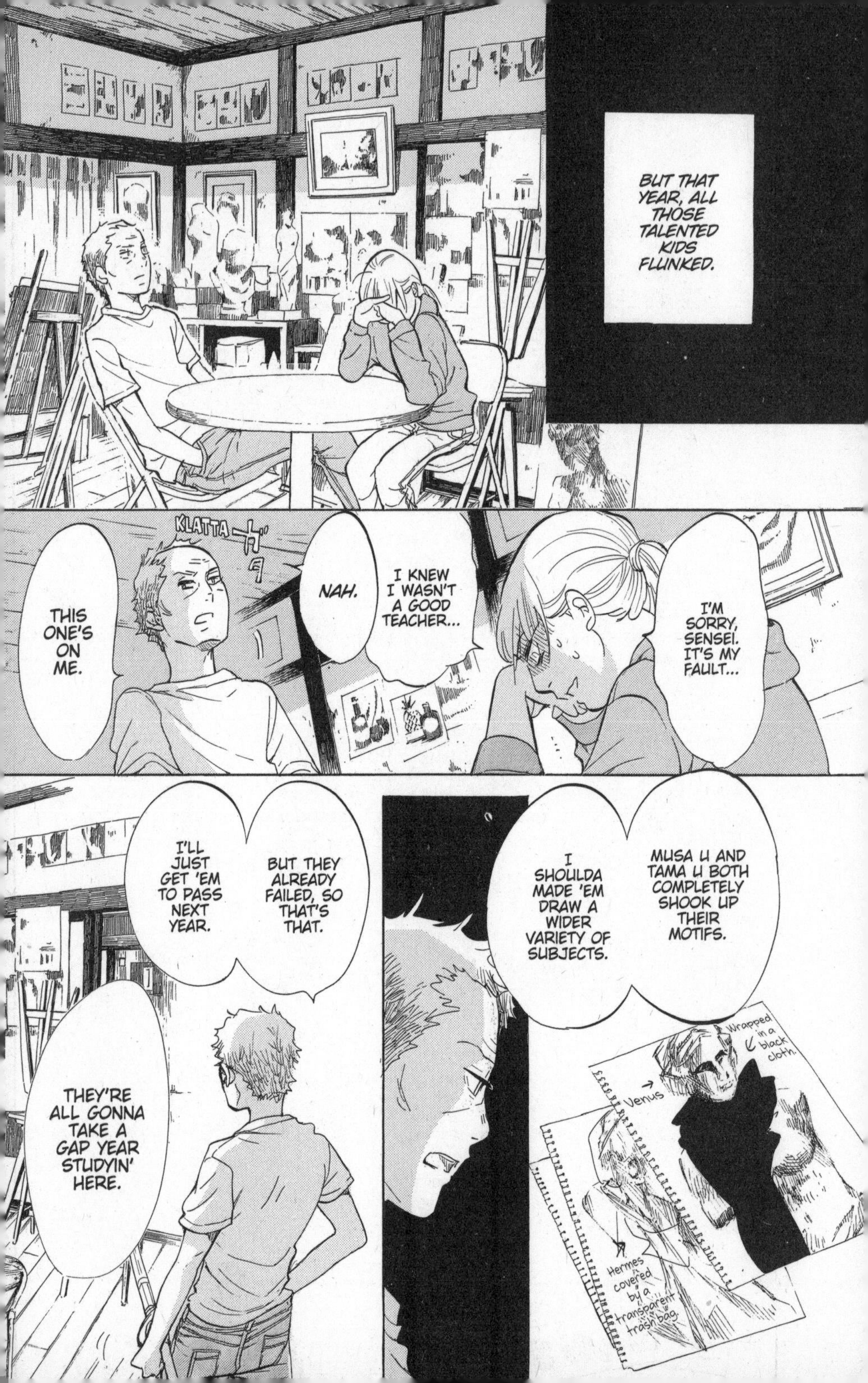
BUT THAT YEAR, ALL THOSE TALENTED KIDS FLUNKED.
I'M SORRY, SENSEI. IT'S MY FAULT...
I KNEW I WASN'T A GOOD TEACHER...
NAH.
KLATTA
THIS ONE'S ON ME.
MUSA U AND TAMA U BOTH COMPLETELY SHOOK UP THEIR MOTIFS.
I SHOULDA MADE 'EM DRAW A WIDER VARIETY OF SUBJECTS.
Wrapped in a black cloth.
Venus
Hermes covered by a transparent trash bag.
BUT THEY ALREADY FAILED, SO THAT'S THAT.
I'LL JUST GET 'EM TO PASS NEXT YEAR.
THEY'RE ALL GONNA TAKE A GAP YEAR STUDYIN' HERE.

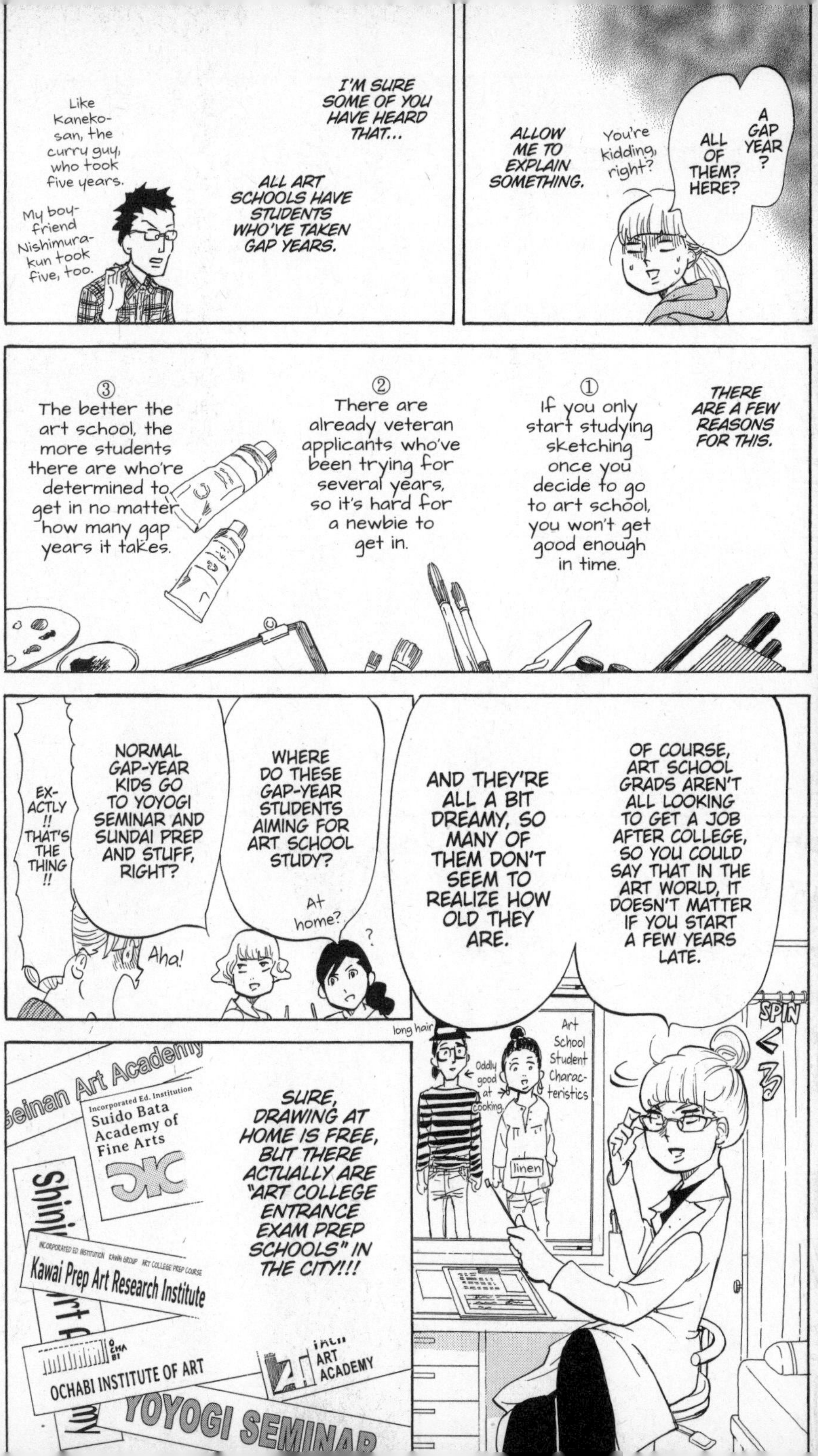

A GAP YEAR?
ALL OF THEM? HERE?
You're kidding, right?
ALLOW ME TO EXPLAIN SOMETHING.
I'M SURE SOME OF YOU HAVE HEARD THAT...
ALL ART SCHOOLS HAVE STUDENTS WHO'VE TAKEN GAP YEARS.
Like Kaneko-san, the curry guy, who took five years.
My boyfriend Nishimura-kun took five, too.
THERE ARE A FEW REASONS FOR THIS.
① If you only start studying sketching once you decide to go to art school, you won't get good enough in time.
② There are already veteran applicants who've been trying for several years, so it's hard for a newbie to get in.
③ The better the art school, the more students there are who're determined to get in no matter how many gap years it takes.
OF COURSE, ART SCHOOL GRADS AREN'T ALL LOOKING TO GET A JOB AFTER COLLEGE, SO YOU COULD SAY THAT IN THE ART WORLD, IT DOESN'T MATTER IF YOU START A FEW YEARS LATE.
AND THEY'RE ALL A BIT DREAMY, SO MANY OF THEM DON'T SEEM TO REALIZE HOW OLD THEY ARE.
SPIN
Art School Student Characteristics
long hair
Oddly good at cooking
linen
WHERE DO THESE GAP-YEAR STUDENTS AIMING FOR ART SCHOOL STUDY?
At home?
?
NORMAL GAP-YEAR KIDS GO TO YOYOGI SEMINAR AND SUNDAI PREP AND STUFF, RIGHT?
EXACTLY!! THAT'S THE THING!!
Aha!
SURE, DRAWING AT HOME IS FREE, BUT THERE ACTUALLY ARE "ART COLLEGE ENTRANCE EXAM PREP SCHOOLS" IN THE CITY!!!
Seinan Art Academy
Incorporated Ed. Institution
Suido Bata Academy of Fine Arts
INCORPORATED ED. INSTITUTION KAWAI GROUP ART COLLEGE PREP COURSE
Kawai Prep Art Research Institute
OCHABI INSTITUTE OF ART
ART ACADEMY
YOYOGI SEMINAR

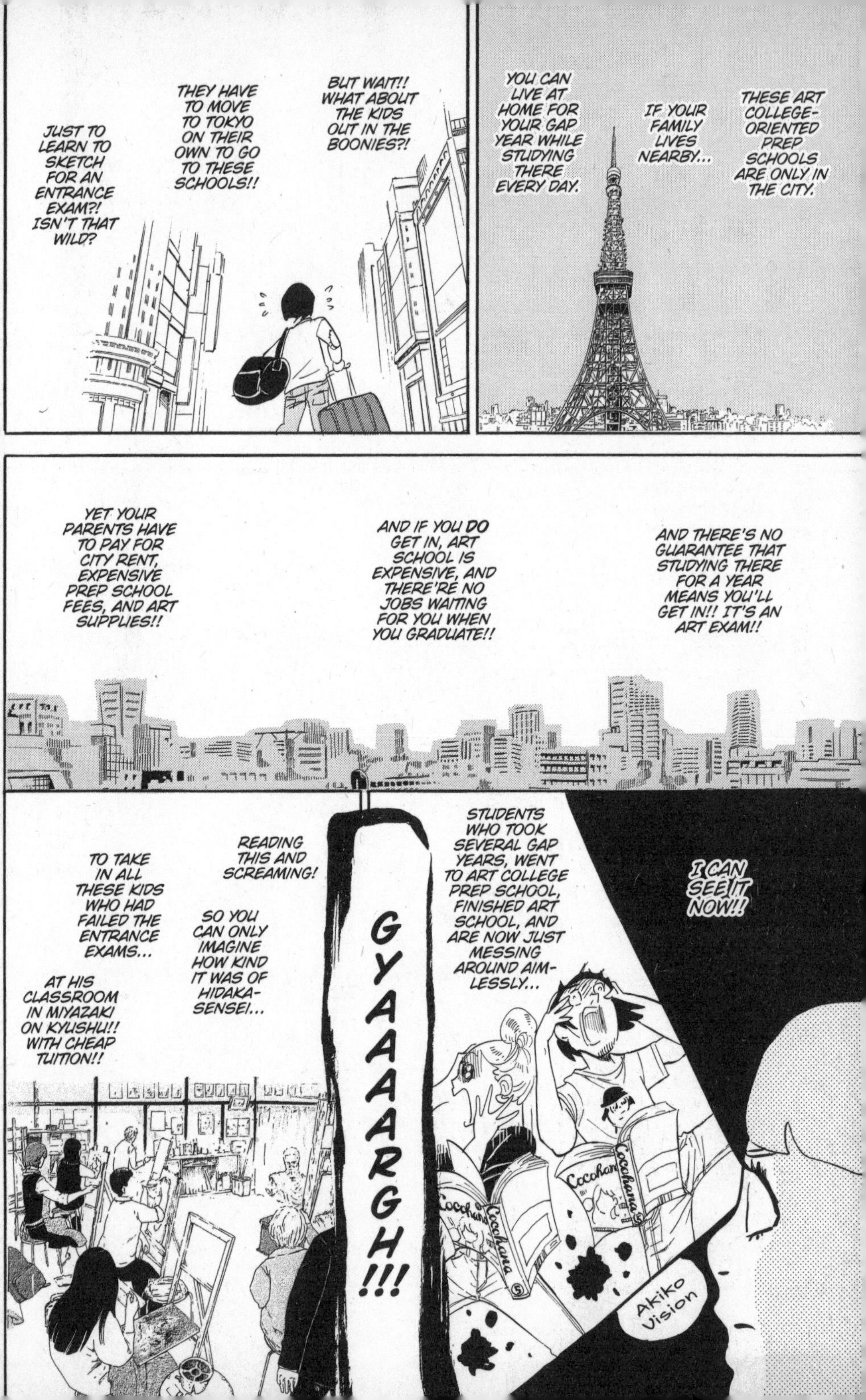

THESE ART COLLEGE-ORIENTED PREP SCHOOLS ARE ONLY IN THE CITY.
IF YOUR FAMILY LIVES NEARBY...
YOU CAN LIVE AT HOME FOR YOUR GAP YEAR WHILE STUDYING THERE EVERY DAY.
BUT WAIT!! WHAT ABOUT THE KIDS OUT IN THE BOONIES?!
THEY HAVE TO MOVE TO TOKYO ON THEIR OWN TO GO TO THESE SCHOOLS!!
JUST TO LEARN TO SKETCH FOR AN ENTRANCE EXAM?! ISN'T THAT WILD?
AND THERE'S NO GUARANTEE THAT STUDYING THERE FOR A YEAR MEANS YOU'LL GET IN!! IT'S AN ART EXAM!!
AND IF YOU DO GET IN, ART SCHOOL IS EXPENSIVE, AND THERE'RE NO JOBS WAITING FOR YOU WHEN YOU GRADUATE!!
YET YOUR PARENTS HAVE TO PAY FOR CITY RENT, EXPENSIVE PREP SCHOOL FEES, AND ART SUPPLIES!!
I CAN SEE IT NOW!!
STUDENTS WHO TOOK SEVERAL GAP YEARS, WENT TO ART COLLEGE PREP SCHOOL, FINISHED ART SCHOOL, AND ARE NOW JUST MESSING AROUND AIM-LESSLY...
Akiko Vision
Cocohana
GYAAAAARGH!!!
READING THIS AND SCREAMING!
SO YOU CAN ONLY IMAGINE HOW KIND IT WAS OF HIDAKA-SENSEI...
TO TAKE IN ALL THESE KIDS WHO HAD FAILED THE ENTRANCE EXAMS...
AT HIS CLASSROOM IN MIYAZAKI ON KYUSHU!! WITH CHEAP TUITION!!

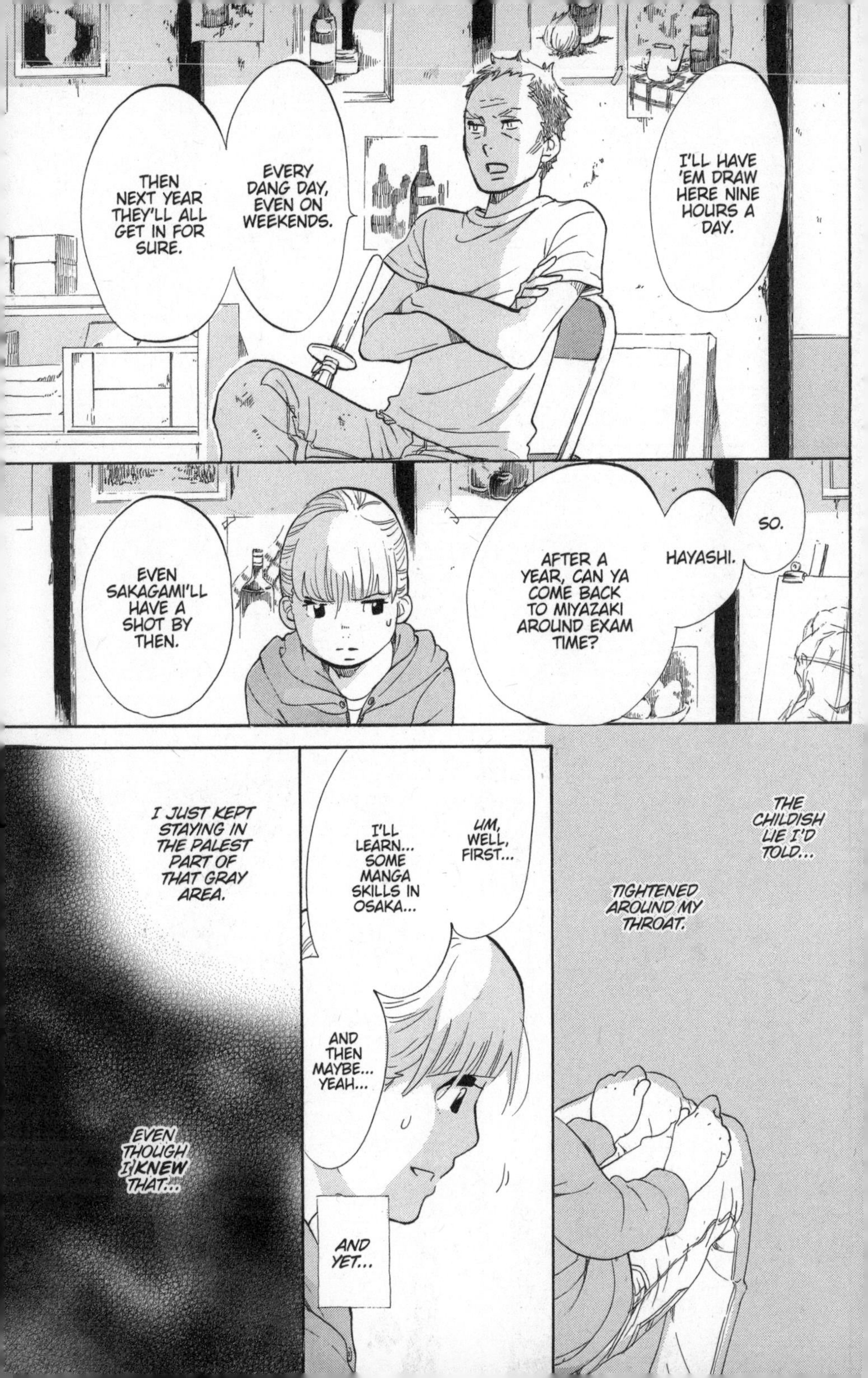
I'LL HAVE 'EM DRAW HERE NINE HOURS A DAY.
EVERY DANG DAY, EVEN ON WEEKENDS.
THEN NEXT YEAR THEY'LL ALL GET IN FOR SURE.
SO.
HAYASHI.
AFTER A YEAR, CAN YA COME BACK TO MIYAZAKI AROUND EXAM TIME?
EVEN SAKAGAMI'LL HAVE A SHOT BY THEN.
THE CHILDISH LIE I'D TOLD...
TIGHTENED AROUND MY THROAT.
UM, WELL, FIRST...
I'LL LEARN... SOME MANGA SKILLS IN OSAKA...
AND THEN MAYBE... YEAH...
AND YET...
I JUST KEPT STAYING IN THE PALEST PART OF THAT GRAY AREA.
EVEN THOUGH I KNEW THAT...

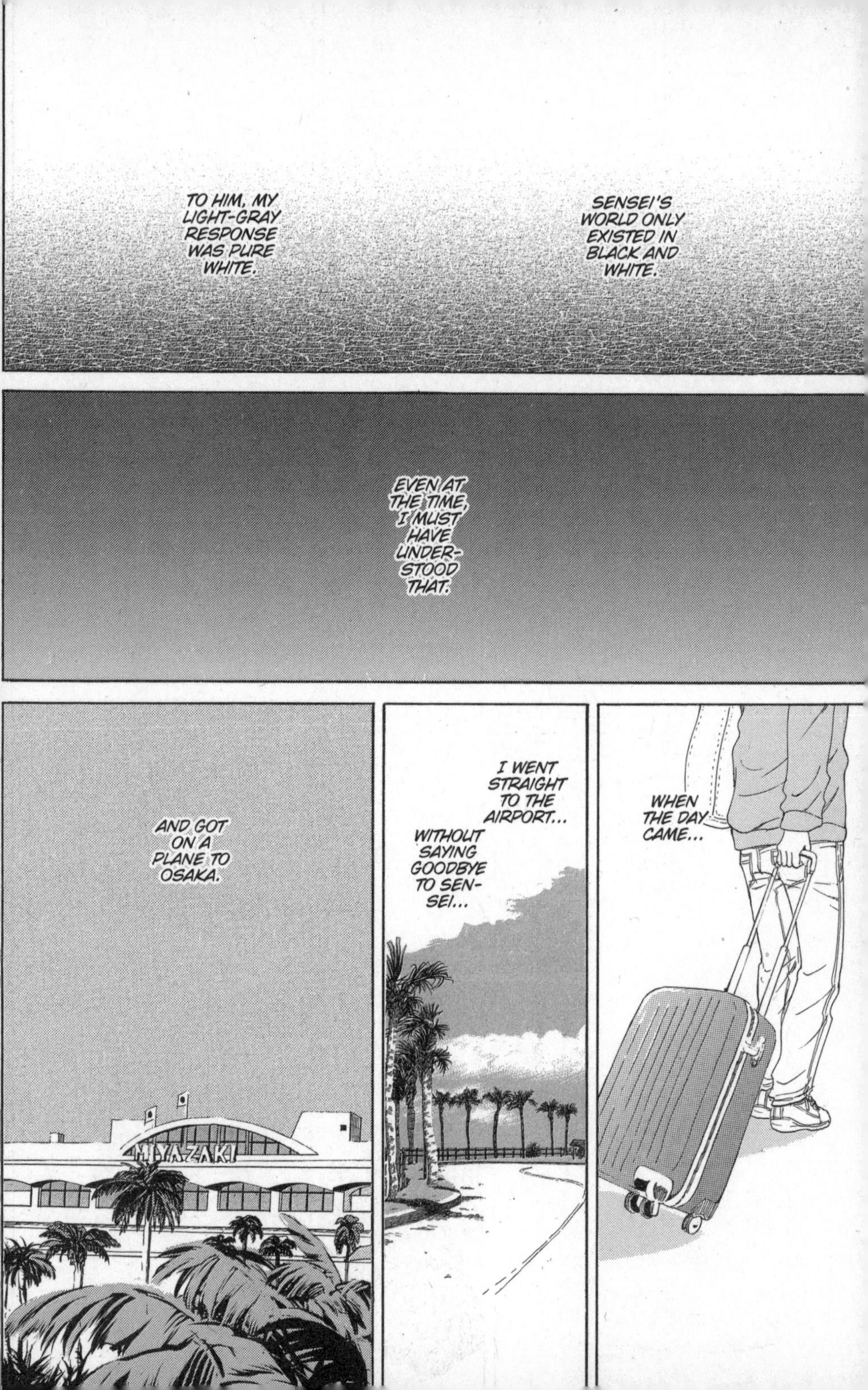
SENSEI'S WORLD ONLY EXISTED IN BLACK AND WHITE.
TO HIM, MY LIGHT-GRAY RESPONSE WAS PURE WHITE.
EVEN AT THE TIME, I MUST HAVE UNDER-STOOD THAT.
WHEN THE DAY CAME...
I WENT STRAIGHT TO THE AIRPORT...
WITHOUT SAYING GOODBYE TO SEN-SEI...
AND GOT ON A PLANE TO OSAKA.
MIYAZAKI

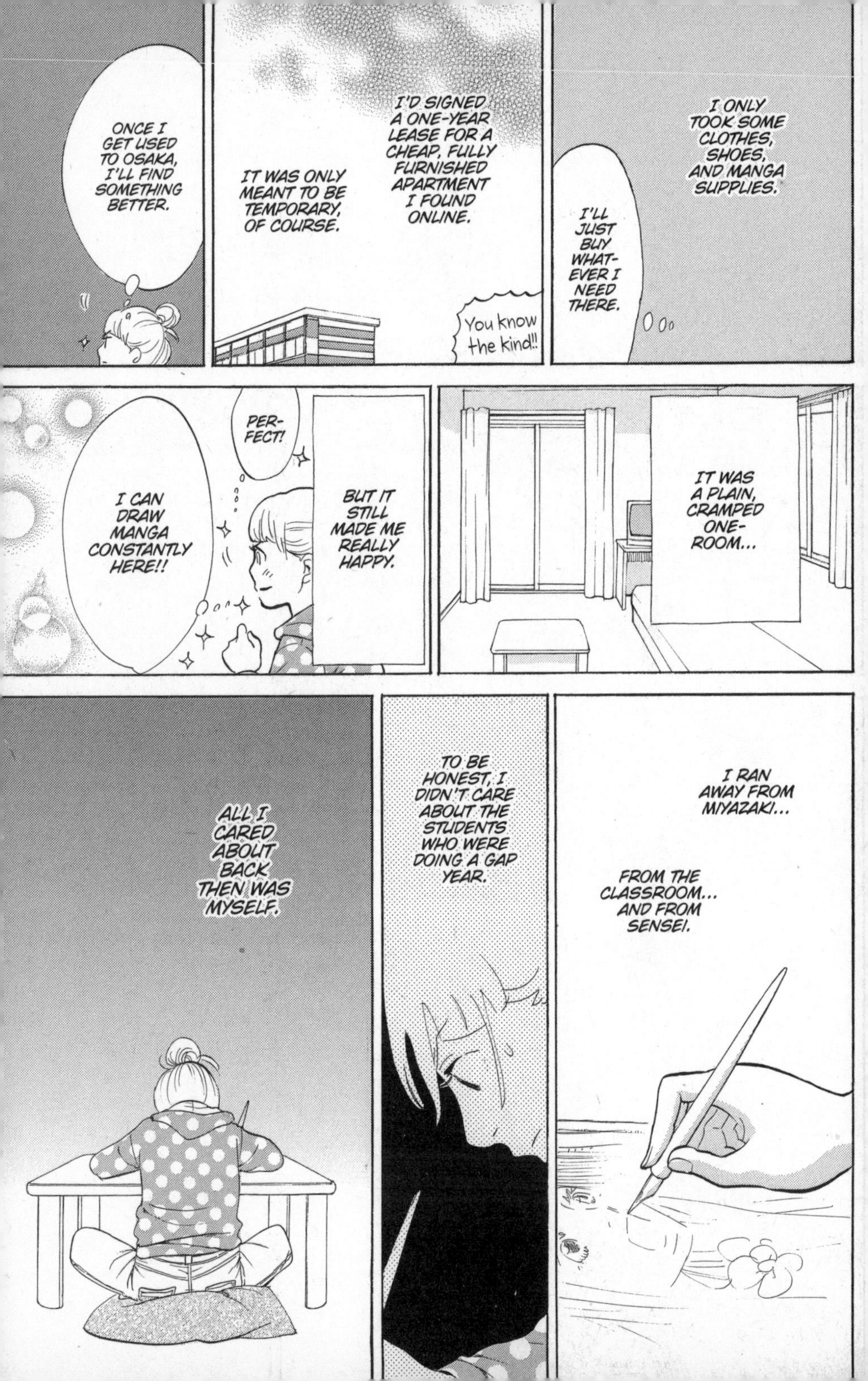
I ONLY TOOK SOME CLOTHES, SHOES, AND MANGA SUPPLIES.
I'LL JUST BUY WHATEVER I NEED THERE.
I'D SIGNED A ONE-YEAR LEASE FOR A CHEAP, FULLY FURNISHED APARTMENT I FOUND ONLINE.
You know the kind!!
IT WAS ONLY MEANT TO BE TEMPORARY, OF COURSE.
ONCE I GET USED TO OSAKA, I'LL FIND SOMETHING BETTER.
IT WAS A PLAIN, CRAMPED ONE-ROOM...
BUT IT STILL MADE ME REALLY HAPPY.
PERFECT!
I CAN DRAW MANGA CONSTANTLY HERE!!
I RAN AWAY FROM MIYAZAKI...
FROM THE CLASSROOM... AND FROM SENSEI.
TO BE HONEST, I DIDN'T CARE ABOUT THE STUDENTS WHO WERE DOING A GAP YEAR.
ALL I CARED ABOUT BACK THEN WAS MYSELF.

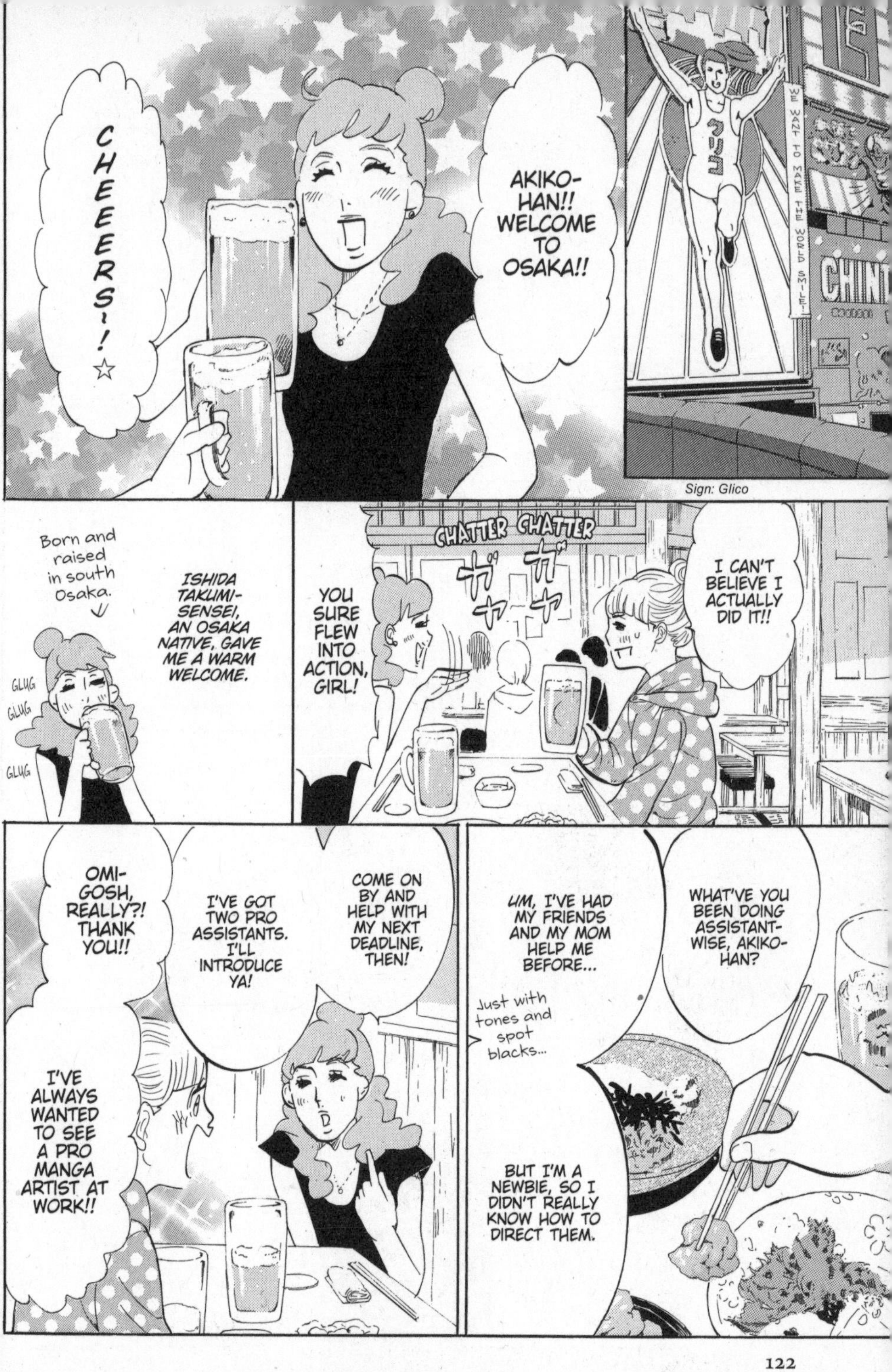
WE WANT TO MAKE THE WORLD SMILE!
Sign: Glico
AKIKO-HAN!! WELCOME TO OSAKA!!
CHEEEERS~!☆
I CAN'T BELIEVE I ACTUALLY DID IT!!
CHATTER CHATTER
YOU SURE FLEW INTO ACTION, GIRL!
ISHIDA TAKUMI-SENSEI, AN OSAKA NATIVE, GAVE ME A WARM WELCOME.
Born and raised in south Osaka.
GLUG GLUG GLUG
WHAT'VE YOU BEEN DOING ASSISTANT-WISE, AKIKO-HAN?
UM, I'VE HAD MY FRIENDS AND MY MOM HELP ME BEFORE...
Just with tones and spot blacks...
BUT I'M A NEWBIE, SO I DIDN'T REALLY KNOW HOW TO DIRECT THEM.
COME ON BY AND HELP WITH MY NEXT DEADLINE, THEN!
I'VE GOT TWO PRO ASSISTANTS. I'LL INTRODUCE YA!
OMI-GOSH, REALLY?! THANK YOU!!
I'VE ALWAYS WANTED TO SEE A PRO MANGA ARTIST AT WORK!!

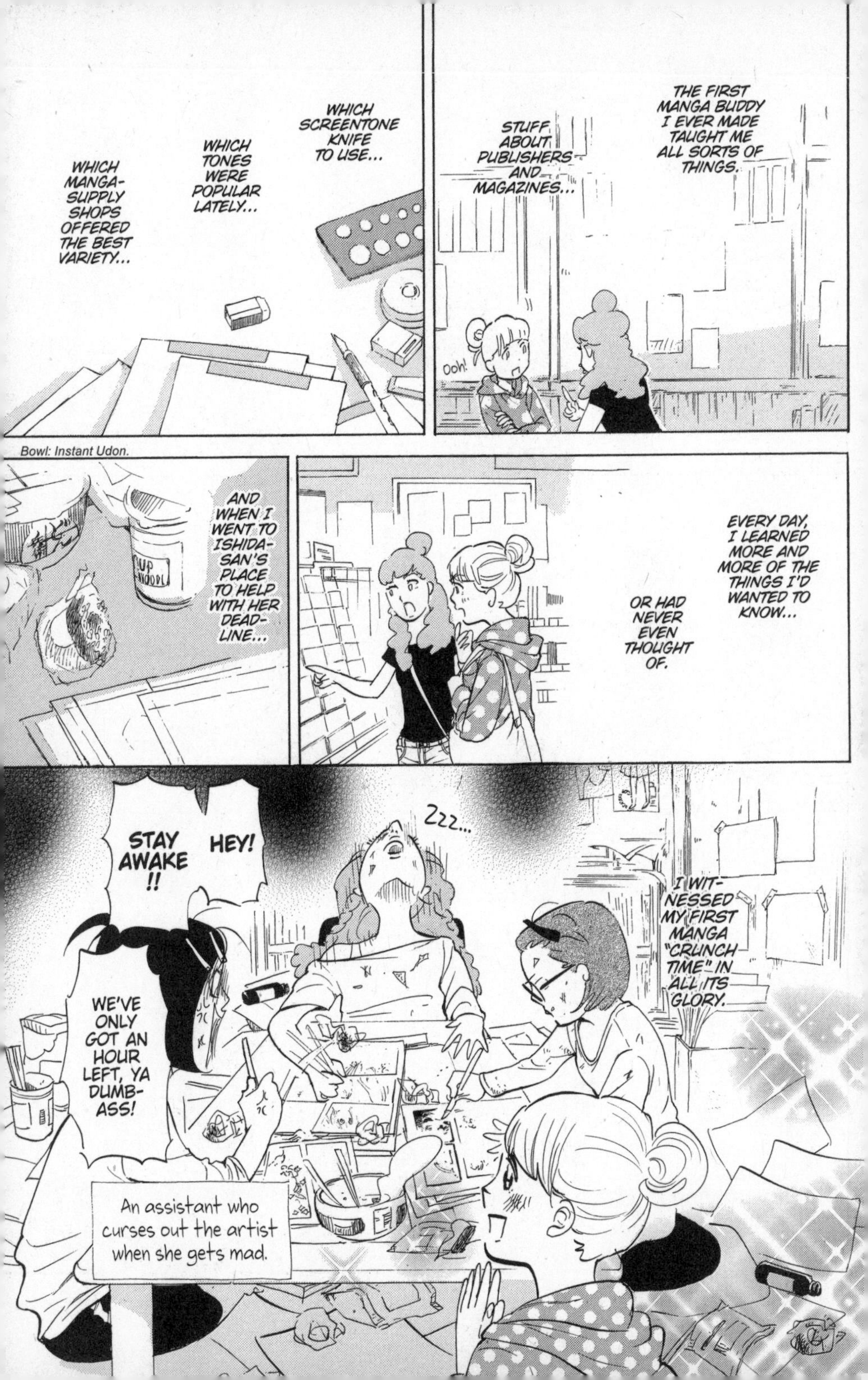
THE FIRST MANGA BUDDY I EVER MADE TAUGHT ME ALL SORTS OF THINGS.
STUFF ABOUT PUBLISHERS AND MAGAZINES...
Ooh!
WHICH SCREENTONE KNIFE TO USE...
WHICH TONES WERE POPULAR LATELY...
WHICH MANGA-SUPPLY SHOPS OFFERED THE BEST VARIETY...
Bowl: Instant Udon.
EVERY DAY, I LEARNED MORE AND MORE OF THE THINGS I'D WANTED TO KNOW...
OR HAD NEVER EVEN THOUGHT OF.
AND WHEN I WENT TO ISHIDA-SAN'S PLACE TO HELP WITH HER DEAD-LINE...
I WIT-NESSED MY FIRST MANGA "CRUNCH TIME" IN ALL ITS GLORY.
Zzz...
HEY!
STAY AWAKE!!
WE'VE ONLY GOT AN HOUR LEFT, YA DUMB-ASS!
An assistant who curses out the artist when she gets mad.

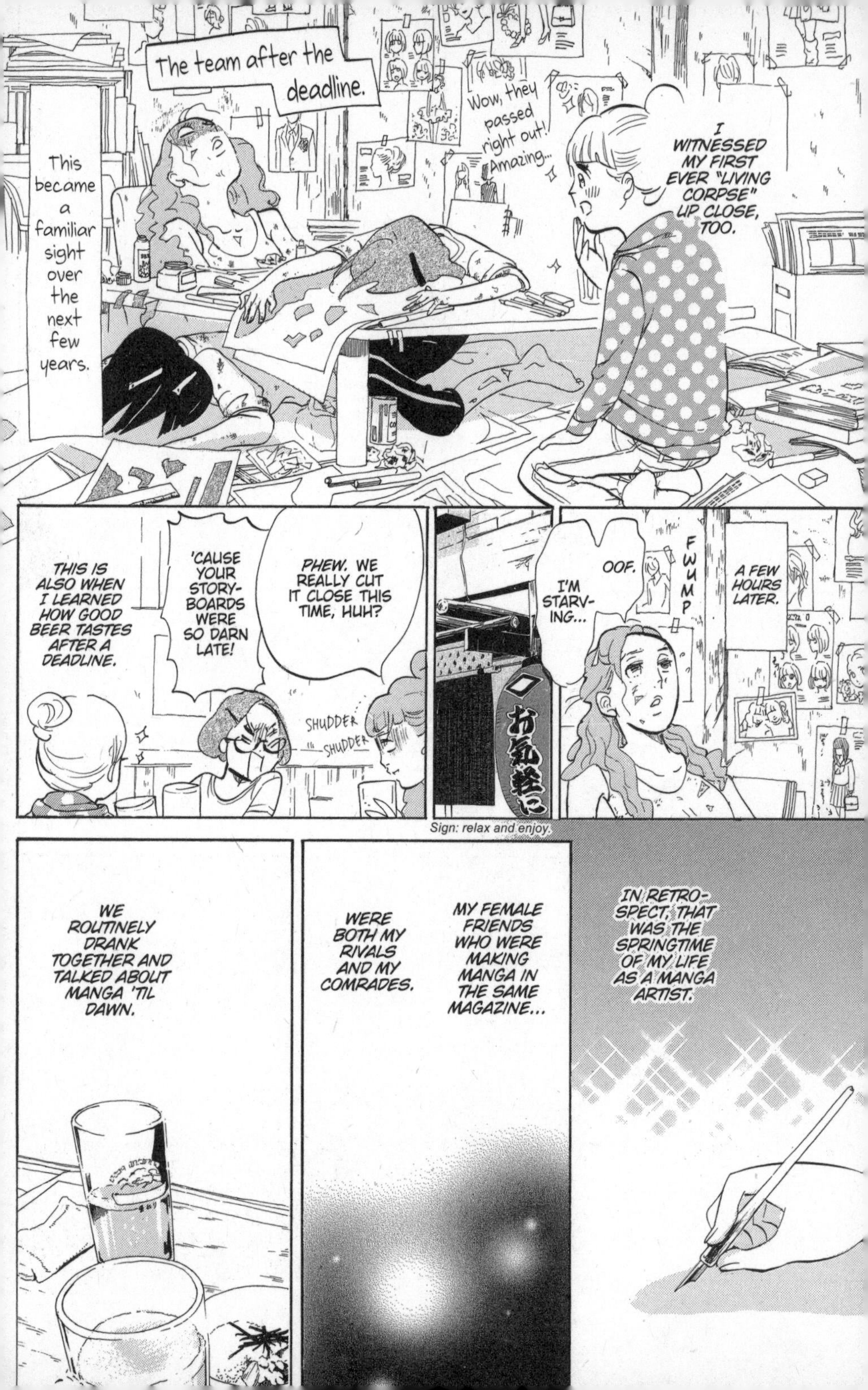
I WITNESSED MY FIRST EVER "LIVING CORPSE" UP CLOSE, TOO.
Wow, they passed right out! Amazing...
The team after the deadline.
This became a familiar sight over the next few years.
A FEW HOURS LATER.
FWUMP
OOF.
I'M STARVING...
お気軽に
Sign: relax and enjoy.
PHEW. WE REALLY CUT IT CLOSE THIS TIME, HUH?
'CAUSE YOUR STORYBOARDS WERE SO DARN LATE!
SHUDDER SHUDDER
THIS IS ALSO WHEN I LEARNED HOW GOOD BEER TASTES AFTER A DEADLINE.
IN RETROSPECT, THAT WAS THE SPRINGTIME OF MY LIFE AS A MANGA ARTIST.
MY FEMALE FRIENDS WHO WERE MAKING MANGA IN THE SAME MAGAZINE...
WERE BOTH MY RIVALS AND MY COMRADES.
WE ROUTINELY DRANK TOGETHER AND TALKED ABOUT MANGA 'TIL DAWN.

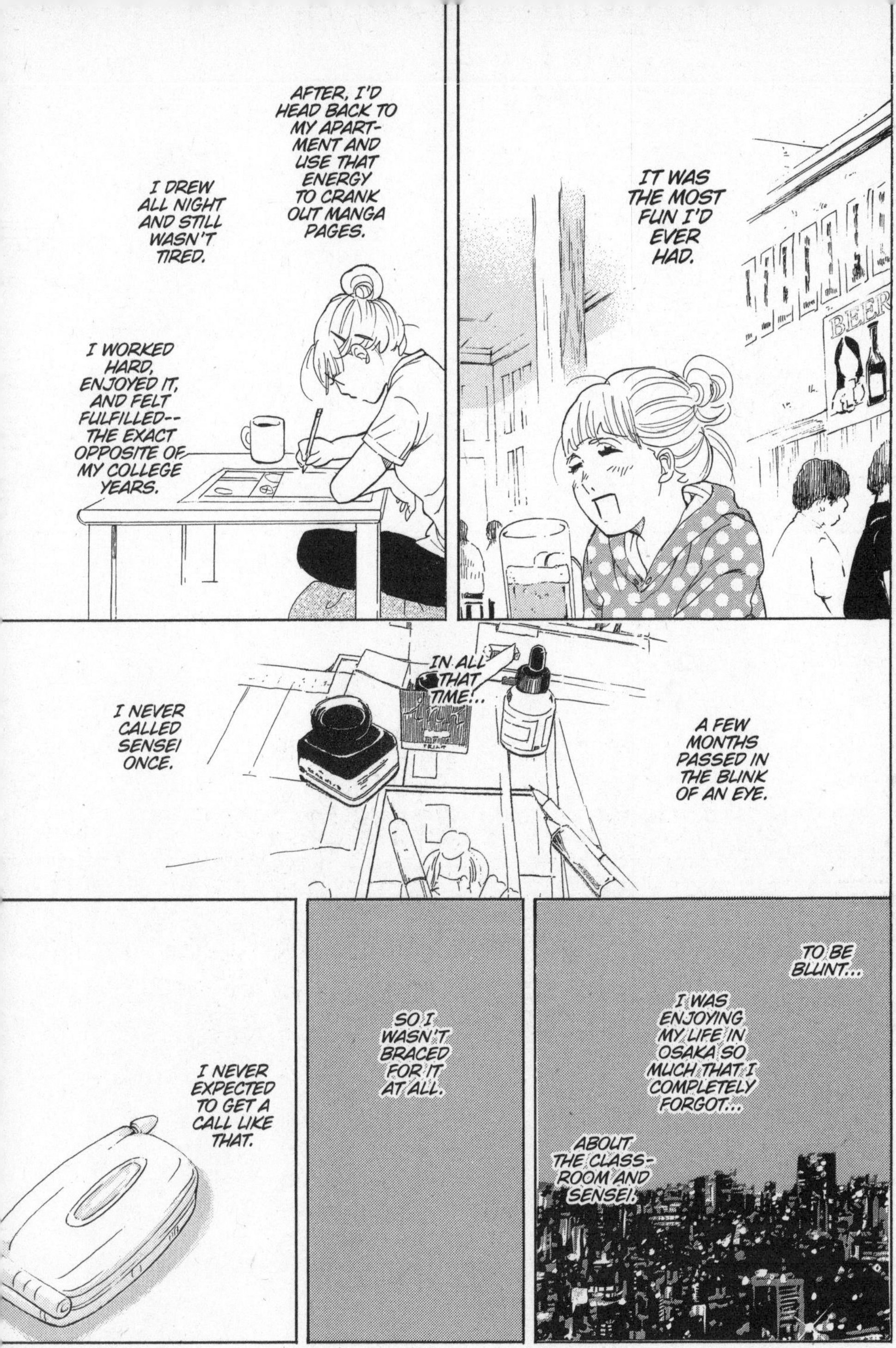
IT WAS THE MOST FUN I'D EVER HAD.
BEER
AFTER, I'D HEAD BACK TO MY APARTMENT AND USE THAT ENERGY TO CRANK OUT MANGA PAGES.
I DREW ALL NIGHT AND STILL WASN'T TIRED.
I WORKED HARD, ENJOYED IT, AND FELT FULFILLED-- THE EXACT OPPOSITE OF MY COLLEGE YEARS.
A FEW MONTHS PASSED IN THE BLINK OF AN EYE.
IN ALL THAT TIME...
I NEVER CALLED SENSEI ONCE.
TO BE BLUNT...
I WAS ENJOYING MY LIFE IN OSAKA SO MUCH THAT I COMPLETELY FORGOT...
ABOUT THE CLASSROOM AND SENSEI.
SO I WASN'T BRACED FOR IT AT ALL.
I NEVER EXPECTED TO GET A CALL LIKE THAT.

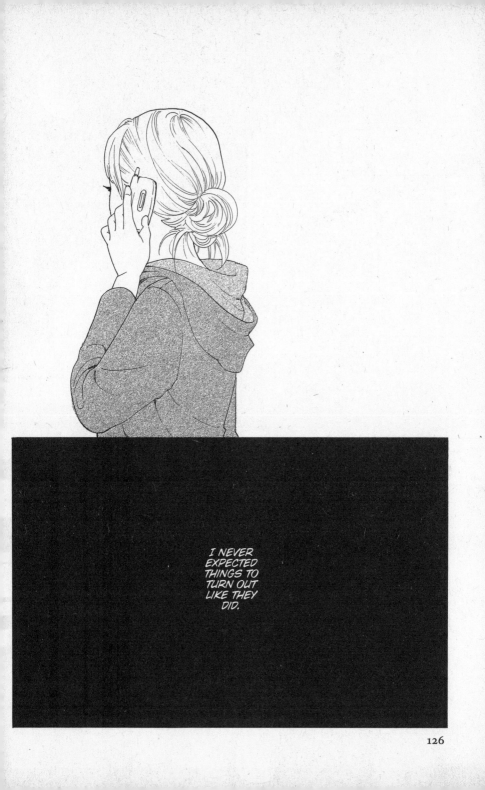

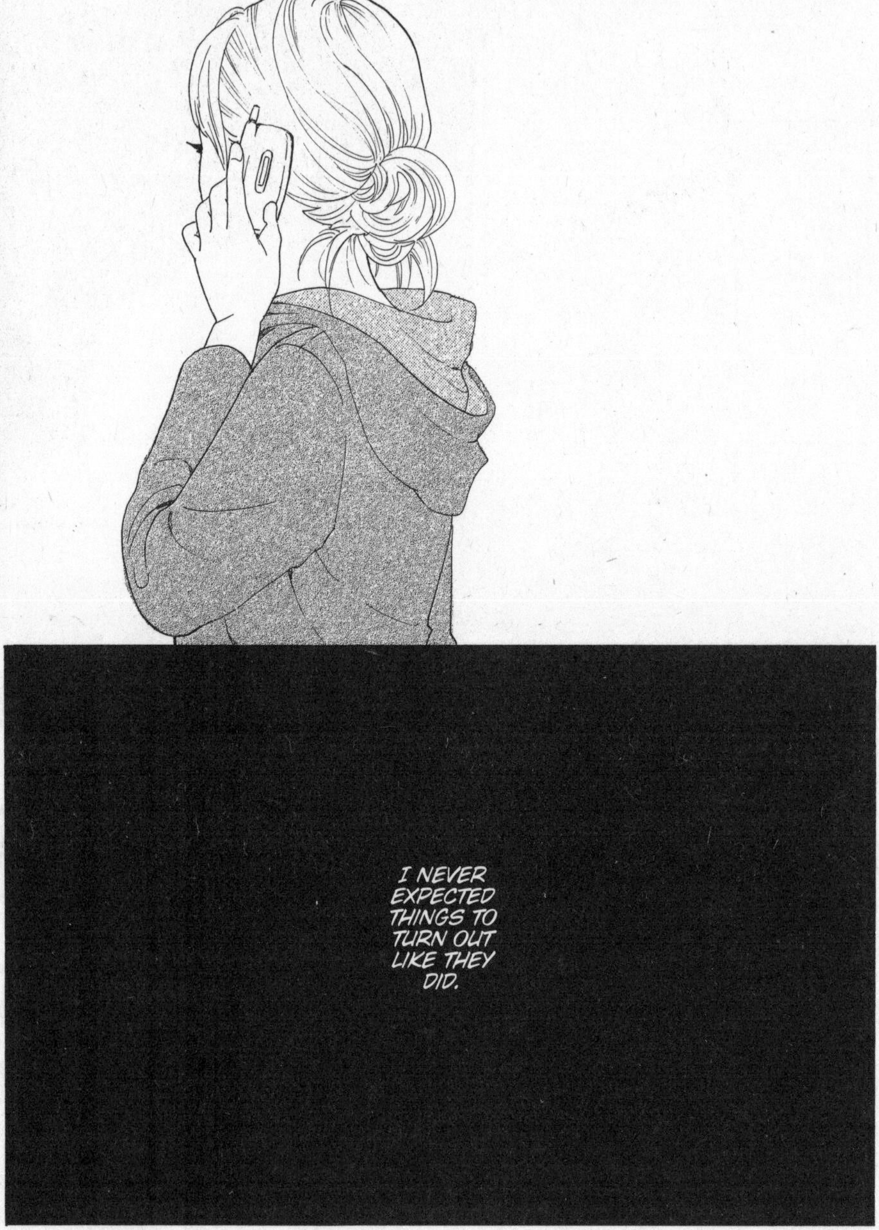
I NEVER EXPECTED THINGS TO TURN OUT LIKE THEY DID.

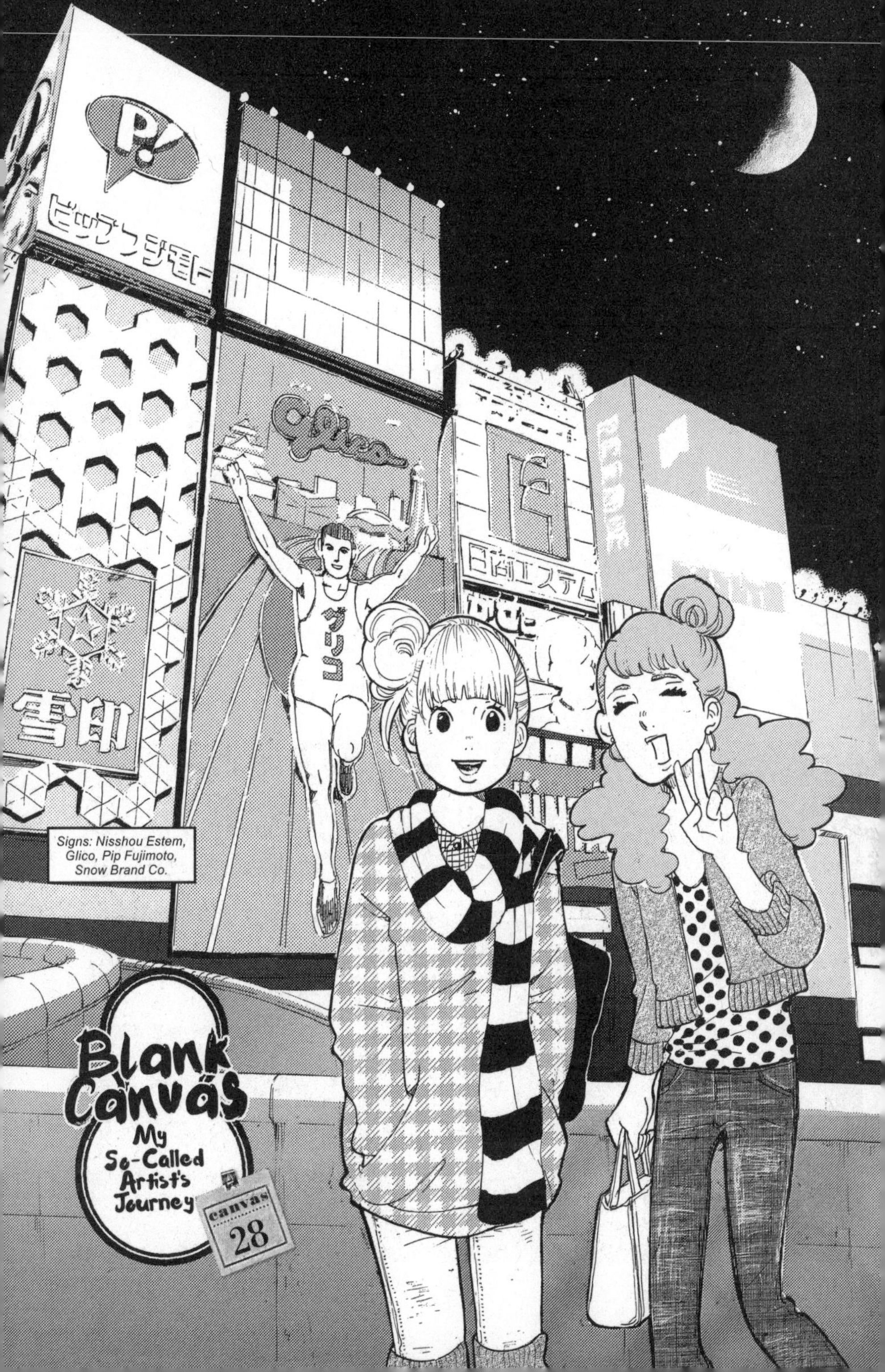
ピップフジモト
グリコ
日商エステム
雪印
Signs: Nisshou Estem, Glico, Pip Fujimoto, Snow Brand Co.
Blank Canvas
My So-Called Artist's Journey
canvas
28

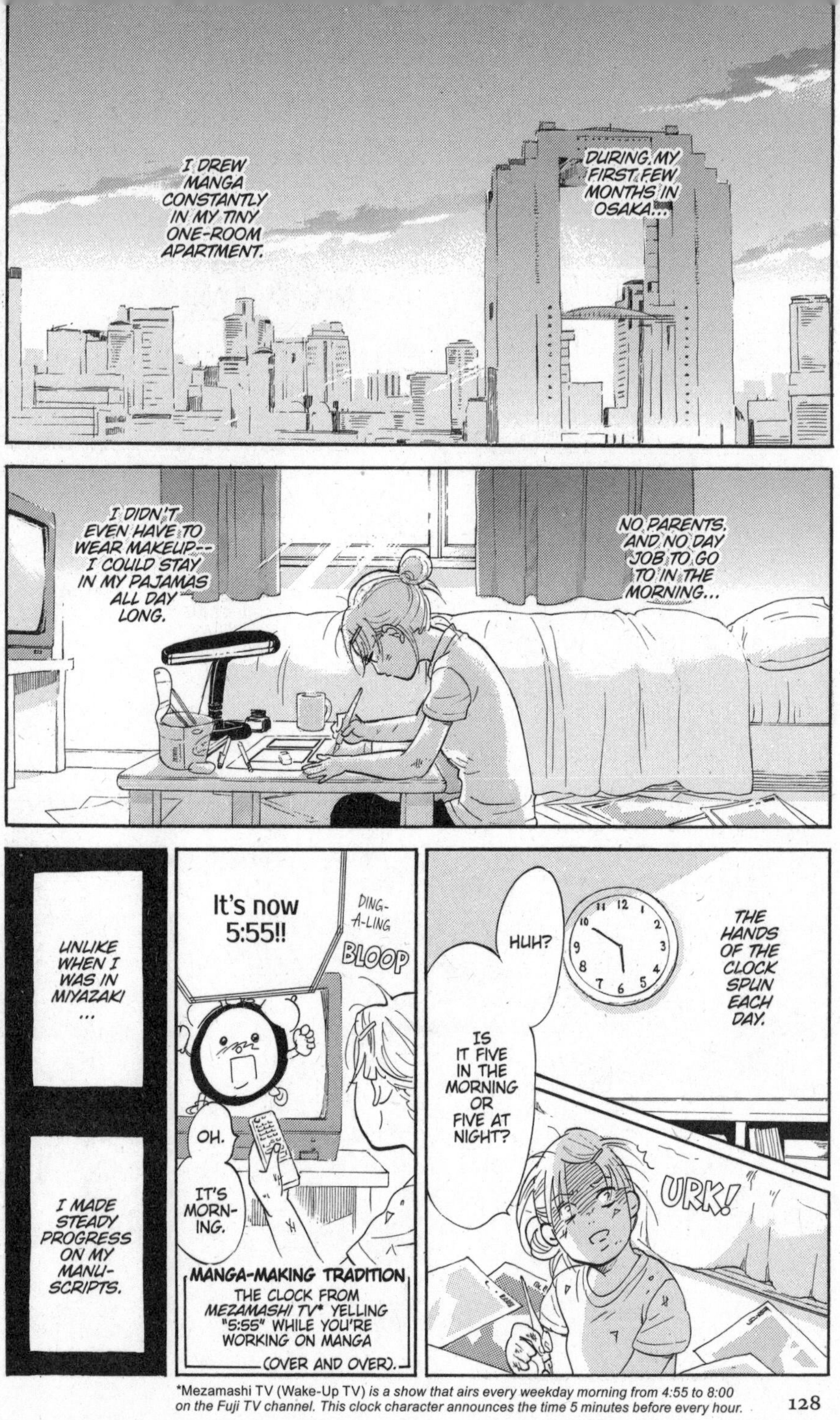
DURING MY FIRST FEW MONTHS IN OSAKA...
I DREW MANGA CONSTANTLY IN MY TINY ONE-ROOM APARTMENT.
NO PARENTS, AND NO DAY JOB TO GO TO IN THE MORNING...
I DIDN'T EVEN HAVE TO WEAR MAKEUP-- I COULD STAY IN MY PAJAMAS ALL DAY LONG.
THE HANDS OF THE CLOCK SPUN EACH DAY.
HUH?
IS IT FIVE IN THE MORNING OR FIVE AT NIGHT?
URK!
It's now 5:55!!
DING-A-LING
BLOOP
OH.
IT'S MORNING.
MANGA-MAKING TRADITION
THE CLOCK FROM *MEZAMASHI TV** YELLING "5:55" WHILE YOU'RE WORKING ON MANGA (OVER AND OVER).
UNLIKE WHEN I WAS IN MIYAZAKI...
I MADE STEADY PROGRESS ON MY MANUSCRIPTS.

*Mezamashi TV (Wake-Up TV) *is a show that airs every weekday morning from 4:55 to 8:00 on the Fuji TV channel. This clock character announces the time 5 minutes before every hour.*

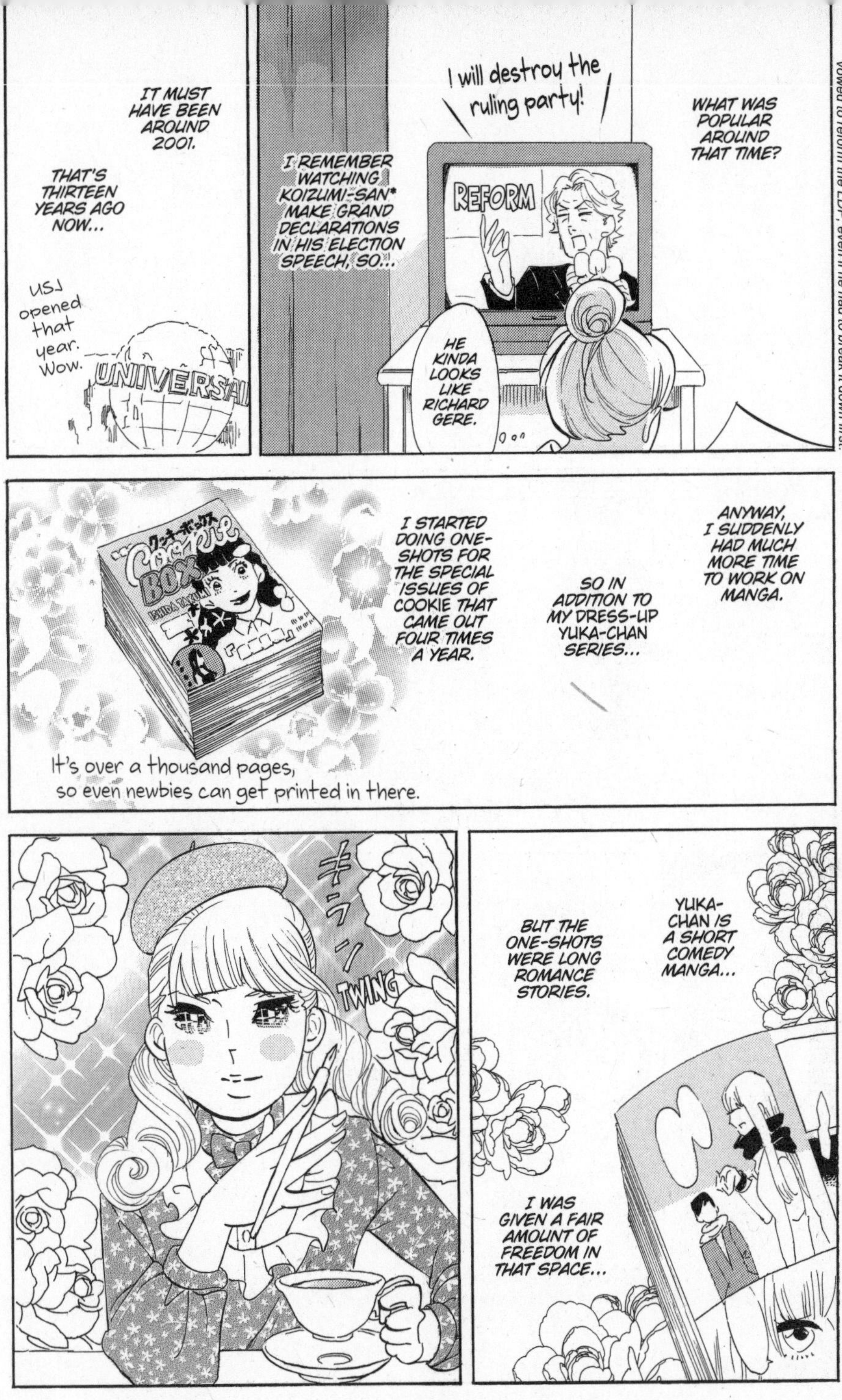
WHAT WAS POPULAR AROUND THAT TIME?
I will destroy the ruling party!
REFORM
I REMEMBER WATCHING KOIZUMI-SAN* MAKE GRAND DECLARATIONS IN HIS ELECTION SPEECH, SO...
HE KINDA LOOKS LIKE RICHARD GERE.
IT MUST HAVE BEEN AROUND 2001.
THAT'S THIRTEEN YEARS AGO NOW...
USJ opened that year. Wow.
UNIVERSAL
ANYWAY, I SUDDENLY HAD MUCH MORE TIME TO WORK ON MANGA.
SO IN ADDITION TO MY DRESS-UP YUKA-CHAN SERIES...
I STARTED DOING ONE-SHOTS FOR THE SPECIAL ISSUES OF COOKIE THAT CAME OUT FOUR TIMES A YEAR.
It's over a thousand pages, so even newbies can get printed in there.
YUKA-CHAN IS A SHORT COMEDY MANGA...
BUT THE ONE-SHOTS WERE LONG ROMANCE STORIES.
I WAS GIVEN A FAIR AMOUNT OF FREEDOM IN THAT SPACE...
TWING

well as president of the Liberal Democratic Party. He famously vowed to reform the LDP, even if he had to break it down first.

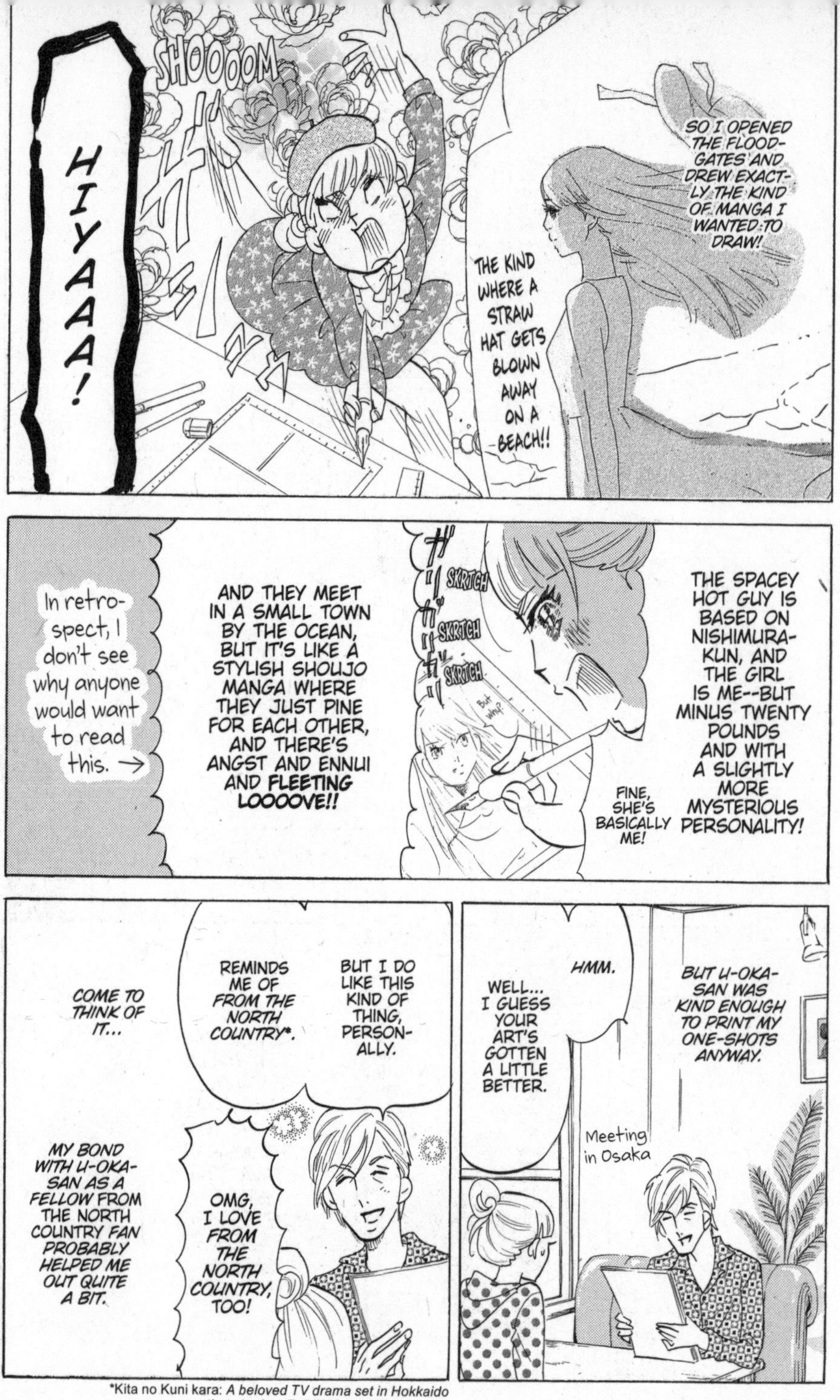
SO I OPENED THE FLOOD-GATES AND DREW EXACTLY THE KIND OF MANGA I WANTED TO DRAW!
THE KIND WHERE A STRAW HAT GETS BLOWN AWAY ON A BEACH!!
SHOOOOM
HIYAAA!
THE SPACEY HOT GUY IS BASED ON NISHIMURA-KUN, AND THE GIRL IS ME--BUT MINUS TWENTY POUNDS AND WITH A SLIGHTLY MORE MYSTERIOUS PERSONALITY!
FINE, SHE'S BASICALLY ME!
SKRTCH
SKRTCH
SKRTCH
But why?
AND THEY MEET IN A SMALL TOWN BY THE OCEAN, BUT IT'S LIKE A STYLISH SHOUJO MANGA WHERE THEY JUST PINE FOR EACH OTHER, AND THERE'S ANGST AND ENNUI AND **FLEETING LOOOOVE!!**
In retrospect, I don't see why anyone would want to read this. →
BUT U-OKA-SAN WAS KIND ENOUGH TO PRINT MY ONE-SHOTS ANYWAY.
HMM.
WELL... I GUESS YOUR ART'S GOTTEN A LITTLE BETTER.
Meeting in Osaka
BUT I DO LIKE THIS KIND OF THING, PERSONALLY.
REMINDS ME OF FROM THE NORTH COUNTRY*.
COME TO THINK OF IT...
OMG, I LOVE FROM THE NORTH COUNTRY, TOO!
MY BOND WITH U-OKA-SAN AS A FELLOW FROM THE NORTH COUNTRY FAN PROBABLY HELPED ME OUT QUITE A BIT.

*Kita no Kuni kara: *A beloved TV drama set in Hokkaido that aired on Fuji TV from 1981 to 2002.*

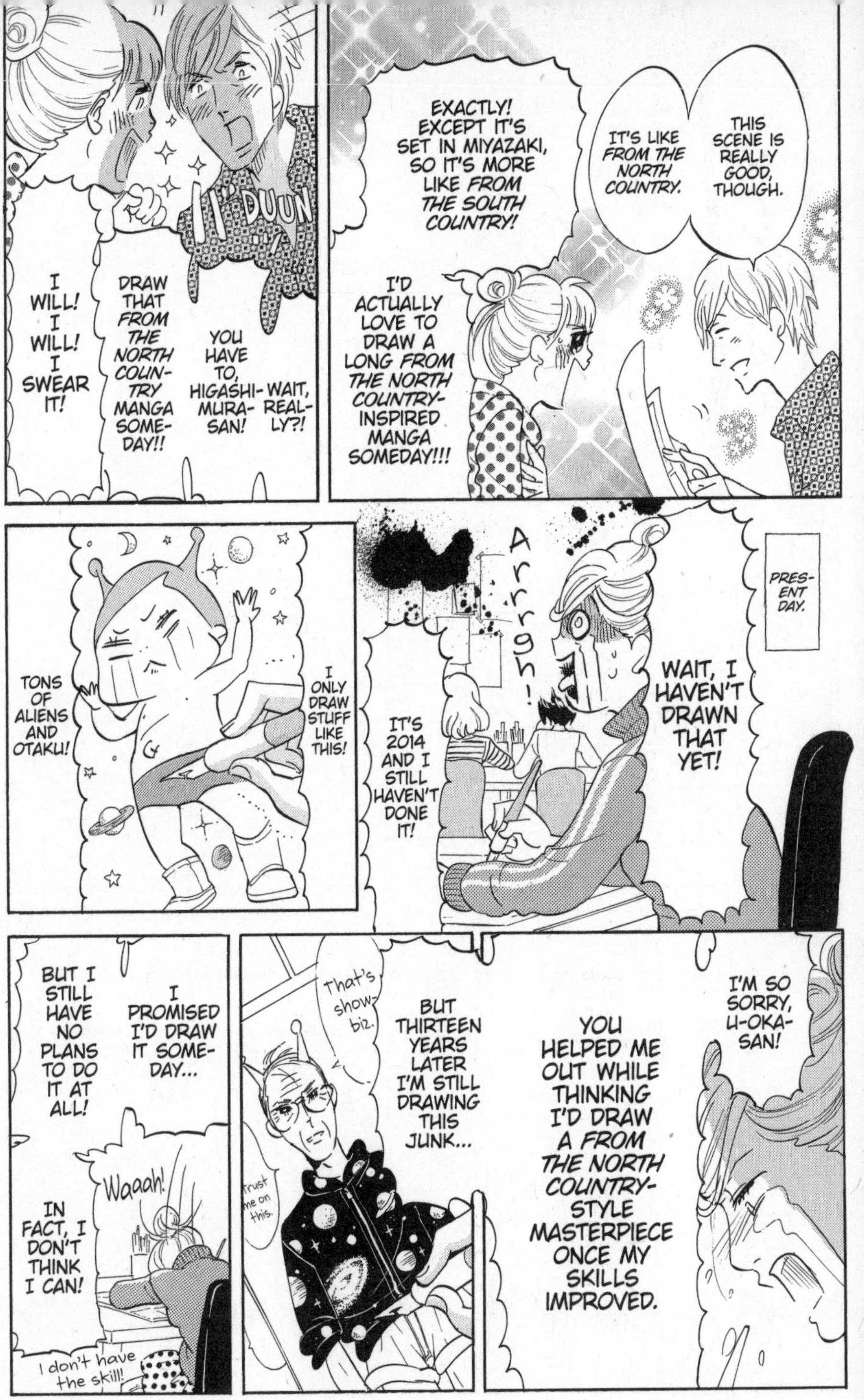
THIS SCENE IS REALLY GOOD, THOUGH.
IT'S LIKE *FROM THE NORTH COUNTRY.*
EXACTLY! EXCEPT IT'S SET IN MIYAZAKI, SO IT'S MORE LIKE *FROM THE SOUTH COUNTRY!*
I'D ACTUALLY LOVE TO DRAW A LONG *FROM THE NORTH COUNTRY*-INSPIRED MANGA SOMEDAY!!!
I'DUUN
WAIT, REALLY?!
YOU HAVE TO, HIGASHIMURA-SAN!
DRAW THAT *FROM THE NORTH COUNTRY* MANGA SOMEDAY!!
I WILL! I WILL! I SWEAR IT!
PRESENT DAY.
WAIT, I HAVEN'T DRAWN THAT YET!
Arrrgh!
IT'S 2014 AND I STILL HAVEN'T DONE IT!
I ONLY DRAW STUFF LIKE THIS!
TONS OF ALIENS AND OTAKU!
I'M SO SORRY, U-OKA-SAN!
YOU HELPED ME OUT WHILE THINKING I'D DRAW A *FROM THE NORTH COUNTRY*-STYLE MASTERPIECE ONCE MY SKILLS IMPROVED.
BUT THIRTEEN YEARS LATER I'M STILL DRAWING THIS JUNK...
That's show-biz.
Trust me on this.
I PROMISED I'D DRAW IT SOMEDAY...
BUT I STILL HAVE NO PLANS TO DO IT AT ALL!
Waaah!
IN FACT, I DON'T THINK I CAN!
I don't have the skill!

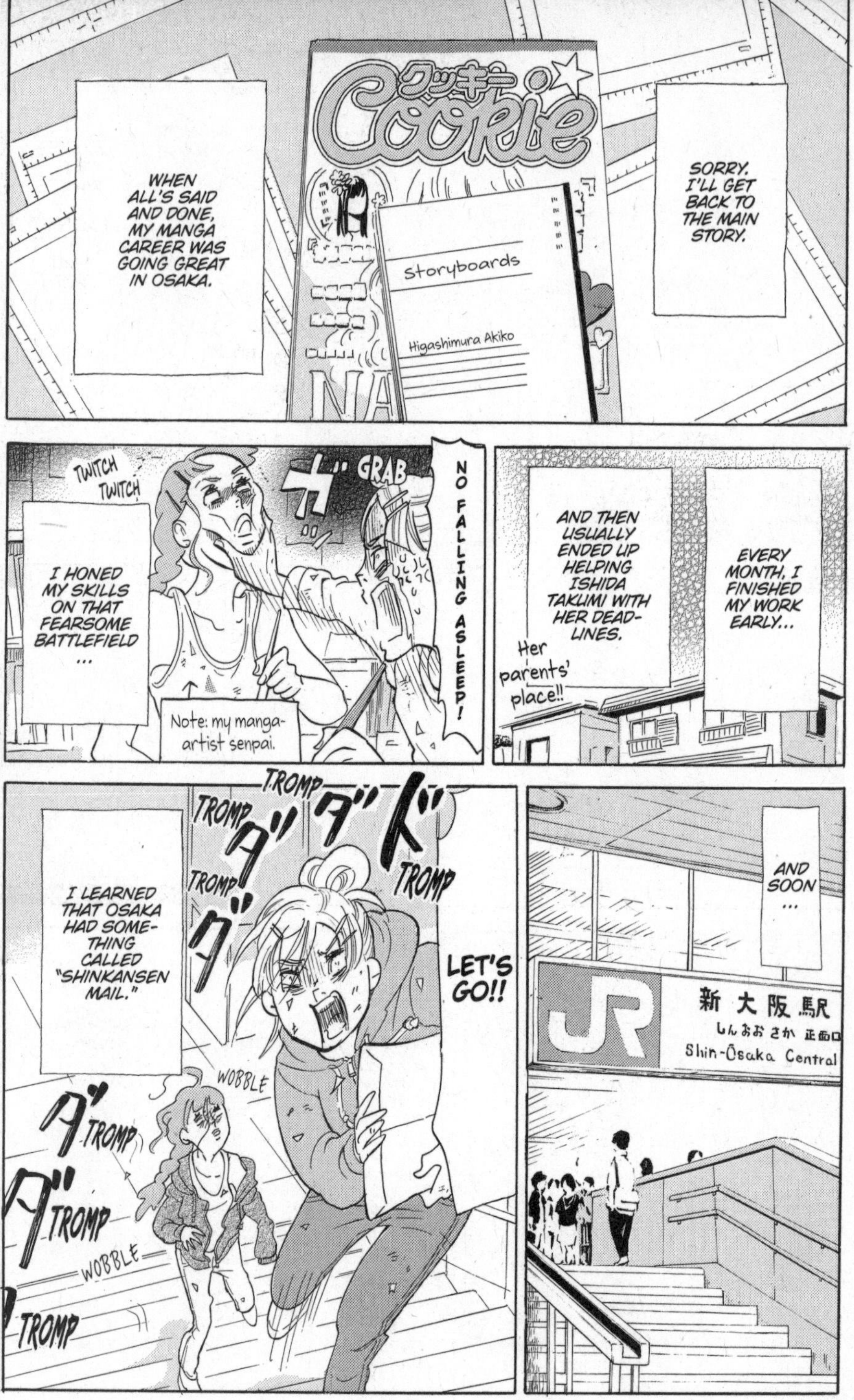
SORRY. I'LL GET BACK TO THE MAIN STORY.
クッキー Cookie
Storyboards
Higashimura Akiko
WHEN ALL'S SAID AND DONE, MY MANGA CAREER WAS GOING GREAT IN OSAKA.
EVERY MONTH, I FINISHED MY WORK EARLY...
AND THEN USUALLY ENDED UP HELPING ISHIDA TAKUMI WITH HER DEAD-LINES.
Her parents' place!!
NO FALLING ASLEEP!
GRAB
TWITCH TWITCH
I HONED MY SKILLS ON THAT FEARSOME BATTLEFIELD ...
Note: my manga-artist senpai.
AND SOON ...
新大阪駅
しんおおさか 正面口
Shin-Ōsaka Central
TROMP
TROMP
TROMP
TROMP
LET'S GO!!
I LEARNED THAT OSAKA HAD SOME-THING CALLED "SHINKANSEN MAIL."
WOBBLE
TROMP
TROMP
WOBBLE
TROMP

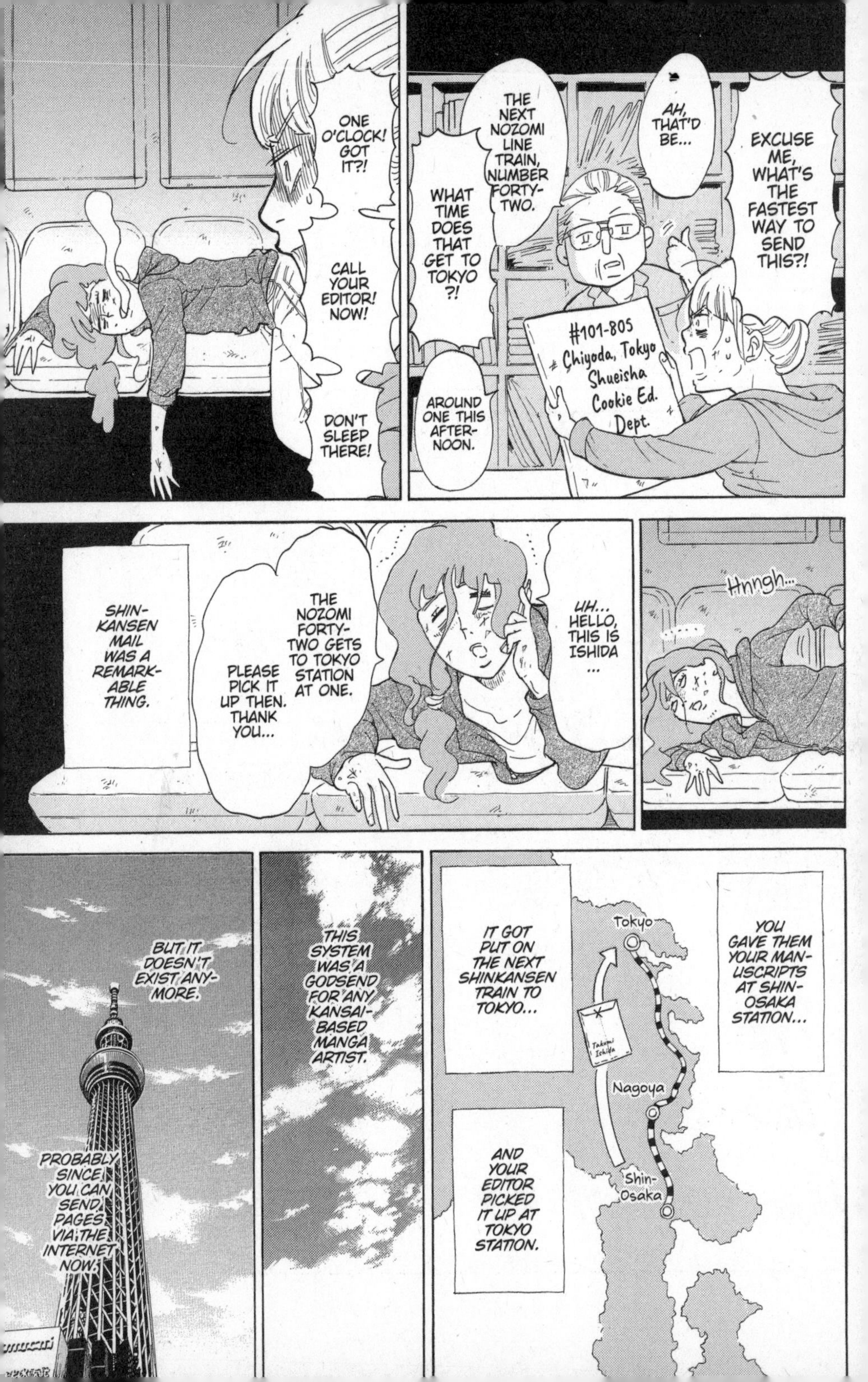
EXCUSE ME, WHAT'S THE FASTEST WAY TO SEND THIS?!
AH, THAT'D BE...
#101-805 Chiyoda, Tokyo Shueisha Cookie Ed. Dept.
THE NEXT NOZOMI LINE TRAIN, NUMBER FORTY-TWO.
WHAT TIME DOES THAT GET TO TOKYO?!
AROUND ONE THIS AFTERNOON.
ONE O'CLOCK! GOT IT?!
CALL YOUR EDITOR! NOW!
DON'T SLEEP THERE!
Hnngh...
.....
UH... HELLO, THIS IS ISHIDA...
THE NOZOMI FORTY-TWO GETS TO TOKYO STATION AT ONE.
PLEASE PICK IT UP THEN. THANK YOU...
SHINKANSEN MAIL WAS A REMARKABLE THING.
YOU GAVE THEM YOUR MANUSCRIPTS AT SHIN-OSAKA STATION...
IT GOT PUT ON THE NEXT SHINKANSEN TRAIN TO TOKYO...
Tokyo
Takumi Ishida
Nagoya
Shin-Osaka
AND YOUR EDITOR PICKED IT UP AT TOKYO STATION.
THIS SYSTEM WAS A GODSEND FOR ANY KANSAI-BASED MANGA ARTIST.
BUT IT DOESN'T EXIST ANYMORE.
PROBABLY SINCE YOU CAN SEND PAGES VIA THE INTERNET NOW.

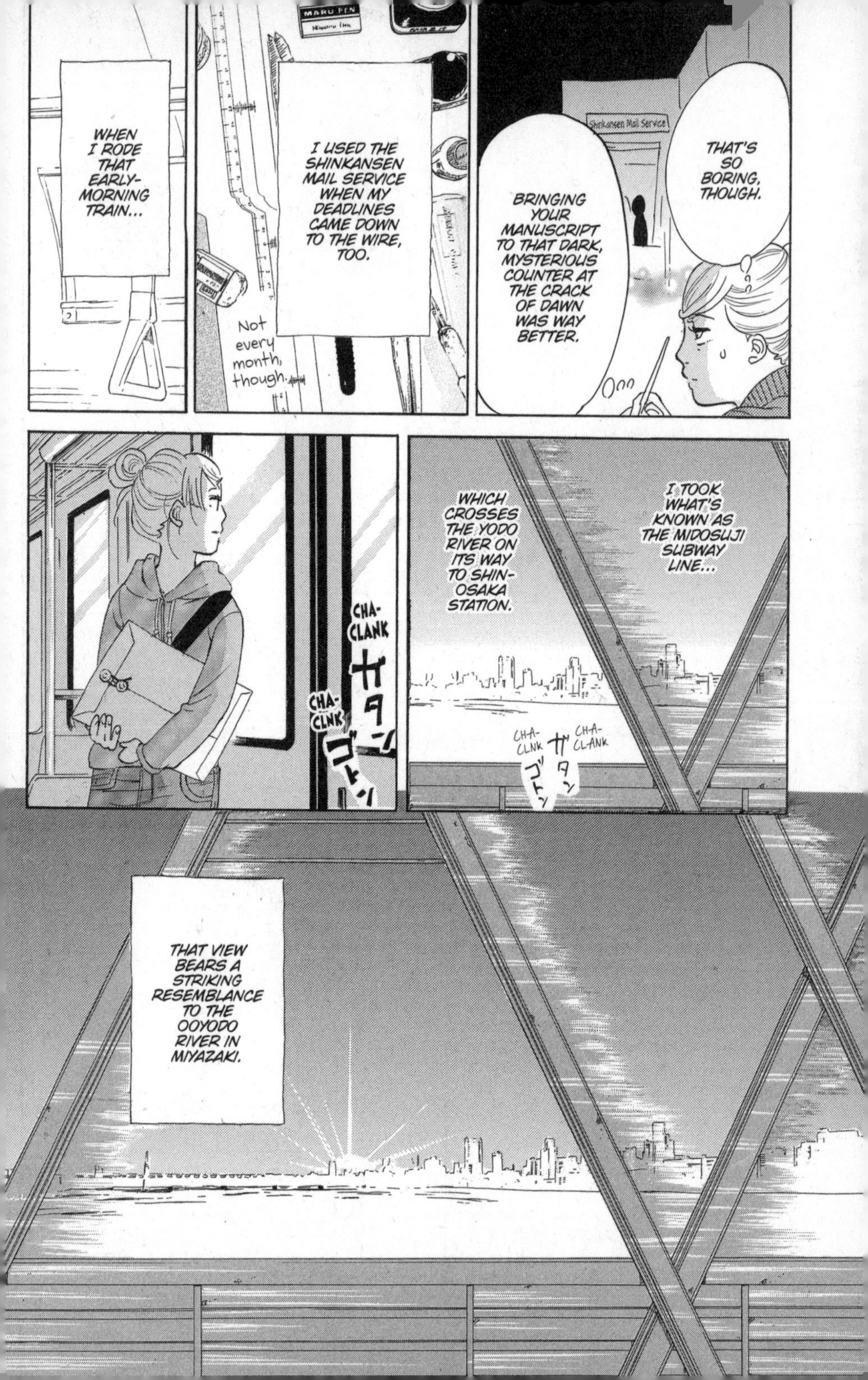
Shinkansen Mail Service
THAT'S SO BORING, THOUGH.
BRINGING YOUR MANUSCRIPT TO THAT DARK, MYSTERIOUS COUNTER AT THE CRACK OF DAWN WAS WAY BETTER.
MARU PEN
I USED THE SHINKANSEN MAIL SERVICE WHEN MY DEADLINES CAME DOWN TO THE WIRE, TOO.
Not every month, though.
WHEN I RODE THAT EARLY-MORNING TRAIN...
I TOOK WHAT'S KNOWN AS THE MIDOSUJI SUBWAY LINE...
WHICH CROSSES THE YODO RIVER ON ITS WAY TO SHIN-OSAKA STATION.
CHA-CLANK
ガタン
CHA-CLNK
ゴトン
CHA-CLANK
ガタン
CHA-CLNK
ゴトン
THAT VIEW BEARS A STRIKING RESEMBLANCE TO THE OOYODO RIVER IN MIYAZAKI.

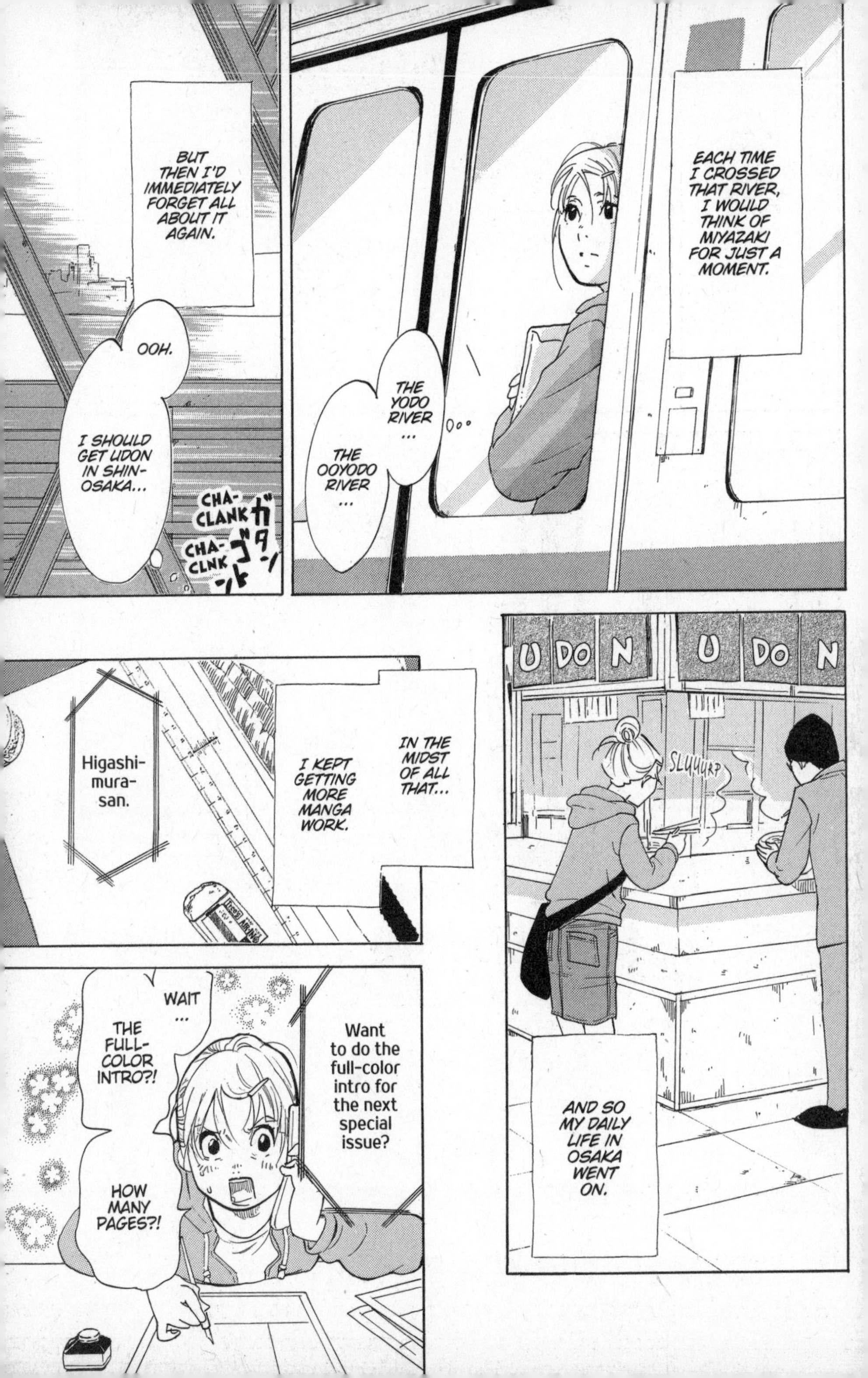

EACH TIME I CROSSED THAT RIVER, I WOULD THINK OF MIYAZAKI FOR JUST A MOMENT.
THE YODO RIVER ...
THE OOYODO RIVER ...
BUT THEN I'D IMMEDIATELY FORGET ALL ABOUT IT AGAIN.
OOH.
I SHOULD GET UDON IN SHIN-OSAKA...
CHA-CLANK
CHA-CLNK
UDON
UDON
SLUUURP
AND SO MY DAILY LIFE IN OSAKA WENT ON.
IN THE MIDST OF ALL THAT...
I KEPT GETTING MORE MANGA WORK.
Higashi-mura-san.
Want to do the full-color intro for the next special issue?
WAIT ...
THE FULL-COLOR INTRO?!
HOW MANY PAGES?!

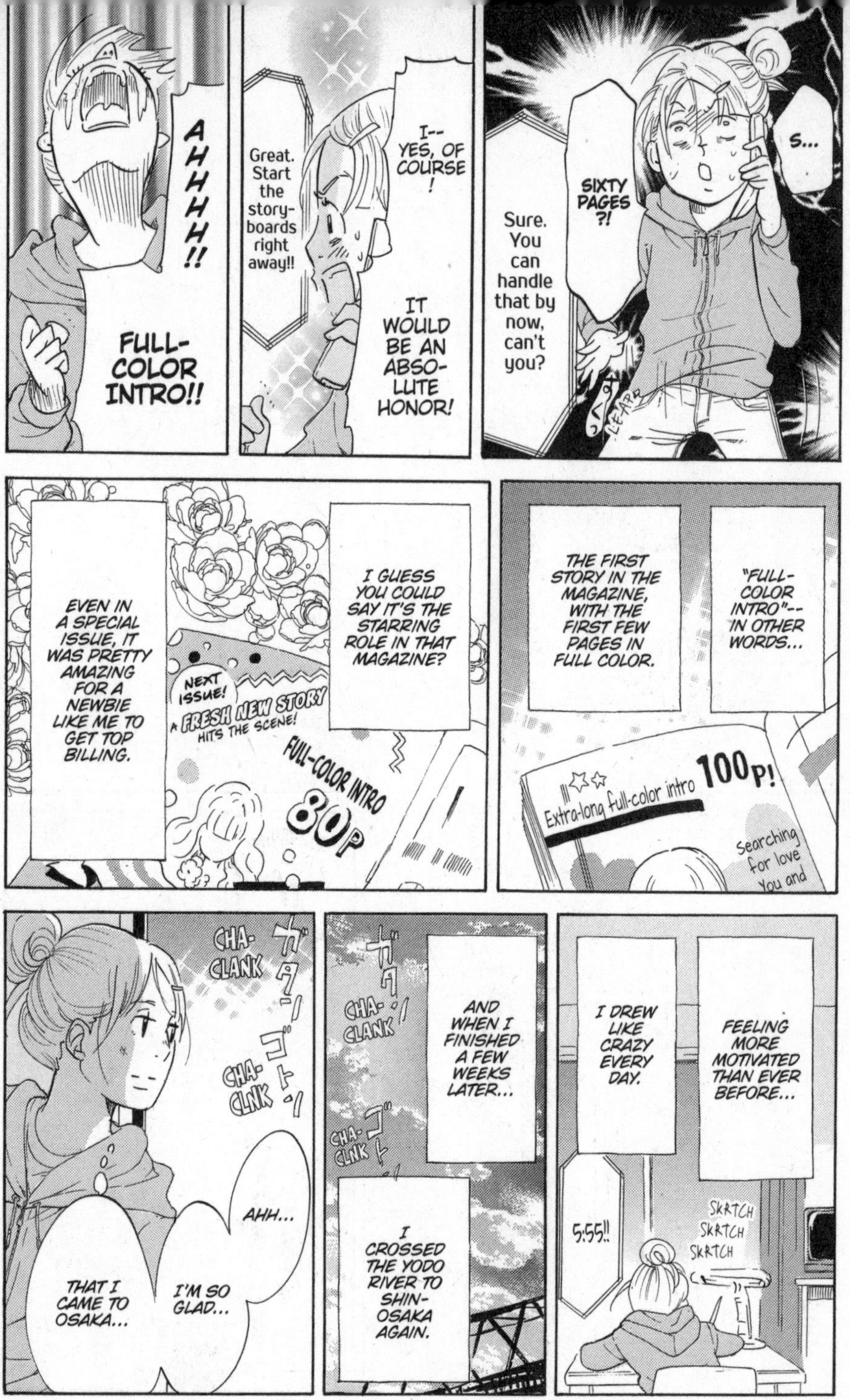
S...
SIXTY PAGES ?!
Sure. You can handle that by now, can't you?
LEAP
I-- YES, OF COURSE!
Great. Start the story-boards right away!!
IT WOULD BE AN ABSO-LUTE HONOR!
AHHHHH!!
FULL-COLOR INTRO!!
"FULL-COLOR INTRO"-- IN OTHER WORDS...
THE FIRST STORY IN THE MAGAZINE, WITH THE FIRST FEW PAGES IN FULL COLOR.
Extra-long full-color intro 100P!
Searching for love You and
I GUESS YOU COULD SAY IT'S THE STARRING ROLE IN THAT MAGAZINE?
NEXT ISSUE!
A FRESH NEW STORY HITS THE SCENE!
FULL-COLOR INTRO 80P
EVEN IN A SPECIAL ISSUE, IT WAS PRETTY AMAZING FOR A NEWBIE LIKE ME TO GET TOP BILLING.
FEELING MORE MOTIVATED THAN EVER BEFORE...
I DREW LIKE CRAZY EVERY DAY.
5:55!!
SKRTCH SKRTCH SKRTCH
AND WHEN I FINISHED A FEW WEEKS LATER...
CHA-CLANK
CHA-CLNK
I CROSSED THE YODO RIVER TO SHIN-OSAKA AGAIN.
CHA-CLANK
CHA-CLNK
AHH...
I'M SO GLAD...
THAT I CAME TO OSAKA...

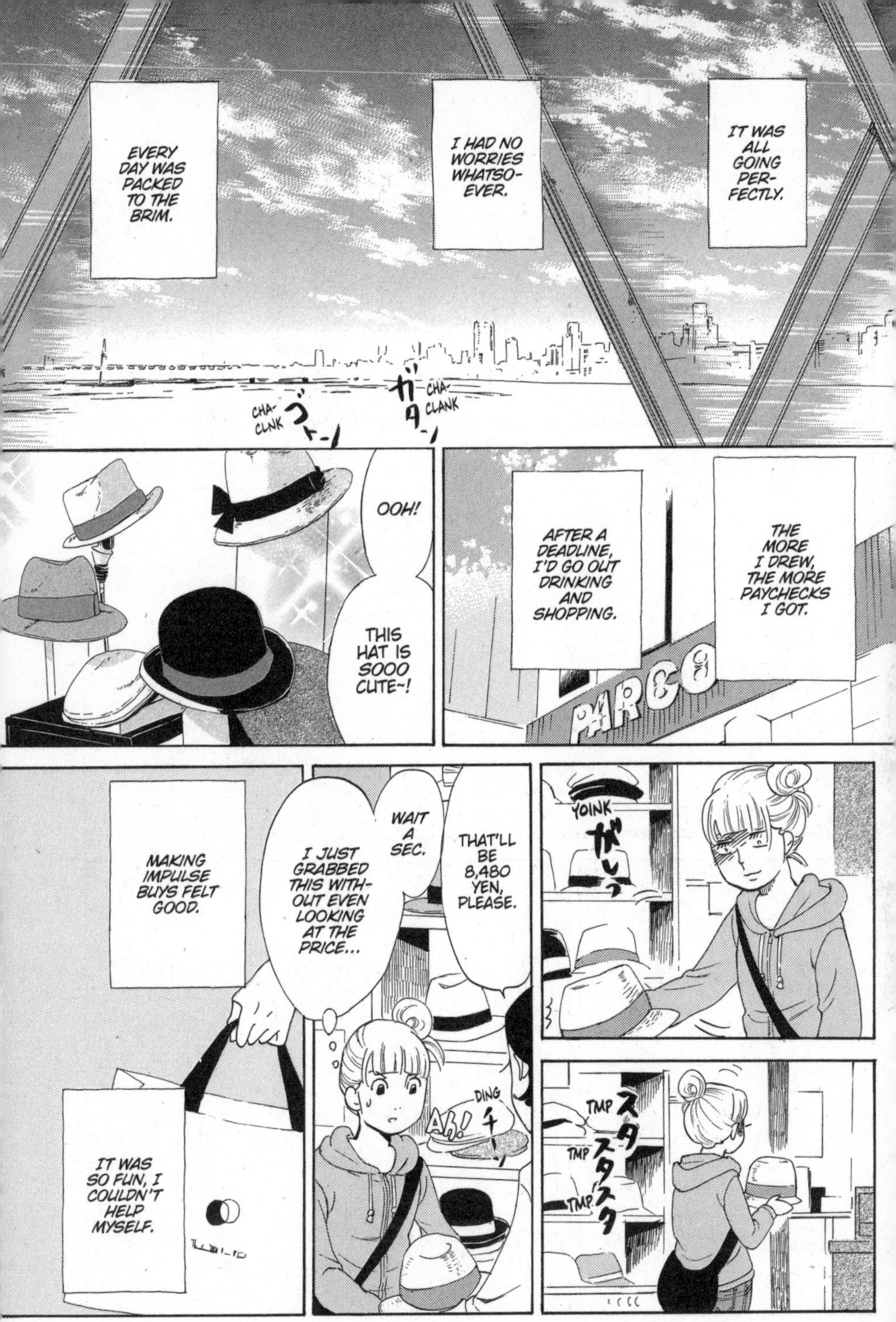
IT WAS ALL GOING PER-FECTLY.
I HAD NO WORRIES WHATSO-EVER.
EVERY DAY WAS PACKED TO THE BRIM.
CHA-CLANK
CHA-CLNK
THE MORE I DREW, THE MORE PAYCHECKS I GOT.
AFTER A DEADLINE, I'D GO OUT DRINKING AND SHOPPING.
OOH!
THIS HAT IS SOOO CUTE~!
YOINK
TMP
TMP
TMP
THAT'LL BE 8,480 YEN, PLEASE.
WAIT A SEC.
I JUST GRABBED THIS WITH-OUT EVEN LOOKING AT THE PRICE...
DING
Ah!
MAKING IMPULSE BUYS FELT GOOD.
IT WAS SO FUN, I COULDN'T HELP MYSELF.

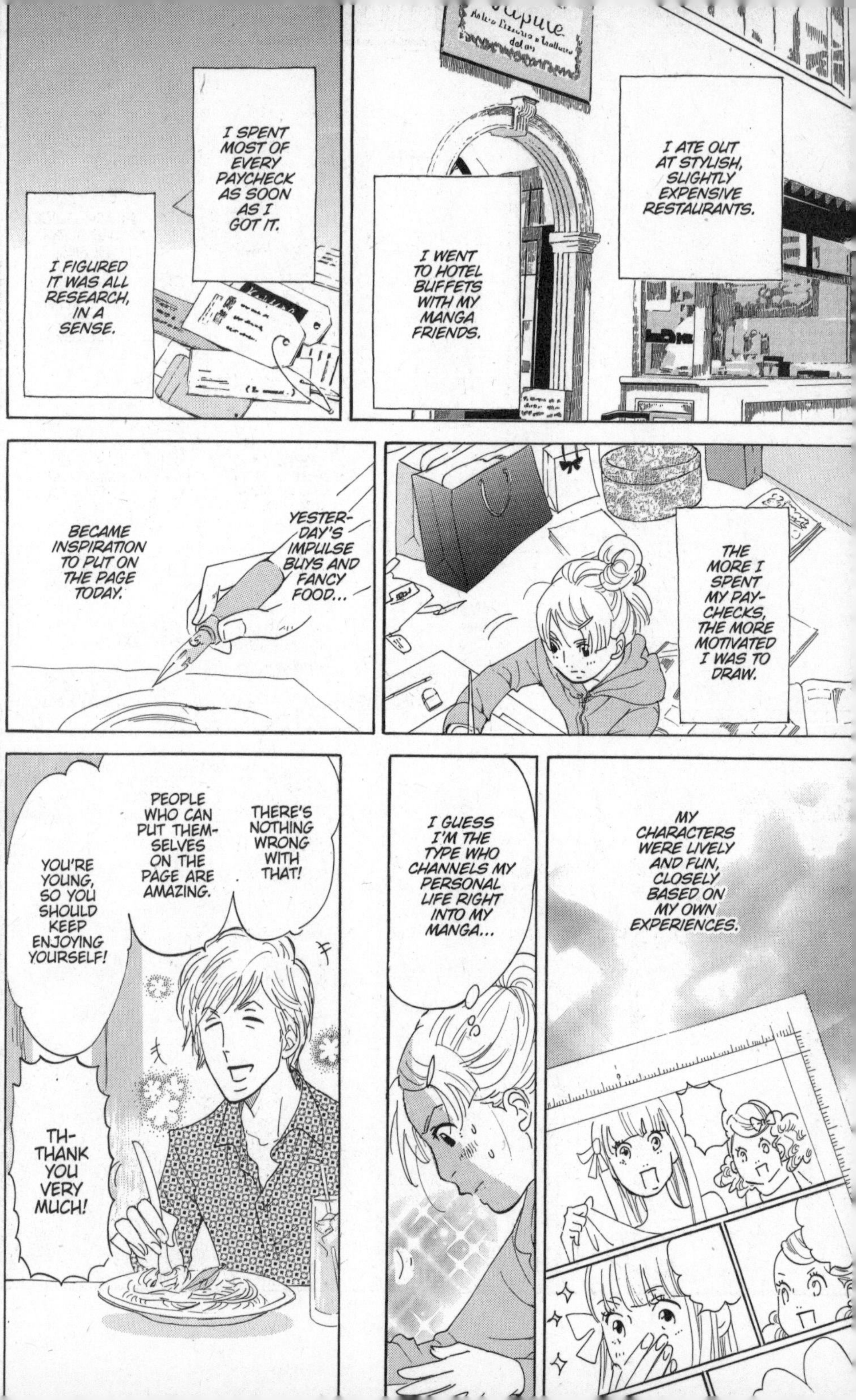
I ATE OUT AT STYLISH, SLIGHTLY EXPENSIVE RESTAURANTS.
I WENT TO HOTEL BUFFETS WITH MY MANGA FRIENDS.
I SPENT MOST OF EVERY PAYCHECK AS SOON AS I GOT IT.
I FIGURED IT WAS ALL RESEARCH, IN A SENSE.
THE MORE I SPENT MY PAYCHECKS, THE MORE MOTIVATED I WAS TO DRAW.
YESTERDAY'S IMPULSE BUYS AND FANCY FOOD...
BECAME INSPIRATION TO PUT ON THE PAGE TODAY.
MY CHARACTERS WERE LIVELY AND FUN, CLOSELY BASED ON MY OWN EXPERIENCES.
I GUESS I'M THE TYPE WHO CHANNELS MY PERSONAL LIFE RIGHT INTO MY MANGA...
THERE'S NOTHING WRONG WITH THAT!
PEOPLE WHO CAN PUT THEMSELVES ON THE PAGE ARE AMAZING.
YOU'RE YOUNG, SO YOU SHOULD KEEP ENJOYING YOURSELF!
TH-THANK YOU VERY MUCH!

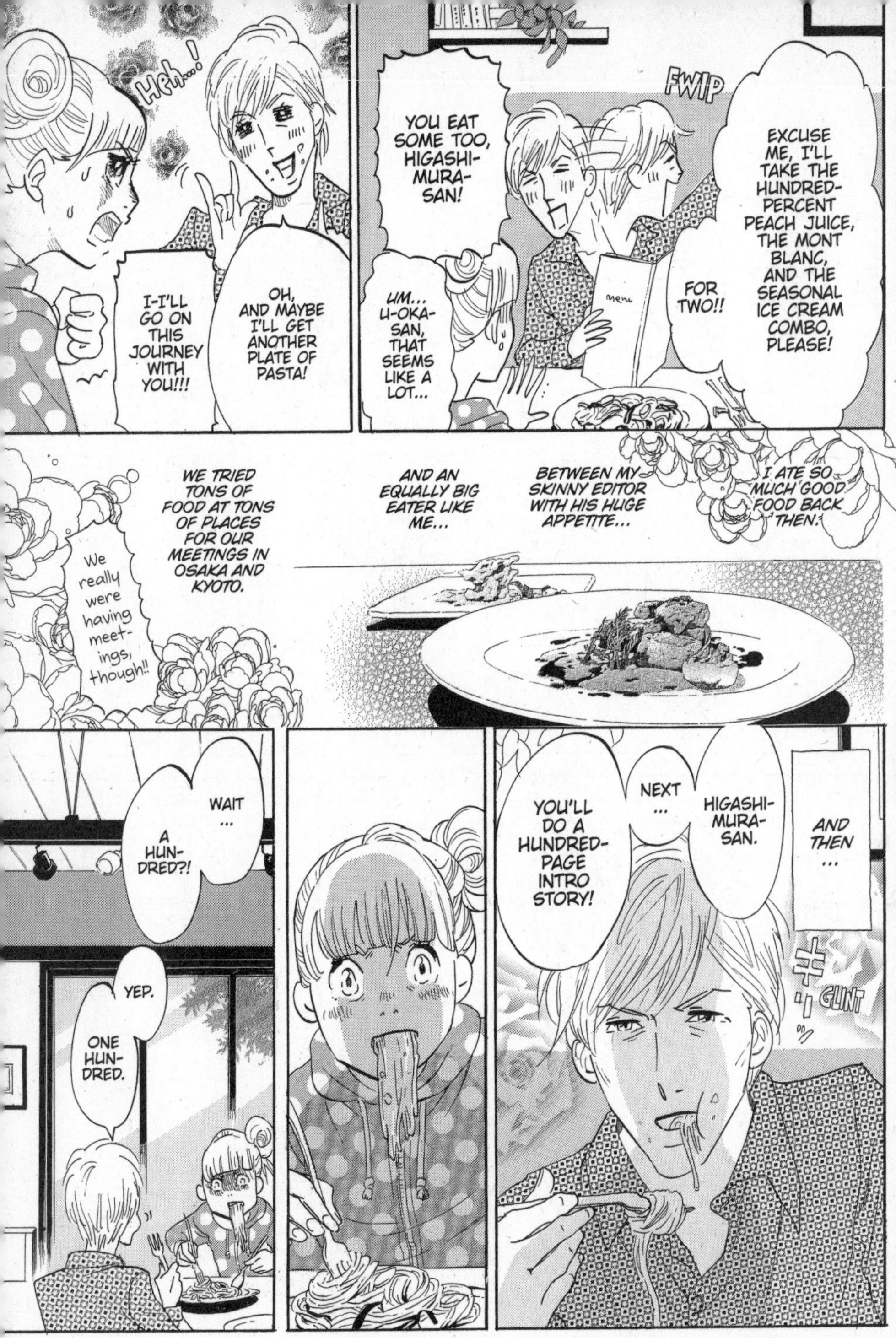
FWIP
EXCUSE ME, I'LL TAKE THE HUNDRED-PERCENT PEACH JUICE, THE MONT BLANC, AND THE SEASONAL ICE CREAM COMBO, PLEASE!
FOR TWO!!
YOU EAT SOME TOO, HIGASHIMURA-SAN!
UM... U-OKA-SAN, THAT SEEMS LIKE A LOT...
Heh...!
OH, AND MAYBE I'LL GET ANOTHER PLATE OF PASTA!
I-I'LL GO ON THIS JOURNEY WITH YOU!!!
I ATE SO MUCH GOOD FOOD BACK THEN.
BETWEEN MY SKINNY EDITOR WITH HIS HUGE APPETITE...
AND AN EQUALLY BIG EATER LIKE ME...
WE TRIED TONS OF FOOD AT TONS OF PLACES FOR OUR MEETINGS IN OSAKA AND KYOTO.
We really were having meetings, though!!
AND THEN...
HIGASHIMURA-SAN.
NEXT...
YOU'LL DO A HUNDRED-PAGE INTRO STORY!
GLINT
WAIT...
A HUNDRED?!
YEP.
ONE HUNDRED.

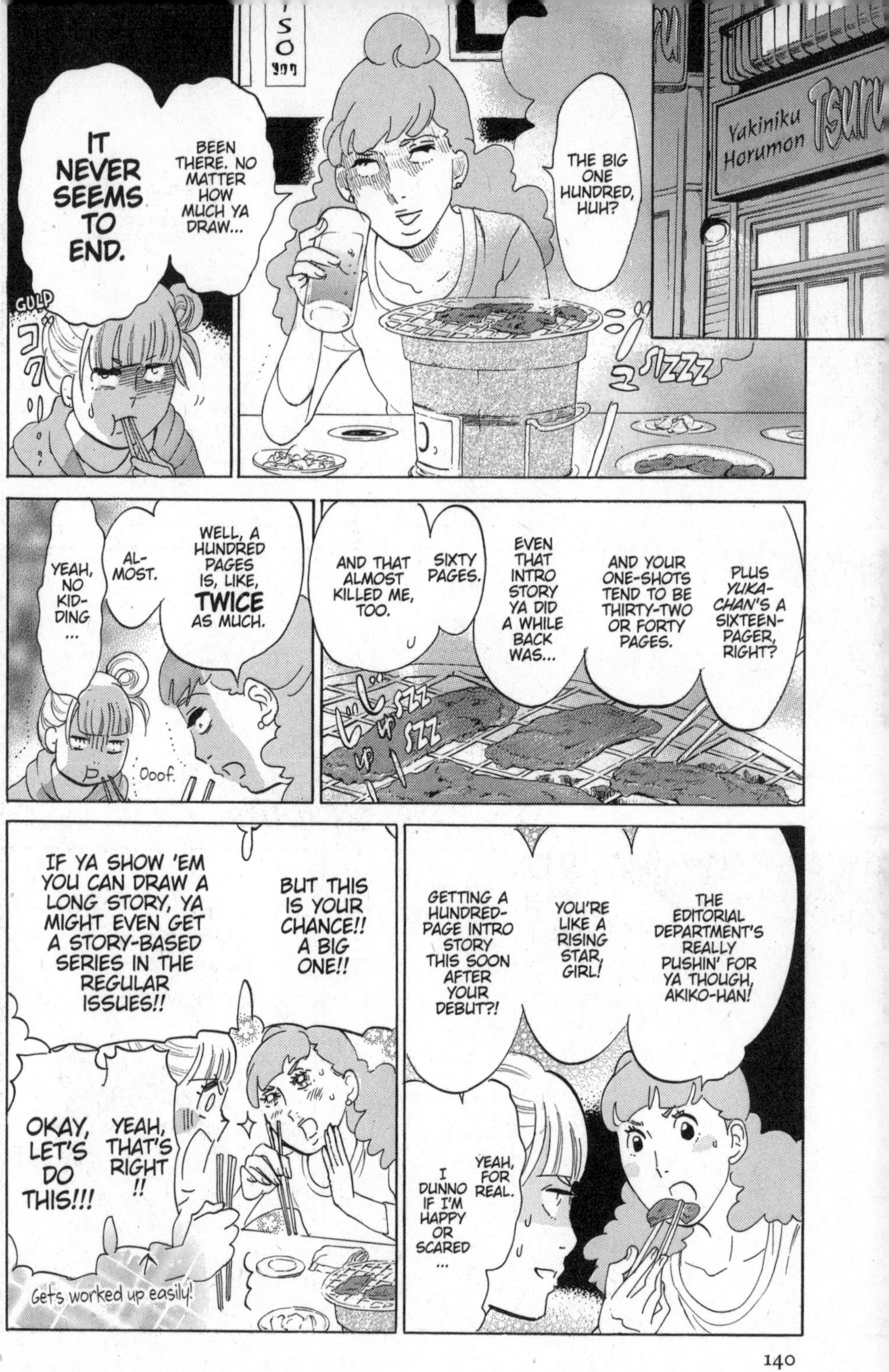
Yakiniku Horumon Tsuru
THE BIG ONE HUNDRED, HUH?
BEEN THERE. NO MATTER HOW MUCH YA DRAW...
IT NEVER SEEMS TO END.
GULP
SIZZZ
PLUS YUKA-CHAN'S A SIXTEEN-PAGER, RIGHT?
AND YOUR ONE-SHOTS TEND TO BE THIRTY-TWO OR FORTY PAGES.
EVEN THAT INTRO STORY YA DID A WHILE BACK WAS...
SIXTY PAGES.
AND THAT ALMOST KILLED ME, TOO.
SZZ
SZZ
WELL, A HUNDRED PAGES IS, LIKE, TWICE AS MUCH.
AL-MOST.
YEAH, NO KID-DING...
Ooof.
THE EDITORIAL DEPARTMENT'S REALLY PUSHIN' FOR YA THOUGH, AKIKO-HAN!
YOU'RE LIKE A RISING STAR, GIRL!
GETTING A HUNDRED-PAGE INTRO STORY THIS SOON AFTER YOUR DEBUT?!
YEAH, FOR REAL.
I DUNNO IF I'M HAPPY OR SCARED...
BUT THIS IS YOUR CHANCE!! A BIG ONE!!
IF YA SHOW 'EM YOU CAN DRAW A LONG STORY, YA MIGHT EVEN GET A STORY-BASED SERIES IN THE REGULAR ISSUES!!
YEAH, THAT'S RIGHT!!
OKAY, LET'S DO THIS!!!
Gets worked up easily!

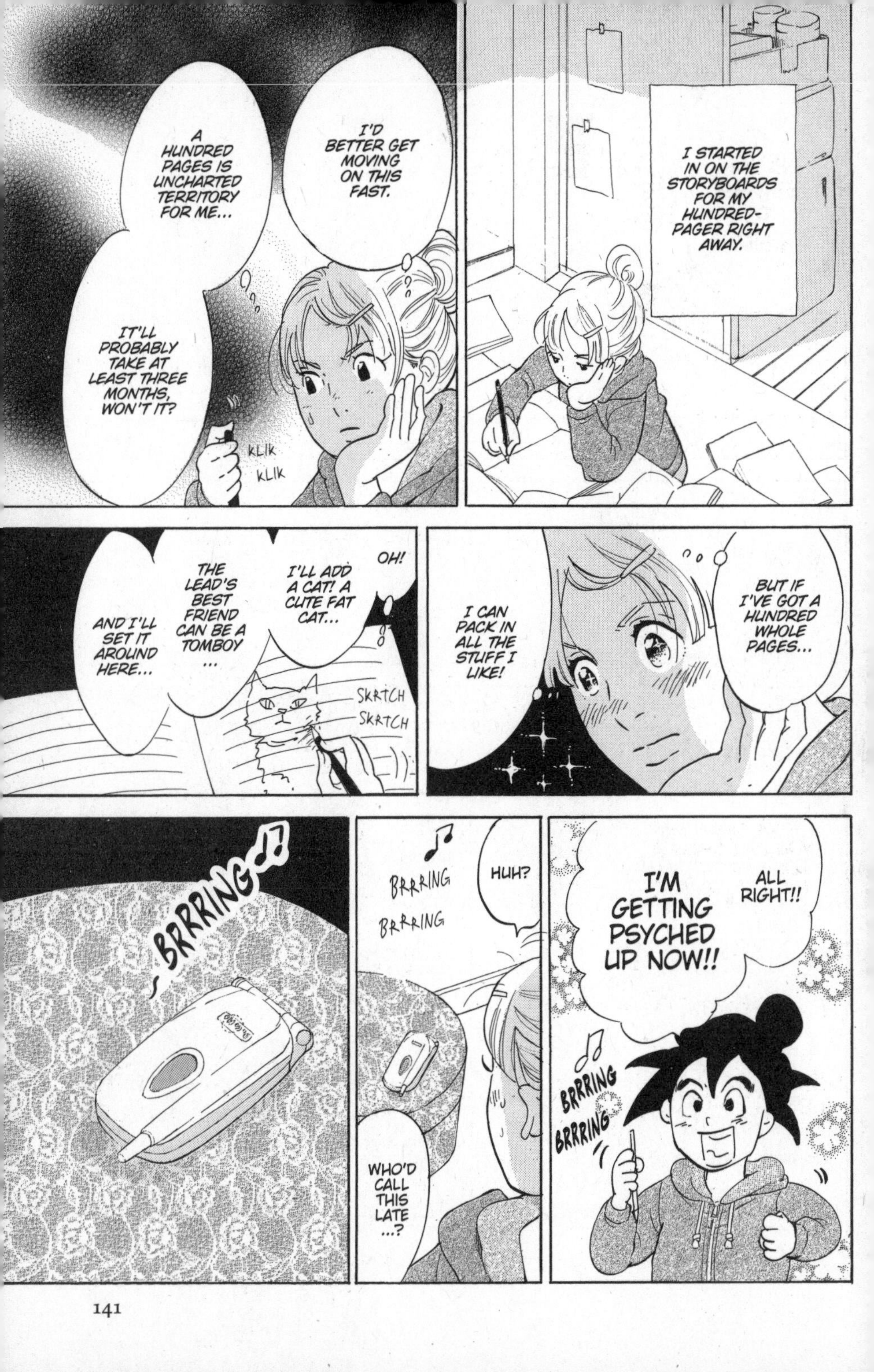
I STARTED IN ON THE STORYBOARDS FOR MY HUNDRED-PAGER RIGHT AWAY.
I'D BETTER GET MOVING ON THIS FAST.
A HUNDRED PAGES IS UNCHARTED TERRITORY FOR ME...
IT'LL PROBABLY TAKE AT LEAST THREE MONTHS, WON'T IT?
KLIK
KLIK
BUT IF I'VE GOT A HUNDRED WHOLE PAGES...
I CAN PACK IN ALL THE STUFF I LIKE!
OH!
I'LL ADD A CAT! A CUTE FAT CAT...
THE LEAD'S BEST FRIEND CAN BE A TOMBOY...
AND I'LL SET IT AROUND HERE...
SKRTCH
SKRTCH
ALL RIGHT!!
I'M GETTING PSYCHED UP NOW!!
BRRRING
BRRRING
HUH?
BRRRING
BRRRING
WHO'D CALL THIS LATE...?
BRRRING

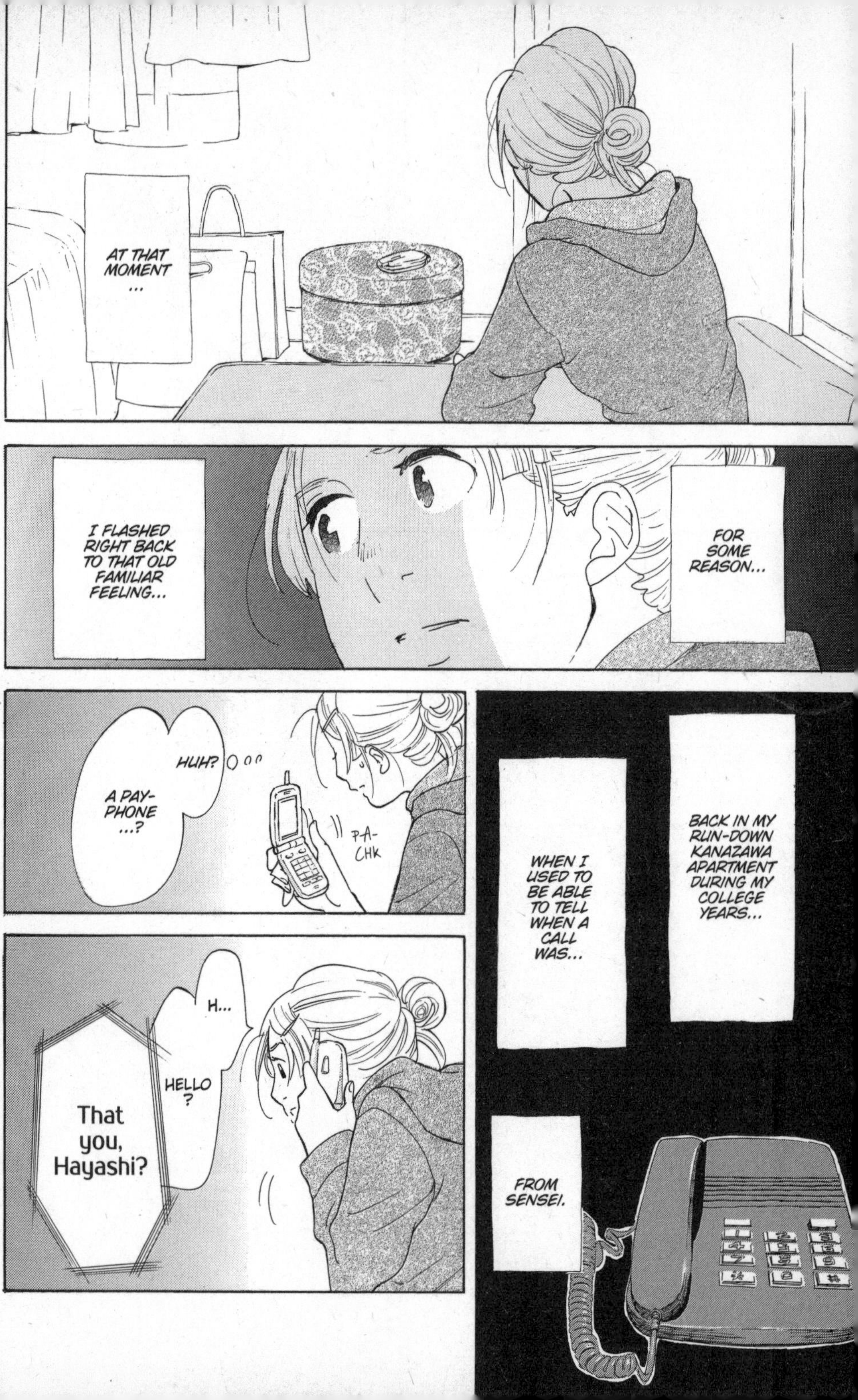
AT THAT MOMENT ...
FOR SOME REASON...
I FLASHED RIGHT BACK TO THAT OLD FAMILIAR FEELING...
BACK IN MY RUN-DOWN KANAZAWA APARTMENT DURING MY COLLEGE YEARS...
WHEN I USED TO BE ABLE TO TELL WHEN A CALL WAS...
FROM SENSEI.
HUH?
A PAY-PHONE ...?
P-A-CHK
H...
HELLO ?
That you, Hayashi?

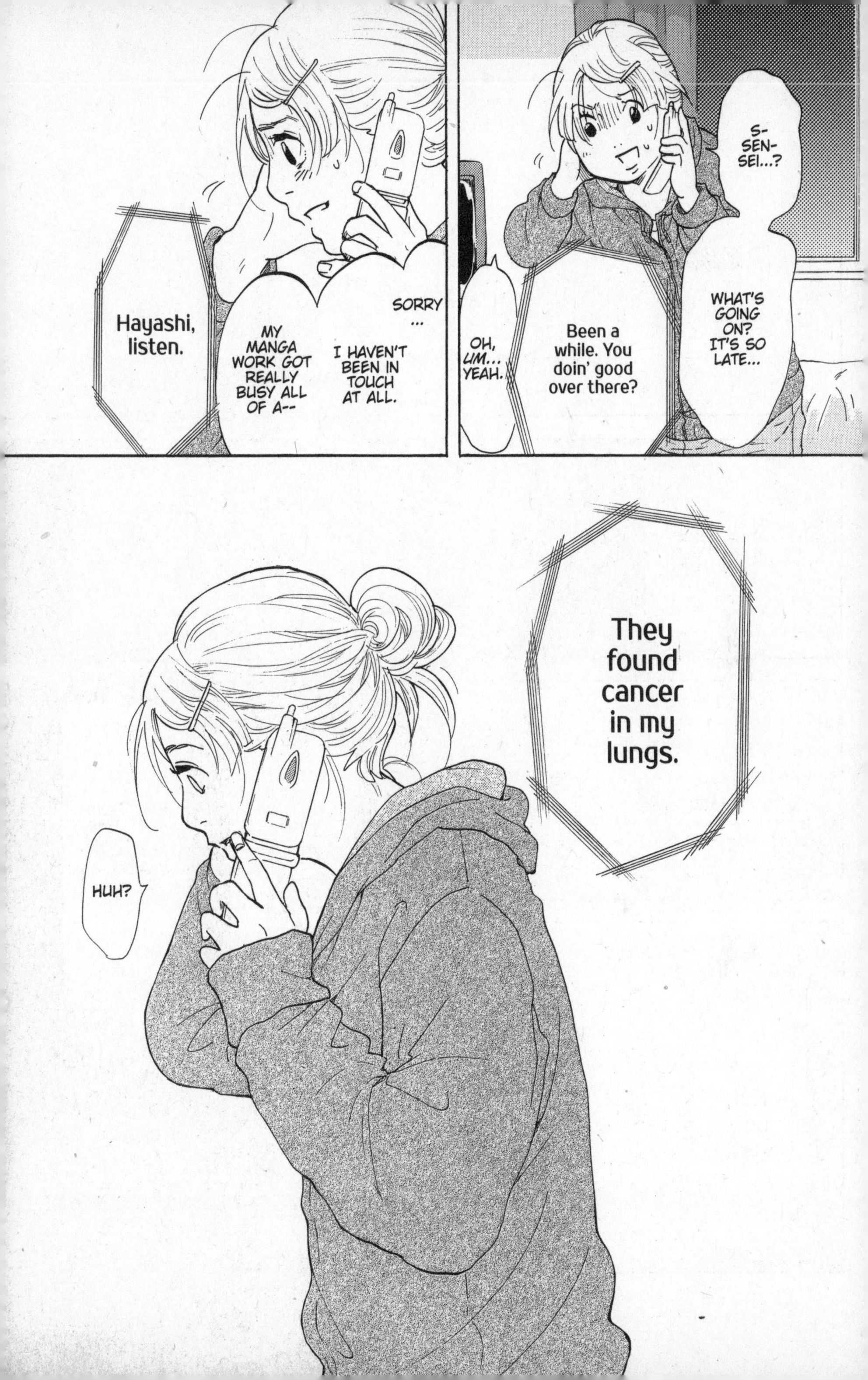
S-SEN-SEI...?
WHAT'S GOING ON? IT'S SO LATE...
Been a while. You doin' good over there?
OH, UM... YEAH.
SORRY...
I HAVEN'T BEEN IN TOUCH AT ALL.
MY MANGA WORK GOT REALLY BUSY ALL OF A--
Hayashi, listen.
They found cancer in my lungs.
HUH?

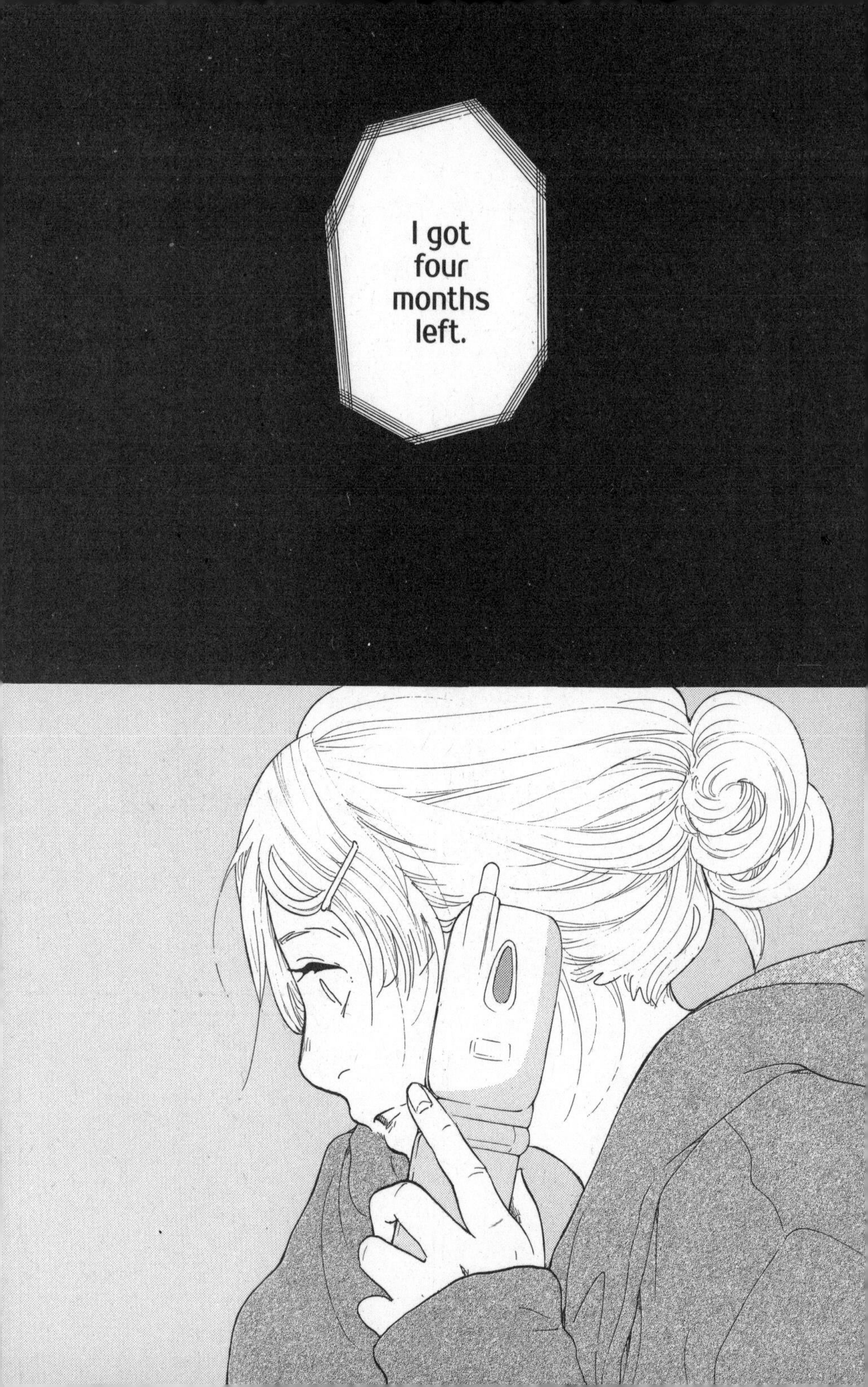
I got four months left.

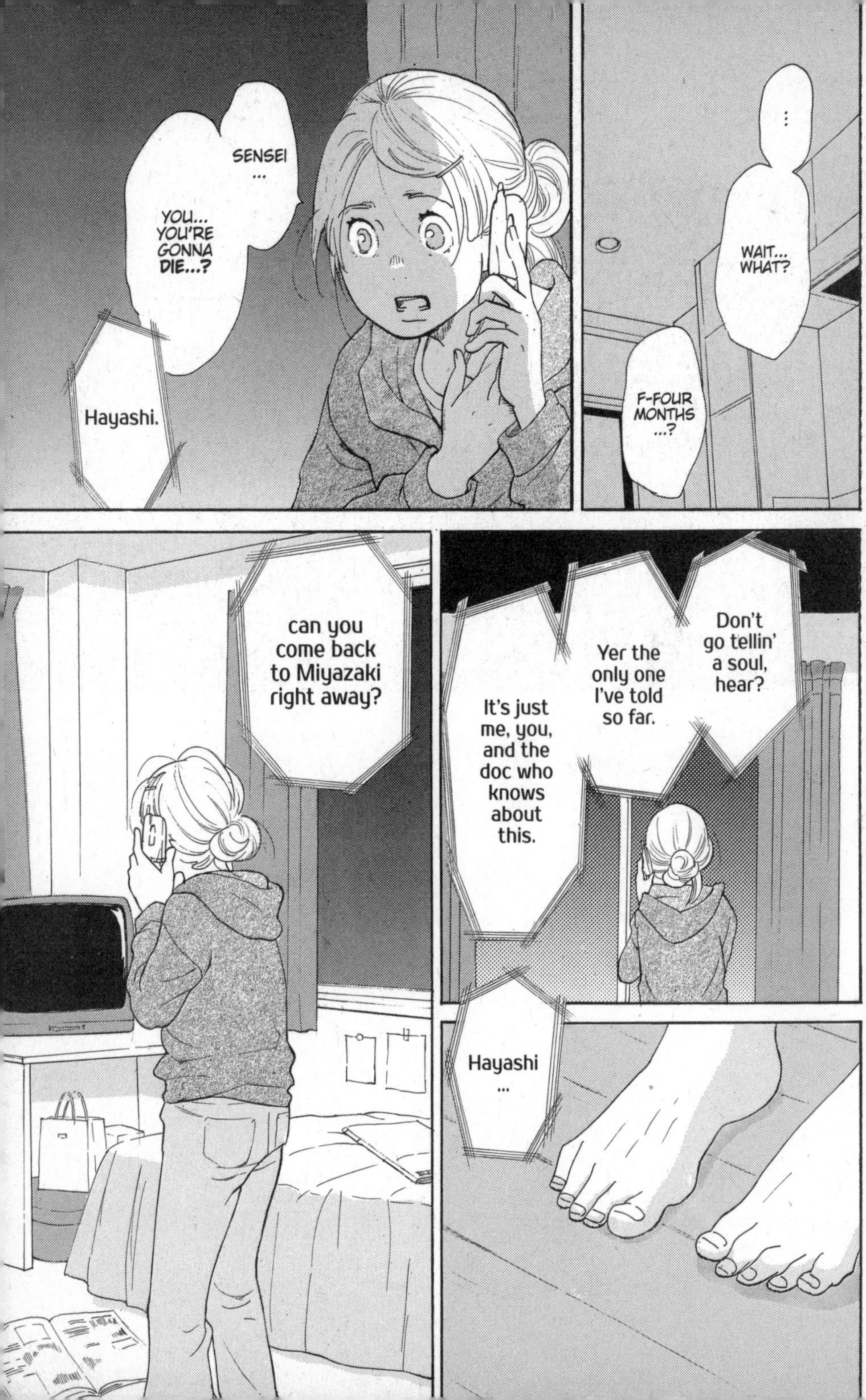
…
WAIT… WHAT?
F-FOUR MONTHS …?
SENSEI …
YOU… YOU'RE GONNA DIE…?
Hayashi.
Don't go tellin' a soul, hear?
Yer the only one I've told so far.
It's just me, you, and the doc who knows about this.
Hayashi …
can you come back to Miyazaki right away?

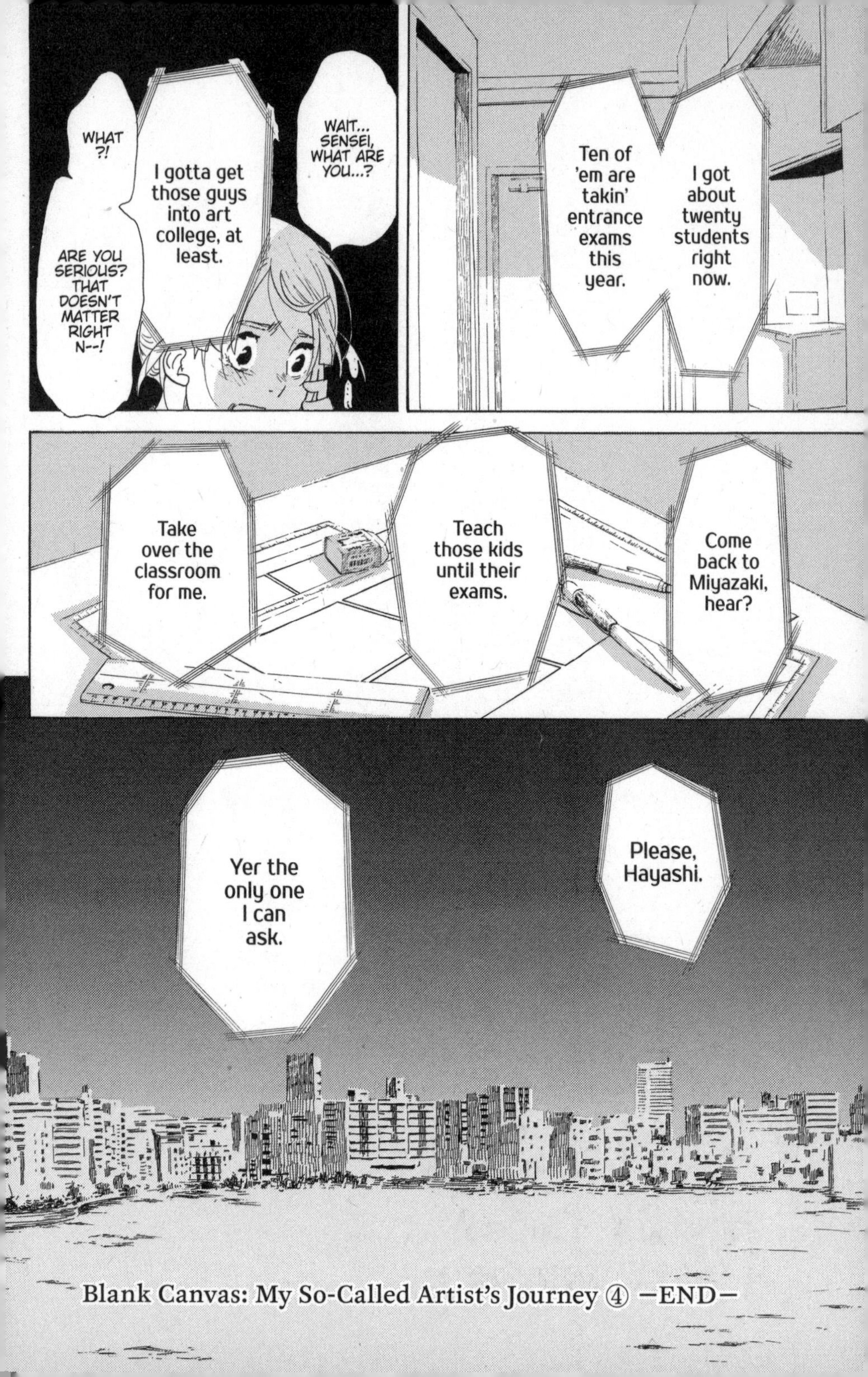
I got about twenty students right now.
Ten of 'em are takin' entrance exams this year.
WAIT... SENSEI, WHAT ARE YOU...?
I gotta get those guys into art college, at least.
WHAT ?!
ARE YOU SERIOUS? THAT DOESN'T MATTER RIGHT N--!
Come back to Miyazaki, hear?
Teach those kids until their exams.
Take over the classroom for me.
Please, Hayashi.
Yer the only one I can ask.
Blank Canvas: My So-Called Artist's Journey ④ —END—

Blank Canvas

My So-Called Artist's Journey

Blank
Canvas
My So-Called
Artist's Journey

When I started working on this series, I went back to Miyazaki to take reference photos.

I borrowed my family's car for the long, long journey to the classroom, where I used to commute on my bike (even driving, it was still far).

Along the way, I took lots of photos.

Luckily for me, the scenery around the classroom had barely changed over the last twenty years.

Back then, we didn't have cell phones, digital cameras, or smartphones.

We just bought disposable cameras for high school field trips and that kind of thing.

Once you took twenty-four pictures with one, you'd bring it to the photo studio to get the film developed and make prints.

It was time-consuming and expensive, so we only took photos on special occasions in those days.

Maybe that's why...

I don't have a single photo of Sensei's classroom, even though I went there just about every day for so many years.

So all of the drawings of the classroom's interior are based on my memories.

The same is true of Sensei's face.

Not just his face--the way he walked, how he looked with that black cat sitting on his shoulders...

The jeans he wore with a patch sewn roughly over the knee with a sewing machine...

There's a whole gallery of pictures and videos in my head that are just as good as any smartphone album.

I didn't realize that until I started drawing this series, so...

I guess I can honestly say now that I'm happy I did.

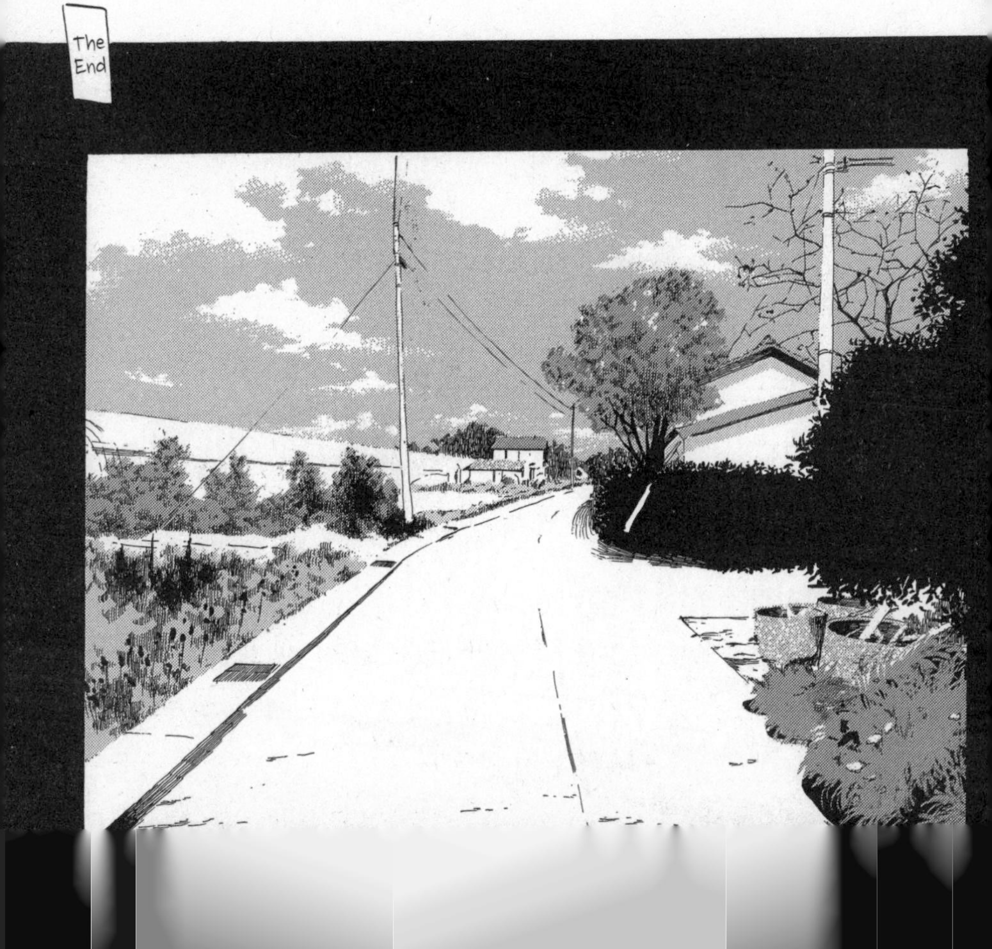

The End

SEVEN SEAS ENTERTAINMENT PRESENTS

Blank Canvas
My So-Called Artist's Journey

story and art by AKIKO HIGASHIMURA VOLUME 4

TRANSLATION
Jenny McKeon

ADAPTATION
Ysabet MacFarlane

LETTERING AND LAYOUT
Lys Blakeslee

COVER DESIGN
KC Fabellon

PROOFREADER
Kurestin Armada

EDITOR
Jenn Grunigen

PREPRESS TECHNICIAN
Rhiannon Rasmussen-Silverstein

PRODUCTION MANAGER
Lissa Pattillo

MANAGING EDITOR
Julie Davis

ASSOCIATE PUBLISHER
Adam Arnold

PUBLISHER
Jason DeAngelis

First published in Japan in 2011 by SHUEISHA Inc., Tokyo.
English translation rights arranged by SHUEISHA Inc.
through TOHAN CORPORATION, Tokyo.

Seven Seas press and purchase enquiries can be sent to Marketing Manager Lianne Sentar at press@gomanga.com. Information regarding the distribution and purchase of digital editions is available from Digital Manager CK Russell at digital@gomanga.com.

ISBN: 978-1-64275-072-0

Printed in Canada

First Printing: March 2020

10 9 8 7 6 5 4 3 2 1

FOLLOW US ONLINE: ***www.sevenseasentertainment.com***

READING DIRECTIONS

This book reads from ***right to left***, Japanese style. If this is your first time reading manga, you start reading from the top right panel on each page and take it from there. If you get lost, just follow the numbered diagram here. It may seem backwards at first, but you'll get the hang of it! Have fun!!

1
2
3
4
5
6
7
8
9

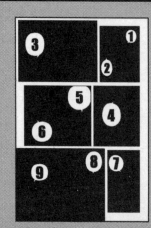